ISTHMIA

―――

VOLUME V

THE HEXAMILION AND THE FORTRESS

ISTHMIA

EXCAVATIONS BY THE UNIVERSITY OF CALIFORNIA AT LOS ANGELES

AND THE OHIO STATE UNIVERSITY

UNDER THE AUSPICES OF

THE AMERICAN SCHOOL OF CLASSICAL STUDIES AT ATHENS

VOLUME V

THE HEXAMILION
AND THE FORTRESS

BY

TIMOTHY E. GREGORY

AMERICAN SCHOOL OF CLASSICAL STUDIES AT ATHENS

PRINCETON, NEW JERSEY

1993

Library of Congress Cataloging-in-Publication Data

Gregory, Timothy E.
    The hexamilion and the fortress / by Timothy E. Gregory
        p.   cm. — (Isthmia ; v. 5)
    Includes bibliographical references and index.
    ISBN 0-87661-935-9
    1. Hexamilion (Greece). 2. Fortification—Greece—Corinth, Isthmus of.
3. Corinth, Isthmus of (Greece)—Antiquities. I. Title. II. Series.
DF556.G74   1993
938'.7—dc20   92-22211
                                                                            CIP

TYPOGRAPHY BY THE AMERICAN SCHOOL OF CLASSICAL STUDIES PUBLICATIONS OFFICE
C/O INSTITUTE FOR ADVANCED STUDY, PRINCETON, NEW JERSEY
PLATES BY THE MERIDEN-STINEHOUR PRESS, LUNENBURG, VERMONT
PRINTED IN THE UNITED STATES OF AMERICA
BY THE JOHN D. LUCAS PRINTING COMPANY, BALTIMORE, MARYLAND

TO THE MEMORY OF

PAUL A. CLEMENT

PREFACE

THE STUDY of the Hexamilion and the Fortress at Isthmia provides important information related to the "decline and fall of the Roman Empire," especially as it affected the classical lands of Greece in the late Roman and Byzantine periods. The Hexamilion, constructed during the reign of Theodosius II (A.D. 408–450), was a barrier wall or lateral fortification, similar to Hadrian's Wall in Britain, stretching across the Isthmus of Corinth, from the Corinthian to the Saronic Gulf. Its construction was a feat requiring considerable energy and organizational strength, a testimony not to the weakness of the empire but to its resilience, and an indication of its willingness to experiment and try new approaches to the military problems of the age. The examination of the Hexamilion, however, requires a variety of approaches, involving traditional analysis of historical texts, archaeological excavation, and detailed topographic exploration. What follows is, in large part, the results of investigations at Isthmia conducted by the University of California, Los Angeles (UCLA) and the Ohio State University for the American School of Classical Studies at Athens. It will focus on the history of the Hexamilion as a Byzantine fortification, but it will consider material that is both earlier and later. What gives the work unity, however, is the Hexamilion itself and the effort it represented to stem the tide of barbarism that threatened to engulf the Greek peninsula at the end of antiquity. This study reflects the recent increased interest in the fortification efforts of late antiquity (witness the studies of Pringle, Karnapp, Johnson, and others). For this reason, the focus is on the Hexamilion as an architectural and military unit, and no systematic attempt has been made to discuss the abundant spolia used in the fortification.

In the pages that follow I have attempted to present this disparate matter in a reasonably organized way. After an introduction, which discusses earlier attempts to wall the Isthmus, comes a chapter on the geographical setting of the Hexamilion (Chap. II). Next are the testimonia (Chap. III), which include the most important texts needed for the historical interpretation of the archaeological remains. For the period of late antiquity, therefore, I have been as full and inclusive as possible, presenting all texts that might bear on the issue. From the fifteenth century onward the historical data become more plentiful, and I have had to be more selective. The independence of the modern Greek state from Ottoman rule (1821) seemed to be a reasonable cut-off for the testimonia, and I have not included later texts here. Translations, except where noted, are my own, and they express for the reader how I understand a given passage. After the testimonia comes a chapter tracing the course of the Hexamilion, from the Gulf of Corinth to the Saronic Gulf (i.e., from west to east), with the exception of the Fortress (Chap. IV). Figures 3–10 are a series of detailed topographic maps that present the course of the Hexamilion in visual form, while Figure 11 allows a schematic view of the elevation of the Hexamilion, from one sea to the other. Chapters V–IX examine various parts of the Fortress where excavation was carried out, beginning at the two gates (Chaps. V and VI), continuing with the towers at the corners of the Fortress (Chaps. VII and VIII), and concluding with the other Fortress towers (Chap. IX). A summary chapter (Chap. X) discusses matters of military strategy and construction techniques, and a final chapter (Chap. XI) presents the history of the Hexamilion, as revealed by excavation, historical analysis, and topographic exploration.

The Hexamilion was approximately 7,600 meters long (slightly shorter than the six miles that its name implies), and it is, thus, in some ways the largest single archaeological site in Greece. The area in the vicinity of the Sanctuary of Poseidon at Isthmia has been largely enclosed in fences and so is relatively safe from further deterioration; the large proportion of the Hexamilion, however, is in open territory and is therefore in continuous danger of further collapse and destruction. It is unlikely that a better opportunity will ever occur to combine excavation with topographic exploration of the Hexamilion since residential and industrial projects continue to grow at alarming rates throughout the Corinthia. Moreover, even during the time in which this study was conducted, significant amounts of ancient evidence have simply disappeared as a result of modern development. It has therefore seemed appropriate to be as full as possible in the presentation of all archaeological and topographic evidence concerning the Hexamilion. This study will, it is hoped, serve as a record and a document for future scholars who may want to make use of this evidence for their own research. The interpretations and historical conclusions drawn in the present study will probably be revised by others, but the basic documentation should remain as a primary research tool.

I realize that the title of this volume and the running text involve an anachronism: the early Byzantine wall across the Isthmus of Corinth was probably not called the Hexamilion until about the twelfth century. For reasons of style, however, it has seemed acceptable to call the fortifications by this name from the very beginning, since we do not know an earlier designation.

In the present study I have had to face the difficulty of determining the amount of documentation to be included. In light of the comments above, I naturally chose to document the architectural details of the Hexamilion as fully as possible; this has included hypothetical restoration (at the Northeast Gate and Tower 6) where the evidence warranted and as an indication, if only *exempli gratia*, of how the fortifications looked when preserved to their full height. Coins, lamps, pottery, and other material have provided the primary evidence for the date of the Hexamilion and its subsequent rebuildings and re-uses. I have followed different practices in detailing this evidence, determined primarily by the availability of the material in other publications. At the time of this writing, volumes on the coins (by Paul A. Clement) and the lamps (by Birgitta L. Wohl) are complete in manuscript, so that it seems unnecessary to present full details of these items in the text when they are used for chronological purposes. Thus, in mentioning coins, I refer to the catalogue numbers in Professor Clement's volume, while for the lamps I give the inventory numbers (either IP [Isthmia Pottery] or IPL [Isthmia Pottery, Lamps]) along with a brief indication of the type. Scholars who wish further information on these items will be able to refer to the appropriate volumes in the Isthmia series. For pottery, however, full publication is not presently forthcoming, and it has seemed best to provide a rather fuller treatment of items that are chronologically diagnostic. Consequently, I have given enough detail so that the reader can decide how much value to accord this evidence. Most of the pottery mentioned has been inventoried and therefore has proper IP, IPR (Roman), or IPB (Byzantine) designations; on occasion, however, it has been necessary to refer to uninventoried context pottery, and this has been done by indicating the Isthmia Lot in which it was found.

I began this study in 1980, when I was Samuel H. Kress Foundation Professor at the American School of Classical Studies at Athens. The project was made possible by the generous support given to Isthmia Excavations by the National Endowment for the Humanities, the Samuel H. Kress Foundation, the David and Lucile Packard Foundation, and Stuart E. Thorne, and to me personally by the College of Humanities and the Graduate School of The Ohio State University. A study such as this is by nature a collaborative effort, and the author is merely the person who assembles and correlates the work of others from over the years. In particular, the present study is dependent upon the work of all those who participated in Isthmia Excavations (UCLA) from 1967 to 1978. I would like to thank the Greek Archaeological Service and a succession of cooperative officials, both from the Classical and Prehistoric Ephoreia in Nauplion and from the Byzantine Ephoreia in Patras. Thanks are also due to Professors Henry Immerwahr and Stephen G. Miller, successive directors of the American School of Classical Studies at Athens, and Professor Elizabeth R. Gebhard, Dr. Charles K. Williams, II, and Professor Demetrios Pallas, who kindly allowed me to use material under their authority. David Wilson carried out a preliminary study of the Hexamilion, and I owe much to his earlier work. Various individuals prepared the drawings assembled in this volume; among them I may mention Joseph Shaw, William Dinsmoor, Jr., Karen Hutchinson, and Charles Peirce, to whom I am especially indebted for many insights, suggestions, and unfailing good humor. I was not always able to use Charlie's drawings and reconstructions, many of which seemed to have a life and a logic all their own, but each of them, in its own way, contributed to this volume. Special thanks are due to Harrianne Mills, Birgitta Wohl, and Michael Mills for much assistance and advice.

Most of all, however, I would like to thank Paul A. Clement, who first undertook the full-scale investigation of the Hexamilion and who invited me to publish the excavations concerned with it. He always remained interested in the work and offered sound advice about matters of both style and content. It is a great sadness that he did not live to see final publication of this volume, but I am pleased that he was able to inspect the manuscript and to know that the work was complete. It is with respect that I dedicate this book to his memory.

Kyras Vrysi
31 July 1986*

---

* This volume was completed in 1986. Information from fieldwork since that date has been selectively added to the text, but the book stands essentially as it was written in 1986.

TABLE OF CONTENTS

LIST OF ILLUSTRATIONS

ILLUSTRATIONS IN TEXT

FIGURES

PLATES

SELECTED BIBLIOGRAPHY AND ABBREVIATIONS

PRIMARY SOURCES

Aed. See Procopius

Anekdota. See Procopius

Ammianus Marcellinus, *Rerum gestarum*, edited by V. Garthausen, 2 vols., Leipzig 1974–1975

Bees, *Inschriften = Corpus der griechisch-christlichen Inschriften von Hellas*, I, *Die griechisch-christlichen Inschriften des Peloponnes*, edited by N. A. Bees, Athens 1945

Chalkokondyles, L., *Historiarum demonstrationes (CSHB)*, edited by I. Bekker, Bonn 1843

CTh = Codex Theodosianus, edited by T. Mommsen and P. Meyer, 2 vols., Berlin 1905, translated by C. Pharr, Philadelphia 1952

Cyriacus of Ancona, *Cyriacus of Ancona and Athens*, edited by E. W. Bodnar (*Collectio Latomus* 43), Brussels 1960

De re strategica, edited by H. Köchly and W. Rustow, in *Griechische Kriegschriftsteller* II, ii, Leipzig 1885, pp. 1–209, 311–355

Dölger, F., *Regesten der Kaiserurkunden des oströmischen Reiches von 565–1453*, V, *Regesten von 1341–1453*, Munich 1965

Ducas, *Historia byzantina*, edited by I. Bekker (*CSHB*), Bonn 1834; edited by V. Grecu, Bucharest 1958

Eunapius, *Vitae sophistorum*, edited and translated by W. C. Wright, London 1968

Evagrius, *Historia ecclesiastica*, edited by J. Bidez and L. Parmentier, London 1898, reprinted Amsterdam 1964

Kedrenos, G., *Historiarum compendium (CSHB)*, edited by I. Bekker, 2 vols., Bonn 1838–1839

Lambros, S. P., and K. Amantos, Βραχέα χρονικά. Ἀκαδημία Ἀθηνῶν, Μνημεῖα τῆς ἑλληνικῆς ἱστορίας, I, Athens 1932–1933

Manuel II = *The Letters of Manuel Palaeologus*, edited by G. T. Dennis, Washington 1977

Mazaris, *Descent into Hades*, edited by Seminar Classics 609, SUNY Buffalo (*Arethusa Monographs* 5), Buffalo 1975

Philo of Byzantium, *Liber mechanicus*, edited by Y. Garlan, in *Recherches de poliorcétique grecque* (Bibliothèque des Écoles françaises d'Athènes et de Rome 223), Paris 1974, pp. 279–404

Procopius of Caesarea, *De aedificiis*, edited by J. Haury, revised by G. Wirth, Leipzig 1964

Procopius, *Anekdota* = Procopius of Caesarea, *Anekdota*, edited by J. Haury, revised by G. Wirth, Leipzig 1964

Procopius, *Vand.* = Procopius of Caesarea, *De bello vandalico*, edited by J. Haury, revised by G. Wirth, 2 vols., Leipzig 1963

Pseudo-Phrantzes, *Chronicon maius*, edited by I. Bekker (*CSHB*), Bonn 1838; edited by V. Grecu, Budapest 1966

Sathas, *Documents inédits* = *Documents inédits relatifs à l'histoire de la Grèce au moyen age*, 9 vols., edited by K. Sathas, Venice/Paris 1880–1890

Schreiner, *Kleinchroniken = Die byzantinischen Kleinchroniken (CFHB)*, edited by P. Schreiner, 3 vols., Vienna 1975–1979

Skylitzes, I., *Synopsis historiarum (CFHB)*, edited by H. Thurn, Berlin 1973

Sphrantzes, G., *Chronicon minus*, edited by V. Grecu, Budapest 1966

Strategicon = Cecaumeni strategicon, edited by B. Wassiliewsky and V. Jernstedd, St. Petersburg 1896, reprinted Amsterdam 1965

Theophanes Continuatus, *Chronikon*, edited by I. Bekker (*CSHB*), Bonn 1838

Thiriet, *Régestes* = F. Thiriet, *Régestes des délibérations du Sénat de Venise concernant la Romanie*, 3 vols., Paris 1958–1961

Vitruvius, *De architectura*, edited by F. Granger, 2 vols., London 1931–1934

Zonaras, Ioannes, *Epitome historiarum*, edited by L. Dindorf, 4 vols., Leipzig 1868–1875

Zosimus, *Historia nova*, edited by L. Mendelssohn, Leipzig 1887

SECONDARY SOURCES

Agora V = H. S. Robinson, *The Athenian Agora, V, Pottery of the Roman Period: Chronology*, Princeton 1959

Agora XXIV = A. Frantz, *The Athenian Agora, XXIV, Late Antiquity: A.D. 267–700*, Princeton 1986 (with contributions by H. A. Thompson and J. Travlos)

Aupert, "Céramique slave" = P. Aupert, "Céramique slave à Argos (585 ap. J.-C.)," in *Études argiennes* (*BCH*, Suppl. 6, pp. 373–395), Paris 1980

Aupert, "Objets" = P. Aupert, "Objets de la vie quotidienne à Argos en 585 ap. J.-C.," in *Études argiennes* (*BCH*, Suppl. 6, pp. 395–457), Paris 1980

Barker, *Manuel II* = J. W. Barker, *Manuel II Palaeologus (1391–1425): A Study in Late Byzantine Statesmanship*, New Brunswick, N.J. 1969

Barker, "Chronology" = J. W. Barker, "On the Chronology of the Activities of Manuel II Palaeologus in the Peloponnesus in 1415," *Byzantinische Zeitschrift* 55, 1962, pp. 39–55

Beaton and Clement, "Date of Destruction" = A. E. Beaton and P. Clement, "The Date of the Destruction of the Sanctuary of Poseidon on the Isthmus of Corinth," *Hesperia* 45, 1976, pp. 267–279

Broneer, "Corinthian Isthmus" = O. Broneer, "The Corinthian Isthmus and the Isthmian Sanctuary," *Antiquity* 32, 1958, pp. 80–88

Broneer, 1953 = O. Broneer, "Isthmia Excavations, 1952," *Hesperia* 22, 1953, pp. 182–195

Broneer, 1955 = O. Broneer, "Excavations at Isthmia, 1954," *Hesperia* 24, 1955, pp. 110–141

Broneer, 1958 = O. Broneer, "Excavations at Isthmia, Third Campaign, 1955–1956," *Hesperia* 27, 1958, pp. 1–37

Broneer, 1959 = O. Broneer, "Excavations at Isthmia, Fourth Campaign, 1957–1958," *Hesperia* 28, 1959, pp. 298–343

Broneer, 1966 = O. Broneer, "The Cyclopean Wall on the Isthmus of Corinth and Its Bearing on Late Bronze Age Chronology," *Hesperia* 35, 1966, pp. 346–362

Broneer, 1968 = O. Broneer, "The Cyclopean Wall on the Isthmus of Corinth, Addendum," *Hesperia* 37, 1968, pp. 25–35

———. *See also Isthmia*

Clement = P. A. Clement, forthcoming *Isthmia* volume on coins

Clement, 1968 = P. A. Clement, "Isthmia Excavations," Δελτ 23, 1968, Β' 1 (1969), pp. 137–143

Clement, 1969 = P. A. Clement, "Isthmia," Δελτ 24, 1969, Β' 1 (1970), pp. 116–119

Clement, 1970 = P. A. Clement, "Isthmia Excavations," Δελτ 25, 1970, Β' 1 (1972), pp. 161–167

Clement, 1971 = P. A. Clement, "Isthmia Excavations," Δελτ 26, 1971, Β' 1 (1974), pp. 100–111

Clement, 1972 = P. A. Clement, "Isthmia Excavations," Δελτ 27, 1972, Β' 2 (1977), pp. 224–231

Clement, 1973 = P. A. Clement, "Isthmia Excavations," Δελτ 28, 1973, Β' 1 (1977), pp. 143–149

Clement, "Alaric" = P. A. Clement, "Alaric and the Fortifications of Greece," *Ancient Macedonia*, Thessaloniki 1977, pp. 135–137

Clement, "Date of the Hexamilion" = P. A. Clement, "The Date of the Hexamilion," *Essays in Memory of Basil Laourdas*, Thessaloniki 1977, pp. 159–164

Corinth: Results of Excavations Conducted by the American School of Classical Studies

    I, [i]. H. N. Fowler and R. Stillwell, *Introduction, Topography, Architecture*, Cambridge, Mass. 1932

    III, ii. R. Carpenter and A. Bon, *The Defenses of Acrocorinth and the Lower Town*, Cambridge, Mass. 1936

    VI. K. M. Edwards, *Coins*, Cambridge, Mass. 1933

    VIII, iii. J. H. Kent, *The Inscriptions, 1926–1950*, Princeton 1966

    XI. C. H. Morgan, *The Byzantine Pottery*, Cambridge, Mass. 1942

Evans, J. A. S., "The Walls of Thessalonica," *Byzantion* 47, 1977, pp. 361–362

Fimmen, "Isthmos" = E. Fimmen, "Isthmos," *RE* IX, 1916, cols. 2256–2265

Frazer, *Pausanias* = J. G. Frazer, *Pausanias's Description of Greece*, 6 vols., 2nd ed., London 1913

Freyberg, *Geologie* = B. von Freyberg, *Geologie des Isthmus von Korinth* (*Erlanger geologische Abhandlung* 95), Erlangen 1973

Gerster, B., "L'Isthme de Corinthe," *BCH* 8, 1884, pp. 225–232

Gebhard, *Theater* = E. R. Gebhard, *The Theater at Isthmia*, Chicago 1973

Gregory, "Fortified Cities" = T. E. Gregory, "The Fortified Cities of Byzantine Greece," *Archaeology* 35, fasc. 1, 1982, pp. 14–21

Gregory, "Late Roman Wall" = T. E. Gregory, "The Late Roman Wall at Corinth," *Hesperia* 48, 1979, pp. 264–280

Gregory and Mills, "Roman Arch" = T. E. Gregory and H. Mills, "The Roman Arch at Isthmia," *Hesperia* 53, 1984, pp. 407–445

Groag, *Reichsbeamten* = E. Groag, *Die Reichsbeamten von Achaea in spätrömischer Zeit*, Budapest 1949

Hayes = J. W. Hayes, *Late Roman Pottery*, London 1972

Hayes, *Roman Glass* = *Roman and Pre-Roman Glass in the Royal Ontario Museum*, Toronto 1975

Iorga, "Notes" = N. Iorga, *Notes et extraits pour servir à l'histoire des croisades au XVe siècle*, 4 vols., Paris/Bucharest 1899–1916

Isthmia, Results of Excavations Conducted by the University of Chicago
    I. O. Broneer, *Temple of Poseidon*, Princeton 1971
    II. O. Broneer, *Topography and Architecture*, Princeton 1973
    III. O. Broneer, *Terracotta Lamps*, Princeton 1977

Jenkins and Megaw, "Researches" = R. J. H. Jenkins and H. Megaw, "Researches at Isthmia," *BSA* 32, 1931/32, pp. 68–89

Johnson, *Late Roman Fortifications* = S. Johnson, *Late Roman Fortifications*, London 1983

Karnapp, *Stadtmauer* = W. Karnapp, *Die Stadtmauer von Resafa in Syrien* (*Denkmäler antiker Architektur* XI), Berlin 1976

Kenchreai, Eastern Port of Corinth
    II. L. Ibrahim, R. Scranton, and R. Brill, *The Panels of Opus Sectile in Glass*, Leiden 1976
    III. R. L. Hohlfelder, *The Coins*, Leiden 1978
    IV. B. Adamscheck, *The Pottery*, Leiden 1979
    V. H. Williams, *The Lamps*, Leiden 1981

Kirchen, Fritz, *Die Befestigungen von Herakleia am Latmos, Milet*, III, ii, Berlin 1922

Kirchen, *Landmauer* I = F. Kirchen, *Die Landmauer von Konstantinopel* I (*Denkmäler antiker Architektur* I), Berlin 1938

Kordosis, Michael, S., Συμβολὴ στὴν ἱστορία καὶ τοπογράφια τῆς περιοχῆς Κορίνθου στοὺς μέσους χρόνους (Βιβλιοθήκη ʿΙστορικῶν Μελέτων 159), Athens 1981

Lambros, «Τὰ τείχη» = S. P. Lambros, «Τὰ τείχη το ἰσθμοῦ Κορίνθου κατὰ τοὺς μέσους αἰῶνας», Νέος ʿΕλληνομνήμων 2, 1905, pp. 435–489; 4, 1907, pp. 20–26, 240–243; 5, 1908, pp. 115–116

Lambros, Παλαιολόγεια = S. P. Lambros, Παλαιολόγεια καὶ Πελοποννησιακά, 4 vols., Athens 1912–1930

Lawrence, *Greek Aims* = A. W. Lawrence, *Greek Aims in Fortification*, Oxford 1979

Lawrence, "Skeletal History" = A. W. Lawrence, "A Skeletal History of Byzantine Fortification," *BSA* 78, 1983, pp. 171–233

Leake, W. M., *Peloponnesiaca*, London 1846, repr. Amsterdam 1967 (not cited)

Leake, *Travels* = W. M. Leake, *Travels in the Morea*, 3 vols., London 1830, repr. Amsterdam 1968

MacDowall, "Byzantine Coin Hoard" = D. MacDowall, "The Byzantine Coin Hoard Found at Isthmia," *Archaeology* 18, 1965, pp. 264–267

MacKay, "More Byzantine Pottery" = T. S. MacKay, "More Byzantine and Frankish Pottery from Corinth," *Hesperia* 36, 1967, pp. 249–320

Martindale, *Prosopography* = J. R. Martindale, *Prosopography of the Later Roman Empire* II, Cambridge 1980

Meyer-Plath and Schneider, *Landmauer* II = B. Meyer-Plath and A. M. Schneider, *Die Landmauer von Konstantinopel* II (*Denkmäler antiker Architektur* VIII), Berlin 1943

Monceaux, "Fouilles" = P. Monceaux, "Fouilles et recherches archéologiques au sanctuaire des Jeux Isthmiques," *Gazette archéologique* 1884, pp. 273–285, 354–363; 1885, pp. 205–214

Pallas, Τὸ «ʿΕξαμίλιον» = D. Pallas, «Τὸ «ʿΕξαμίλιον» τεῖχος ἐπὶ τοῦ ᾿Ισθμοῦ», Δελτ 17, 1961/1962, Β′ 1 (1963), pp. 78–83

Peppers = J. M. Peppers, *Selected Roman Pottery, Isthmia Excavations, 1967–1972*, diss. University of Pennsylvania, 1979

Pringle, *Defence* = D. Pringle, *The Defence of Byzantine Africa from Justinian to the Arab Conquest* (*British Archaeological Reports, International Series* 99), 2 vols., Oxford 1981

Stein, *Histoire* = E. Stein, *Geschichte des spätrömischen Reiches*, Vienna 1928, edited and translated by J.-R. Planque as *Histoire du bas-empire*, I, Paris 1959; II, Paris 1949

Winter, *Greek Fortifications* = F. E. Winter, *Greek Fortifications*, London 1971

Wiseman, *Corinthian Walls* = J. R. Wiseman, *Corinthian Trans-Isthmian Walls and the Defense of the Peloponnesos*, diss. University of Chicago, 1966

Wiseman, "Gymnasium Area" = J. R. Wiseman, "Excavations in Corinth, the Gymnasium Area, 1967–1968," *Hesperia* 38, 1969, pp. 64–106

Wiseman, *Land* = J. R. Wiseman, *The Land of the Ancient Corinthians (Studies in Mediterranean Archaeology* 50), Göteborg 1978

Wiseman, 1963 = J. R. Wiseman, "A Trans-Isthmian Fortification Wall," *Hesperia* 32, 1963, pp. 248–275

Wohl, "Deposit of Lamps" = B. L. Wohl, "A Deposit of Lamps from the Roman Bath at Isthmia," *Hesperia* 50, 1981, pp. 112–140

Yassi Ada = *Yassi Ada* I, G. F. Bass and F. H. van Doornick, Jr., edd., College Station, Tex. 1982

Zakythinos, *Despotat* = D. A. Zakythinos, *Le despotat grec de Morée* I, Paris 1932

CORPUS AND PERIODICAL ABBREVIATIONS

AJA = *American Journal of Archaeology*

BCH = *Bulletin de correspondance hellénique*

BM = W. Wroth, *Catalogue of the Imperial Byzantine Coins in the British Museum*, 2 vols., London 1908

BSA = *The Annual of the British School in Athens*

CTh = *Codex Theodosianus*

CFHB = *Corpus Fontium Historiae Byzantinae*

CSHB = *Corpus Scriptorum Historiae Byzantinae*

Δελτ = Ἀρχαιολογικόν Δελτίον

Dittenberger, *Syll.*³ = W. Dittenberger, *Sylloge Inscriptionum Graecarum*, 3rd ed., Leipzig 1915–1924

DOC = A. R. Bellinger and P. Grierson, *Catalogue of the Byzantine Coins in the Dumbarton Oaks Collection and in the Whittemore Collection*, 3 vols. to date, Washington 1966–

DOP = *Dumbarton Oaks Papers*

GRBS = *Greek, Roman and Byzantine Studies*

IG = *Inscriptiones Graecae*

JHS = *Journal of Hellenic Studies*

JRS = *Journal of Roman Studies*

LRBC = P. V. Hill, J. P. C. Kent, and R. A. G. Carson, *Late Roman Bronze Coinage, A.D. 324–498*, London 1965

Πρακτικά = Πρακτικὰ τῆς ἐν Ἀθήναις Ἀρχαιολογικῆς Ἑταιρείας

RE = *Realencyclopädie der klassischen Altertumswissenschaft*, edited by A. Pauly, G. Wissowa, and G. Kroll, Stuttgart 1894–

RIC = *Roman Imperial Coins*, edited by H. Mattingly and E. A. Sydenham, London 1923–

SEG = *Supplementum Epigraphicum Graecum*

TAPA = *Transactions of the American Philological Association*

ZPE = *Zeitschrift für Papyrologie und Epigraphik*

I

INTRODUCTION

THE HEXAMILION and the Fortress at Isthmia have long been familiar features in the landscape of the Corinthia. Constructed with facing walls of large ashlar masonry, they provided a convenient quarry for builders over the centuries, and the practice of robbing these walls has continued into modern times. The core of the Hexamilion, however, is made of mortar and rubble, and the mixture has been extraordinarily resistant to both natural and human agencies. Accordingly, even when the facing blocks of the Hexamilion have been stripped away, the core remains in most places to provide evidence of its course across the Isthmus.

The Hexamilion was designed to protect the Peloponnesos from invasion from the north. As such, it was of little use to a power that controlled the whole of the Balkans and thus did not feel threatened from a northerly direction. For that reason, the last time the Hexamilion seems to have been put into commission was in the seventeenth century, when the Venetians attempted to hold the south of Greece against the Ottoman Turks. The Ottomans, of course, had little use for the fortification since Greece was only a small part of their far-flung empire, and after the expulsion of the Venetians in 1715, their control of the land was nearly uncontested. As a result, the Hexamilion was allowed to decay. Over the past two and a half centuries, its towers have fallen into ruin and the curtain walls have collapsed. Squatters established themselves in parts of the fortifications, although not, apparently, in the towers or gates of the Fortress itself. Modern development has caused further destruction, and large sections of the Hexamilion were buried by debris from construction of the Corinth Canal.

EXPLORATIONS OF THE SITE

The ruins of the Hexamilion, however, remained largely visible. They naturally attracted the attention of European visitors, from at least the seventeenth century onward.[1] Thus, in 1676 Spon and Wheler noted the Hexamilion, which they identified as a wall that ran from sea to sea (see Testimonia, 24). As late as 1821 the ruins of the Hexamilion were well enough preserved to prompt the suggestion that they be reconditioned and again put into service. In that year Charles James Napier published an anonymous pamphlet, *War in Greece*, which offered practical help for the struggle of the Greek people against the Turks. A key element in his plan was the fortification of the Isthmus of Corinth by the restoration of the Hexamilion: "The whole of the Isthmus is covered with ruins, among which are found vast quantities of squared stones. . . : from this circumstance all masonry would be easily executed, and the Greeks may, without difficulty, throw up a bastioned line with demi-lunes from sea to sea. . . ." This, he argued, might be done "in less than a week."[2]

Modern study of the Hexamilion may be said to have begun with the visit of Colonel Leake to the Corinthia in 1806 (see Testimonia, 26). It was Leake who first identified the Fortress wall as the temenos of the Sanctuary of Poseidon, and he described it as constructed in "the most regular kind of Hellenic masonry." Leake was also the first to execute a plan of the Fortress, which was included at the end of volume III of *Travels in the Morea*. This plan, which was copied without any significant

[1] Cf. *Isthmia* II, pp. 5–6.

[2] *War in Greece*, London 1821, pp. 31–32. See also the plan of the Isthmus, which shows that Napier's suggested fortification ran along the course of the Hexamilion. He also proposed the cutting of a canal through the Isthmus.

alterations by Curtius, Bursian, Burnouf, and others, was schematic and simplistic. It did not show the correct location of the gates, and it ignored all the towers of the western Fortress Wall.[3]

In 1883, at the time the French were beginning to construct the Corinth Canal, Paul Monceaux came to Isthmia and carried out the first systematic campaign of excavations along the Hexamilion.[4] He published a plan of the Fortress (his plate 38), which corrected Leake's in many specifics and added considerable detail. Monceaux accepted Leake's identification of the Fortress wall as the temenos of the Sanctuary of Poseidon, and all his conclusions were affected by that fact. For some reason he thought that the Hexamilion was constructed without mortar and that it was to be dated no later than the first century after Christ.[5] In the area of the Fortress, Monceaux conducted excavations in three separate areas: at the Northeast and South Gates and at the small gate north of Tower 14. He identified the last as the "West Gate", and he thought that it was in use from antiquity through the Middle Ages.[6]

At the South Gate Monceaux carried out a larger excavation and dug down to what he thought was ancient ground level, five meters below the modern surface.[7] In the course of this excavation he discovered the famous Victorinus inscription (*IG* IV, 204; see Testimonia, 4) "le long de ce mur"; inexplicably, he thought the inscription had originally come from one of the chapels whose ruins he noted inside the Fortress.[8] Monceaux apparently excavated the whole of the South Gate, for he identified the two flanking towers and the large foundations on which they rest. He concluded that "le tour polygonale était d'un joli travail et peut être attribuée à l'époque hellénique."[9]

But Monceaux devoted most of his attention to the Northeast Gate, where he dug through the center of the gate and exposed nearly the whole of the structure. He was the first to identify the Roman Arch within the military architecture of the gate, but he thought that it was an addition to the Greek temenos wall which was, in turn, rebuilt in the third century under the emperor Valerian.[10] Monceaux attributed his failure to find any classical Greek buildings to the many destructions that the site had undergone in antiquity.

In September of 1903 Efstathios Staïs carried out a 15-day excavation at Isthmia, largely to test Monceaux's conclusion that nothing classical survived in the "sanctuary".[11] Staïs laid out many trenches, primarily within the Fortress, and he encountered the remains of no ancient structures and no sherds older than Roman. Instead, he uncovered the ruins of some nine Byzantine houses and churches, although he provided no details or plans of these. Staïs concluded that Monceaux was correct, but he noted the shallowness of the fill in the "sanctuary" (normally 1–2 meters) and suggested that this lack of cover was the reason for the disappearance of the classical buildings seen by Pausanias at Isthmia.

---

[3] Leake, *Travels* III, pl. 3. This shows a "Temple of Neptune" in the southern part of the Fortress and a "Temple of Palaimon" in the north, the two connected by an "Avenue".

[4] Monceaux, "Fouilles," 1884, pp. 273–285, 354–363; 1885, pp. 205–214.

[5] Monceaux, "Fouilles," 1884, p. 275.

[6] Monceaux, "Fouilles," 1884, pp. 276–277; his reasoning for thinking the gate was used in antiquity was that it led to the Theater.

[7] Monceaux, "Fouilles," 1884, pp. 277–279.

[8] Monceaux's plan ("Fouilles," 1884, pl. 38) includes three buildings identified as "chapelles byzantines". One of these is on the site of the modern church of St. John, but the other two are clearly oriented north–south, and they were probably not churches.

[9] Monceaux, "Fouilles," 1884, pp. 279–285.

[10] Monceaux, "Fouilles," 1884, p. 282, note 1. It is difficult to understand Monceaux's chronology for the Fortress Wall; at one moment he says it was classical while at another he opts for a Roman date.

[11] Πρακτικά 1903, pp. 14–17.

A Greek date for the Hexamilion and the Fortress continued to be generally accepted in the early years of the twentieth century.[12] Fimmen, however, in 1916 described the masonry technique used in the Fortress as in the "Charackter justinianischer Bauten," and he was first to conclude that the whole fortification was of Early Byzantine date.[13]

In 1932 and 1933 R. J. H. Jenkins and H. Megaw again studied the surviving remains of the Fortress and carried out a series of selective excavations in the area.[14] They concluded that, with the exception of the Roman Arch, the Hexamilion and the Fortress are the work of one period, certainly post-Roman and probably to be identified with the fortification work of Justinian. Megaw and Jenkins prepared improved plans of the Fortress and the Northeast Gate. They sank several pits within the Fortress, excavated along its outer wall between Towers 10 and 11, and dug a long trench north of the Hexamilion between the Fortress and the Roman Bath. Within the Fortress they were able to show that the land had once sloped down considerably along the eastern side but that the early Byzantine builders had leveled the area by bringing in enormous quantities of fill. In the area north of the Hexamilion they identified what they thought was an outer fortification wall and defensive trench, which they equated with the *proteichisma* and *taphros* of Procopius, the Land Walls of Constantinople, and the Byzantine military manuals.

Oscar Broneer took an interest in the Fortress, and he carried out small-scale excavations in 1952 and 1954.[15] More substantial work was done in the area of the South Gate and Towers 6 and 7 in 1956 and 1958.[16] In the early 1960's and subsequently, Demetrios Pallas excavated sections of the Hexamilion, especially in the area of the National Highway.[17] Both Broneer and Pallas accepted a Justinianic date for the Fortress and the Hexamilion. Pallas, in fact, devoted considerable attention to the building techniques used in the section of the Hexamilion he investigated. He concluded that the Hexamilion was constructed in two phases, one between 540 and 542 and the other between 542 and 551.[18]

From 1967 to 1978 Paul A. Clement undertook for Isthmia Excavations (UCLA) a detailed investigation of selected areas of the Fortress and the Hexamilion, and these form the basis of the present volume.[19] The primary areas explored were the Northeast Gate (1967, 1969), Tower 2 (1968), Tower 10 (1968, 1972), Tower 14 (1967, 1969), Tower 15 (1968), the Hexamilion Bastion (1970), the Hexamilion Outworks (1972), the Fortress Towers (1972), and the Roman Bath (1970–1978). In addition, important topographic exploration was carried out along the course of the Hexamilion in various years. An important stage in this research was the execution of detailed topographic maps showing the course of the Hexamilion across the Isthmus, the work of Efstratios Papanis in 1969–1971.

[12] For example, J. G. O'Neill, *Ancient Corinth*, I, *From the Earliest Times to 404 B.C.*, Baltimore 1930, pp. 13–14; Fowler in *Corinth* I, i, pp. 51–55.

[13] Fimmen, *s.v.* "Isthmos," cols. 2256–2265.

[14] Jenkins and Megaw, "Researches," pp. 68–89.

[15] Broneer, 1953, p. 185 (a trench "on either side of the west wall of the Justinian Fortress"), Broneer, 1955, p. 124 (Tower 13), and Broneer, 1958, pp. 20–22.

[16] Broneer, 1959, pp. 320–321. These excavations were supervised by Demetrios Pallas, under the direction of Oscar Broneer. I would like to thank Professors Pallas and Broneer, and Professor Broneer's successor Professor Elizabeth Gebhard, for giving me full access to the records and finds from them.

[17] Pallas, Τὸ «Ἑξαμίλιον», pp. 78–83.

[18] Pallas, Τὸ «Ἑξαμίλιον», pp. 81–82.

[19] Clement, 1968, pp. 137–143; 1969, pp. 116–119; 1970, pp. 161–167; 1971, pp. 100–111; 1972, pp. 224–231; 1973, pp. 143–149.

During the first half of 1992 the 6th Ephoreia of Byzantine Antiquities carried out the excavation of a 200-meter stretch of the Hexamilion southeast of the National Highway. Thanks to the kind offices of the ephoreia I have been able to inspect this area and examine the finds from the excavation, but this occurred only when the present volume was in final proof. Thus, I have been able to make only cursory mention of the results of this important work (p. 34 below), which must await full publication by our Greek colleagues.

Of nonarchaeological studies, the work of Spyridon Lambros is of foremost importance. Lambros presented a detailed history of the Hexamilion, especially in the later Middle Ages, frequently basing his research on then-unpublished texts. More recent archaeological evidence requires the modification of some of Lambros' conclusions, and new editions of many of his texts have appeared over the past eighty years, but his is still the fundamental study of the literary evidence for the history of the Hexamilion.[20] Crucial for an understanding of the topography of the Corinthia, especially in late antiquity, is the work of Wiseman,[21] while the study of Michael Kordosis adds important details for the Middle Ages.[22]

EARLIER WALLS ACROSS THE ISTHMUS

The Isthmus of Corinth is a natural place to focus the defense of the Peloponnesos, and ancient literature contains a number of references to such attempts.[23] Probably because of the imposing ruins of the Hexamilion, modern observers have frequently wished to identify earlier walls across the Isthmus, and they have naturally sought archaeological support for such a view.

Oscar Broneer maintained that the earliest wall across the Isthmus was constructed in Mycenaean times.[24] Broneer's evidence for this wall is seven individual stretches of masonry between the Saronic Gulf and the Sanctuary of Poseidon at Isthmia; two of these are located on the sides of the gully between Mytikas and the Rachi, while another has been identified just south of the Palaimonion at Isthmia. Unquestionably, Broneer found sections of various walls, and some of these may indeed be Mycenaean, but there is no evidence to connect these short sections into a great defensive work across the Isthmus; some of the sections may not be Mycenaean at all. Fortification walls are notoriously difficult to date, and one can applaud Broneer's effort to supply chronological precision, but the evidence he adduces for a Mycenaean date does not inspire much confidence. For example, in the section south of the Palaimonion (Section Ge)[25] Broneer admits that pottery from above the wall and beside the faces ranges from modern to Mycenaean, while within the fill between the faces there was pottery as late as Late Roman. In other areas, the ceramic evidence is not much better (e.g., Late Roman sherds and Hellenistic tiles in Section Pe, although the pottery from Sections Sk and St seems more convincing).[26]

More serious objections have to be raised concerning the course of the "Mycenaean Wall" and the apparent disappearance of all trace of the wall in other parts of the Isthmus. Thus, only by a difficult stretch of the imagination can we see a fortification wall running along the east side of Mytikas, turning the head of the ravine, and then returning along the east side of the Rachi.[27] In its

---

[20] Lambros, «Tὰ τείχη», 1905, pp. 435–489; 1907, pp. 20–26, 240–243; 1908, pp.115–116.

[21] Wiseman, *Land*; Wiseman, 1963; Wiseman, *Corinthian Walls*.

[22] M. S. Kordosis, Συμβολὴ στὴν ἱστορία, Athens 1981.

[23] For a convenient survey of such attempts, see Wiseman, *Land*, pp. 59–63, esp. p. 77, note 91, where Wiseman cites eight instances between 369 and 146 B.C. when defenses along the line of Mt. Oneion were manned.

[24] Broneer, 1968, pp. 25–29.

[25] *Ibid.*

[26] Broneer, 1966, p. 351.

[27] See C. P. Kardara, "The Isthmian Wall," *Athens Annals of Archaeology* 4, 1971, pp. 85–89.

upper reaches this ravine is not deep, and it makes no sense for a defensive wall to have followed this extraordinarily tortuous course. Further, as Broneer admits, his attempts to locate the Mycenaean wall along its projected course were frequently unsuccessful; he attributes this to later robbing of the wall, but just as likely, the wall simply did not continue in one uninterrupted line and, in all probability, Broneer's wall is a series of walls of different kinds and different periods. The wall on the slopes of Mytikas probably retained a road, but it is useless to speculate about the other sections.[28]

Herodotos (8.71) provides the first good evidence for the fortification of the Isthmus. He says that after the Battle of Thermopylai (480 B.C.) all the Peloponnesians rushed to the Isthmus and broke up the Skironian Road. Then they decided to build a wall across the Isthmus, bringing in stones, bricks, and wood. Herodotos (9.7–10) further testifies that this wall was completed, presumably by the summer of 479 B.C., and that it was topped by a parapet. The material described by Herodotos makes this undertaking sound like a temporary fortification, otherwise known from various parts of Greece.[29] The addition of a parapet, however, suggests that this may in fact have been a more substantial wall. Wiseman identified a stretch of wall *ca.* 1,700 m. long, primarily on the Agios Demetrios ridge south of the road between Isthmia and Ancient Corinth, as the remains of this early fifth-century fortification.[30] This wall has eleven rectangular towers[31] and is dated by Wiseman to *ca.* 480 B.C. on the basis of pottery, loomweights, and the general style of masonry. According to Wiseman, this wall was at least partly built over by another wall constructed in 279 B.C. by the Macedonians under Antigonos Gonatas. This wall supposedly ran from Kenchreai to a point near modern Corinth, although traces of it have been found only as far north as a knoll near Boikiana, half-way across the Isthmus.[32] Undoubtedly, Wiseman discovered a fortification or series of fortifications in the eastern part of the Isthmus, and his evidence concerning dates seems reasonable. It is less certain, however, that the stretches he excavated were all once part of the same fortification (witness the difficulty caused by the discovery of another stretch of the Hellenistic wall above Kenchreai).[33] As Wiseman himself has shown,[34] the heights of Oneion have repeatedly been used as a defense of the Peloponnesos, and the walls on the Agios Demetrios ridge may not have continued all the way across the Isthmus. It is, as Wiseman himself noted, odd that his Classical and Hellenistic walls (as well as Broneer's Mycenaean wall) left the site of the Sanctuary of Poseidon to the attacker. This would naturally not have bothered the Mycenaeans, but it is peculiar in Classical and Hellenistic times, especially when a line further to the north would have been shorter and probably of greater strategic advantage.[35]

Zosimus (see Testimonia, 1) says that a wall across the Isthmus was planned at the time of the emperor Valerian (A.D. 253–260), and on this evidence many Byzantine sources and modern

[28] Concerning Wiseman's objections to Kardara (*Land*, p. 60), it may be noted that (1) a roadway may well have been stepped out in the manner of the preserved section and (2) the road may have been designed to rise into the hills, requiring that it wind its way into, but not out of, the ravine.

[29] Lawrence, *Greek Aims*, pp. 160–172.

[30] Wiseman, 1963, pp. 248–275; Wiseman, *Corinthian Walls.*

[31] Note the comment of Lawrence (*Greek Aims*, p. 169): "The eleven large towers above precipices cannot have been needed for flanking, but provided quarters for troops."

[32] Wiseman, 1963, pp. 248–275; Wiseman, *Land*, pp. 62–63.

[33] Wiseman, *Land*, pp. 62, 77, note 100.

[34] Wiseman, *Land*, pp. 59, 77, note 91.

[35] It is difficult to know what to make of Wiseman's statement (*Land*, p. 60) that the wall on the Agios Demetrios ridge "puts the attacker at a greater disadvantage through height than any section of the late Roman wall." A wall along this course had to cross into very low-lying territory northeast of Mt. Oneion, while the Hexamilion, as will be seen below, took advantage of every natural height. Lawrence (*Greek Aims*, p. 169) found the fortifications on Agios Demetrios "mysterious—to modern eyes superfluous."

observers have thought that the Hexamilion was first built by that emperor. This view may also have arisen from the language of Procopius (see Testimonia, 3), who says that Justinian rebuilt the fortification. As will be seen, however, absolutely no archaeological evidence exists for a "Valerian" Hexamilion, and if work was actually begun on such a wall, it was certainly never completed. Probably, as Clement suggested, the text of Zosimus should be interpreted to say that the Peloponnesians planned to fortify the Isthmus but that the work was never carried out.[36]

The Hexamilion was constructed under the emperor Theodosius II (A.D. 408–450), and it may well have been the one and only wall across the Isthmus. Clearly, attempts to defend the Peloponnesos often focused at the Isthmus, and a wall across it must frequently have been contemplated. Temporary barriers were probably built in the face of urgent danger, and forts or fortresses may have been constructed to complement the powerful position of Acrocorinth in barring passage through the Corinthia. Nevertheless, there is little evidence of any successful attempt to fortify the whole Isthmus until the early Byzantine age. As we have seen, a project of this nature required both effective control of the whole of the Peloponnesos and the ability to bring tremendous resources, material and human, to bear on the project. There were few periods in the history of Greece when all these conditions were met. The brief era of cooperation in the face of Xerxes' invasion (480–479 B.C.) may have been one of these, and there may have been times during the Hellenistic period when such a wall could have been built. But the early Byzantine wall was possibly the only successful fortification of the whole of the Isthmus. In any case, the Hexamilion was visible to writers of later days, and the ruins of towers and curtain walls inspired speculation and perhaps scholarly invention.

Excavation now shows that the Hexamilion was built in one period, as part of a carefully coordinated plan to defend the early Byzantine world from the Germanic invasions. The Byzantines brought great resources and technological superiority to this struggle, and the Hexamilion is an example of Byzantine strength and an indication of their strategy against the barbarians. Detailed study of the Hexamilion will thus shed light on the larger question of the "Fall of the Roman Empire", and the successes and failures of the Hexamilion may provide lessons of use to those interested in broader issues of military strategy and planning.

[36] Clement, manuscript on coins from Isthmia.

II
THE GEOLOGICAL AND MORPHOLOGICAL SETTING

THE HEXAMILION extends across the southern edge of the Isthmus of Corinth, the narrow land bridge that connects central Greece and the Peloponnesos (Figs. 1 and 2). Running roughly east and west, the Hexamilion lies near the shortest line between the Corinthian and the Saronic Gulfs.[1]

Geologically, the Isthmus consists of low and relatively recent marine deposits. To the northeast are the heights of Mt. Geraneia and to the south the mountains of the northeast Peloponnesos.[2] These two land masses were once separate, but the land bridge of the Isthmus was formed as the result of tectonic activity. The relatively low-lying area along the north side of the Isthmus, however, was built up by marine deposition in geologically recent time.[3]

The surface of much of the southern part of the Isthmus is characterized by a thin layer of red, clayey sand.[4] This upper layer is only 5 to 10 meters thick, and it contains small marine fossils, indicating a near-shore formation. This material is easily eroded, and the erosion of the upper surfaces, along with the series of natural plateaus discussed below, are the dominant features of the Isthmus.[5] Underlying this uppermost layer of sand are Tyrrhenian deposits of conglomerates, marls, marly limestones, and sand. Perhaps the best example of this formation is the "Corinthian sandstone" visible in the large ancient quarries between Kyras Vrysi and the village of Hexamilia.[6] Underlying these Tyrrhenian deposits in much of the Corinthia and in the eastern part of the Isthmus are the light-colored Pliocene marls that give Corinthian pottery its characteristic hue.[7] These marls frequently occur between layers of conglomerate, but they are visible only when the surface has been exposed through erosion or uplifted by tectonic activity.

Along both the Corinthian and the Saronic coasts of the Isthmus, the sea once reached much further inland than it does now, so that what is now the city of New Corinth and the eastern and western mouths of the Corinth Canal (Isthmia and Poseidonia) were under water.[8] Alluvial deposits developed in these areas, probably before the beginning of the historical era (although they must have remained marshy), and a precipitous line of coastal cliffs is still visible in places (e.g., above New Corinth) to mark the earlier shore line of the Corinthian Gulf. Inland from the sea the land rises in a series of terraces, running roughly northeast–southwest, which dominates the topography of the southern part of the Isthmus. These terraces were formed by tectonic activity in geologically recent time, and their geological structure does not vary significantly from one area to another. As many as five terraces can be identified between the sea and the village of Hexamilia, and these provide a significant barrier to north–south communications.[9]

[1] See *Isthmia* II, pp. 1–3.

[2] A. Philippson, *Die griechischen Landschaften* III, i, *Der Peloponnes. Der Osten und Norden der Halbinsel,* Frankfurt 1955.

[3] Freyberg (*Geologie*, pp. 148–157) argues that formation of the Isthmus was the result of antitilted fault blocks (*Kippschollenkreuzung*); cf. idem, "Der Bau des Isthmus von Korinth," *Ann. Geol. pays helléniques* 4, 1952, pp. 157–188.

[4] See Korinthos Sheet, Institute for Geology and Subsurface Research, Athens 1971.

[5] This leading Strabo (8.6.23) to describe the Corinthia as "beetle-browed and full of hollows."

[6] See Korinthos Sheet (footnote 4 above); Freyberg ("Korinthischer Bausandstein"), pl. 15, fig. 1; pl. 16, fig. 2; pl. 23, figs. 3, 4; pl. 31 (map 2) and Wiseman, *Land*, pp. 68, 78–79, fig. 76.

[7] Korinthos Sheet (footnote 4 above); Freyberg, *Geologie*, pl. 1, fig. 1; pl. 15, fig. 2.

[8] Freyberg, *Geologie*, p. 11.

[9] A. Philippson, "Der Isthmos von Korinth," *Zeitschrift Ges. Erdkde.* 25, 1890, p. 9; Wiseman, *Land*, pp. 9, 64.

The northeastern part of the Isthmus is defined by Mt. Geraneia, which all but blocks communication through the Isthmus. On the east the mountain reaches the southern side of the Isthmus at the Scironian Rocks, falling almost vertically into the waters of the Saronic Gulf. The western outrunners of Mt. Geraneia form the Perachora Peninsula, which extends out into the Corinthian Gulf and further inhibits north–south communications. Thus, on the west there is a narrow alluvial coastal plain from modern Loutraki south to the Hexamilion, but further north and west, the cliffs of Mt. Geraneia extend nearly down to the sea.[10]

Southwest of the Scironian Rocks the eastern side of the Isthmus is more low-lying and more open to the sea, and this must have provided the normal means of access to the Peloponnesos by land. What was probably the primary road in antiquity descended from Thebes to join the road from Athens, probably just west of Eleusis.[11] It continued south and west through the Megarid and then crossed over the tops of the Scironian Rocks before descending into the coastal plain near Krommyon (modern Agioi Theodoroi) and proceeding through Schoinos, reaching the Peloponnesos in the vicinity of the Sanctuary of Poseidon. Sea traffic from the east would naturally have landed at Corinth's eastern port at Kenchreai or, less frequently, at Schoinos, before proceeding overland to the city.

South of the Isthmus the eastern coastal plain is constricted by a series of east-west ridges (e.g., the Rachi, immediately south of the Sanctuary of Poseidon and Agios Demetrios ridge further to the southwest), which approaches closer to the sea the further south one goes. Finally, the heights of Mt. Oneion reach the sea just south of Kenchreai and effectively block north–south communications along the coast.[12] From Kenchreai to Epidauros there is only one good means of access to the interior from the sea, at Korfos, where an ancient road certainly ascended to the vicinity of modern Sophiko and the rough high country to the west.[13]

As mentioned above, the Hexamilion is located on the south side of the depression that forms the southern end of the Isthmus. Immediately to the north of it, the southernmost ridges of Mt. Geraneia reach nearly to the sea, at Harma (elev. +171 m.) just to the northeast of the Bay of Kalamaki. To the south is the great mass of Mt. Oneion (+584 m.) and to the southwest Acrocorinth (+524 m.). The modern Corinth Canal follows the shortest line between the two gulfs and the one that is generally the lowest. The land through the Isthmus along this line rises from sea level to a maximum elevation of *ca.* 81 meters, at a point between the modern railroad and automobile bridges. The rise in the west is slightly more gradual than that in the east. The landscape of the Isthmus, however, is far from even, in part because of the series of plateaus and in part because of the erosion, which has led to the creation of a complex network of ravines and arroyos.

Since the plateaus run roughly northeast–southwest, any wall across the Isthmus could not avoid crossing them, and the Hexamilion had to be designed to do this most economically, ascending the plateaus on either side in a manner that did not weaken the defenses (Fig. 2). A second problem confronting the military engineers was the series of ravines that run down across the plateaus (i.e., roughly south to north) and then turn obliquely toward the sea (at least in the case of the ravines on the eastern half of the Isthmus). The Hexamilion had to cross several of these ravines perpendicularly, and the crossings were especially dangerous locations. The ravines would tend to "funnel" an enemy toward the Hexamilion, and the crossings were especially difficult engineering feats.

[10] See Wiseman's discussion of the roads through Geraneia and Oenoe (*Land*, pp. 20–27).
[11] Wiseman, *Land*, pp. 17–20; Gregory and Mills, "Roman Arch," pp. 428–429, note 55.
[12] Wiseman, *Land*, pp. 52–56.
[13] The construction of the modern Epidauros road has, of course, changed all that. Wiseman, *Land*, pp. 127–142.

On the west, two of these ravines are just to the east of New Corinth (at 0+500 m. and 0+1,200 m.; Figs. 3 and 4).[14] They cut down steeply into the first plateau, and they once brought water directly into the Gulf of Corinth at the foot of that plateau. The alluvial fill between New Corinth and Poseidonia, with the exception of the canal dump, was brought down largely by those ravines, but the absence of any significant degradation shows that there was no river or outlet to the sea in the western part of the Isthmus. This means that the lowest area must have been covered by the sea or at least marshy when the ravines were cut into the surface of the plateau. The first of these ravines involved a drop of 12 meters, while the second fell 20 meters. Further on, at *ca.* 0+2,000 m. there is another ravine that must have led off to the Gulf of Corinth, although changes in the landscape since construction of the canal make its course uncertain.

Across the central part of the Isthmus the land is rather flat and featureless, with, as we have seen, a maximum elevation of *ca.* 81 meters. After *ca.* 0+3,600 m., however, the land begins to descend toward the Saronic Gulf (Fig. 6). The dominant feature in this area is the Great Ravine, which rises from three main sources and runs roughly toward the east into the Saronic Gulf (Fig. 1).[15] This Great Ravine has many tributaries joining it from the south, and it was certainly a dominant consideration for construction of the Hexamilion in the eastern part of the Isthmus. The first of these tributaries, the so-called Kyras Vrysi Ravine, is the ravine that rises in the village of Kyras Vrysi and runs roughly northward, crossing the line of the Hexamilion between 0+4,900 and 0+5,100 m. (Fig. 7). The second of these primary tributaries of the Great Ravine originally ran through the Sanctuary of Poseidon, where it had to be channeled through a drain in the northwest corner of the temple area. It then ran northward and emptied into the Great Ravine along the western side of the Roman Bath.

The landscape in the area of the Sanctuary of Poseidon has been altered considerably over the centuries, first by the construction of buildings associated with the Sanctuary and later by the Hexamilion and its subsequent abandonments. A smaller tributary ravine ran along the eastern side of the Theater (perhaps through the Theater before its construction) and emptied into the Great Ravine through the so-called North Drain.[16] Another larger tributary rose east of the Rachi (between the Rachi and Mytikas), ran through the depression of the New Stadium, and crossed the line of the Hexamilion just south of Tower 2. Before this point, however, the Great Ravine turned slightly to the north, where it seems to have followed the course taken by the modern canal into the sea at the head of the Bay of Kalamaki.

East of the Rachi the sandstone outcrop of Mytikas rises steeply to a height of 83 meters and descends gradually to the east in the direction of the Saronic Gulf. The area east of Mytikas is today covered with dumped material from construction of the Corinth Canal at the end of the nineteenth century.[17] This dump now presents a flat surface, 12–14 meters above sea level, from Mytikas to the sea, and it forms a cliff at the modern shoreline. Canal dump is visible in the scarp along the sea right down to sea level, which suggests that the level of the land along the sea was not very high before construction of the canal. It is naturally difficult now to be certain, but in antiquity probably either the sea came directly up to the foot of Mytikas or the land between the sandstone outcrop and the sea was low-lying and marshy.

Two deep ravines run down from the crest of Mytikas toward the Saronic Gulf, one rising in the west and the other in the south. These ravines converge as they approach the sea, but their

---

[14] See p. 27 below for an explanation of the running-distance measurements.

[15] Broneer (*Isthmia* II, pp. 1–2) calls this the "Northwest Gully".

[16] Broneer, *Isthmia* I, p. 2; Gebhard, *Theater*, p. 1.

[17] B. Gerster, "L'Isthme de Corinthe," *BCH* 8, 1884, pp. 225–232; Freyberg, *Geologie*, pl. 31.

courses are now blocked by the canal dump. The modern bottom of the southern ravine is at an elevation of *ca.* 6 meters above sea level (i.e., 6–8 meters below the level of the dump), although it is approximately 400 meters away from the present seashore, another indication that the land covered by the canal dump was originally very low. These ravines ran just north of a rounded outcrop from Mytikas, whose crest of 24 meters is now cut through by the modern road to Epidauros. This hill effectively represents the end of the Isthmus on the southeast, and the hill must originally have stood directly above either the sea or the marshy land to the east. Further to the south, as we have seen, passage is possible to Kenchreai and beyond into the mountainous interior of the southeastern Corinthia, but the road rises continuously and passes through hilly land along its course. Thus, access into the interior of the Peloponnesos was effectively blocked south of Kenchreai. A strong detachment of troops there, combined with the Hexamilion, would have provided a strong defense against attacks from the north or northeast.

III

THE TESTIMONIA

Dates preceding each citation or group of citations pertain to the events in the passages cited.

A.D. 253–260

1. Zosimus 1.29.

Παρελθὼν δὲ Βαλεριανὸς κοινῇ γνώμῃ πρὸς τὴν τῶν ὅλων ἀρχὴν σπουδὴν ἐποεῖτο τὰ πράγματα εὖ δια-
θεῖναι. Σκυθῶν δὲ ἐξ ἠθῶν ἀναστάντων καὶ Μαρκομαννῶν πρὸς τούτοις ἐξ ἐφόδου τὰ πρόσοικα τῇ ῾Ρω-
μαίων ἀρχῇ χωρία λεηλατούντων, εἰς ἔσχατον μὲν ἡ Θεσσαλονίκη περιέστη κινδύνου, μόλις δὲ καὶ σὺν
πόνῳ πολλῷ τῆς πολιορκίας λυθείσης τῶν ἔνδον καρτερῶς ἀντισχόντων, ταραχαῖς ἡ ῾Ελλὰς ἐξητάζετο
πᾶσα. καὶ ᾿Αθηναῖοι μὲν τοῦ τείχους ἐπεμελοῦντο μηδεμιᾶς, ἐξότε Σύλλας τοῦτο διέφθειρεν, ἀξιωθέντος
φροντίδος, Πελοποννήσιοι δὲ τὸν ᾿Ισθμὸν διετείχιζον, κοινὴ δὲ παρὰ πάσης φυλακὴ τῆς ῾Ελλάδος ἐπ᾿
ἀσφαλείᾳ τῆς χώρας ἐγίνετο.

Valerian, by common consent, became emperor, and he tried valiantly to administer things well. But the
Scythians and the Makromanni were rising up from their lairs and devastating those towns that bordered on
the Roman empire. Thessalonica was in the gravest danger, and the siege was lifted only with the great effort
of those who resisted staunchly. All Greece was sorely tried by these disturbances. The Athenians began to
take care of their wall, which had not received any attention since its destruction by Sulla. The Peloponnesians, however, planned to wall the Isthmus, and from all Greece there arose a common concern for the safety
of the country.

This is the only evidence for a so-called "Valerian" fortification of the Isthmus, but many scholars
have been willing to accept this interpretation of the text (Fimmen, "Isthmos," col. 2263; *Corinth* I, i,
p. 55; Lawrence, "Skeletal History," p. 193, quoting Broneer, "Corinthian Isthmus," p. 80). The archaeological evidence seems to support a Valerian wall in Athens, but there is absolutely none for a
third-century fortification on the Isthmus. Zosimus' use of the imperfect form διετείχιζον might
show that the Peloponnesians "had it in mind to wall" or "were in the process of walling" the Isthmus, a task which they probably never finished. I owe this interpretation of the "imperfect of attempted action" to Michael Mills; see also the discussion in Clement's forthcoming volume on the
coins from Isthmia.

A.D. 396

2. Zosimus 5.6.

᾿Αλλάριχος δὲ τὴν ᾿Αττικὴν πᾶσαν ἀπόρθητον ἀπολιπὼν δέει τῶν φανέντων φασσάτων φασμάτων ἐπὶ
τὴν Μεγαρίδα παρῄει, καὶ ταύτην ἑλὼν ἐξ ἐπιδρομῆς τῆς ἐπὶ τὴν Πελοπόννησον ἐλάσεως εἴχετο, μηδεμιᾶς πειρώμενος ἀντιστάσεως. ἐνδόντος δὲ αὐτῷ Γεροντίου τὸν ᾿Ισθμὸν διαβῆναι, πάντα λοιπὸν ἦν αὐτῷ
δίχα πόνου καὶ μάχης ἁλώσιμα, τῶν πόλεων σχεδὸν ἁπασῶν διὰ τὴν ἀσφάλειαν ἣν ὁ ᾿Ισθμὸς παρεῖχεν
αὐταῖς ἀντειχίστων οὐσῶν.

Alaric then left all Attica unravaged because of the phantoms that appeared [on the wall of Athens], and he
descended on the Megarid and, taking it by a sudden attack, he advanced on the Peloponnesos, meeting
absolutely no opposition. Gerontius allowed him to cross the Isthmus, and everything then was his for the
taking, without trouble or a battle, for nearly all the cities were unwalled because of the security that the
Isthmus provided.

This passage says nothing about a fortification of the Isthmus at the time of Alaric's invasion of
Greece. The geographical setting of the Isthmus, combined presumably with Gerontius' troops,
was thought to provide adequate defense for the country. Gerontius was commander of the guard at

Thermopylai (τὸν ἐφεστηκότα τῇ Θερμοπυλῶν φυλακῇ) who, according to Zosimus, withdrew to the Isthmus to resist the Visigoths there. For one reason or another, he decided against a stand and allowed the barbarians to pass. Eunapius (*Vita Maximii*, p. 438, ed. Loeb) thought that Christian monks had somehow allowed Alaric to pass through Thermopylai.

A.D. 548–560
3. Procopius, *De aedificiis* 4.2.27–28.

Ταῦτα διαπεπραγμένος Ἰουστινιανὸς βασιλεύς, ἐπεὶ τὰς ἐν Πελοποννήσῳ πόλεις ἁπάσας ἀτειχίστους ἐμάνθανεν εἶναι, λογισάμενος ὅτι δή οἱ πολὺς τετρίψεται χρόνος, εἰ κατὰ μιᾶς ἐπιμελοῖτο, τὸν Ἰσθμὸν ὅλον ἐν τῷ ἀσφαλεῖ ἐτειχίσατο, ἐπεὶ αὐτοῦ καταπεπτώκει τὰ πολλὰ ἤδη. φρούριά τε ταύτῃ ἐδείματο καὶ φυλακτήρια κατεστήσατο. τούτῳ δὲ τῷ τρόπῳ ἄβατα τοῖς πολεμίοις ἅπαντα πεποίηκεν εἶναι τὰ ἐν Πελο-ποννήσῳ χωρία, εἰ καί τι ἐς τὸ ἐν Θερμοπύλαις ὀχύρωμα κακουργήσοιεν. ἀλλὰ ταῦτα μὲν τῇδε κεχώρηκε.

Having accomplished all these things [the fortification of Greece between Thermopylai and the Isthmus], the emperor Justinian learned that all the cities of the Peloponnesos were unwalled. He reasoned that a very long time would be consumed if he attended to them one by one, and so he securely walled the whole of the Isthmus because so much of it had already collapsed. And he built fortresses and guardstations there. In this way he made all the towns of the Peloponnesos inaccessible to the enemy, even if somehow they should force the fortifications at Thermopylai. And thus these things were accomplished.

The evidence of Procopius makes it clear that Justinian did not build the Hexamilion, but that he rebuilt an already existing structure that had suffered considerable damage (καταπεπτώκει τὰ πολλά). Procopius says that the fortification of the Isthmus was completed later than that of central and northern Greece and that the emperor adopted a different policy in the Peloponnesos from that in central Greece: the Hexamilion was to serve as the main defense, and the cities further south were left unwalled. He seems to suggest, however (4.2.24), that the wall at Corinth was rebuilt. There is some archaeological evidence that this was done (Gregory, "Late Roman Wall," pp. 272–274). This contradicts Procopius' statement in the *Anekdota* (26.33) that Justinian carried out no public works in Greece. Φρούριον was Procopius' normal term for a fortress, as opposed to a walled city or a part of a fortification (cf. *Aed.* 3.4.10; 4.1.35 [fortified farms]; 4.1.38 [fortress built above low-lying cities]). The term φυλακτήριον is more difficult to understand; it may refer to the towers, although elsewhere (e.g. *Aed.* 4.1.33) Procopius seems to use it for small, independent fortresses.

4. *IG* IV, 204   Pl. 1:a

     + Φῶς ἐκ φωτός, θεὸς
     ἀληθινὸς ἐκ θεοῦ ἀληθινοῦ,
     φυλάξῃ τὸν αὐτοκράτορα
     Ἰουστινιανὸν καὶ τὸν
     πιστὸν αὐτοῦ δοῦλον
     Βικτορῖνον ἅμα τοῖς
     οἰκούσειν ἐν Ἑλάδι τοὺς κ(α)τ(ὰ) Θεῶν
     ζῶντας. +

Light of light, true God of true God, guard the emperor Justinian and his faithful servant Victorinus along with those who dwell in Greece according to God.

BIBLIOGRAPHY: *Corinth* VIII, iii, no. 508, pp. 168–169; Monceaux, "Fouilles," 1884, pp. 277–278; A. Skias, «Ἐπιγραφαὶ Κορίνθου», Ἀρχαιολογικὴ Ἐφημερίς 1893, p. 123; Lambros, «Τὰ τείχη», pp. 268–269; G. Lampakis, «Ἕτεραι Χριστιανικαὶ ἀρχαιότητες, 3ων», Δελτίον τῆς Χριστιανικῆς Ἀρ-χαιολογικῆς Ἑταιρείας 6, 1906, pp. 46–47; Dittenberger, *Syll.*[3], no. 910; Groag, *Reichsbeamten*, p. 79; Bees, *Inschriften*, no. 1, pp. 1–5.

The syntax and spelling of the inscription are peculiar (the presumed use of the subjunctive φυ-λάξη or φυλάξῃ, the parallel use of dative and accusative participles) or incorrect (οἰκούσειν for οἰκοῦσιν, Ἑλάδι for Ἑλλάδι, and θεῶν for θεόν). This stone is now in the museum in Ancient Corinth. Many previous observers have noted that the inscription was cut on a re-used Ionic cornice block, but the block is rounded, presumably from one of the several round buildings of the Sanctuary of Poseidon. According to the Short Chronicle 35 (Testimonia, 8, below) and Pseudo-Phrantzes (p. 108, ed. Bonn), this inscription was found during the reconstruction of the Hexamilion by Manuel II in 1415. The literary texts do not indicate clearly where the stone was found or whether it was still *in situ* in the fifteenth century. These texts also variously correct the last line of the inscription to reflect a singular divinity. A similar text is found in a scholion to the Paschal Chronicle (II, p. 254, ed. Bonn).

In 1883 Monceaux rediscovered the inscription in the ruins of the South Gate, at a depth of 2 meters below ground level, but 3 meters above the level of the roadway (Monceaux, "Fouilles," 1884, p. 278). Against much modern opinion, however (e.g., *Corinth* VIII, iii, p. 168), the block was not *in situ* at that time but rather loose in the fill, since Monceaux thought that it had originally been in one of the Byzantine chapels he identified inside the Fortress. Monceaux concluded that the South Gate had been closed for some centuries by the time of Manuel's reconstruction, and he apparently felt that the inscription lay on what was ground level in the fifteenth century, a confirmation that it was not set into the wall when he found it. The inscription was probably built into the South Gate at the time of Justinian's reconstruction (but see discussion in Testimonia, 8). For the placement of a similar and roughly contemporary inscription above the arch of a gateway, see Pringle, *Defence* II, inscription 29, pl. L:b.

The date of the inscription must be after June 28, 548, when Theodora died, since the empress is not mentioned. The work of reconstruction must have been completed before 553–560, when Procopius wrote the *De aedificiis* (J. A. S. Evans, "The Dates of the *Anecdota* and the *De Aedificiis* of Procopius," *Classical Philology* 64, 1969, pp. 29–30; G. Downey, "The Composition of Procopius, *De Aedificiis*," *TAPA* 78, 1947, pp. 171–183; Stein, *Histoire* II, p. 837).

Victorinus is not mentioned in Martindale, *Prosopography*, but he was certainly an imperial official and not an architect, as some modern authorities assert. His probable involvement in fortification efforts elsewhere in the Balkans suggests that he may have been *praefectus praetorio*. Thus, Groag (*Reichsbeamten*, p. 80) suggests that the fortress at Viktoriania in Dardania (Procopius, *Aed.* 4.4.3) may have been named after him. *SEG* II, 377, from Balsi, is an epigram, again connecting Victorinus with Justinian, although in this case a decidedly pagan sentiment has replaced the Christian tone of the Isthmian inscription:

[Ο]ὐκ ἄν ποτε Λήθης τοῖς ῥίθροις δοθήσεται
['Ι]ουστινιανοῦ τὸ κράτιστον οὔνομα.
ἀλλ' οὐδ' ὁ μακρὸς καὶ ἀναρίθμητος χρόνος
γηρῶν καλύψει τοὺς πόνους Βικτωρίνου
εἰς ὕψος αὐτοῦ τῶν ἀρετῶν ἐπηρμένων.

Never will the most powerful name of Justinian be given over to the streams of Forgetfulness. And neither will long and unmeasured time, growing old, conceal the toils of Victorinus, unto the height of his exalted virtues.

5. *IG* IV, 205

> + Ἁγ(ία) Μαρία, θεοτόκε, φύλαξον
> τὴν βασιλείαν τοῦ φιλοχρίστου Ἰουστινιανοῦ
> καὶ τὸν γνησίως
> δουλεύοντα αὐτῷ
> Βικτορῖνον σὺν τοῖς
> οἰκοῦσιν ἐν Κορίνθῳ κ(ατὰ) Θεὼν
> ζῶντας. +

Holy Mary, Theotokos, safeguard the empire of the Christ-loving emperor Justinian and his faithful servant Victorinus, along with those who dwell in Corinth living according to God.

Sigismond Alberghetti brought this inscription to Venice, and it is now in Verona. Certainly, the Victorinus of this inscription is the same as in *IG* IV, 204 = Testimonia, 4, above (notice the same misspelling of θεόν), but it is not clear whether *IG* IV, 205 has any connection with the Hexamilion. More likely, it stood on the early Byzantine wall of Corinth, probably also repaired by Justinian (Gregory, "Late Roman Wall," pp. 272–274).

A.D. 1415
6. Sphrantzes (p. 4, Grecu).

> Τὸν δὲ Ἰούλιον μῆνα τοῦ κα‑ου ἔτους ἐξελθὼν ἀπὸ τῆς Πόλεως ἀπῆλθεν εἰς τὴν νῆσον Θάσον ὁ ἅγιος βασιλεὺς κῦρ Μανουὴλ καὶ ἀπῆρεν αὐτὴν τὸν Σεπτέμβριον τοῦ κβ‑ου ἔτους. Εἶτ' ἀπ' ἐκεῖ ἀπῆλθεν εἰς τὴν Θεσσαλονίκην καὶ εἰς τὸν Μορέαν καὶ ἔκτισε τὸ Ἑξαμίλιον.

In the month of June in the 21st year (1413) the emperor Manuel left the City and landed on the island of Thasos; he departed from there in September of the 22nd year (1414). He went from there to Thessalonica and to the Morea, and he built the Hexamilion.

Sphrantzes' simple account makes no mention of the events surrounding construction of the Hexamilion. He also errs in assigning the date to 1414 rather than to 1415.

7. Laonikos Chalkokondyles (pp. 183–184, ed. Bonn).

> διὸ καὶ Ἐμμανουὴλ ὁ Βυζαντίου βασιλεὺς ἐπὶ Πελοπόννησον ἀφικόμενος τόν τε Ἰσθμὸν ἐτείχισε, καὶ τοὺς Πελοποννησίους αὐτοῦ μεταπεμψάμενος, ἐπειδὴ ἐτείχισε τὸν Ἰσθμόν. ὁ δὲ Ἰσθμὸς οὗτος ξύμπασαν τὴν Πελοπόννησον, ὥστε νῆσος γενέσθαι, διείργει, ἐς δύο καὶ τεσσαράκοντα σταδίους ἀπὸ θαλάττης εἰς θάλατταν καθήκων, καθ' ὃν δὴ χῶρον καὶ Ἴσθμια ἐτελεῖτο τοῖς Ἕλλησι. διήκει δὲ ἀπὸ Κορίνθου πόλεως σταδίους πέντε καὶ εἴκοσι. τοῦτον τὸν Ἰσθμὸν ἐλαύνοντος Ξέρξεω τοῦ Δαρείου ἐπὶ τὰς Ἀθήνας ἐτειχίσαντο Πελοποννήσιοι, διακωλύειν βουλόμενοι μὴ παριέναι εἴσω τῆς Πελοποννήσου τὸν βάρβαρον. μετὰ δὲ ταῦτα Ἰουστινιανὸς ὁ Ῥωμαίων βασιλεὺς τὸ δεύτερον ἐτείχισε. καὶ οὗτος δή, ὡς εἰρηναῖα αὐτῷ πρὸς Μεχμέτη τὸν Παιαζήτεω, ἐς Πελοπόννησον ἀφικόμενος τόν τε ἀδελφὸν αὐτοῦ καθίστη ἐπὶ τὴν ἀρχὴν τῆς Πελοποννήσου καὶ τὸν Ἰσθμὸν ἐτείχισεν, ὥστε αὐτῷ τελέσαι τοὺς Πελοποννησίους ἐπὶ τὴν τοῦ Ἰσθμοῦ φυλακὴν χρήματα. προηγόρευε μὲν οὖν ἐς τὸν Ἰσθμὸν συλλέγεσθαι· οἱ δὲ ἐπείθοντο καὶ συλλεχθέντες ἐτείχιζον, συμβαλλόμενος ἕκαστος τὴν ἑαυτοῦ δύναμιν. ἐπείτε δὴ ἐς τέλος ἤγαγε τὸ τείχισμα, ἐνταῦθα συλλαμβάνει τοὺς Πελοποννησίων ἄρχοντας, οἳ πολὺν κατέχοντες χρόνον τὴν χώραν οὐδέν τι πάνυ πείθεσθαι τοῖς Ἑλλήνων ἡγεμόσι βούλοιντο, ὅ τι μὴ σφίσιν αὐτοῖς δοκοῦν ἔστι τι ὠφελεῖν αὐτούς. τότε μὲν δὴ συλλαβὼν τούτους ἐκομίζετο ἐπὶ Βυζάντιον, ἔχων καὶ τοὺς Πελοποννησίους ἐν φυλακῇ.

Meanwhile, Emmanuel, the emperor of Byzantium, arrived in the Peloponnesos and walled the Isthmus. He summoned his Peloponnesians [i.e., his vassals], after which he walled the Isthmus. This Isthmus shuts off the whole Peloponnesos so that it becomes an island, extending for four hundred and two stades, from sea to sea, and it's the place where the Isthmian games used to be celebrated by the Greeks. It is twenty-five stades from the city of Corinth. The Peloponnesians walled the Isthmus when Xerxes, the son of Darius, was advancing on Athens, wishing to prevent the barbarian from entering the Peloponnesos. After that, the Roman emperor Justinian walled it a second time. And then when there was a peace between him and Mehmet, the son of Beyazid, he [Manuel II] arrived in the Peloponnesos, established his brother as governor, and walled the Isthmus so that the Peloponnesians paid him money for the fortification of the Isthmus. He ordered [them] to assemble at the Isthmus; they obeyed and, gathering together, they built the wall, each one contributing according to his ability. When the building of the wall was completed he seized the nobles of the Peloponnesos, who, occupying the country for a long time, were unwilling to obey the rulers of the Greeks in any matter at all, which they did not think likely to bring them any profit. Then, when he had seized them, he returned to Byzantium, keeping the Peloponnesians also under guard.

Writing sometime after 1463, Chalkokondyles provides only sketchy details about the rebuilding of the Hexamilion in 1415 and the revolt of the Peloponnesian nobles. He shows that the nobles were required to assist in the construction and that they had to attend personally. His excursus into the history of the Hexamilion is a literary flourish without any solid basis, although it demonstrates contemporary concern with the antiquity of the task of defending the Isthmus. See the discussion in Testimonia, 15.

8. Short Chronicle 35 (p. 286, Schreiner, I).

ἐν ἔτι, ͵ϛϡκγ', ἰνδικτιῶνος η', μαρτίῳ κθ', ἡμέρα παρασκευῇ μεγάλῃ, ἦλθεν ὁ βασιλεύς, ὁ μακαρίτης κῦρ Μανουήλ, ἐν τῷ λιμένι τῶν Κεχρεῶν. καὶ τῇ η' ἀπριλλίου ἤρξατο ἀνακαθαίρειν καὶ ἀνοικοδομεῖν τὸ Ἑξαμίλιον, ὅπερ ἔνι τὸ μῆκος οὐργιάς, ͵γω'· ἀνέστησε δὲ πύργους ἐπ' αὐτῷ ρνγ'. εὑρέθησαν δὲ καὶ γράμματα ἐν μαρμάρῳ λαξευτὰ κατὰ τὸ μέρος τὸ ἐν τῇ Ἑλλάδι λέγοντα οὕτως· φῶς ἐκ φωτός. Θεὸς ἀληθινός. ἐκ Θεοῦ ἀληθινοῦ. φυλάξη τὸν αὐτοκράτορα Ἰουστινιανόν. καὶ τὸν αὐτοῦ δοῦλον Βικτορῖνον. καὶ πάντας τοὺς ἐν τῇ Ἑλλάδι οἰκοῦντας. τοὺς ἐκ Θεοῦ ζῶντας.

On Good Friday, March 29, 1415 (year 6923, 8th indiction), the blessed lord emperor Manuel arrived at the harbor of Kenchreai; and on April 8 he began to clear and to build the Hexamilion, which is 3800 ourgias long. And he set upon it 153 towers. And there was found an inscription in marble on the side in Hellas, saying: 'Light of light, true God of true God, guard the emperor Justinian and his faithful servant Victorinus and all those dwelling in Greece, those living according to God.'

Also edited by S. P. Lambros (Βραχέα Χρονικά, Athens 1932, no. 18, p. 35). See the discussion in Bees, *Inschriften*, no. 1 (Testimonia, 4); Barker, "Chronology," pp. 42–43, 52–53; R.-J. Loernertz, "Épître de Manuel II Paléologue aux moines David et Damien, 1416," *Silloge Byzantina in onore di Silvio Giuseppe Mercati = Studi Byzantini e neoellenici* 9, 1957, p. 295. This notice is the earliest extant narrative source (as opposed to Manuel's letter and Mazaris, Testimonia, 9 and 10) for details surrounding reconstruction of the Hexamilion. It is likely that Chalkokondyles, Pseudo-Phrantzes, and others derived their information from it. Particularly interesting is the detail about the number of towers and the indication that the inscription was found on the "side called Hellas" (the text in Lambros reads κατὰ τὸ μέρος τῆς Ἑλλάδος). Pseudo-Phrantzes (p. 108, ed. Bonn) identifies the "mainland of Hellas" (χέρσος τῆς Ἑλλάδος) as the "land of Attica" (τῆς Ἀττικῆς γῆ). Cf. P. Charanis, "Hellas in the Greek Sources of the Sixth, Seventh, and Eighth Centuries," in *Late Classical and Medieval Studies in Honor of Albert Mathias Friend, Jr.*, Princeton 1955, pp. 161–176, reprinted in *Studies on the Demography of the Byzantine Empire*, London 1972. This phrase might suggest that the Victorinus inscription was at the Northeast Gate (i.e., the side toward central Greece), but it is more likely that the source has simply erred. Several other short chronicles (e.g., Lambros, nos. 19 [p. 36], 23 [p. 42], 27 [p. 47]) mention the reconstruction of the Hexamilion in very similar language, but they contribute no additional information.

9. Manuel II (p. 68, Dennis).

καὶ πρό γε πάντων ἐκεῖνο τοὖργον, τὸ τοῖς πλείοσι δοκοῦν παντάπασιν ἀνήνυτον, τὸ τειχίζειν λέγω τὸν
Ἰσθμόν, ὡς ἄν, συναιρομένης τῆς θείας χάριτος, ἅπασι τοῖς ἔνδον οἰκοῦσιν ἀφοβίαν χαρισαίμεθα.

Ἐξῆν γὰρ φόβου χωρὶς ἀροῦν καὶ ὕλας ἡμεροῦν, καὶ σπείρειν ἄλση τέμνοντας, καὶ ἡδὺ κυμαίνοντα
βλέπειν τὰ λήϊα καὶ ἥδιον ταῦτα ἀμᾶν καὶ φυτῶν ἠμελημένων ἐπιμελεῖσθαι καὶ ἀμπελῶνα κεχερσωμένον
ἀνακαινίζειν, καὶ ἐπὶ τούτοις καινὰ φυτεύειν, καὶ τοῖς ἐξ ἁπάντων καρποῖς ἑστιᾶν μὲν ὀφθαλμόν, ἑστιᾶν δὲ
φίλον, τρυφᾶν δὲ τούτοις ἔχειν εἰς κόρον, καὶ πρός γε ἔτι πολλοῦ πιπράσκειν τὸ περιττεῦον εἰ βούλοιτο.
προσῆν τὸ τούτου κρεῖττον, ἢ μηδαμῶς ἔλαττον, βουκόλιά τε καὶ ποίμνια, καὶ τἆλλ’ ὁπόσα χειροήθη τῶν
τετραπόδων, τρέφειν εἰς πιμελήν. ἐκώλυε γὰρ οὐδέν, ἅτε δὴ τῆς τῶν βαρβάρων ἐφόδου δεδιττομένης
μηκέτι, χρῆσθαι μὲν ἐσχατιαῖς, χρῆσθαι δὲ ἄρκαις, καὶ διαιτᾶσθαι κατ’ ἐξουσίαν, κἂν τοῖς πεδίοις κἂν τοῖς
ἀβάτοις τὸ πρίν. . . . Οὐδὲ γὰρ ἠνάγκαζέ τι ἄντρον τε καὶ φρούριον ἔτι ζητεῖν ὥστε νυκτὸς αὐτοὺς κα-
θειργνύειν, οὐδὲ κρημνώδη χωρία αἰεὶν ἀγρίαις μόναις βατὰ ἤ τινα βαθεῖαν λόχμην δυναμένην ἀφανίζειν
τοὺς ἐν αὐτῇ καταφεύγοντας, ὡς ἂν μὴ θήραμα γένοιτο τοῖς ἐχθροῖς. μανίαν γὰρ εἶναι σαφῆ μετὰ τὸ
ἀνεγηγέρθαι τὰ πάλαι τείχη μακρᾶς γε αὖθις κακοπαθείας ἄλλως ἀνέχεσθαι. . . .

οἱ μὲν, οἱ κρείττους τὸν τρόπον τε καὶ τὴν σύνεσιν—οὗτοι δ’ εὐαρίθμητοι πάντως—μάλ’ ἐπήνουν τὸ μὴ
σφᾶς ἀεὶ προκεῖσθαι λάφυρον ἕτοιμον καὶ βοράν, χερσὶ καὶ στόμασι τῶν ἐχυρῶν, ἀλλὰ προθύμως ἐθέλειν
ἀλλάττεσθαι τῶν φανερῶν καὶ εἰωθότων κινδύνων τοὺς ἐν ἀδηλίᾳ κειμένους καὶ οὐ μονίμους. τούτοις δὲ
καὶ ὡμοφρόνουν καὶ ὡμολόγουν καὶ τὰ τῶν Ἰλλυριῶν ἅπαντα σμήνη, ἅτε καὶ μᾶλλον βλαπτόμενοι παρὰ
τῶν ἐχθρῶν, ἀπόλιδές τε ὄντες καὶ ἐν ἀγροῖς καὶ σκηναῖς εἰθισμένοι διαβιοῦν. τοῖς πόνοις τοίνυν εὐθὺς
αὐτοὺς ὅσοι τῶν ὀρθῶν εἴχοντο λογισμῶν, ὡς ὤφελόν γε καὶ πάντες, ἐκδεδωκότες, ἅμα τῷ τὴν γνώμην
παρρησιάσθαι, οὐ τῶν ποδῶν, οὐ τῶν χειρῶν, οὐ τοῦ παντὸς ἐφείδοντο σώματος, νύκτωρ τε καὶ μεθ’
ἡμέραν κομίζοντες ὧνπερ ἔδει τείχεσιν, εἰ δεῖ συντόμως εἰπεῖν, ἀνεγειρομένοις.

ἓν τὸ πάντων αἴτιον, τὸ τούτους εἴσω τειχῶν μὴ βούλεσθαι γεγονέναι τουτωνί, τῶν ἐν τῷ Ἰσθμῷ λέγω.
τοῦτο γὰρ βρόχος ἄντικρυς ἦν αὐτοῖς, ὡς οὐκ ἐπιτρέπον τὸ σύνολον, οὔτε τοῖς προτέροις πονηρεύμασιν
ἔτι χρῆσθαι, οὔτε μὴν μὴ καὶ τοῖς ἔργοις τῷ δεσπότῃ τὴν εὐγνωμοσύνην δεικνύναι, μέχρι δὲ τοῦ σφᾶς
αὐτοὺς εὔνους ἐκείνῳ προσαγορεύειν, ἀλλὰ καὶ προσαναγκάζον αὐτοὺς πράγμασιν αὐτοῖς βεβαιοῦν τοῦθ’
ὃ καλοῖντο. καὶ γὰρ καὶ τῷ δεσπότῃ ῥοπὴν ἐδίδου ταὐτὸ ποιεῖν.

ὁ γὰρ δὴ πολέμιος θήρ, εἰ καὶ ἐδόκει ξυνευδοκεῖν, οὐ τῇ ψυχῇ καὶ τοῖς πράγμασι. καὶ οὔτ’ αὐτὸς οὔθ’ οἱ
σατράπαι, οἵ τε γειτονοῦντες ἡμῖν, καὶ οἱ ἀμφ’ αὐτὸν ὄντες, οἷοί τε φέρειν ἐφαίνοντο τὸ παρ’ ἐλπίδα
φαινόμενον. ᾤοντο γὰρ ὡς ἔοικεν χρόνου περιόδων ἡμῖν προσδεῖν, εἰ μέλλοιμέν τι τῆς οἰκοδομῆς ἐκτε-
λέσειν. καὶ διὰ τοῦτο, λήσειν ἡμᾶς ἐλπίζοντες, σφᾶς αὐτοὺς λελήθασιν εὐγνωμοσύνην ὑποκρινόμενοι.
ὁρῶντες δ’ ὥσπερ αὐτόματα φυόμενα τὰ τείχη ἀλλ’ οὐ κατὰ τὰς αὐτῶν προσδοκίας σχολῇ, καὶ οἷον
χωλεύοντα καὶ ὅλως τούτοις ἁλώσιμα, θελήσασί γε μόνον ἑλεῖν, κρύπτειν οὐκ ἐδύναντο, καίτοι σφόδρα
θέλοντες, τὴν ὀργήν, εἰ δὲ βούλεσθε, λαμπρὰν μανίαν ἢ λύτταν, ἢ ὅ τι χεῖρον τούτων ἐστὶν εἰπεῖν. καὶ
μέντοι καὶ ἐξήμουν τὸν ἰὸν τὸν ταῖς αὐτῶν ψυχαῖς ἐμφωλεύοντα, ἠπατῆσθαι λέγοντες, καὶ μὴ φέρειν
δύνασθαι ζημίαν αἰσχύνῃ συγκεκραμένην.

Above all, there was that task which most people thought was absolutely futile, the fortification of the Isthmus, so that, with the aid of God's grace, we might favor those dwelling therein with freedom from fear. . . .

[After reconstruction of the Hexamilion] they could now till the fields without fear, reclaim woodlands and
sow where trees had once stood. They could look with pleasure upon the billowing crops and with still greater
pleasure reap them. They were able to attend to plants that had been neglected, replant the vineyard that had
been left dry, and plant new crops besides, while feasting their eyes, as well as a friend, on the fruits of all
these and luxuriate to satiety. What is more, they were able to sell their surplus at a high price if they wished.
Even better, or by no means worse, they were able to fatten herds of cattle and flocks of sheep and their other
livestock. For since they no longer lived in fear of barbarian incursion, nothing hindered them from making
use of their outlying borders, cultivating them as they wanted, be it in the plains or in formerly inaccessible
places. . . . No longer were these people forced to seek some cave or fortress to shut themselves in at night, or
precipitous places accessible only to wild goats, or some thicket deep enough to hide in and keep them from

becoming the prey of their enemies. . . . For once the ancient walls had been raised up, it would be sheer madness to endure long and pointless periods of distress again.

. . . .

First of all, those who are superior in character and wisdom—and these may be counted very quickly— strongly approved the idea of not leaving themselves constantly exposed as easy spoils and prey to the hands and mouths of their enemies; they eagerly desired to exchange obvious and familiar dangers for those which might not come at all or would pass away. All the swarms of Illyrians [Albanians] thought and said the same, inasmuch as they suffered more serious damage from the enemy, for they did not dwell in cities but were accustomed to spend their lives in the fields and in tents. Once they had freely expressed their decision, there- fore, all those men who were of sound judgment immediately set to work, as indeed, every one of them ought to have done, and they did not spare their feet, their hands, or their entire body as night and day, to put it briefly, they brought in whatever was needed to raise up the walls. . . .

. . . .

[Concerning those who were opposed,] everything can be attributed to one cause, their desire not to be within those walls, those on the Isthmus, I mean. For this was a veritable noose around their necks, inasmuch as it completely prevented them from continuing to perpetrate their former outrages and from manifesting their loyalty to the despot, not by deeds but by the mere claim to be well disposed toward him. It forced them into the position of having to confirm by their actions that they were, in fact, what they professed to be. The wall, of course, would tilt the scale in favor of the despot and enable him to compel them to act according to their profession. . . .

. . . .

For that hostile beast [Mehmet I], even though he gave the appearance of agreeing to the project, did not really do so in his soul and in his actions. Neither he nor his satraps, both those on our borders and those about him, seemed able to endure the sight of what they had not expected. They believed we were likely to need a considerable amount of time if we were going to complete any of the building. In expecting to fool us, consequently, they have fooled themselves by feigning indulgence. But when they saw the walls going up spontaneously, as it were, and not so slowly as they had expected, just limping along and an easy prize for them to take whenever they wanted, they could not conceal—despite their strong desire to do so—their anger, or, if you prefer, their wild madness or fury or whatever else worse than these can be named. They spewed forth the poison buried in their souls and claimed they had been deceived and were unable to endure this injury which had been compounded by shame.

See the analysis by Dennis, p. 218; translation and discussion by Barker, *Manuel II*, pp. 301–320; also Loenertz, "Épître de Manuel II" (see Testimonia, 8), pp. 294–304. The letter was written in late 1415 or 1416, and it is thus nearly contemporary with reconstruction of the Hexamilion. It is also remarkable for the light it sheds on the attitudes of several groups toward the project. Accord- ing to the emperor, the sultan gave his approval to the rebuilding, thinking that it would take a considerable time to be accomplished. (The reasoning for this, assuming Manuel is correct in his interpretation, is rather difficult to comprehend. It is more likely that Mehmet was simply busy elsewhere and did not feel he could actively oppose the project.) Once the reconstruction was com- plete the Turks were furious. Some few people welcomed the rebuilding. Interestingly enough, these included the large Albanian population settled in the Peloponnesos, who (according to the emperor) supported the project because they were especially vulnerable to attack. On the other hand, at least some of the Peloponnesian nobility resisted, since this reduced their independence from the despot. (See the discussion of Mazaris [Testimonia, 10, below] for further information on this resistance.)

Manuel's logic on this point is not entirely clear, since he says that reconstruction of the Hexamilion prevented them from perpetrating "their former outrages" and forced them to demon- strate their loyalty with deeds rather than words. The magnates lived in the Peloponnesos, that is, inside the fortifications, and it is unclear how the Hexamilion curtailed their independence. Per- haps they stood to lose influence with the populace when the despot provided effective defense against invasion. Alternatively, the despot may have used the Hexamilion as a large fortress or castle which gave him a solid base from which to operate in the northeastern Peloponnesos.

Manuel does not say specifically that the aristocrats were required to assist in the reconstruction, even though this offers a more plausible reason for their opposition to the project. Presumably, the aristocrats were expected to help maintain the fortification after construction, although—again—this is not the complaint Manuel mentions. The emperor does say that his supporters wore themselves out in bringing supplies for the task; to the degree that the project involved any Peloponnesian nobles, this is a confirmation that corvée labor was used. Although we should naturally be wary of the emperor's hyperbole, his comments on the state of the Peloponnesos, before and after the reconstruction, suggest the effect the Hexamilion could have. Before 1415, the Corinthia was obviously open to the ravages of whatever hostile power happened along, whether these were the troops of the sultan or not.

10. Mazaris, *Descent into Hades* (pp. 80–82, Buffalo).

Τοῦ θειοτάτου καὶ γενναιοτάτου καὶ μάλα ὑψηλοτάτου αὐτοκράτορος καὶ ἐκ Κωνσταντίνου ἀπάραντος κατὰ τὴν πέμπτην καὶ εἰκοστὴν ἰουλλίου τῆς ἑβδόμης ἰνδικτιῶνος μετὰ νηός τε μεγάλης μιᾶς καὶ πέντε τριήρων, κατέπλευσεν ἐπὶ τῇ στασιασάσῃ πολυυμνήτῳ Θάσῳ, κἀκεῖσε τρεῖς μῆνας ἐνδιατρίψας ὑφ' ἑαυτὸν ἐποιήσατο πᾶσαν, ὥσπερ ἦν πρότερον, μετὰ δυνάμεώς τε καρτερᾶς καὶ πετροβόλων μηχανημάτων, συχνῶν πρότερον καὶ μεγάλων ἐν αὐτῇ γεγονότων πολέμων. Εἶτα μέχρι καὶ Θεσσαλονίκης τοῦ τοιούτου ἐλθόντος καὶ τὰ ἐκεῖσε πάντ' εὖ καὶ ὡς εἰκὸς διαθεμένου, ἐπανῆκε μετὰ τῆς τοιαύτης δυνάμεως καὶ πρὸς τὴν τοῦ Πέλοπος χαίρων. Ἐπανῆκεν οὖν οὐ πρὸς θοίνην οὐδὲ θήραν, ἀλλ' οὐδὲ πρὸ ἄνεσιν καὶ πόνων ἀνακωχήν, τῶν πολλῶν καὶ γενναίων ἐκείνων ἔργων ὧν ἐν Θεσσαλονίκῃ καὶ Θάσῳ πεποίηκεν· ἀλλὰ τὸν ἀπ' αἰῶνος κατεσκαμμένον ἰσθμὸν τῆς Πελοποννήσου καὶ βατὸν τυγχάνοντα τῷ βουλομένῳ παντί, ὃν οὐδ' ἐν ὕπνοις ὠνειροπόλησέ τις τῶν πρὸ τοῦ βασιλέως, πρὸς τὸ τειχίσαι τε καὶ παφρῶσαι τοῦτον, παρὰ πᾶσαν προσδοκίαν ἐν πέντε πρὸς ταῖς εἴκοσιν ἡμέραις μετ' ἐπάλξεων καὶ πυργωμάτων τὸν τοιοῦτον τετείχικε περίβολον, καὶ σὺν αὐτῷ ἀνῳκοδόμησε καὶ τὰ ἐν ἄκροις κατεσκαμμένα δύο πολίχνια εἰς φρουρὰν μὲν τῶν ἔνδον συναναστρεφομένων, λιμένα δὲ τῶν χειμαζομένων ἔξωθεν ὑπ' ἀνάγκαις βαρβαρικαῖς.

Οὔπω δὲ τοῦ περιωνύμου τούτου ἔργου ἀπαρτισθέντος, οἱ πάντ' ἄνω καὶ κάτω κυκῶντές τε καὶ ταράττοντες τὰ τῶν Πελοποννησίων τὸν ἄπαντα τῆς ζωῆς αὐτῶν χρόνον, οἱ μάχαις μὲν ἀεὶ χαίροντες καὶ ταραχαῖς, φόνιον δ' ἐς ἀεὶ πνέοντες τοπάρχαι, οἱ ἀπάτης καὶ ψεύδους καὶ δόλου μεστοί, οἱ βεβαρβαρωμένοι καὶ τετυφωμένοι καὶ ἄστατοι καὶ ἐπίορκοι καὶ ἄπιστοι πρὸς βασιλέας τε καὶ δεσπότας ἀεί, οἱ ὄντες μὲν ταλάντατοι, Ταντάλου δὲ πλέον φρονοῦντες τυραννίδα τούτων ἕκαστος ἐμελέτησε, καὶ ὅρκους καὶ συμβούλια χαλεπὰ πρὸς ἀλλήλους συνέθεντο καὶ δόλους κατὰ τοῦ γενναιοτάτου βασιλέως ἔρραψαν, καὶ πρὸς τοῖς ἐργαζομένοις ἠπείλησαν ἵνα καὶ τὸν ἀνοικοδομηθέντα πρὸς σωτηρίαν αὐτῶν τε καὶ τῶν μετ' αὐτῶν περίβολον κατασκάψωσι.

When His Most Divine and Gracious Majesty the Emperor had set sail from Constantinople on July 25, 1414, with one large warship and five galleys, he landed on the far-famed island of Thasos, which had rebelled. He spent three months there, and with a powerful force supported by artillery he reduced the entire island to its former state of submission, thus putting an end to a period of frequent and heavy fighting. Next he proceeded to Thessalonica and having set everything in good and proper order there, he gladly took the opportunity to revisit with such a force also the land of Pelops. He came not to feast or hunt nor to rest and relax from his labors after all those noble exploits of his in Thessalonica and Thasos. He came to fortify with a wall and a ditch the Isthmus of the Peloponnesos, which had been dismantled for ages and lay open to anyone who wished to pass through. None of the emperors before him had even dreamed of it. But he, contrary to every expectation, needed only twenty-five days to complete such a wall with battlements and towers; and at the same time he rebuilt the two dismantled forts at either end, to provide protection for those who lived inside the wall and a refuge for those outside when threatened by pressure from the barbarians.

Even before this illustrious work had been completed, however, the local barons, that turbulent, subversive crowd, who spend all their lives upsetting the peace in the Peloponnese, men delighting in battles, riots, and always redolent of bloodshed, always full of deceit, treachery and falsehood, barbarized and demented, fickle, perjured, and forever disloyal to the emperors and despots, despicable wretches, but prouder than Tantalus . . . had the insolence, the impudence, to rise against their benefactor and savior, each of them planning to usurp power on his own behalf, and they conspired and schemed with each other, hatching plots against His Majesty; they also threatened the workmen, to get them to destroy the wall that was built for their own protection and that of their fellow citizens. . . . (Translation modified from that of the SUNY Buffalo seminar.)

Mazaris' account was written in late 1415 or early 1416. It tells us that Manuel dug a ditch in front of the Hexamilion (ταφρῶσαι τοῦτον, cf. p. 84, line 3) and that the reconstruction was completed in twenty-five days. This confirms the implication in Manuel's letter (Testimonia, 9, above) that the work was carried out remarkably quickly, before the Turks fully understood what Manuel was doing. This implies, of course, that the reconstruction cannot have been terribly extensive, although Mazaris claims that the "isthmus" had been dismantled for ages (τὸν ἀπ' αἰῶνος κατεσκαμμένον ἰσθμόν).

It is odd that Mazaris says that no earlier emperor had dreamed of fortifying the Isthmus; presumably this statement is mere hyperbole. The two fortresses at the ends of the wall must refer to the Sea Bastions on the Corinthian and the Saronic Gulfs, proving that there was such a bastion on the Saronic and that the bastions had been built previously, since Mazaris describes them as being reconstructed. He shows that the fortresses on the Hexamilion served as places of refuge, not only for those in the Peloponnesos but also for those who lived to the north of the fortifications. Mazaris goes on, beyond the exerpt quoted here, to discuss the revolt of the nobles and even to name two of them.

A.D. 1423
11. Sphrantzes (p. 16, Grecu).

Καὶ τὸ Μάιον τοῦ αὐτοῦ ἔτους ἐχάλεσε καὶ ὁ Τουραχάνης τὸ ʽΕχαμίλιον εἰς τὸν Μορέαν καὶ πολλοὺς τῶν Ἀλβανιτῶν ἐσκότωσεν.

In May of this year Turahan destroyed the Hexamilion in the Morea, and he killed many Albanians.

This attack on the Hexamilion was in response to Manuel II's would-be interference in the succession to the sultanate. See Barker, *Manuel II*, pp. 370–371, and Iorga, *Notes* I, pp. 334–335; the latter gives more details, dating the battle to May 21 and charging that the defenders deserted their posts.

A.D. 1431
12. Sphrantzes (p. 50, Grecu).

Καὶ τῷ τέλει τοῦ ἔαρος αὐτοῦ δὴ τοῦ ἔτους ἦλθεν ὁ Τουραχάνης καὶ κατεχάλασε καὶ ἔτι τὸ ʽΕξαμίλιον.

And at the end of spring in this same year Turahan came and again totally destroyed the Hexamilion.

This passage suggests that before 1431 the Hexamilion provided at least some defense for the Morea, since the Turks bothered to destroy it.

A.D. 1435
13. Sphrantzes (p. 52, Grecu).

ἐγύρισα ἀπὸ τὸ ʽΕξαμίλιον. . . .

I returned [from central Greece] by way of the Hexamilion. . . .

This passage shows that in the fifteenth century, even after the destruction of 1431, the Hexamilion was regarded as a geographical location as well as a fortification, a way-station on the road between central Greece and the Morea. It is uncertain whether the "Hexamilion", as Sphrantzes uses it here, was the Fortress at Isthmia or the wall as a whole. This geographical usage continued in later centuries, where Ξαμίλι is the generalized name for the Corinthia in the Greek portulans (the simplified geographical treatises that provided sailing directions for travel in the Mediterranean; they are preserved in many languages from the thirteenth century onward). It presumably explains the name of the modern village of Hexamilia.

A.D. 1436
14. Cyriacus of Ancona (p. 168, Bodnar).

> Ad K. Maias ad peloponensiacum Isthmom venimus, antiquis olim moenibus Lacedaemonum ope clausum; nobile quippe opus, sed longa temp. labe collapsum, bifariam a Iustiniano, atque Manuele Palaeologo Constantinopolitanus Principibus restitutum, & iterum per Achaemenidum genus dirutum. adhuc eius non paruae ruinae conspectantur [Insulum].

> On April 22 we came to the Peloponnesian Isthmus, which was shut off once upon a time by ancient walls by the Lacedaemonians; indeed this was a fine work but had collapsed in ruin through the long passage of time and was twice restored, by Justinian and Manuel Palaeologos, the emperor of Constantinople, and then again destroyed by the race of the Achaemenids [Turks]. And to this day the visible ruins of this are not insubstantial.

Cyriacus obviously refers to the destruction wrought by Turahan in 1423 and 1431. This is the earliest securely dated reference to the three-fold chronology of construction and reconstruction, with the original construction in the classical age and rebuildings by Justinian and Manuel II. Cf. the discussion in Testimonia, 15, below.

A.D. 1431–1446
15. Pythian Oracle (pp. 166–167, Bodnar).

> Δίζεαι μαθέειν τριαινοκράτορος αὐλαίης ἔρκους πέρι. οὔ ποτε τανυσίπεπλος ἐστήξει περίβολος, ἀλλά γε τείχεος ὀλοὸν ἐσσεῖται κάρτος· οἵ κέν μιν ἐγείρωσιν, οὗτοι κατερείψουσι. δύσμορον κακόμορον τοξοφόρον Ἀχαιμενιδῶν πάρα γένος ὀλεῖται τληπαθῶν Ἑλλήνων, τεθνήξεται δ' ὅτι πλεῖστον, οἰωνοῖσί τε πᾶσι καὶ θηρσὶν ἐλώρια γενήσεται.
>   ἀλλ' ἥξει τίσιος ἑκατόγχειρος δίκη, Ποσειδάονος δ' ἐς βένθε' ἁλὸς οἰχομένου, μιξοβαρβάρων ἑσπερίων θ' ἑῴων τ' ἐθνῶν ἀρχηγὸς ἰσθμὸν τειχίσει, λειοπώγων πολυμήχανος ἀνὴρ δουλοσύνης Ἑλλήνων ταλαῶν ὕπερ, τοξοφόρων δ' ὑπερβορέων μάρψει γένος, κῆρας τληπαθῶν Ἑλλήνων ἄξον ἀν' Ἑλλάδα πᾶσαν· ἄκρα δ' ἀίκητα μενεῖ.
>   ἐν τριτάτῃ δὲ μοίρᾳ ξανθὸς μέροψ, γρυπὸς πολιὸς βραχὺς Ἑλλήνων ἀρχηγὸς ἰσθμὸν τειχίσει· τύχη δ' οὐκ ἔσται πάρα. ἐν αὐτῷ γὰρ ὀλεῖται πάλιν τειχέων κρήδεμνα τοξοφόρων ἑλκεσιπέπλων πάρα κοὐκ' ἔτ' ἐσσεῖται μένος Ἑλλήνων ἀρηιφίλων.
>   ἥξει δὲ καὐτοῖς χαλκόπους Ἐρινὺς πολύπους καὶ πολύχειρ καὶ καραβαλεῖ μένος τούτων. ὅταν κόνις πίτυν δέξηται καὶ πίτυς λύθρον, τότε καρτερὸς γενήσεται περίβολος ἰσθμοῦ· δίκη δ' ἐς Ἑλλήνων γένος οὐρανόθεν ἥξει τύχης μέτα, καὶ τοὺς πρὶν αὐτῶν ἀναιδέας ὀλετῆρας ὑποθήσει ζεύγλῃ. μακάρτατος δ' ἐστὶν ὁ τὸ τέταρτον ἰσθμὸν τειχίσων, ἐνοσίχθονος πέδον.

> You desire to learn about the screen, the defense wall of him who is powerful with the trident. Never shall the long-robed enclosure stand, but its own strength will destroy the wall; those who erect it will cast it down. Ill-fated, evil fated, the race of suffering Hellenes will be destroyed at the hands of the bow-bearing Achaemenids and will die to the greatest number possible and will be prey to all the birds and beasts.

But the justice of hundred-handed vengeance will come, and, when Poseidon shall have gone into the depths of the sea, a leader of peoples half barbarian and half Hellenic, from west and east will wall the Isthmus—a smooth-bearded, resourceful man—to ward off slavery from the wretched Hellenes, and he will overtake the race of bow-bearing northerners as they are on the point of bringing death to the suffering Hellenes throughout all Hellas; and the citadels shall remain untenanted.

In the third time a fair-haired mortal, hook nosed, grizzled, short, a prince of the Hellenes, will wall the Isthmus; but good fortune will not be with him. For in his presence will be destroyed again the battlements of the walls at the hands of a bow-bearing, trailing-robed foe, and the Hellenes, dear to Ares, will no longer be mighty.

But upon these foes, too, will descend a brazen-footed Erinys, many handed and many footed, and she will overthrow their might. When dust holds pine, and pine receives gore, then will the Isthmus' enclosure grow strong; and justice will come to the race of the Hellenes from heaven, along with good fortune, and she will subject to the yoke their former shameless destroyers. Most blessed is he who for the fourth time will fortify the Isthmus, the land of the earth-shaker.

Text in Edward W. Bodnar, "The Isthmian Fortifications in Oracular Prophecy," *AJA* 64, 1960, pp. 165–172, and Lambros, «Tὰ τείχη», 1905, pp. 472–477; translation adapted from Bodnar. The prophecy is in the form of an "oracle", supposedly delivered by Pythian Apollo. Lambros identified the three constructions mentioned in the oracle and concluded that the fourth event was the refortification by Constantine (despot, later Constantine XI) of the Hexamilion in 1443 («Tὰ τείχη», 1905, p. 472). Bodnar ("Fortifications," p. 168), however, argued that a variant reading in the MS of Cyriacus, bishop of Ancona, shows that there was an epigram actually inscribed and set into the Hexamilion when the bishop visited the Isthmus in 1436, seven years before Constantine's reconstruction. He concluded that the earlier version was written sometime after the disaster of 1423 as a pious and patriotic hope for the reconstruction of the battered defenses. As we have seen, however, the Hexamilion was apparently still defensible until Turahan's incursion of 1431, and so it is preferable to date the original oracle to the period between 1431 and 1443.

In Bodnar's view, the longer version of the oracle, quoted here, is a literary embellishment of the earlier inscription. The presence of an early inscription, perhaps in place by the time of Cyriacus' visit in 1436, might explain the bishop's mention of the three-fold construction of the Hexamilion, something he could have taken from the inscription. In considering the alleged first construction of the Hexamilion, the oracle says that the Greeks themselves "will cast it down" and that they "will die to the greatest number possible." This is a strange misreading of ancient history, since the Persians never crossed the Isthmus. Both Lambros and Bodnar identified the second builder as Justinian, although Bodnar notes that a scholion on the Florence MS says that the "smooth-bearded" emperor was Nero (Bodnar, "Fortifications," p. 166, note 6). In its present form, of course, the "oracle" must have been composed after Constantine's reconstruction of 1443. See Testimonia, 16 and 17, below.

A.D. 1443

16. Sphrantzes (p. 66, Grecu, speaking of 1444).

Διερχόμενος δὲ εὗρον καὶ τὸ Ἑξαμίλιον κτισθὲν παρὰ τοῦ αὐθεντός μου καὶ δεσπότου τῷ παρελθόντι καιρῷ τοῦ ἔαρος.

Passing through [from Euboea to Mystra] I found that the Hexamilion had been [re]built by my lord and despot [Constantine] during the previous spring.

See the discussion in Zakythinos, *Despotat*, p. 226, and the letter of Cardinal Bessarion, ed. Lambros, Παλαιολόγεια, 3, pp. 32–45.

17. Laonikos Chalkokondyles (pp. 319–320, ed. Bonn).

συναγαγὼν δὲ καὶ ξύμπασαν τὴν Πελοπόννησον ἐς τὸν Ἰσθμὸν ἐτείχισεν αὐτόν, ὡς ἠδύνατο τάχιστα, συγκαλέσας αὐτοῦ καὶ τὸν ἀδελφόν, καὶ ἧς αὐτὸς ἦρχε χώρας, ξύμπαντας ἐνταῦθα μεταπεμψάμενος ἐληλάκει τὸ τεῖχος, παραδοὺς ἐνὶ ἑκάστῳ ὅσον ἐν τοσῷδε χρόνῳ παρέχοιτο ᾠκοδομημένον. ὡς δὲ τὸ τεῖχος τοῦ Ἰσθμοῦ αὐτῷ παρεσκεύαστο, στρατόν τε ἔπεμπεν ἐπὶ τὴν βασιλέως χώραν, καὶ ἐδῄου τε τὴν χώραν καὶ πολεμῶν διεγένετο.

[Constantine] gathered together the whole of the Peloponnesos at the Isthmus, and as quickly as possible he walled it. He summoned his brother also, and from the land which he ruled he summoned everybody thither and had the wall built, having assigned to each as much as he should have built within so much time. And when the wall of the Isthmus had been built for him, he sent an army to the territory of the sultan, and he passed through, ravaging the land and making war.

By summoning his subjects to help rebuild the wall, Constantine used the same means as Manuel II, except in this case Chalkokondyles specifies that the despot divided the wall into sections and assigned each to an individual. We hear nothing about a revolt against corvée labor in 1443.

A.D. 1446
18. Sphrantzes (p. 70, Grecu).

«Νῦν δ' ἐγὼ μὲν ἀπέρχομαι πρὸς οἰκοδομὴν καλίω τοῦ Ἑξαμιλίου....» ἀπῆλθον εἰς τὸ Ἑξαμίλιον τῇ η⁻ῃ τοῦ αὐτοῦ Σεπτεμβρίου μῆνος.... τῇ δὲ κζ⁻ῃ τοῦ Νοεμβρίου μηνὸς τοῦ αὐτοῦ ἔτους ἦλθεν ὁ ἀμηρᾶς κατὰ Ἑξαμιλίου καὶ τῇ ι⁻ῃ Δεκεμβρίου ἀπῆρεν αὐτὸ καὶ τὸ ἐξάλασε· καὶ ἀπελθόντος αὐτὸν καὶ ἕως εἰς τὴν Πάτραν, τὴν χώραν καὶ τὴν μόνην ἀπῆρε καὶ κατέκαυσε καὶ ἠφάνισε.

"Now I am departing for the structure called the Hexamilion...." I arrived at the Hexamilion on the eighth day of that same month of September.... On November 27 of this same year the emir came against the Hexamilion, and on December 10 he took it and destroyed it. Going as far as Patras, he took the countryside and the monastery and burned and destroyed them.

19. Short Chronicle 33 (p. 252, Schreiner, I).

δεκεβρίω γ', ἡμέρᾳ σαββάτῳ, ἦλθεν μετὰ φοσσάτου χιλιάδων ϛ' Τοῦρκος ἀμηρᾶς ὁ Ἀμωράτης, εἰς τὸ Ἑξαμίλι Κορίνθου, καὶ τῇ ἄλλῃ ἐρχομένῃ παρασκευῇ ἑσπέρα, ἤρξατο τοῦ πολέμου καὶ δι' ὅλης τῆς νυκτὸς γεναμένης ἰσχυρᾶς τῆς ἀμάχης τῷ πρωὶ ἀφείθη ὁ τεῖχος παρὰ τῶν ἐπιβούλων καὶ ἐτράπησαν εἰς φυγὴν οἱ Ῥωμαῖοι καὶ ἐσέβησαν οἱ Τοῦρκοι καὶ ἐδίωκων αὐτούς, καὶ ἐπῆραν ἄπειρα πλήθη καὶ ἅρματα καὶ ζῶα καὶ χρήματα πολλά.

On the third of December, a Saturday, the Turkish emir Murad came to the Hexamilion of Corinth with a force of six thousand troops. On the following Friday evening the battle began, and the fighting was violent throughout the night; early in the morning the wall was taken by the attackers, and the Romans were put to flight. The Turks were in control, and they pursued [the Romans], and as many as they captured they made prisoners. And they took an innumerable multitude, along with much weaponry, animals, and money.

This text shows that the despots offered considerable resistance to the Turks. We do not know how large the Byzantine force was, but the despots clearly carried out a spirited defense of the Hexamilion. Chronicle 47 (Schreiner, *Kleinchroniken* I, p. 346) has essentially the same information as the text above, although it identifies the Turkish commander as Turhan and gives the size of the Ottoman force as 50,000; it also says specifically that the despots Constantine and Thomas defended the Hexamilion in person. It concludes: καὶ ἐγίνεται θρῆνος καὶ οὐαὶ πολὺ εἰς τοὺς Ῥωμαίους. ὤ, τί θρῆνος γέγονε.

20. Laonikos Chalkokondyles (pp. 345–346, ed. Bonn).

καὶ ἕκαστοι παρασκευσάμενοι ἐπήεσαν ἐς τὸ τεῖχος, αὐτίκα τειχομαχοῦντες κατὰ τὸ ἰσχυρόν. βασιλεύς τε
αὐτὸς καὶ οἱ νεήλυδες κατὰ τὸ μέσον τοῦ Ἰσθμοῦ, ἧπερ ἐσκήνουν, καθίσαντο ἐς μάχην, καὶ κλίμακάς τε
προσέφερον, καὶ διορύσσοντες τὸ τεῖχος ἠγωνίζοντο ὡς ἐξαιρήσοντες. καὶ τούς τε τηλεβολίσκους ταύτῃ
ταξάμενος οὐκ εἴα τοὺς Πελοποννησίους προκύπτειν. δεινὸν γάρ τοι ὁ τηλεβολίσκος, καὶ οὐδὲν τῶν ὅπλων
ἀντέχει ὥστε μὴ διαχωρεῖν διὰ πάντων καθικνούμενος. δοκεῖ δὲ κἀπειδάν τι αὐτῷ ἀντέχῃ, τότε δὴ μάλιστα
καθικέσθαι ἐπὶ πλέον, ἐπεὶ ἔς τε βάμβακα καὶ κρόκην καὶ τὸ ἔριον οὐκ ἂν οὕτω καθίκοιτ’ ἂν ἐπὶ πολύ. ἐπεὶ δ’
ἐν ἀδείᾳ τε ἐγένοντο οἱ νεήλυδες, καὶ τάς τε κλίμακας ἐς τὸ τεῖχος ἐνεγκάμενοι ἀνέβαινον, καὶ ὑπερέβησαν
ταύτῃ ᾗ ἐθεᾶτο ἑστὼς ὁ βασιλεύς, ἀνέβη ἐπὶ τὸ τεῖχος νήελυς Χιτήρης, Τριβαλλὸς τὸ γένος, καὶ εἷλέ τε
τὸ τεῖχος, καὶ τοὺς ταύτῃ διωσάμενος ἐς φυγὴν ἐτρέψατο.

When every one [of the Turks] was ready, they attacked the wall and immediately began fighting fiercely.
The sultan himself and the Janissaries were fighting at the middle of the Isthmus, where they had their camp,
and they brought ladders, and digging under the wall they struggled to destroy it. They focused the bombardment there, and the Peloponnesians could not even look out. Artillery bombardment is a terrible thing,
let me tell you, and no weapon can resist it so as to prevent it penetrating through everything when it lands.
And it seems that whenever anything does hold out, then it rains down even more, since it could do no more
against cotton, cloth, or wool. When the Janissaries were given the nod, they brought ladders to the wall and
ascended. They scaled the wall where the sultan stood watching, and the first on the wall was the Janissary
Chitris, a Serbian, and he took the wall, and thrusting through those who were there, he put them to flight.

Chalkokondyles' account provides many details, some perhaps drawn from family sources since he
says that his father served as an ambassador of the despot in the latter's attempt to secure a peace
before the battle (p. 343, lines 9–10). He gives 6,000 as the size of the Turkish army (p. 343, lines
13–14), and he shows that the Hexamilion was still in defensible condition since Murad saw that
ἔχει τε φυλακῆς τὸ τεῖχος καὶ παρασκευῆς ἐς τὸν πόλεμον (p. 343, lines 14–15). Indeed, it was
necessary to bring ladders against it and attempt mining operations. From this text it is clear that
the main attack came in the "middle of the Isthmus" and that the determining factor was the
artillery bombardment. The Hexamilion was never designed to withstand an attack with cannon,
although the resistance was nevertheless apparently spirited and determined. Cf. Chronicle 36
(Schreiner, *Kleinchroniken* I, p. 293), Ducas 32, line 6 (p. 223, ed. Bonn), and the discussions in
Lambros, «Τὰ τείχη», 1905, pp. 479–486 and Schreiner, *Kleinchroniken* II, pp. 467–469.

Νεήλυδες literally mean "newcomers", "converts", or "recruits", but the word presumably represents a translation of the Turkish *veniceri* (from *veni*, "new"), and refers to the Janissaries.
Particularly interesting is the information about the Serbian Janissary Chitiris; his name in Old
Church Slavonic means "fast, quick, clever, adroit" (Fr. Miklosich, *Lexicon Palaeslovenico-Grae-
co-Latinum*, Vienna 1862–1865, p. 1103; cf. M. Vasmer, *Russisches etymologisches Wörterbuch*
IV, Moscow 1973, p. 240). He was thus probably an actual historical figure, although it is possible
that the name was an appropriate fiction for the first attacker over the wall. Chalkokondyles, however, was writing only a few years after the event. It seems unlikely that he would record a story of a
legendary name created in Slavonic.

A.D. 1452

21. Pseudo-Phrantzes (p. 235, ed. Bonn).

ἐλθόντος οὖν τοῦ Τουραχάνη καὶ τὰ τείχη τοῦ Ἰσθμοῦ αὖθις ἀώσαντος, καὶ ἀμφοτέρων τῶν μερῶν
πλεῖστοαι ἀπεκτάνθησαν, λέγω Χριστιανῶν καὶ ἀπίστων, μάλιστα ἐκ τῶν Χριστιανῶν, οἳ καὶ εἰς φυγὴν
ἐτράπησαν. αὐτὸς δὲ καταλιπὼν τὴν Κόρινθον καὶ διὰ μέσσου τῆς νήσου ἐρχόμενος. . . .

> When Turahan arrived and again took the walls of the Isthmus, many from both sides indeed were killed, both Christians and infidels, but especially Christians, who indeed fled. And he left Corinth and went into the interior of the peninsula. . . .

This attack on the Peloponnesos was apparently designed to neutralize the despots Demetrios and Thomas and prevent them from aiding in the defense of Constantinople. Again, the Hexamilion seems to have been strongly defended, although once again the Turks prevailed after heavy casualties.

A.D. 1458

22. Laonikos Chalkokondyles (p. 443, ed. Bonn).

ὡς δὲ εἰσέβαλε καὶ ἐντὸς τοῦ Ἰσθμοῦ ἐγένετο, ἐπελαύνων αὐτίκα τὴν Κόρινθον ἐπολιόρκει.

> When he [Mehmet II] invaded and came within the Isthmus, he marched straight for Corinth and beseiged it.

This text suggests that in 1458, when Mehmet began the Ottoman conquest of the Peloponnesos, the Hexamilion was undefended. At least, Chalkokondyles mentions no struggle at the Isthmus, as had been the case in 1446 and 1452.

A.D. 1462

23. Sphrantzes (p. 128, Grecu).

καὶ ἐλθόντος τοῦ τζενεράλη καπετάνου Ἀλωΐζου Λορδᾶ ἐκείνου μετὰ πολλῆς ὅτι παρασκευῆς καὶ δυνάμεως, ἐπίασε τὸ Ἐξαμίλιον καὶ ἔκτισεν αὐτό, κακῶς δὲ ἀπὸ τῆς συντομίας, Οὐ γὰρ ἐν συντόμῳ τὰ ἀσφαλές, ὡς ὁ λόγος, ἀλλ᾽ ὡς ἐπεὶ ἐπολέμησε τὴν Κόρινθον καὶ οὐκ ἔτυχε τοῦ ἐλπιζομένου, ἀφείς καὶ τὸ Ἐξαμίλιον ἀπῆλθε.

> Coming there with considerable preparation and power, the captain general Aloizo Lorda took the Hexamilion and [re]built it, poorly as it turned out because of the shortness of time. "For security doesn't come in a short time," as the saying goes. And when he attacked Corinth and didn't accomplish what he hoped, he left the Hexamilion also and went away.

This refortification of the Hexamilion shows that the Venetians hoped to gain control of the whole Morea shortly after the Ottoman conquest. The Venetians had recently taken Argos, and by securing the Isthmus they planned to keep the Turks at bay while they solidified their hold on the peninsula. Chronicle 36 (Schreiner, *Kleinchroniken* I, p. 294) reports that in September of 1463 ἐπίασαν οἱ Φράγγοι τὸ Ἐξαμίλιον. Presumably, this refers to the same event, although Greek texts usually distinguish between the Venetians and the "Franks". Cf. also Chalkokondyles, pp. 557–558 (ed. Bonn), Chronicles 33 (Schreiner, *Kleinchroniken* I, p. 255) and 37 (p. 300), for 1463.

A.D. 1676

24. George Wheler, *A Journey into Greece*, London 1682, p. 437.

> We alighted to visit the Ruins of that famous Place, where the Isthmian Games were celebrated; which was on the Hill, being part of Mount Oneius before mentioned. There are yet to be seen the Ruins not only of the Town, old Walls, and several old Churches, but also the Remains of the Isthmian Theatre.

Cf. Jacob Spon and G. Wheler, *Voyage d'Italie, de Dalmatie, de Grèce et du Levant*, Lyon 1678, II, p. 293: "Examiglia . . . quelques restes d'une muraille qui traversoit d'une mer à l'autre." See also A. Bon, *Corinth* III, ii, pp. 146–149, especially on the veracity of Wheler. Wheler and Spon were in the Corinthia in February of 1676.

A.D. 1802

25. Mary Nisbet, *The Letters of Mary Nisbet, Countess of Elgin*, arranged by Lieutenant Colonel Nisbet Hamilton Grant, London 1926, p. 181.

> Next morning we rode to the foot of Acrocorinthus from whence we had a view of Mount Helicon, Parnassus, the Gulph of Lepanto, the City of Sicyon, and the commencement of the wall which crosses the Isthmus, separating Greece from the Peloponnesus.

A.D. 1806

26. Leake, *Travels* III, pp. 286–287, 297–298, 302–305.

> [286] At about fifty yards from this wall, to the northward, and about double that distance eastward of the theatre, are the remains of an ancient enclosure, which was undoubtedly the peribolus of the temple of Neptune. The wall which surrounded the sacred ground is now a heap of ruins; it was of the most regular kind of Hellenic masonry externally, but was filled up with rubble between the casings. It was flanked with square towers; the northern side formed [287] part of a line of fortification, which stretched across the isthmus. Among the stones of the peribolus I find a few fragments of a large Doric edifice, particularly that of a column, of which the chord of the fluting is ten inches and a half in length; this is the only measurable dimension, but it is sufficient, I think, to shew that the column belonged to the Temple of Neptune, though I could not find a vestige of the foundations of that building. The enclosed space is now a level pasture. The northern wall of the peribolus, or Isthmic wall, takes a southerly direction eastward of the peribolus, and is traced as far as a brow which overhangs, on the northern side, a small torrent bed, terminating in a level at the head of the Bay of Kalamaki. Another wall crossed from the same brow to a height on the southern side of the level, where probably stood a small fortress, forming part of a plan of defense toward the sea; all these walls were flanked with square towers. Westward of the peribolus the Isthmus wall is traced, for about 300 yards, to the foundations of another small fortress; and from thence, westward across the isthmus, as far as the bay of Lechaeum, and thus the whole appears clearly to have been a connected system of permanent fortification for the defense of the Isthmus, as well as for the safety of the Hierum.
>
> [297] As nothing can be more obvious and natural than the project of erecting works of defense across the Isthmus, for the protection of the peninsula, or than the more important design of cutting a canal through it, by which its defensive strength would be increased, at the same time that a circuitous and often a dangerous navigation round the southern end of the peninsula would be avoided; so we find, that both these operations are often alluded to in ancient [298] history.
>
> [302] To fortify it is a much easier operation, and accordingly we still trace, as I have already remarked, the remains of a Hellenic wall, flanked with towers from the bay of Schoenus to that of Lechaeum. Wheler, who observed this fortification, supposed it to have been the work of the Lacedaemonians. The only authority that I can find to countenance this supposition is Diodorus, who states, that the Peloponnesians, at the time of the Persian invasion, *strengthened* the wall across the Isthmus; which seems as if some permanent work had previously existed. The far better evidence of Herodotus, however, speaks only, on that occasion, of one of those field works often executed in the wars of Greece for temporary purposes, and which were composed of rude stones, bricks, timber, and earth. Neither Thucydides nor Xenophon allude to any lines of defense, as having formed an obstacle on any of the occasions on which they describe the hostile pro[303]gress of troops through the Isthmus; and Diodorus describes that which was erected when Athens, Sparta, and Corinth endeavoured to defend the Isthmus against the Boeotians [B.C. 368] as nothing more than a ditch and palisade.
>
> Nevertheless, it is certain, that there was at one time a permanent fortification, since its remains, built in the manner of the best times, still attest the fact. It began on the shore of the bay of Lechaeum, about three quarters of a mile southward of the canal of Nero, and extended across the narrowest part of the Isthmus to the bay of Schoenus. It was constructed of a masonry rather regular, and such as does not seem to indicate a very remote antiquity. It was flanked with square towers on the northern side, shewing that it was intended for the protection of the Isthmus toward the Megaris. It followed the crest of the low cliffs already mentioned wherever this natural advantage offered itself; and in some parts there are traces of the [304] wall having had the additional defense of a ditch. Some wells are visible also in the line of the ditch, which were, perhaps, no more than excavations for the purpose of ascertaining the nature of the soil when the formation of a canal was

intended. At the western end the line terminated in a square fortress, standing upon the shore of the bay of Lechaeum. Of this the foundations still remain, and have served to form part of a similar work, which in later times has been erected upon it; and of which the last repairs were probably made by the Venetians. I have already described the termination of the Isthmic wall at the eastern end; and thus no doubt can remain, that a line of permanent fortifications existed at some period of ancient history. It seems most probable, that it was a work of the Corinthians, and was, perhaps, a [305] part of their system for defending the Corinthia, and at the same time for obtaining the command of the entrance into the Peloponnesus, which the position of Corinth naturally suggested, and of the existence of which some proofs have already been given from ancient history.

Until the beginning of modern excavations, most modern scholarship was based on Leake's account. It contains details about many features no longer visible today, but it is also susceptible of considerable error. Thus, Leake is incorrect about the date of the Hexamilion and the characterization of the masonry as classical, but he is right to question the evidence of Diodoros and Herodotos about the date of the fortification. More important, Leake provides crucial evidence about the fortresses at either end of the Hexamilion and about its course near the Saronic Gulf.

A.D. 1819

27. E. Dodwell, *A Classical and Topographical Tour through Greece* II, London 1819, pp. 183–184.

[Coming from Mt. Geraneia,] we soon after crossed a large foss near the sea of Corinth. Our *agiogiates* informed us that it was excavated by the Hellenes, in order to unite the two seas, but that the undertaking was abandoned when blood was perceived to issue from the earth where they dug. A quarter of an hour more brought us to a place called Kastro-Teichos, where three thick parallel walls, which commence at the sea, extend towards the Saronic Gulf. They are composed of small stones, bricks, and rubbish, and were constituted to guard the entrance into the Peloponnesos. A little further on are some other remains of a similar kind. They are not built in a straight line across the Isthmus, but follow the sinuosities of the ground. The remains of the square towers with which they were fortified are also visible.

Dodwell's description parallels and complements that of Leake, although it is not nearly so full or so accurate. The Kastro-Teichos is undoubtedly the Fortress at Isthmia. It is likely that the road Dodwell took led from Schoinos to Isthmia and thence to Corinth (it was thus on the line of the primary ancient road). He was certainly wrong to see three parallel walls, and his testimony has led to much confusion among subsequent authors who seem to have followed Dodwell without careful autopsy. After this passage Dodwell gives a brief history of the fortifications, as he understood it (*Tour*, pp. 184–187).

IV

THE HEXAMILION FROM SEA TO SEA

THE HEXAMILION ran between the Gulf of Corinth and the Saronic Gulf, a length of some 7,500 meters. The course of the fortification is described in the pages below, beginning at its western termination on the Gulf of Corinth and proceeding eastward toward the Saronic Gulf. Because the Fortress at Isthmia has been extensively excavated, it is not described here but rather in Chapters V–IX below. The course of the Hexamilion across the Isthmus may be followed in the series of plans, Figures 3–10 (cf. Figs. 2, 11). The visible traces of the Hexamilion are shown as a solid line, while its presumed course is indicated with dashed lines. On these plans the towers west of the Fortress at Isthmia, beginning at the Gulf of Corinth, are designated with a "W" and numbered consecutively, 1–26, from west to east.[1] To the southeast of the Fortress the towers are designated with an "S" and numbered consecutively, 1–21, from the Fortress to the Saronic Gulf. These plans also show the running distance along the Hexamilion from the Sea Bastion in the west to the presumed eastern termination of the Hexamilion near the Saronic Gulf; this distance is shown in 100-meter increments: 0+100 m., 0+200 m., and so on. Hatched lines, parallel to the face of the Hexamilion (e.g., along the eastern face between S-3 and S-8, Fig. 8), indicate that traces of the *taphros*, the defensive trench in front of the wall, are visible in a given area. The elevation of the Hexamilion may also be followed on Figure 11, which shows sections through the Isthmus along the course of the Hexamilion, with the towers and the running distance recorded as on Figures 3–10 and heights above sea level clearly indicated at either end of the sections.

FROM THE GULF OF CORINTH TO THE KYRAS VRYSI RAVINE

The termination of the Hexamilion on the Corinthian Gulf was W-1, the powerful Sea Bastion (Figs. 3, 12; Pl. 1:b–d). This fortress was built on a small northerly projection of the coastline at a point of considerable natural strength. It was designed not only to protect the low-lying shoreline but to discourage an enemy from turning the western end of the Hexamilion by sea. Immediately above the Bastion is a line of cliffs that marked the shore in earlier geological time.[2] These cliffs run in a generally northeast–southwest direction, and they now approach the sea just above the Sea Bastion. From this point, however, the cliffs swing around to the south, forming the depression in which the city of New Corinth is situated. Thus, to the east and northeast of the Sea Bastion is the coastal plain which sweeps around the head of the Gulf of Corinth toward Loutraki. To the south, however, is a line of high cliffs, while to the west is the low-lying land that was probably marshy and partially impassible in antiquity (seen in Plate 1:b).

The position occupied by the Sea Bastion, therefore, was admirably suited to block the path of an invader who sought to cross into the Peloponnesos along the flat land on the west side of the Isthmus. An invader approaching the Hexamilion by sea from the west would, of course, have landed far to the west, but the Hexamilion was not designed against such an enemy. On the other hand, the artillery, which was surely stationed on the Sea Bastion, would easily attack a land-based enemy who might embark in ships in an attempt to turn the western end of the Hexamilion by sea.

---

[1] No attempt has been made on these plans to represent the actual width of the Hexamilion or the shape of the individual towers. For information on this, consult the running text and the tables in the Appendix.

[2] Freyberg, *Geologie*, pp. 52–56, pl. 31.

Until quite recently, at least the lower part of the Sea Bastion was well preserved, and in 1806 Leake noted that on the west the Hexamilion terminated in a "square fortress". "Of this," he said, "the foundations still remain, and have served to support part of a similar work," which he thought the Venetians had probably erected.[3] Much of this was apparently still standing in 1932 when Fowler described "a rounded structure serving to support a small house and garden";[4] his figure 23 presents a view of the northeastern face of the Bastion as it was at that time. As recently as 1980, a large section of the landward part of the Bastion remained *in situ* until it was destroyed in a road-widening operation (Pl. 2:a). At present, all that remains of the Sea Bastion is a large foundation, broken into several parts and rising up from the sea just below the modern road between New Corinth and the western crossing of the Corinth Canal at Poseidonia (Fig. 12).

The foundations of the Sea Bastion were laid on a thin layer of crumbly conglomerate that overlay a deep deposit of clay. Over the centuries the waves wore away much of the clay layer, and the upper parts of the Bastion tilted unevenly and collapsed. During those years, as both Leake and Fowler noted,[5] the superstructure of the Bastion was rebuilt and re-used; in its latest phases the uneven floor was leveled with liberal applications of mortar.

For the sake of convenience, the remains of the Sea Bastion may be divided into three sections (Fig. 12: A, B, and C). Section A is a large mass of masonry, generally constructed of medium-sized stones, roughly coursed and laid in mortar. The western face, now visible above the beach (Pl. 1:d), was probably never intended to be seen, as it would have been underground when the Bastion was built. This explains why it was not faced at this level, although there were probably ashlar facing blocks higher up. The deep foundations of the eastern part of Section A, however, are made of large cut blocks, obviously taken from ancient buildings. Section A preserves straight edges on its west and south sides, although it tilts downward considerably from west to east. The topmost part of this section is made of small, uneven stones set in thick mortar. Section A is preserved to a height of 5.40 m. above sea level. On the west the conglomerate ledge has been washed away, but on the east the top of the ledge is at an elevation of +2.30 m.

Section B is made entirely of large cut blocks, like the eastern part of Section A. In the preserved eastern face are two Ionic architrave-frieze blocks (one of which is shown in Plate 2:b; cf. *Corinth* I, i, p. 57, fig. 23[6]), and a third lies on the beach just to the east of the Bastion. This section preserves an interior corner which is in line with the southern face of Section A, showing that the two pieces were once part of the same structure. The alignment is also clear on the western face of Section B near the water, where it is possible to see how the two sections once fitted together and where one block was broken in two at the time the Bastion collapsed. The eastern face of Section B as preserved has no even surface, and it must at one time have extended farther in this direction. Like Section A, Section B tilts slightly toward the west, and it has a covering of small rubble and mortar, added in a late phase of the structure (but obviously before the collapse).

Section C is made of small stones and mortar, with a facing of cut blocks along the eastern side. It is clearly preserved farther south into the scarp, but the overburden of washed-in soil makes any further investigation impossible. Section C seems to be on the same line as the section of wall

---

[3] Leake, *Travels* III, p. 304; see Testimonia, 25. Cf. Frazer, *Pausanias* III, p. 5.

[4] *Corinth* I, i, p. 53.

[5] Leake, *Travels* III, p. 304 (Testimonia, 26), repeated by many scholars, including Frazer, in his commentary on Pausanias. *Corinth* I, i, p. 53: "At the point where Frazer says the wall 'ended in a square fortress,' there is a rounded structure serving to support a small house and garden. In the foundation are ancient blocks, none of which is in the position for which it was intended." Cf. Fig. 23.

[6] This photograph shows how little the east face of Section B has changed in the past 75 years, while the area beyond Section C has been nearly completely covered with soil.

destroyed in 1980 (Pl. 2:a). This masonry was on the south side of the road between New Corinth and Poseidonia and on a line with the Hexamilion as it ascends the cliff to the south (see Fig. 3 and below).

The poor state of preservation of the remains makes reconstruction difficult, especially since it is impossible to know how much of the Bastion may have been destroyed by the sea on the north. As we have seen, the southwest corner of the Bastion is preserved, as is an internal corner on the west side of Section B. In addition, the face of the wall in Section C may be taken as the eastern face of the Bastion, allowing us to reconstruct the normal width of the Hexamilion (2.95 m.), with a stairway (*ca.* 0.80 m. wide) added to the internal face, beginning *ca.* 10.60 m. south of the south wall of the Bastion.

The rest of the reconstruction must be based on analogy. The south side of the Bastion may be hypothetically restored by projecting it to a point that meets the line of the east face of Section C (see plan, Fig. 12). This makes the south side approximately 10 meters long, the same size as the large square towers of the Land Walls of Constantinople, and we may accordingly suggest that the Sea Bastion was originally a square about 10 meters on a side.

The Sea Bastion may thus be restored as a large tower that rose at least one story above the level of the fighting platform on the curtain wall. The large upper surface of the Bastion would have been designed to carry artillery to fire on any ships that attempted to turn the western end of the Hexamilion. In addition, the Bastion was placed so as to offer fire along the entire face of the Hexamilion as it ascended the cliffs above the narrow coastal plain in this vicinity. This would naturally have been a particularly vulnerable section of the wall, but fire from the Sea Bastion below and the first tower above (W-2) would have considerably strengthened the fortifications.

The closest parallel for the Sea Bastion is the so-called Mermer-Kule at the southwest corner of the Land Walls of Constantinople.[7] The Mermer-Kule projected out from the course of both the Land Walls and the later Sea Walls, providing a formidable barrier for an enemy who hoped to turn the corner of the fortification. It was faced with blocks of well-cut ashlar and stood to a height of one story above the fighting platform of the curtain wall. The Mermer-Kule survives today in reasonably good condition and thus provides an indication of the original appearance of the Sea Bastion on the Hexamilion.

Above the Sea Bastion the Hexamilion ascends a low cliff to reach the first plateau above the narrow coastal plain (Figs. 3, 11). At this point (0+82 m.) the first regular tower (W-2) is located on a rock outcrop overlooking the approach of the wall from the sea (Pl. 2:c). As will be seen frequently in this study, over the centuries the remains of the Hexamilion have been used as building materials, foundations, and convenient, ready-made walls for later buildings. Tower W-2 is located in the outskirts of modern Corinth, in a courtyard of the Disco Vrachos, where it is partially buried by later walls. It is quite overgrown with vegetation. The clay below the conglomerate-rock footing for the tower has been hollowed out to form a room, sometime well after the construction of the Hexamilion. Vegetation and the encroachment of modern buildings make measurement, and even identification of the Hexamilion, difficult. It is impossible to give the full dimensions of the tower, but the western façade is preserved to a height of three courses. The stones used in the tower are not all of an even size, and some of them are quite small and only partially squared.

East of Tower W-2 the Hexamilion follows the top of a cliff, which becomes increasingly steep (Figs. 3, 11). Defenders stationed along this stretch of wall held the high ground above the western coastal plain as it approached the Sea Bastion. Invaders who hoped to breach the Hexamilion along

---

[7] Kirchen, *Landmauer* I, pl. 40; Meyer-Plath and Schneider, *Landmauer* II, pls. 1 (plan), 12:a (photograph).

this natural approach would thus have been funneled into a narrow defile between the sea and the cliff. There they would have been exposed to fire from above and from the front.

Although the dense vegetation and modern construction make identification frequently difficult, the course of the Hexamilion is clear and its foundations are occasionally visible. Just before reaching a distance of 0+200 m., the Hexamilion passes the church of Agios Spyridon, and in this area the rubble-and-mortar core of the Hexamilion can be clearly discerned (Pl. 3:a). Some cuttings in bedrock are visible near the apse of this church. It is possible that a tower in the Hexamilion once stood here, although no certain trace of it survives. The Hexamilion, however, continues to overlook the narrow coastal plain at this point, and it would have been an ideal location for a tower.

East of Agios Spyridon the foundations of the Hexamilion are sporadically visible as it passes north of the Hospital of New Corinth, still hugging the edge of the cliff and slowly gaining height. Just before it reaches the first of the several gullies that lay in its path (between 0+400 and 0+600 m.; Fig. 3), all trace of the Hexamilion disappears. Presumably, it continued along the edge of the cliff until it reached the side of the gully, on either side of which towers were undoubtedly located. Unfortunately, no trace of the Hexamilion can be seen in this area, and it is impossible to say how it spanned the gully, which is *ca.* 70 meters wide and 12 meters deep. On the east side of the gully, however, the Hexamilion is once again visible, running eastward from the ruins of a World War II artillery emplacement that was constructed at this strategic location (just west of 0+600 m.). It is noteworthy that in crossing this first gully, the Hexamilion gained several meters in elevation; east of the gully it continues to rise slowly, reaching an elevation of more than 34 meters above sea level. The gully also marked another transition, since at this point the Hexamilion left the lowest plateau above the coastal plain and began to turn inland, running along the northern edge of an interior plateau. The land north of the Hexamilion in this area slopes away more gradually toward the coast, making the fortifications more vulnerable to an attack from the north. Even here, however, the Hexamilion could be built on a small ridge, where the descent became steeper, allowing the defenders to make use of this geographical advantage. Although there may have been a *taphros* in this stretch of the Hexamilion, no trace of it is visible today.

Between 0+600 and 0+700 m. the Hexamilion is very well preserved, standing occasionally to a height of 1.5 m. in three courses. Just beyond 0+700 m., it spans a small gully and then turns slightly to follow a course almost directly east. On the east side of the gully the Hexamilion preserves a face of regular masonry, and there is evidence of a sizable spillway to allow water from the gully to pass under the wall. Midway between 0+700 and 0+800 m., a modern road crosses the Hexamilion, giving access from the coastal plain below. This is the first modern road encountered along the course of the Hexamilion east of the coast road at the Gulf of Corinth, and it is presumably on the line of an ancient roadway. This area therefore would have been especially vulnerable to attack. We should probably assume that a tower stood at this point, although no trace of one survives. Investigation in this vicinity revealed an inscribed block (IΣ 70-3, Pl. 3:b), which was probably built into the Hexamilion, although it was found lying detached on the ground. The block contains a crudely cut cross with abbreviations [IC] XC NK = Ἰησοῦς Χριστὸς Νικᾶ, loosely translated as "Jesus Christ, Victory," a common sentiment in Byzantine inscriptions and graffiti. Although the inscription was probably built into the Hexamilion as a prayer and an apotropaic device, it was unlikely to have been placed there at the time of the original construction, since inscriptions of this type are usually attributed to the Middle Byzantine period.[8]

---

[8] See, for example, Meyer-Plath and Schneider, *Landmauer* II, p. 123, inscription 1. Cf. Hans Lietzmann, *Die Landmauer von Konstantinopel*, Berlin 1929, p. 21, who argues that the phrase arose in reaction to the earthquake of

In the area just east of 0+800 m. the Hexamilion follows the line of an increasingly steep cliff. The builders of the Hexamilion enhanced this natural feature, cutting the face of the cliff down sharply and creating a nearly vertical line (Pl. 3:c). The Hexamilion in this area appears to have been rebuilt in several phases, and much of the facing material has been robbed away. In one section a facing of roughly cut, medium-sized blocks was set over the rock-cut surface using large quantities of mortar (Pl. 3:d). In other sections larger cut blocks were set over the rock face. In at least one instance, the cut surface of the cliff seems to have been used as the outer face of the Hexamilion, since large cut blocks were set directly on top of the line of bedrock.

East of 0+800 m. the Hexamilion again begins to rise. Just past 0+900 m. (Fig. 4), it reaches a height of 40 meters above sea level. Beyond 0+1,000 m. the land below the Hexamilion becomes steeper, while the plateau above is almost completely flat. Just beyond 0+1,100 m. the foundations of the Hexamilion have been removed by modern earthworking. The Hexamilion, however, must have approached the second large gully in much the manner shown on Figure 4. There is, unfortunately, no trace of the fortification either in the gully or on the bank immediately to the east. It is impossible, therefore, to tell whether the Hexamilion spanned the gully as suggested or whether it followed the sides of the gully for a distance and crossed somewhere to the southwest, making the actual crossing narrower and less deep: at its mouth the gully is over 80 meters wide and 20 meters deep. Once again, there were presumably towers on either face of the gully crossing, although no trace of them has survived.

Less than 10 meters east of the east edge of the gully, however, the foundations of the Hexamilion are once again visible, and these follow a relatively straight line to the southeast, past 0+1,300 and 0+1,400 m. The landscape becomes noticeably flatter, and the wall ascends gradually to a height of 48 meters above sea level. Traces of the foundations disappear briefly beyond 0+1,400 m., but they reappear just east of 0+1,700 m., making the course of the Hexamilion clear. About 20 meters west of 0+1,800 m. are the remains of a rectangular tower (W-3), the first one clearly visible since Tower W-2, immediately above the Sea Bastion. Almost directly north of this tower is the beginning of the *taphros*, the deep cutting excavated in front of the wall to help defend it from a frontal attack and to prevent an enemy from bringing siege engines up against it. Along much of the Hexamilion the *taphros* was unnecessary because of the steep declivity in front of the wall, but in this area, as we have seen, the land drops off slowly to the northeast, and the *taphros* was seen as a necessary defensive addition. Here the *taphros* was cut directly in the bedrock; it is now much eroded and difficult to delimit, but it appears to have been *ca.* 4.50 m. wide.

Just past 0+2,100 m. there is a jog in the wall that presumably marks the spot of another tower (W-4), one that would have offered flanking fire to the lower and more exposed area to the west but that would have been of little use for fire toward the east. Somewhat before 0+2,000 m. the Hexamilion begins to climb slightly more steeply as it ascends to the central plateau of the Isthmus (Fig. 5). The ground in the area is quite flat, and this would have been the most vulnerable part of the central section of the Hexamilion. The *taphros* continues to be visible in this area, from 0+1,800 m. to well past the place where the National Highway crosses the Hexamilion at 0+2,900 m., and the ruins of the Hexamilion are well preserved throughout this stretch.

Very close to 0+2,800 m. begins the area that Demetrios Pallas systematically investigated, beginning in 1961 when large-scale grading operations were carried out in preparation for a

---

740; see Clive Foss ("Historical Note on the Church at Sige," *Jahrbuch der österreichische byzantinische Gesellschaft* 16, 1967, p. 310), who questions Meyer-Plath and Schneider's reading and assigns the inscription in Constantinople to the end of the eighth century.

widening of the National Highway as it crosses the Hexamilion.[9] As Pallas pointed out,[10] the original exposure of the area was made with earth-moving equipment and without proper archaeological supervision. Pallas was later able to clear both sides of the Hexamilion and expose a series of six towers that had been built to defend this almost completely level stretch of land (W-5 to W-10). In addition, he was able to record another tower (W-6A), located directly under the modern roadway and thus destroyed.

The towers are unevenly spaced, between 27.4 m. and 69.2 m. apart. The Hexamilion in this area is uniformly between 2.90 m. and 2.95 m. wide, and its outer (northeast) face is made of carefully squared ashlar blocks, while the core is the usual rubble and mortar (Pl. 4:a, c). The interior (southwest) face of the wall is less well preserved; the lowest visible course seems to have been made of ashlar blocks, but the upper sections of the wall were constructed of small, irregularly shaped stones set in and surrounded by a heavy brown mortar (Pls. 4:b, 5:a). Double lines were frequently incised between the stones, forming either x- or diamond-shaped patterns, in a style of masonry that is still practiced throughout the Greek countryside. Basing his argument on these two distinct styles of masonry, Pallas concluded that the Hexamilion was here constructed in two phases. The work, he suggested, was begun by Justinian *ca.* 540 but was interrupted by the terrible plague of 542. The Hexamilion was then completed sometime between 542 and the earthquake of 551, after which, he believed, the region was unable to support such a vast undertaking.[11] Pallas' argument was partially based on his observation (Tὸ «Ἐξαμίλιον», p. 81) that the style of masonry on the southwest face of the Hexamilion could not be found in the Fortress at Isthmia. This same style, however, has now been discovered in the piers of the Hexamilion along the north side of the Roman Bath, in the area of Tower 15, and elsewhere (see pp. 35, 40, 98 below). Although one may disagree with the date Pallas assigned to the original masonry technique, he is probably correct in assigning the later masonry to the time of Justinian.

The Hexamilion in this area is unevenly preserved; it reaches a maximum height of 2.90 m. in five courses. The towers are all rectangular in shape, but their dimensions vary widely; two of the towers are wider than they are long, while four are longer than they are wide (see Appendix). The walls of most of the towers are constructed with separate exterior and interior faces. The outer sides of the walls are all built of regularly coursed ashlar blocks, while the interior faces are normally built of uncoursed small stones set in large quantities of mortar. Frequently, the exterior faces of the towers bond into the exterior (northeast) face of the Hexamilion, while the interior faces of the towers normally do not bond. This difference probably has no chronological significance.

Two of the towers have doorways cut through the width of the Hexamilion. One of these doorways is in the westernmost tower of the group (W-5, just past 0+2,800 m., Pl. 5:b); the passageway is *ca.* 1.12 m. wide, and its threshold is *ca.* 0.72 m. above the preserved floor of the tower, thus providing access into the tower from ground level on the interior of the Hexamilion. The northwest side of the passageway is faced with cut blocks, while on the southeast side the core of the Hexamilion protrudes roughly into the passageway, suggesting that this doorway is a later addition to the fortification. The other preserved doorway is in the tower just northwest of 0+3,100 m. (W-9). This doorway is *ca.* 1.05 m. wide, and its floor is *ca.* 3.65 m. above the floor of the tower, suggesting that it gave entrance into the second level of the tower. On the inner side of the doorway are pivot holes, and there are horizontal lines on the adjoining blocks where the door was presumably set. The well-cut masonry surrounding this doorway suggests that it was probably a part

---

[9] Pallas, Tὸ «Ἐξαμίλιον», pp. 78–83.

[10] Tὸ «Ἐξαμίλιον», p. 79.

[11] Pallas, Tὸ «Ἐξαμίλιον», pp. 81–82.

of the original construction. Just southeast of this tower, but before the easternmost tower in the area, is a gateway cut through the curtain wall of the Hexamilion. This gateway was undoubtedly a later construction, and there is no evidence to date the period of its use. It was, however, later filled with rubble and mortar, and so the gateway was presumably both cut through the Hexamilion and then blocked while the fortification was still in use.

This area is an ideal location for a gate, and the towers would have provided appropriate protection. In his survey of the Corinthia, Wiseman makes no mention of an ancient road through the central Isthmus, along the line of the modern National Highway,[12] and it is clear that the Corinth Canal and the founding of modern Corinth changed the political geography of the Isthmus. Nevertheless, at least as early as the seventeenth century, a road crossed the Hexamilion more or less in the vicinity of the modern highway: a Venetian plan shows a "Strade di Thebe a Corinthe" following this route.[13]

Southeast of W-6, exactly beside the cutting for the National Highway, there is a wall running southwestward from the northeast face of the Hexamilion for about 15 meters (Pl. 5:c). This wall is made of small irregularly cut blocks set on a foundation of mortar and small rubble. It is reminiscent of those on either side of the roadway in the Northeast Gate (see Chap. V) and those in the South Gate of the Fortress (see Chap. VI). At first sight, it might be thought that this wall, which clearly extended through the width of the Hexamilion, was cut through at some later date, perhaps even in modern times. Its foundation, however, is at a level below that of the curtain of the Hexamilion. Ground level in the immediate area until 1961 was nearly two meters higher (this level can be seen on the south side of the road, where the former road surface appears at a level above the preserved top of the Hexamilion). Although the masonry of this wall and that of the Hexamilion do not directly bond, the area where bonding would have occurred has been disturbed by road construction. The mortar used in both sections is the same, suggesting that the wall was part of the original Hexamilion construction. Such evidence would indicate the presence of a gate between Towers W-6 and W-6A, along the line of the modern National Highway.

In addition, several architectural members from ancient structures can be seen built into or near the Hexamilion in this area. This suggests that there were one or more ancient buildings in the vicinity, presumably cannibalized in the construction of the Hexamilion. In addition, some of the finer architectural pieces may have been used to decorate the façade of the Hexamilion in this area and give it a monumental appearance. Thus, in Tower W-5, just east of 0+2,800 m., a half column was placed in the exterior face of the southwest wall, with only its bottom surface exposed; Tower W-7 has a cornice with dentils built into the exterior face of the northeast wall, and on the interior face of the southwest wall is a block with two T-clamp cuttings.

More significant are three blocks that must have come from one or more impressive buildings of Roman date (Pl. 5:d). These include a Doric frieze block and two Ionic epistyle-frieze blocks. None of these blocks, unfortunately, were found *in situ* (their present position on the Hexamilion is a result of Pallas' *anastylosis*), but they almost certainly had been built into the Hexamilion at or near the point where the modern National Highway crosses it (near Tower W-6). Although there is no secure evidence, they might have decorated the façade of the Hexamilion, perhaps even at an important gateway. As can be seen from the account of Chalkokondyles (Testimonia, 20), this vulnerable stretch of the fortification was where the Sultan Murad broke through the Hexamilion in December of 1446. This was the crucial event in the Turkish attack on the Hexamilion and the

---

[12] Wiseman, *Land*, p. 64.
[13] *Corinth* III, ii, p. 151, fig. 94.

only instance in which we know where an attacker massed his forces against the fortifications. It is surely significant that it took place here.

Southeast of the last tower in this group (W-10), the Hexamilion continues in a straight line along the northeast side of the road to Kyras Vrysi (Fig. 6). This area has not been excavated, and no further towers are visible in this direction. This may be because the land in this area drops off more sharply to the northeast, making an attack less likely, but further excavation might also reveal other towers along this stretch.

Just past 0+3,500 m. the Hexamilion makes a sharp turn to the east (Fig. 6). After about 100 meters it turns to the southeast, and after another 100 meters it turns again to follow a more easterly course. This section represents the highest point on the Hexamilion (80 meters above sea level; see Fig. 11). The area enclosed by the jog in the wall offered a powerful strategic location: not only was it the highest point along the fortification, but it also overlooked and dominated the vulnerable section near the National Highway. Demetrios Pallas explored this area of the Hexamilion, and he revealed a tower (W-11, Pl. 6:a) just east of the first turn. Pallas' excavation showed that the builders of the Hexamilion leveled the bedrock here and cut the face of the stone away on a line that sloped down to the north from the face of the wall outside the Hexamilion, thus making the approach to the fortifications more precipitous and difficult for an attacker (Pl. 6:b).

The Hexamilion in this area has obviously been rebuilt several times; in its most recent rebuilding it was only 1.90–2.20 m. wide. In several sections, the south face of the rebuilt wall is in place directly above the face of the original Hexamilion, but the rebuilt north face is approximately a meter inside the similar face of the original wall. Pallas' clearing revealed another tower just northwest of 0+3,700 m. (W-12), but it is perhaps surprising that there were not more towers here and that no tower existed at the corner midway between W-11 and W-12. Fire from these two towers was presumably thought sufficient to protect this point, which might itself have been heavily armed as a small fortress. During World War II an Axis antiaircraft artillery position was built behind the Hexamilion at this point.

East of 0+3,900 m. the Hexamilion continues in almost a straight line to the east-southeast. It begins to descend slightly but follows a distinct ridge that gives it a commanding view over the land to the north. After 0+4,100 m. that position is strengthened by the beginning of the Great Ravine, which runs from west to east, rising in the center of the Isthmus and flowing to the Saronic Gulf. For much of the rest of its course, the Hexamilion hugs the southern slope of this ravine, a position that will have forced any attacker to descend into the ravine and ascend its south side in order to attack the Hexamilion. The ravine, however, might also serve as a "funnel", bringing attackers inland from the unprotected coast north of the Hexamilion, and so the fortification had to be carefully guarded where the upper reaches of the ravine approached the central plateau in the vicinity of 0+4,000 m. This must certainly have been the reason for the construction of two towers, one just east and one just west of 0+4,200 m. In this vicinity, the Hexamilion runs on a more or less straight line at about 63 meters above sea level.

The stretch of the Hexamilion from west of 0+4,400 m. to east of 0+4,600 m. was excavated by the Archaeological Service during the first half of 1992.[14] This investigation, carried out in preparation for construction of a new highway, cleared the surface of the Hexamilion and the land 2 m. on either side of the wall, and it resulted in the discovery of one tower, W-14A, that was not previously known. The results of this excavation will be published in due time, but one may note that the towers in this section were all (at least in one phase or another) entered by doorways cut from ground level on the interior of the wall and that the bedrock all along this section was significantly cut down

[14] See p. 4 above.

to the north of the fortification. In addition, several construction techniques are visible in the masonry, most notably a brownish smoothed mortar that seems to be characteristic of the first phase of construction and a paler mortar, marked by incised lines, that is clearly from a later phase.[15]

At approximately 0+4,060 m. a small gully cuts through the Hexamilion and joins the Great Ravine. In this cut a section of the Hexamilion is preserved, standing to a height of *ca.* 2.6 m. (Pl. 6:c). The outer (northeast) facing of this section has fallen away, but the inner face is well preserved, made of small uneven stones, generally laid in relatively regular horizontal courses. East of 0+4,300 m. (Fig. 7) the Hexamilion begins to descend again, riding a ridge that drops to 56 meters above sea level, and at 0+4,500 m. a small but deeply cut gully crosses the line of the Hexamilion, between Towers W-15 and W-16, on its course toward the Great Ravine. This gully ran across relatively level ground south of the Hexamilion, but it then descended rapidly, over a waterfall or steep rapids to the northeast. The Hexamilion was built straight across the gully just above the descent, and the bedrock below the wall was cut away sharply, forming a scarp *ca.* 5 meters high as a further protection of the wall. The blocks of the Hexamilion here were set in cuttings in bedrock (Pl. 7:a), and the builders must have made some provision to allow the water from the gully to flow through the wall, although no trace of this construction has been preserved. Towers (W-15 and W-16) were placed on either side of the gully to protect against infiltration of the Hexamilion along this section. The eastern one of these towers (W-16), like W-4, was apparently built into a small jog in the Hexamilion, allowing enfilading fire across the gully but not affording much protection back along the wall to the southeast.

East of this small gully, between 0+4,500 and 0+4,900 m., the Hexamilion runs southeast along a ridge, overlooking a series of triangular-shaped plateaus just south of the Great Ravine. The land immediately below the Hexamilion slopes off gradually toward the north, and so this section was vulnerable to attack; behind the Hexamilion, to the south, the land was also unusually flat. A series of at least five relatively closely spaced towers protected this area (W-17 to W-21). As in the area near the National Highway, the towers that have been identified are not evenly spaced (see Appendix). The four towers east of 0+4,700 m. (W-18 to W-21), however, are all between 37 and 43 meters apart, while W-17 is *ca.* 89 meters away from W-18, and W-21 is *ca.* 84 meters from the point where the Hexamilion turns southward at the Kyras Vrysi Ravine. Perhaps two towers are missing in this stretch, giving a total of eight (including the last, overlooking the Ravine), each at relatively even intervals of just over 40 meters.

Tower W-20 is unfortunately very poorly preserved, and nearly all trace of the Hexamilion disappears in this immediate area because of the uncommonly thick covering of soil and debris. The surface, however, is littered with small cut blocks, chunks of mortar, and quantities of pottery of the thirteenth and fourteenth centuries after Christ. This evidence suggests that there was considerable mediaeval activity in the area, whether connected with a military use of the Hexamilion or not is impossible to say. Immediately east of W-19 a modern cart road cuts through the line of the Hexamilion and continues northward to the National Highway. As mentioned above, this area is readily approachable from both the north and the east, and the towers at this point would have provided important protection against attack.

This whole section, from Tower W-17 to the Kyras Vrysi Ravine, was additionally protected by a *taphros*, whose southern edge appears to have been 8 to 9 meters in front of the exterior face of the Hexamilion (Pl. 7:b). Erosion and modern land use prevent an accurate measurement of the

[15] Thanks are extended to the Sixth Ephoreia of Byzantine Antiquities (Patras) for an opportunity to visit this excavation and to examine both the finds and the archaeological features. Obviously, I have not taken measurements or made drawings or photographs of this area, which will be published by the Archaeological Service.

width of the *taphros*, but it was in places partly cut in the bedrock, and a cutting with a minimum width of *ca.* 2.50 m. is preserved just north of W-17 (Pl. 7:c). Presumably, this represents only the lowest part of the *taphros*, and the whole was wider than this. Parenthetically, it may be noted that the excavation of bedrock for the *taphros* must have provided considerable quantities of stone for construction of the Hexamilion itself.

Between 0+4,900 and 0+5,100 m. the Hexamilion crosses the Kyras Vrysi Ravine just before it empties into the Great Ravine. This area provides important evidence about how the Hexamilion crossed the deep gullies that lay in its path, since the masonry here is better preserved than at other ravine crossings. The floor of the ravine is *ca.* 18 meters below the level of the ridge on which the Hexamilion approached it (Figs. 7, 11), and its sides are steep, especially on the west (Pl. 8:a). The course of the Hexamilion is visible almost all the way to the western cliff in the form of a rock-cut ledge, *ca.* 1.10 m. high and 1.20 m. wide. This cutting was presumably designed to hold the facing blocks of the Hexamilion as it approached the ravine (Pl. 8:b). In this area, the *taphros* is still visible, cut in bedrock right up to the edge of the ravine, some 12 meters north of the face of the Hexamilion.

The surface of the bedrock behind (i.e., south of) this cutting has been leveled. There is little trace of the superstructure of the east–west section of the Hexamilion as it approached the ravine, but there are several large sections of masonry from the Hexamilion as it turned southeastward and ran along the side of the ravine. No facing blocks survive in this area, and large parts of the Hexamilion clearly have fallen into the ravine. Nevertheless, this masonry can be traced for a distance of *ca.* 19.20 m. along the western face of the ravine. In the southern part of this area, both faces of the rubble-and-mortar core are visible, *ca.* 1.50 m. apart. The mortar here contains large quantities of tile fragments, and it closely resembles the mortar used, for example, in the area of Tower 2 within the Fortress (see Fig. 8). It is clear that foundations existed to the east of the southernmost part of this masonry, indicating the remains of a tower, which we have restored as W-22 (Pl. 8:c). The area behind this bend in the Hexamilion forms a large plateau that projects eastward well into the ravine, offering a commanding position high above it. This would be an ideal place for one of the *phrouria* (fortresses) known from literary sources to have been located along the course of the Hexamilion.

Below this tower (W-22), the remains of the Hexamilion are sporadically visible where it descends the almost vertical face of the cliff. On the floor of the ravine many cut blocks are still *in situ*. A large masonry structure, now much overgrown, is probably part of the arrangement for sluices that were necessary to allow water to flow through the fortification. Few traces of the Hexamilion remain, however, as it ascends the eastern side of the ravine. Tower W-23 has been restored at the eastern top of the ravine, although no traces of its foundation are still visible. The Hexamilion was especially vulnerable as it crossed the ravine, and towers must have stood guard on both sides.

FROM THE KYRAS VRYSI RAVINE TO THE FORTRESS

After crossing the Kyras Vrysi Ravine, the Hexamilion first runs northeast, following the line of precipitous cliffs that form the eastern edge of the ravine (Fig. 7). For *ca.* 38 meters a stretch of the rubble-and-mortar core is visible running along the surface. No facing blocks are preserved *in situ*, but below the remains of the core is a ledge *ca.* 0.30 m. high and 0.40 m. wide in the bedrock, probably cut for the foundations of the face of the wall at this point. After this stretch, all traces of the wall disappear, as does the cut shelf; it is possible that the cliffs fell into the valley below, carrying along with them the remains of the Hexamilion.

At 0+5,100 m., however, the Hexamilion turns once again to the east, as the sides of the ravine become less steep, and traces of the wall appear, running along a low ridge (Figs. 7, 8). At this point several blocks from ancient buildings, including sills and an Ionic cornice, are lying loose on the debris of the wall where they had undoubtedly been used in the construction of the Hexamilion. These are the first pieces of spolia encountered since the blocks near the National Highway.

The Hexamilion between 0+5,100 m. and 0+5,300 m. is founded directly on the bedrock, and at the beginning of this stretch only one course is preserved. As the Hexamilion runs to the east, its ruins assume a characteristic rounded shape, with the core projecting higher than the faces, only one of which is usually clearly visible. The Hexamilion is ca. 2.95 m. thick at this point. The northern (exterior) face, where preserved, is consistently made of a good ashlar construction, while the southern face seems less carefully built, often with smaller stones set roughly in mortar.

In this area are three preserved towers (W-24 to W-26; Figs. 7, 8), spaced unevenly between 44 and 70 meters apart. The land slopes off gently toward the north, and the Hexamilion was thus particularly vulnerable here. Beginning just east of W-24, the *taphros* is visible (indicated with hatching in Figures 7 and 8), continuing along the northern face of the wall for a distance of some 210 meters until the land becomes more precipitous again in the region of the Roman Bath. Naturally, the *taphros* is much eroded, and it is difficult to determine precisely its original shape: it appears to have been about 7 meters wide, with its southern side about 10 meters north of the north face of the Hexamilion. Just west of 0+5,200 meters, the *taphros* was cut in the soft bedrock, and here are preserved the best traces in this area. It is impossible to say anything about how deep the *taphros* was, and there is no evidence of a *proteichisma*[16] here.

All along the stretch between 0+5,100 and 0+5,300 m., the *taphros* is littered with huge cut blocks, many of them nearly two meters in length. At approximately 0+5160 m. and 11 meters north of the Hexamilion, a large circular structure is built in the *taphros*. It is constructed mostly of large limestone blocks formed into a rough circle with an exterior diameter of ca. 4.0 m. and an interior diameter of 2.80–2.95 m. The interior of the structure is filled with debris, and only two courses of masonry are visible above the modern fill. At the east side is a rectangular passageway ca. 0.60 m. wide that extends through the thickness of the circular wall. The upper course of preserved masonry forms the lintel of this passageway, which extends down to the rubble fill. Because of its location in the middle of the *taphros*, this structure was clearly not part of the defensive system but must have been built sometime later, after the Hexamilion went out of operation. Since Manuel II seems to have dug out the *taphros* along the Hexamilion in 1415 (Mazaris, Testimonia, 10), the passageway must have been created sometime after that. Undoubtedly, the structure was one of the several lime kilns located along the Hexamilion (although there are no preserved traces of burning), and the blocks in the area may have been on their way to the kiln. This round structure may have been one of what Leake called "wells" that were "visible also in the line of the ditch" (Testimonia, 26, p. 304).

Between W-25 and W-26, at approximately 0+5,238 m., a modern cart road crosses the Hexamilion, allowing easy transit between the village of Kyras Vrysi and the valley below. This passageway was undoubtedly not an original gate in the Hexamilion, since there are no lateral facing blocks and the pavement of the passage through the wall is simply the remains of the ordinary rubble-and-mortar core. There are, however, wheel ruts, ca. 2 meters apart, and the northern facing block between these ruts has a series of four rectangular cuttings, ca. 0.09 m. wide by 0.14 m. long and ca. 0.09 m. deep. The cuttings are unevenly spaced 0.15 to 0.22 m. apart, and their northern face

[16] A low forewall outside and running parallel to the main wall, known from literary sources and such examples as the Land Walls of Constantinople.

slopes gradually down to the floor of each. The purpose of these cuttings is unclear, although they may have been connected with some form of gateway in a later period of the Hexamilion.

At approximately 0+5,340 m. the Hexamilion reaches the small ravine near the Roman Bath, which was probably constructed in the middle of the second century after Christ (Fig. 8). At this point the *taphros* comes to an end, and the wall makes an oblique turn to the southeast, following the side of the small ravine for about 28 meters. The wall then cuts directly across the ravine until it reaches the west side of the Roman Bath. Along the western side of the ravine the Hexamilion is poorly preserved, since most of the outer (eastern) face and considerable sections of the core fell into the ravine, while the inner face is concealed in the soil. Midway along this stretch of wall three blocks of ashlar masonry are preserved *in situ*, representing the lowest course of the outer face of the Hexamilion at this point. These are resting on a shallow rubble-and-mortar foundation, much of which has washed away. The preserved height of the Hexamilion here, from the bottom of the ashlar blocks to the top of the rubble core, is *ca.* 7 meters. Since the interior face of the wall is not visible, it is difficult to measure its thickness, but the width from the outer surface of the preserved facing blocks to the innermost piece of exposed masonry in the core is more than 2 meters.

The Hexamilion along the west side of the ravine and the Roman Bath on the east side were undoubtedly built on natural slopes, but construction of the Hexamilion and subsequent erosion have changed the landscape. Originally, the ravine began far to the south, beyond the Temple of Poseidon, and the water was channeled under the northwest corner of the Sanctuary through the so-called Northwest Tunnel (see Chap. II).[17] The ravine then continued north of the Temple to empty into the Great Ravine just west of the spot where the Roman Bath was constructed. The Hexamilion crossed this small ravine in the manner discussed above, and there were undoubtedly sluices at its bottom, although no trace of them survives. These sluices may have become clogged over the course of time so that soil backed up against the south face of the Hexamilion, forming the present landscape. The water that still flowed through this course until modern times, however, found an underground outlet somewhere along the wall, causing a great subsidence and forming the two great depressions that now dominate the area west and southwest of the Roman Bath.

As it crosses the eastern part of the ravine (Fig. 13), the Hexamilion is *ca.* 2.95 m. thick. The outer (north) face is constructed with huge ashlar blocks, preserved in three courses to a height of up to 2.70 m. above the rubble-and-mortar foundations. The south face is also set on foundations of rubble and mortar that project *ca.* 0.18 m. beyond the face of the wall. Above these foundations is a leveling course of tiles, over which the face of the wall was constructed. The south face of the Hexamilion here is made of small stones and an occasional cut block, all set in smoothed mortar.

The Hexamilion reached the northwest corner of the Roman Bath at Room XIV, whose foundations it apparently overran (Figs. 13, 14). It then turned obliquely to the northeast and followed the east side of the ravine (Pl. 8:d). As will be seen several times below, in many places the Hexamilion was constructed over the ruins of earlier buildings to save time and material and to provide a secure foundation for the fortification. In this area, however, the Hexamilion struck out in a different direction and did not immediately use the walls of the Roman Bath, probably to protect two entrances into the Bath (one into Room III, the other into the furnace room below it), which would have been exposed had the Hexamilion simply followed the exterior walls of the Bath.

This diagonal section of the Hexamilion follows a course that strikes the northwest corners of Rooms V and IV of the Roman Bath. The upper portion of the wall is preserved to a height of *ca.* 1.60 m., but this section is very poorly constructed, using small stones, including several pieces of

---

[17] *Isthmia* II, pp. 81–82, plan IV. Compare also the observations of Frazer (*Pausanias* V, p. 544), who seems to mention the Hexamilion in this area.

marble, and large quantities of tile chinking, in a manner totally unlike that of other sections of the Hexamilion, especially on its outer face (Pl. 8:d). This type of construction certainly reflects a later period of rebuilding, and parallels can be found in the Frankish walls at Penteskouphi[18] and the late mediaeval and Turkish repairs at Acrocorinth.[19]

Traces of the original Hexamilion construction in this area are perhaps visible in the lowest course of blocks, exposed for a distance of *ca.* 11.70 m. from the corner of Room XIV (Pl. 8:d). These blocks are set on a shallow rubble-and-mortar foundation laid directly on bedrock, and they describe a rather careless S-shaped curve in plan. This course was probably never meant to be seen, which would explain its poor construction, but rather formed part of the foundations of the Hexamilion. These foundations, in fact, project *ca.* 0.25 m. from the second course of ashlar blocks, which is only partially preserved. Even so, at best, the Hexamilion was extraordinarily thin in this area, reaching only about half of its normal width.

At the west wall of Room IV, the northwest corner of the Bath, the Hexamilion turned eastward along the north wall of the Bath.[20] This wall (from the original phase of the Bath construction) was only 0.75–0.80 m. thick as it ran along the north sides of Rooms IV and II, far too thin for defensive use in the Hexamilion. The wall was strengthened by constructing rectangular rubble-and-mortar piers, *ca.* 1.85–2.00 m. thick, up against the inner (south) face of the walls in Rooms IV, II, and I (Pl. 9:a), making the total thickness of the new wall 2.70 to 2.80 m., close to the normal width of the Hexamilion. The piers were joined together by a series of brick vaults, the springing for which is preserved in all three niches in Room II (Pl. 9:a, b). This is the only part of the Hexamilion where we can be certain that the fighting platform was supported on an arcade. This technique is paralleled at many other early Byzantine fortifications: the middle of the three walls of the Theodosian circuit in Constantinople,[21] the lower fighting platform at Resafa,[22] and, closer at hand, at Daphne just outside Athens.[23] In addition, Procopius refers to Justinian's addition of vaults to various fortifications to increase their height.[24]

The east side of the easternmost vault and the west side of the central vault in Room II rested on the original piers of the Bath at elevations of +44.20 m. and +44.17 m., respectively. None of these vaults were found intact, but their collapsed masonry fell into the space below. It has been possible to restore the easternmost of these vaults, which was the best preserved. The springing began at an elevation of +43.60 m. The highest masonry preserved *in situ* was at +44.74 m., 3.82 m. above the mosaic floor of the Bath. The original height of the top of the vault, of course, was somewhat more; the restored elevation of +44.89 m. gives a reasonable approximation, and one should imagine some packing above the top of the vault. The construction of these vaults on the stumps of the piers of the Roman Bath shows that at least the northern part of the Bath had lost its roof by this time. The cutting of a long channel across the north side of Room VI and the removal of the east wall in Rooms VI and I are also probably part of this demolition.[25]

---

[18] *Corinth* III, ii, pp. 265–267.

[19] E.g., *Corinth* III, ii, pp. 241–244. A. Bon, *La Morée franque* (*Bibliothèque des Écoles françaises d'Athènes et de Rome* 213), Paris 1969, I, p. 674.

[20] There is no evidence of original-phase masonry northeast of the northwest corner of Room V. In a subsequent phase of rebuilding, perhaps in the 15th century, the diagonal wall may have been continued to the northwest corner of Room IV.

[21] Kirchen, *Landmauer* I, figs. 2–4, pls. 4, 22; Meyer-Plath and Schneider, *Landmauer* II, pp. 33–36, fig. 21, pl. 34.

[22] Karnapp, *Stadtmauer*, pp. 16–18, pls. 7, 8, 24, and *passim*.

[23] G. Millet, *La monastère de Daphni*, Paris 1899; A. Orlandos, Ἀρχεῖον τῶν Βυζαντινῶν μνημείων τῆς Ἑλλάδος II, Athens 1955–1956, p. 68.

[24] *Aed.* 2.1.16 (Dara), 4.9.16 (Toperus in Rhodope); cf. Pringle, *Defence* I, p. 147.

[25] See Wohl, "Deposit of Lamps," pp. 116–118.

The purpose of this vaulting, in the original Hexamilion phase at least, is clear. The piers along the inner face of Rooms IV and II were designed to strengthen the wall by thickening it, while the corner piers on the east wall of Room IV and in Room I were intended to buttress the wall where it made a turn. The vaults were undoubtedly designed to support the upper part of the Hexamilion, including the fighting platform and the parapet wall. If we assume a packing of 1.5 m. above the top of the vault, the fighting platform would have been at an elevation of *ca.* +46.39 m.; if we allow a parapet wall of 2.0 m., the top of the Hexamilion in this area would have been at an elevation of *ca.* +48.39 m. Excavation just outside the Bath to the north of Room II revealed foundations at +41.03 m., which would make the fighting platform *ca.* 5.36 m. above ancient ground level on the north side of the Bath. This information, imperfect as it is, provides the first indication of the original height of the Hexamilion.

The piers along the north side of the Bath were constructed entirely of rubble and mortar, but the visible surfaces were almost completely plastered over, leaving only parts of individual stones visible in the wall face (Pl. 9:b). The light-brown plaster was carefully finished, leaving an almost completely flat surface. This technique, which must belong to the original construction of the Hexamilion, finds a parallel in one of the masonry techniques on the south face of the Hexamilion near the National Highway and in Tower 15 (pp. 32 and 35 above and p. 98 below). Rectangular scaffolding holes, usually aligned vertically in two rows, are visible on the face of each pier.

The piers were bedded directly on the mosaic floor of the Bath without other foundations (Pl. 9:c). Excavation in Rooms I and II revealed a thin layer of hard-packed dirt, *ca.* 0.19 m. thick, directly on top of the mosaic; along the south side of the piers in Room II and the two free sides of the pier in Room I, the hard soil was cut away and a section of soft dirt, some 0.25 m. wide, rested on the mosaic floor and up against the Hexamilion piers. The hard layer undoubtedly represents a period of disuse in the Bath, when soil washed in and settled over these rooms, while the softer section represents the cleaning away of the accumulated dirt by the builders of the Hexamilion in preparation for construction of the piers. Material found in the hard layer provides a rough *terminus post quem* for construction of the piers. Birgitta L. Wohl discussed this evidence fully,[26] and its significance for the history of the Roman Bath will be considered further in the full-scale study of that building. It is sufficient to note here that none of the lamps and other material associated with the hard layer in Room I can be assigned to a date later than the first or second decade of the fifth century after Christ.

At some time after the original Hexamilion construction, the four spaces between the piers in Rooms II and IV were filled with rubble and mortar (Pl. 9:a, b). The style of this work is easily distinguished from that of the original piers: overall it is rougher, using larger and less evenly faced stones and less careful trowel work on the exterior mortared surface. This filling cannot have been designed to help support the superstructure of the Hexamilion, since the height of the fill never reaches the springing of the vaults; the purpose must have been to strengthen the wall by adding greater bulk along this stretch. There is no secure evidence to date this addition to the Hexamilion, although the massiveness of the construction would accord well with Justinianic rebuilding in the sixth century.[27]

---

[26] Wohl, "Deposit of Lamps," pp. 112–140.

[27] It should be noted that the same footing trench (i.e., the softer layer) mentioned above was encountered in front (to the south) of the easternmost of the filling constructions in Room II. Since it was not present in front of the other piers, however, we should simply conclude that a footing trench longer than necessary was cut in this area when the Hexamilion was built.

Wohl noticed some sixth-century pottery in the northern end of the Bath, above the floor level but below the rubble that characterized the collapse of the building.[28] In these same layers were several fragments of so-called Slavic pottery dating from the later sixth and seventh centuries (IPR 72-60, IPB 72-28-33). This same kind of pottery was found in other parts of the Fortress (see pp. 85–86 below). Whether or not this pottery indicates military or civilian use of the Hexamilion, it does show continuity, probably into at least the middle of the seventh century.

In the area north of the Roman Bath the situation is less clear, in part because excavations there were only of an exploratory nature; further excavation is necessary for a full understanding of what was obviously a complex building sequence. In the area north of Room IV is a series of walls that seems generally to continue the course of the diagonal wall from the northwest corner of Room IV toward the northeast following the steep edge of the ravine. No full excavation was carried out in this area, but, evidently, the walls are not all contemporary. No clear plans of rooms or buildings can be recovered, in part because the buildings collapsed into the ravine below. Some construction occurred in this area during the Roman imperial era, shown by floors made of the diamond-shaped tiles characteristic of that era, encountered at several places elsewhere at Isthmia and Corinth. All the Roman buildings, however, seem to have been destroyed either by the events that brought about the end of the Sanctuary or as a result of the building of the Hexamilion. At some later date, structures were once again built in this area, in either late antiquity or the Middle Ages, but none seem to represent original Hexamilion construction. Some of this later building may have involved the strengthening of the Hexamilion by the addition of a forward wall or a small fortress overlooking the ravine; alternatively, the preserved walls may simply come from civilian structures built at one of the many times when the Hexamilion was in disrepair. In the corner of an earlier building, most of which apparently fell over the cliff, are the remains of a small kiln made of broken tiles.

Three Venetian Levantine colonial coins were found in this area; all date from the period A.D. 1368–1413.[29] None was found in any clear archaeological context, but it may be significant that they represent three-fourths of the coins discovered in this area. As mentioned above, some of the walls in this area seem to represent a continuation of the diagonal wall from the northwest corner of Room IV. The coins suggest that Manuel II may have been responsible for the construction, making this one of the few areas of the Hexamilion where he built new fortifications from the ground up rather than utilizing the remains of the original structure.

Clearly, however, in its original phase the Hexamilion followed the north walls of Rooms IV and II, and then turned north following the projected line of the wall between Rooms I and II. Immediately to the north of Rooms I and II, the west face of this wall is constructed of well-coursed bricks on a foundation of large blocks (Ill. 1, Pl. 10:a); this is undoubtedly original Bath construction, strengthened and used in the Hexamilion. The builders of the latter added a filling of rubble and mortar to the east side of the Bath wall, making the total ca. 2.60 m. thick. This is slightly less than the normal Hexamilion width, but the back (east) face of the wall is directly on a line with the east face of the pier in Room I (Fig. 13); the two constructions are undoubtedly contemporary. For just over two meters, the north–south wall preserves its original brick facing on the west, but then there is a doorway, blocked with rubble masonry in the Hexamilion phase (Ill. 1). Thus, along the north side of the Roman Bath and as the Hexamilion turns north from the Bath, the outer face of the Hexamilion was not of the normal ashlar but rather of brick, small, coursed stones, and rubble

[28] Wohl, "Deposit of Lamps," p. 116.

[29] a) Clement, 575 (IC 70-38), Andreas Contarini (A.D. 1368–1382). Cf. *Corinth* VI, no. 53, p. 159.
b) Clement, 605 (IC 70-73), Antonio Venerio (A.D. 1382–1400). Cf. *Corinth* VI, no. 55, p. 159.
c) Clement, 616 (IC 70-72), Michele Steno (A.D. 1400–1413). Cf. *Corinth* VI, no. 56, p. 159.

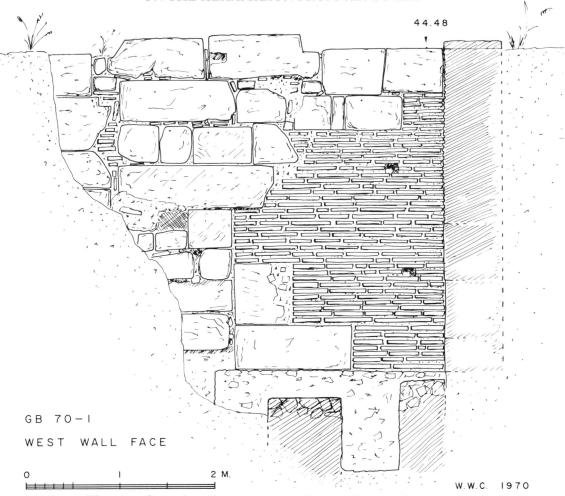

ILL. 1. Elevation of west face of north–south wall north of Roman Bath Rooms I and II

and mortar. Further to the north the Hexamilion is less well preserved, although it seems to represent the same combination of Bath construction strengthened in the Hexamilion period.

At a distance of *ca.* 6.80 m. north of Rooms I and II there is a cross wall running east and west. It is made of well-cut ashlar blocks and is preserved in four courses resting on an ashlar foundation course. The two westernmost blocks of the upper preserved course have matching swallowtail-clamp cuttings. The eastern block has another on its east edge; the next block in this course fell away, and we cannot tell if it had a matching cutting. On the south face of two adjoining blocks in the second course above the foundations of this wall is the inscription Καλαῖς Μυτιληνίαις ("To the beautiful women of Mytilene" [IΣ 70-9]). Exactly at the point where this wall meets the interior (east) face of the Hexamilion is a vertical edge in the masonry that extends from the bottom of the wall to the course immediately below the highest one currently preserved. This was undoubtedly a doorway in the original Roman construction that was blocked when the Hexamilion was built or possibly even sometime earlier.

North of this cross wall the Hexamilion continues the same course for a further 6.40 m. This area has not been systematically excavated, and so it is impossible to know how far the wall of the Bath continued in this direction. The interior (east) face of the Hexamilion in this area is extremely rough, and many architectural members, including no less than nine column drums, are built into it. The Hexamilion here is *ca.* 3.20 m. thick. Built up against the corner of this wall and the north face of the east–west cross wall is a rubble-and-mortar buttress constructed in the same style as the piers inside the Bath. Excavation in this area was not carried to any great depth, and it is not possible to establish clearly the relationship between the buttress and the thick, more amorphous north–south wall, although there is no reason to doubt their contemporaneity.

About 25 meters north of the wall of Rooms I and II, the Hexamilion is once again clearly visible, in an area described by the excavators as the Hexamilion Outworks (Fig. 15; see p. 45 below). As it approaches the side of the ravine, the Hexamilion is faced with large ashlar blocks on both sides, and it is *ca.* 3.20 m. wide. Near the end of this stretch and about 3 meters before it reaches the edge of the ravine is an east–west wall that butts up against the west face of the Hexamilion (Fig. 13). This wall is preserved along the south side for a distance of *ca.* 11 meters, and it is faced with large, well-cut blocks along the exterior for a distance of *ca.* 6.5 m. This wall, however, has no well-defined southern face. The rubble interior is not set in lime mortar, but it was apparently either laid dry or set in a mud mortar that has since washed away. This section may have formed part of the rebuilding of the Hexamilion; presumably, it was not part of the earliest phase.

About 25.25 m. north of the wall of Room I, the Hexamilion makes a sharp turn to the east, and both faces are preserved in well-cut ashlar blocks. Excavation within the interior corner of the wall revealed the floor of a kiln or oven at a level of 41.58 m. above sea level. Below this floor, at +41.48 m., is a surface of hard white earth, which may represent ground level at the time the Hexamilion was built. Cut into this soil is a grave (Gully Bastion Grave 2), with its top at *ca.* +41.08 m. and bottom at +40.18 m. (Fig. 13). On the east and south, the grave was lined with tiles, while the interior face of the Hexamilion formed the west and north sides. On its north side, the grave slightly undercuts the Hexamilion (to a maximum of 0.20 m.), but there can be no doubt that the grave was built either at the same time as the Hexamilion or sometime after it (but obviously before the kiln above it).

The grave was covered by large tiles, including one stamped tile (IA 70-49) and another (IA 70-92) that was a hypocaust cover slab from the near-by Roman Bath. This tile is *ca.* 0.71 m. on a side and *ca.* 0.07 m. thick; it is heavily smoke-stained on one side, except at the corners where it rested on the hypocaust piers.[30] Among the cover tiles, either lost at the time the grave was built or placed there as part of the religious ceremony in honor of the dead, was a fragment of a lamp.[31] A line of vertical tiles running east and west divided the grave into two sections; the heads of the skeletons were all at the west. The north compartment contained two skeletons, the south compartment eight. On the floor of the south compartment, below the lowest burial, were found a bowl, a bronze buckle, and a bead on a wire.[32]

[30] This tile would just fit the spacing of the preserved hypocaust piers in the Bath.

[31] Lamp (IPL 70-100): Athenian glazed (second half 4th century after Christ); cf. Wohl, "Deposit of Lamps," no. 24. For the use of lamps in burials in Christian Corinth, see Wiseman, "Gymnasium Area," pp. 79–86.

[32] a) Bowl (IPR 70-26): H. 0.050–0.054 m., Diam. rim 0.162 m. Intact. Heavy, coarse, dark reddish gray fabric (5YR 4/2) with large orange and white inclusions. Shallow, on a flat base. Flaring sides, folded flanged concave rim; faint wheel ridging on interior. Cf. IP 3758, from the Northeast Gate, found with lamps IP 3690 and 3591, dated to the second half of the 4th century after Christ. Bibl.: Clement, 1971, p. 110, pl. 95:a; Peppers, L343, p. 298, figs. 92:c, d.

b) Bronze buckle (IM 70-32): max. Diam. of ring 0.024 m., L. of tongue 0.024 m. Body badly corroded; small bronze ring, round in section; ends do not join. Linked to it a straight segment of bronze as a tongue, round in section but flattened where it folds over the ring. Cf. Wiseman, "Gymnasium Area," p. 79, pl. 25:c, from the Lerna Hollow Cemetery, grave no. 86 (5th century); best parallel is IM 70-31, from the East Field (which seems generally to have gone out of use at the end of the 4th century); G. R. Davidson, *Corinth*, XII, *The Minor Objects*, Princeton 1952 (repr.

All the items can be dated to the latter part of the fourth or the very early fifth century. The lamp found within the tiles above the burial provides the best date for the grave. Its type is very much like that of the lamps found in the Roman Bath and there associated with the period of construction of the Hexamilion.[33] Perhaps this multiple burial represents part of the garrison assigned to build or to guard the wall in its very early years of operation.

Along the stretch immediately east of the grave, the Hexamilion is *ca.* 2.80–3.00 m. wide and is faced with well-cut ashlar blocks along the north. Five of these blocks in the upper preserved course have swallowtail-clamp cuttings that match those in neighboring blocks. Because the clamps align, either these blocks are *in situ* or they have been re-used in the same order in which they were originally laid. The inner (east and south) faces are less well constructed, although here too large cut blocks are common, and the masonry is very different from the south face of the Hexamilion inside the Roman Bath.

After a distance of *ca.* 12.25 m. the Hexamilion makes another jog, first to the north and then to the east, setting a course it then follows until it approaches the Fortress, some 174 meters to the east (Fig. 15). The corner at the second jog does not make a perfect right angle, and the Hexamilion is therefore set at a slightly different orientation, some five degrees off from that of the Bath walls.[34]

From this point to the juncture with the Fortress, the north face of the Hexamilion is exceptionally well built, with large ashlar blocks frequently preserved in three courses above the foundations. The south face was less well constructed; it used few ashlar blocks, little mortar, and many re-used architectural fragments (e.g., two column drums and a block from a Doric frieze), built into the wall in a manner reminiscent of the inner face of the Hexamilion directly north of the Bath. It is possible that here, just as in the area of the Bath, the Hexamilion followed the line of an already existing structure, using a wall of the earlier building as the outer (north) face of the Hexamilion. The inner (south) face was constructed with whatever stones and spolia lay ready to hand.

About 13 meters east of the second jog in the Hexamilion is a gateway, *ca.* 1.50–1.65 m. wide, running north and south through the wall (Figs. 8, 15). A coat of fine red plaster over a layer of gritty mortar covers the lowest course of the ashlar blocks on the north face. This mortar fans out over the foundations, and there can be little doubt that it was applied at the time the north face of the wall was built. The gateway breaks through the mortar, and the jambs have no finished surfaces, which shows that the gateway was cut through the north face sometime after its original construction. The gateway extends through the entire width of the Hexamilion, however, and there is a roughly finished face on the south side, including a threshold block with a pivot hole. This block was apparently once part of the foundations for the south face of the Hexamilion, recut for use in the gate. At a later date the whole gateway was blocked. On the north face, spolia, including a cornice block, and tile chinking were utilized in filling the former gate.

From this evidence we can reconstruct at least four phases in this area. First, the north face was built as part of some previously unknown structure. Second, the Hexamilion was constructed by the

---

1987), no. 2175, p. 270, pl. 113 (4th to 8th century). Bibl.: Clement, 1971, p. 110, pl. 95:c; Peppers, LCon2, p. 297, fig. 93:b.

c) Bead and wire (IM 70-54): p.Diam. of bead 0.016 m., p.L. of wire 0.020 m. Smooth-polished, black stone bead, chipped and broken on one side. Pierced through, off-center, with a large hole (Diam. 0.005 m.). When found, through the hole was a section of heavy, hollow silver wire, twisted in a cable pattern. Cf. Wiseman, "Gymnasium Area," no. 26, p. 428, pl. 9:n, a bead from grave no. 47 (late 4th to 6th century). Bibl.: Clement, 1971, p. 110, pl. 95:b; Peppers, p. 296.

[33] Wohl, "Deposit of Lamps."

[34] Until this point, the Hexamilion appears to have been following either the walls of the Bath or those of some other building to the north, aligned with it.

addition of the south face and the rubble-and-mortar core. Third, the gateway was cut through the wall, and, finally, the gateway was blocked.

The stratigraphy in this area is naturally not entirely clear, but it is possible to make some observations about the chronological sequence. The foundations of both the north and the south faces of the Hexamilion were sunk into a layer of hard red soil containing pottery that dates no later than the third quarter of the first century after Christ (GB 70, Box 58). Above the hard red layer, two other strata can be distinguished directly against the wall blocks on the north face, indicating that this part of the structure at least was in place when the strata were laid down. Material in these layers, then, should provide a *terminus ante quem* for construction of the north face. The pottery in the lower of these two layers (GB 70, Boxes 55, 63–65) can be dated to the late first and second centuries after Christ, while the upper layers (Boxes 53, 61, 62) contain pottery of the second and third centuries. A plate found near the top of the upper of these two layers is probably a local imitation of Eastern Sigillata B II and may be assigned to the middle of the second century after Christ.[35] Also from the area of the north face of the wall was a small deposit of pottery, perhaps connected with the earliest phase of construction, which has been dated to the later part of the first century after Christ.[36] This date may thus be suggested for the large east–west wall that formed the basis of the Hexamilion here.

Unfortunately, the stratigraphy on the south face of the Hexamilion is not well preserved and provides no basis for chronological conclusions. Thus, it is not possible to give anything other than a relative chronology for the construction of the gate and its blocking.

In 1932 A. H. S. Megaw carried out a brief exploration in the area of the Hexamilion Out-works.[37] At a point *ca.* 19.5 m. east of the gateway, he dug a trench running north from the north face of the Hexamilion for a distance of *ca.* 16.4 m. Within this trench, on a line 6.90 m. north of the Hexamilion, he discovered an east–west wall *ca.* 0.70 m. thick (shown at an elevation of +40.23 m. on Figure 15). He sunk pits to the east and west of this trench and discovered that the smaller wall continued in each direction. Further, about 3 meters north of the secondary wall, Megaw found a steep ditch cut in the soil, with a pile of stones heaped up on the southern side. Megaw concluded that these represented the *proteichisma* and *taphros* of classic Byzantine military construction.

Excavation carried out in 1972 further explored the Hexamilion Outworks (Fig. 15).[38] The light east–west wall was evident at intervals over a distance of nearly 46 meters (Pl. 10:b, c). The best-preserved section of this wall lies in the eastern part of the excavated area; there it is made of rectangular cut limestone blocks, *ca.* 0.60–0.80 m. wide, set on a foundation of mortar and rubble. The wall has an even south face, but since the blocks are uneven in width, the north face is irregular.

In the middle of the excavated area, the superstructure of the light east–west wall has completely disappeared, and only the foundations of rubble and mortar, *ca.* 0.80 m. wide, remain. Farther west the wall is very irregular, running out of line with the stretch farther east. The small blocks in this area are simply set on bedrock without foundations. This undoubtedly represents a later phase after the original structure collapsed.

[35] Plate (IPR 70-101): p.H. 0.060 m., p.W. 0.146 m., Diam. rim *ca.* 0.36 m. Mended from four pieces. Soft, light-red (2.5YR 6/8) clay with white and dark inclusions. Part of wall and slightly flaring, rounded rim, horizontally thickened; curved wall set off from floor with a shallow groove; rim set off from wall with a ridge. Painted decoration in red slip on rim: slashes and vine pattern. Cf. *Agora* V, G50 (1st century B.C.); better parallels are Hayes ARS Form 3A (A.D. 60–90) and unpublished examples in Eastern Sigillata B from Corinth (probably first half of 2nd century after Christ); cf. also IPR 70-103 and 70-104, fragments of similar plates found in the same general area.

[36] Peppers, Group K, pp. 295–298, IPR 70-97–100.

[37] Jenkins and Megaw, "Researches," pp. 77–78.

[38] Report in Clement, 1973, pp. 147–149.

About 2.8 m. north of the light east–west wall, the surface was cut away, perhaps to form the *taphros* of the late Roman fortification. In the eastern part of the excavated area this trench was dug in soil, but in the west it was cut in hard bedrock. The exact dimensions of the *taphros* were not ascertained in this area, but the lowest point encountered was at an elevation of +37.03 m., *ca.* 1.75 m. below the surface at the foot of the wall and *ca.* 3.25 m. from its north face.

Excavation in this area also revealed four north–south walls running between the north face of the Hexamilion and the light east–west wall, at intervals of *ca.* 13 m. The surviving masonry in these walls is not everywhere consistent, and there may have been some rebuilding. The original phase seems to have been characterized by foundations of rubble and mortar, *ca.* 0.70–0.80 m. wide, above which the walls were built of ashlar blocks *ca.* 0.70 m. wide, occasionally mixed with smaller coursed limestone blocks. Few of the large ashlar blocks now remain *in situ*, and most of these are on the south ends of the walls near the north face of the Hexamilion. Only the easternmost of the four north–south walls is preserved above foundation level in the middle, and it is built of mortar and rubble faced with small, unevenly cut limestone blocks whose faces have prominent clawtooth-chisel marks. This construction strongly resembles the limestone facing visible in various places in the Roman Bath, in the area around the Palaimonion, and in the so-called East Field, all in a context of the early Roman period.

The second and fourth of these walls (from the west) are bonded to the light east–west wall at foundation level, while all four walls bond with the Hexamilion north face, at least in alternating courses. This bonding shows that all the original walls in this area were contemporary, forming rectangular spaces *ca.* 12.30 m. by *ca.* 6.50 m. Traces of plaster facing on all four of the north–south walls further confirm the arrangement. The north face of the Hexamilion in the area of the later gate had such plaster on the lowest course (see p. 44 above), and similar traces exist on the north face near the base of the north–south walls. The evidence of the pottery discussed above suggests that these walls are all Roman in date, perhaps from the latter part of the first or the early part of the second century after Christ.

Clement found a small group of pots just to the west of the westernmost north–south wall, at the level of the foundations of the walls, and *ca.* 1 meter north of the Hexamilion north face.[39] A few centimeters from these pots and at the same level was a coin of Corinth under Nero, fairly worn.[40] With the pottery, the coin suggests a date for the construction of the walls in this area in the last third of the first or the early part of the second century after Christ.

The light east–west walls, then, should not be seen as original works of the Hexamilion period but as part of the renovation of the Isthmian sanctuary in Roman imperial times. Exactly what building this represented in its original form we cannot presently say. It is, however, tempting to

---

[39] This deposit included two large vessels:

a) Micaceous water jar (IPR 72-38): p.H. 0.352 m., max. Diam. 0.240 m. Mended from many fragments and restored in plaster. Red micaceous clay (2.5YR 4/6). Ovoid body tapering to a tubular foot with thickened collar. Cf. *Agora* V, M13 (late 1st to early 2nd century after Christ); J46 (2nd to early 3rd century). Bibl.: Clement, 1973, p. 149, pl. 133:e; Peppers, J338, pp. 290–291.

b) Amphora (IPR 72-39): p.H. 0.506 m., max. Diam. 0.311 m. Hard, reddish yellow clay (7.5YR 6/8). Mended from many fragments, preserves most of body. Almost cylindrical body with rounded base and knob foot. Broad wheel ridging on exterior and interior. Cf. *Agora* V, G197 (but with different toe and shoulder, late 1st, early 2nd century after Christ); Hayes, *Roman Glass*, no. 359 (late 1st century after Christ). Bibl.: Clement, 1973, p. 149, pl. 133:f; Peppers, J337, p. 290.

[40] Clement, 51 (IC 72-24), Corinth under Nero (A.D. 67/68): P. Memmius Cleander duovir. Cf. *Corinth* VI, p. 7; no. 64, p. 23.

associate it with the near-by Bath and earlier gymnasium complex or, alternatively, to suggest that here may be one of the stoas otherwise known at the site.[41]

In the area between the two central north–south walls, two kilns were discovered in the corners formed by the Hexamilion north face and the north–south walls. Neither of the kilns was fully explored, but each contained apparent kiln debris, and one had a kiln support (IPR 72-22). The western kiln is ill defined, but the eastern structure is well preserved, with tiles and mortar surviving to four and five courses and incomplete dimensions of 1.04 m. by 0.70 m. The latter kiln was built right up against the corner of the two walls, and mortar used in its construction spreads out over the foundations of the north–south wall. Its position shows that the kilns were built after construction of the Roman building; indeed, the Roman structure must have been standing disused and without a roof, since presumably a kiln would otherwise not have been built there.

In the area of the easternmost of the north–south walls, the upper course of the north face of the Hexamilion preserves a group of at least sixteen blocks with cuttings for swallowtail clamps (Fig. 15). Where these are present, the cuttings match those on neighboring blocks. It appears likely that the wall at this point was originally laid using clamps, probably in the Roman period. For the next approximately 60 meters, the Hexamilion remains unexcavated as it continues its progress almost due east along the edge of the ravine.

About 110 meters east of the second jog in this stretch of the Hexamilion, Oscar Broneer in 1961 and the UCLA excavations again in 1967 partially explored the area of the so-called North Drain (Figs. 8, 16, Pl. 11:a).[42] This area had once been a depression through which a ravine ran, but the ravine was built over by a large structure well before the ground was leveled and the Hexamilion constructed. The declivity, however, still made the spot a weak point in the defenses, and the builders made remarkable efforts to protect it.[43] In the western part here, the north face of the Hexamilion is made of large blocks nearly a meter wide with swallowtail-clamp cuttings on many of them. At intervals of either four or eight meters approximately, perpendicular walls are bonded to the Hexamilion north face (Pl. 11:b). In several places the rubble foundations for these walls can be traced northward, and it is likely that they are the walls of rooms dating from the Roman period. The Hexamilion in this area is on exactly the same line as that in the area of the Hexamilion Outworks, and it was built in the same technique, using blocks with swallowtail clamps. The interior (south) surface of the north face of the Hexamilion is straight and apparently finished, suggesting that this was once a freestanding wall. The inner (south) face of the Hexamilion, however, was made of unevenly cut blocks, while rubble and mortar comprise the usual core. In Plate 11:b it is clear that the core was poured up against the already standing north face: no headers project into the core as they do in many other sections of the Hexamilion. The total width of the Hexamilion here is *ca.* 2.84 m. It seems certain that, again in this area, the Hexamilion was constructed by utilizing the earlier east–west wall as its north face, while a less carefully constructed face was built on the south and rubble and mortar were dumped into the interstices.

In the area of the North Drain where the north face was washed away, the Hexamilion makes a slight deviation to the south. It then follows this altered course all the way to Tower 15 and the junction with the west wall of the Fortress. Truncated perpendicular walls, or possibly buttresses,

[41] Stoas, as well as other buildings in the sanctuary, are known from the inscription listing the donations of Poplius Licinius Iuventianus, *IG* IV, 203.

[42] Clement, 1968, p. 142.

[43] In view of the complexity of this area, we can only echo Clement's comment (1968, p. 142): "More digging will be necessary before the nature of the building and its precise relationship with the Trans-Isthmus wall can be understood."

from an unknown Roman structure continue through this area, running off to the north and unevenly spaced between 3.5 and 5 meters apart.

THE HEXAMILION SOUTHEAST OF THE FORTRESS[44]

Southeast of Tower 2, the Hexamilion crosses the deep ravine, ca. 45 m. wide, which once drained a
large area southeast of the Sanctuary of Poseidon between the Rachi and Mytikas (Fig. 8; see
Chap. II). At the time of its construction across the ravine, a series of seven sluices pierced the
Hexamilion to allow water from the ravine to pass through it (Plate 11:c shows the Hexamilion as
it looked in 1970; cf. Corinth I, i, pp. 54–55, figs. 21, 22). Over the course of the centuries, however,
the sluices became clogged, and debris filled up against the west side of the wall, disturbing the
natural lay of the land. Thus, to the west of the Hexamilion the land is level, at a height of ca. 30
meters above sea level, while to the east of the wall the land drops precipitously by about 10 meters.
This area is now much overgrown and covered with trash, and many blocks from the face of the
Hexamilion have fallen into the ravine below. Some thirteen courses of masonry can still be identified, however, rising approximately 6.50 m. above the floor of the ravine.[45] Only two of the sluices
are now visible; the best preserved of these is ca. 0.24 m. wide and preserved ca. 0.23 m. above the
silt and debris at the bottom on the wall. One of the Dinsmoor photographs of 1909 gives a good
impression of this section of the Hexamilion (Pl. 11:d; cf. Corinth I, i, figs. 21 and 22, which are not
exactly identical).

Beyond the ravine the Hexamilion continues in a southeasterly direction (Towers S-2 to S-5)
along relatively flat land. A short distance beyond 0+6,100 m., the Hexamilion begins to ascend
Mytikas hill. It follows a narrow ridge that provides an admirable view to the north and east and
rises increasingly steeply, gaining some 20 meters between 0+6,200 m. and 0+6,300 m. (Pl. 12:b).
The Hexamilion in this area is 3.00–3.10 m. thick, and, perhaps surprisingly, the taphros is visible
practically all the way to the top of the hill. About 35 meters southwest of Tower S-8, the ground
has caved in to reveal a circular cutting in bedrock, ca. 2.80 m. in diameter; this appears to have
been a large cistern. Re-used blocks continue in this area despite its distance from the Sanctuary of
Poseidon; at about 0+6,220 m. a column drum inscribed with a deeply cut cross is built into the
eastern face of the Hexamilion, and three monolithic columns (diameters ca. 0.62 m.) were built
into Tower S-9. Only the lower parts of this tower survive, but its north and south walls have
a leveling course of three bricks, such as that used in the Bastion at the Northeast Gate and in
Tower 15 (see Chap. V below).

Tower S-9 commands a spectacular view back to the Fortress and across the flat land northeast
to the Saronic Gulf. Just beyond this tower the Hexamilion turns eastward and runs along the side
of Mytikas (Fig. 9), reaching its greatest elevation south of the Fortress just past 0+6,300 m., and
beginning a slow descent (Fig. 11). The land behind (i.e., south of) the Hexamilion along the top of
Mytikas forms a gently sloping plateau, and the wall follows the edge of the plateau, while the
ground falls off steeply to the north.

Just east of Tower S-11 the bedrock has been cut away sharply to form a steep face that is as
much as 1.60 m. high. Hexamilion blocks preserved in situ near Tower S-12 show that the bedrock
was cut away deeply to form a flat ledge on which to lay the lowest course of the facing blocks.

---

[44] The Hexamilion within the Fortress is examined in Chapters V–IX. The following section traces the course of the
Hexamilion across the Isthmus from the Fortress to the Saronic Gulf.

[45] Compare Frazer (Pausanias V, p. 544), who says that the Hexamilion here stood to a height of nine courses (in
1895).

Behind the facing blocks, the bedrock was cut to form a sheer face against which the courses of facing blocks were then set. When the wall reached the top of the bedrock, the normal core of rubble and mortar once again formed the inner part of the wall.

Again rather surprisingly, the *taphros* is visible parallel to the Hexamilion and *ca.* 8 meters to the north of Tower S-12. Between 0+6,345 and 0+6,400 m. the bedrock sits above a thick deposit of clay, and two tunnels have been cut into the clay below (i.e., outside) the Hexamilion. Both of these tunnels are semicircular in shape, but the more westerly has two small projections from the main tunnel penetrating farther into the interior of the hill. The purpose of these and their date of construction are unclear, although they may well be recent. Presumably, they had no connection with the Hexamilion, and they do not seem to have had a military function.

Just past 0+6,500 m. the Hexamilion reaches the end of the plateau and turns sharply to the south. At this point another tower (S-13) formed a lookout over the level ground to the east and north (Pl. 12:c). In this area, from 0+6,300 m. to beyond 0+6,500 m., the Hexamilion follows a line suggested by Oscar Broneer for a section of his Cyclopean wall across the Isthmus.[46] According to Broneer, the wall ran along the north edge of the plateau, until the turning at Tower S-13, at which point the Cyclopean wall continued its course eastward on a nearly direct line to the Saronic Gulf. Section Ro of Broneer's wall seems to be located at the bottom of the hill on this line. The wall may be the one that Leake saw (Testimonia, 26, p. 286), as he speaks of two walls descending towards the sea, apparently from this point (S-13). A seventeenth-century Venetian plan[47] describes the Hexamilion as "Antico Recinto di mura con le sue torri rovinate" and shows the western end of the Hexamilion branching in two directions and the towers reversed, facing south. It is possible that the draftsman simply reversed the direction of the Hexamilion; if the towers are made to face north, one might imagine a division of the Hexamilion at Tower S-13 during the Venetian period, with one branch descending directly to the sea and the other turning south at this point. This would explain the situation described by Leake in 1806. There can, however, be no question that in its original phase there was only one wall and that it turned southward at Tower S-13.

The Hexamilion, in fact, inscribes almost a semicircle around the summit of Mytikas, providing an ideal location for a small fortress (*phrourion*) of the kind attested along the Hexamilion in the literary sources. There is, however, no evidence of other walls and practically no trace of ancient pottery in the area.

Midway along the height of Mytikas is another tower, S-14, as the Hexamilion continues to descend slowly. Just past 0+6,600 m., it crosses the head of a rather steep, small ravine. The builders of the Hexamilion leveled the bedrock at the western edge of the ravine and laid the foundation course on that flat surface; in addition, they apparently cut back the vertical face of the stone below the wall to make it sheer and practically impossible to scale (Pl. 12:d). Beyond the head of the ravine, the Hexamilion makes another nearly right-angle turn and runs along the south side of the small ravine, making a slow descent toward the coastal plain below (Pl. 13:a). Later builders made much use of the wall in this area, and modern walls overlie it in many places (Plate 13:b shows a modern house built over the ruins of the Hexamilion and Tower S-16). Three towers survive in this section (S-15 to S-17 from *ca.* 0+6,675 to 0+6,815 m.) as the Hexamilion drops nearly 20 meters over a distance of 230 meters.

At 0+6,875 m. the Hexamilion reaches Tower S-18 and turns sharply southward, running in a straight line over level ground. The outer (east) face of the Hexamilion is made of large rectangular blocks laid in regular courses; it stands to a maximum height of five courses, above which rises the

---

[46] Broneer, 1966, pp. 346–362; 1968, pp. 26–35.
[47] Published in *Corinth* III, ii, p. 151, fig. 4.

rubble-and-mortar core (Pl. 13:c). Four towers (S-18 to S-21) stand along this stretch, unevenly spaced between 38 and 55 meters apart. Both Frazer and Fowler described this part of the Hexamilion as "the best preserved portion." (Cf. *Corinth* I, i, p. 53, fig. 20; this section of the Hexamilion has not suffered much in the three-quarters of a century since this photograph was taken, although olive trees now obscure much of the view.) They also speak of a "less massive wall" about a hundred paces in front of the larger wall in this part of the Isthmus. Dodwell (Testimonia, 27, p. 183) also refers to another wall, and perhaps there was a *proteichisma* in this area, but, if so, debris from construction of the Corinth Canal dumped in this area at the end of the nineteenth century covered it. Fowler, however, wrote after the debris was deposited, and so he could not have seen any ancient structures there; he seems rather to have followed Frazer, blindly on this point.[48] Little weight should be put on his testimony or that of Frazer, who was not much of a topographer.

At 0+7,034 m. all trace of the Hexamilion disappears beneath the canal dump (Figs. 9, 10). Nevertheless, the Hexamilion clearly continued in a straight line for more than 100 meters across the line of yet another ravine that descends toward the sea from the west. Thus, at several points along this stretch, small pieces of the west facing wall are visible in the undergrowth. Further, as a glance at the topographic map in this area (Fig. 9) will show, the ravine comes to a sudden end along a straight line that continues the course of the Hexamilion to the south (Pl. 13:d). What seems to have happened is that at the end of the nineteenth century the builders of the Corinth Canal used the Hexamilion as a boundary and container in which to dump material excavated in digging the canal; to the north of this area, between 0+6,900 and 0+7,000 m., they dumped canal fill right up to the foot of the Hexamilion on the east side. South of 0+7,000 m. they clearly continued to observe this line in dumped material, suggesting that at the time the canal was built the ruins of the Hexamilion stretched across the mouth of the ravine on the line indicated on the plans.

Beyond this point no remains of the Hexamilion survive, and its course must be restored by conjecture. It is inconceivable that the Hexamilion simply ended in this area without a proper termination on the Saronic Gulf. It is also certain that the Hexamilion did not proceed south as far as Kenchreai. The distance between 0+7,000 m. and Kenchreai is about two kilometers, and this whole area has been thoroughly investigated, by Wiseman and then the Isthmia [UCLA] staff, for any trace of the Hexamilion. It is possible that small sections may have disappeared, but a section as long as that required to stretch as far as Kenchreai simply cannot have vanished without a trace. The builders of the Hexamilion must have wanted not to extend the course of the fortification any farther than necessary in order to conserve material, construction effort, and the size of the garrison necessary to defend it. The Hexamilion must certainly have approached the Saronic Gulf somewhere close to its last visible trace.

In the vicinity of 0+7,000 m., the canal dump obscures all trace of the Hexamilion. We may suggest, however, that it skirted the small hill on the south side of the first ravine, then turned east at *ca.* 0+7,280 m. (Fig. 10). This direction is indicated by the sharp break in the ravine that approaches the area from the south and the line of canal dump that comes to an end at just this point. On analogy with the area around 0+7,100 m., the line of canal dump probably indicates the course of the Hexamilion. We may then suggest that it ascended the bare hill (elev. +22 m.) directly to the east. There is no trace of the Hexamilion on this hill, but erosion and building activity through the centuries (most notably during World War II and in recent years) may have removed all remains in

---

[48] Frazer, *Pausanias* III, p. 5. It is difficult to make much of the photograph in *Corinth* I, i, p. 57, fig. 24, which shows the "less massive wall" apparently in the area of Towers S-19 to S-21; this may be nothing more than a line in the canal dump. On the eastern end of the wall, see T. E. Gregory, "An Early Byzantine Complex at Akra Sophia near Corinth," *Hesperia* 54, 1985, pp. 411–428.

the area. This hill is, in fact, a small headland that juts out toward the sea, the first notable height to approach the sea south of the canal. The dumping of canal fill throughout this area considerably changed the landscape, and it is likely that the sea originally came up to the base of this headland (see pp. 9–10 above). This height would therefore have been a natural point of defense, firmly anchoring the eastern end of the Hexamilion and allowing characteristic enfilading fire along its exposed flank.

The evidence of Mazaris (Testimonia, 10) shows that a fortress stood at the eastern termination of the Hexamilion before Manuel II's rebuilding in 1415. This fortress must have been on the hill discussed above. In 1806 parts of this section of the Hexamilion were perhaps still visible. Thus, Leake described the Hexamilion as it passed "to a height on the southern side of the level, where probably stood a small fortress, forming part of a plan of defense toward the sea" (Testimonia, 26, p. 287). Clearly, in his time no fortress stood intact on the hill, but he may have seen the Hexamilion approach the height, through the area now obscured by canal fill. A fortress at this point must have provided a powerful eastern termination for the Hexamilion and discouraged any attempt to turn the fortification by sea in the Saronic Gulf. One should imagine a bastion, similar to that at the western termination of the Hexamilion and fulfilling a similar function.

V

THE NORTHEAST GATE

THE FORTRESS, located directly east and northeast of the Sanctuary of Poseidon, is the best-preserved part of the Byzantine fortifications on the Isthmus of Corinth. It is also the area most fully excavated. The Hexamilion coincides with the northern side of the Fortress, which is relatively straight, running roughly east–west from Fortress Tower 15 to Tower 19 (Fig. 8); at the latter, however, the Hexamilion turns sharply southeast to follow the line of the Roman Arch (pp. 52–56 below). From there the Hexamilion runs virtually straight to Tower 2. At this point the Hexamilion continues its course southeastward toward the Saronic Gulf, but the East Fortress Wall runs southwestward, describing a great, outwardly concave line to Fortress Tower 6. From Tower 6 the South Fortress Wall runs roughly westward as far as Tower 10 to form the short southern boundary of the Fortress; midway along the South Fortress Wall is the South Gate. From Tower 10 the West Fortress Wall runs northward to join the Hexamilion at Fortress Tower 15. Originally, there were only two gates to the Fortress, the Northeast Gate, between Towers 19 and 1, and the South Gate, between Towers 8 and 9.

THE ROMAN ARCH

The Northeast Gate was the primary entrance into the Fortress and, during the Hexamilion period, the formal entry into the Peloponnesos (Figs. 17, 18; Pl. 14:a, b). In original conception and design, the gate was monumental, intended not only for strategic advantage but also for aesthetic effect. In 1883 Monceaux excavated the central part of the gate, apparently in a long trench that exposed the whole of the marble roadway and defined the basic outline of the gate structure.[1] Monceaux seemingly filled in most of his excavation, but some of the gate superstructure was still visible in 1932, when Jenkins and Megaw investigated it (presumably without excavation) and corrected some of Monceaux's mistakes.[2] By 1967, when Clement began new excavations, most of the gate had once again been buried (Pl. 15:a, b), and considerable effort had to be devoted to clearing the debris from Monceaux's trenches. Although Monceaux exposed the whole of the road surface, he left many areas untouched, especially to the north and south of the roadway, and there was ample opportunity to explore the foundations of the gate structure.

    The Northeast Gate, one of the two original entrances into the Fortress, was built around the four piers of a Roman monumental arch that had marked the northern approach to the Sanctuary of Poseidon at Isthmia since the second half of the first century after Christ (Fig. 18).[3] This arch was simple and its decoration plain, but it lay astride the road any traveler must have used to approach the Sanctuary, either from the north or from the port of Schoinos to the northeast. Its triple-arched passageways must have formed an impressive vista from below. The arch was constructed with large blocks of local sandstone laid without mortar and covered with white stucco. By the time of Monceaux's excavation in 1883,[4] the superstructure of the arch had completely

---

[1] Monceaux, "Fouilles," 1884, pp. 279–284.

[2] Jenkins and Megaw, "Researches," pp. 71–73.

[3] Gregory and Mills, "Roman Arch," pp. 407–445.

[4] Monceaux, "Fouilles," 1884, pp. 273–285, esp. pp. 282–285. Monceaux was the first modern scholar to note the existence of the arch and its utilization in the Fortress.

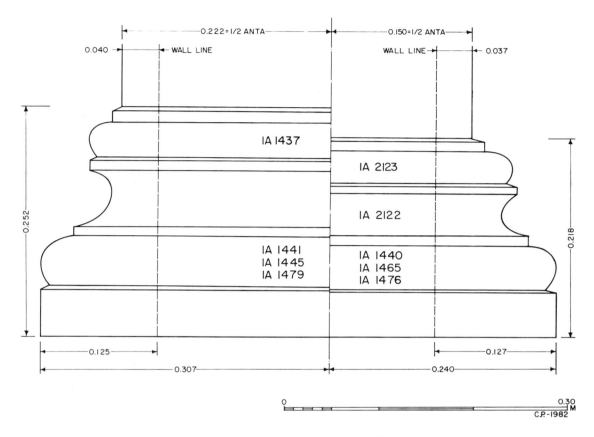

ILL. 2. Roman Arch, anta-base profiles

collapsed. By the beginning of the UCLA excavations in 1967, a maximum of only five courses of blocks was preserved in the piers of the arch.[5] Nevertheless, many of the blocks from the super-structure were discovered in the course of the excavation, and these, along with early photographs and descriptions, and analogy with other Roman monumental arches, allow a hypothetical recon-struction of the arch in its original form (Fig. 19).

The Roman Arch here at Isthmia was an Ionic monument, extraordinarily simple and almost carelessly built. Antas with plain Ionic bases and capitals marked the corners of the passageways (Ill. 2); the ends of the arch, however, had no antas, and neither antas nor columns were used to support the entablature. The entablature consisted of an apparently undecorated Ionic epistyle and frieze and a simple dentilated geison; the attic was crowned by another Ionic geison (Ill. 3). No trace of a dedicatory inscription survives from the arch, and it was probably not decorated with sculpture, either on the façades or on the top.

It is obvious from the plan of the Hexamilion in this area that the wall was aligned with a pre-existing structure at the Northeast Gate. Megaw noticed how the Hexamilion leaves its natural course: "without a pre-existing arch it is difficult to account for this irregularity of plan."[6] The change in direction suggests that the road that ran through the Roman Arch was still in use at the time the Hexamilion was constructed and that the builders decided to make use of the earlier struc-ture in the defenses. It is impossible now to know with certainty whether the arch was still standing

[5] Clement, 1968, pp. 139–143.
[6] Jenkins and Megaw, "Researches," p. 73.

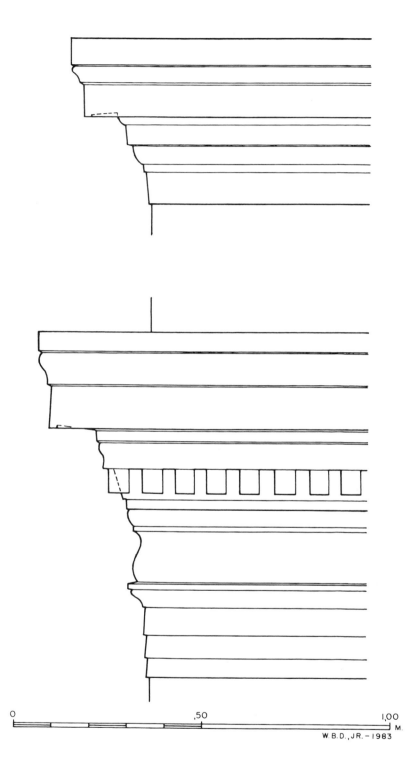

ILL. 3. Roman Arch, superstructure profiles

intact when work on the Hexamilion began. Given the general destruction at the Sanctuary in the fourth century and the especially violent earthquakes at that time, the monument probably suffered some damage.[7] On the other hand, the piers of the arch were still standing to a height of as many as nine courses as late as 1909. Moreover, the excavators found many of the architectural members from the superstructure in the near vicinity, suggesting that they had been built into the Northeast Gate. In fact (see pp. 65–70 below), much of the arch was probably simply incorporated within the structure of the gate, and it may have been standing to nearly its full height at the time construction of the gate began.

Nevertheless, some of the arch must have collapsed or been taken down when the gate was built. This is shown by the three attic geison blocks attributed to the attic of the arch (IA 2069, 2070, 67-1) built into the fabric of the South Tower of the Northeast Gate. Several other blocks assigned to the arch (e.g., IA 69-13, an entablature geison block) are covered with mortar, suggesting that they were built into the Hexamilion, at least in one of its phases. In any case, even after construction of the gate, at least the four anta bases flanking the central roadway were still visible to passers-by. These have all now disappeared, but three of them are visible in a photograph taken by W. B. Dinsmoor, Sr. in 1909 (Pl. 15:c).[8] Some of the anta capitals may also still have been *in situ* at the time of the construction of the gate, since large capital fragments were visible at the time of Monceaux's excavations, and two of these have recently been recovered in the fill.[9] Thus, a monumental façade must still have existed at the time the Fortress was built, and reasons of utility were probably not the only motive for the preservation of the arch.

The utilization of earlier architecture was very much a part of late Roman fortification technique, frequently for aesthetic as much as practical reasons. The Beulé Gate at Athens, for example, was constructed from the choregic monument of Nikias, dismantled specifically for this purpose, but when the gate was built the templelike monument was reassembled in a form that was as close to the original as possible.[10] The re-use of earlier Roman arches in late antique fortifications can be paralleled at several sites. For example, in the Theodosian Walls of Constantinople, built in 413, an earlier arch of Theodosius I may have been incorporated into the Golden Gate, the main ceremonial entry into the capital.[11] Likewise, slightly earlier, several previously standing arches were incorporated as gates in the Aurelian Wall of Rome.[12] Further, at Nicaea an arch dedicated, probably, to Hadrian was transformed into the so-called Istanbul Gate.[13] This arch also had three passageways, although only the central one was arched; by the time the gate was constructed, however (during the reign of Claudius II Gothicus, A.D. 268–270), ground level had risen to make the two side passages unusable. In this instance both façades of the arch were visible in the

[7] For the evidence on the earthquakes of the fourth century in the Corinthia, see *Corinth* VIII, iii, p. 165, and Wiseman, "Gymnasium Area," p. 409, note 19.

[8] Gregory and Mills, "Roman Arch," p. 414, note 19.

[9] Monceaux, "Fouilles," 1884, p. 283, note 1; Gregory and Mills, "Roman Arch," nos. 13 and 14.

[10] Gregory, "Fortified Cities," pp. 14–21. Similar phenomena can be seen at Sparta and elsewhere. Note also the elegant decoration of the gates at Resafa, especially the North Gate: Karnapp, *Stadtmauer*, pp. 37–44, pls. 162–211.

[11] The Golden Gate was constructed to commemorate a victory of the emperor Theodosius, but it is unclear whether this was Theodosius I or Theodosius II. If the former, the gate was originally a freestanding arch outside the Constantinian circuit, later incorporated in the Theodosian Walls. If the latter, the gate was built as an integral part of the Land Walls. See Kirchen, *Landmauer* I, pp. 11–12, fig. 5, pls. 19–22, 42–44.

[12] The Porta Tiburtina was constructed in front of the arch on the Aqua Marcia-Tepula-Julia, and the Porta Praenestina was built around the arch on the Aqua Claudia: I. A. Richmond, *The City Wall of Imperial Rome*, Oxford 1930, pp. 170, 177, 210–213; M. Todd, *The Walls of Rome*, Totowa, N.J. 1978, pp. 35–43.

[13] A. M. Schneider and W. Karnapp, "Die Stadtmauer von Iznik (Nicaea)," *Istanbuler Forschung* 9, 1938, pp. 24–27, pls. 13–19.

gate structure, since two large half-round towers were built up against the short sides of the arch, leaving the façades exposed. A second gate was constructed behind the arch, making what was essentially a double entrance, but the arch itself formed the primary point of defense in the gate. A final example is the triple arch of Caracalla at Theveste/Tebessa, converted into a tower protecting a gateway when the fortifications of that north African town were constructed, sometime between 536 and 544.[14]

CONSTRUCTION OF THE NORTHEAST GATE

THE GATE STRUCTURE

The decisions to incorporate the Roman Arch into the Hexamilion and to make use of the pre-existing road as the primary entrance into the Fortress largely determined the size and shape of the Northeast Gate. The Hexamilion turned an oblique angle at this point to align itself with the axis of the arch, and the central passage through the arch became the passageway through the gate. The transformation of the arch was accomplished by adding a gate mechanism[15] behind (i.e., west of) the central piers of the arch and by building two large towers that projected to the east of the arch and protected the roadway on either side (see Fig. 18). These towers blocked the side entrances of the arch and completely enclosed the North and South Piers within the tower constructions. The two central piers, however, were still visible on the east, and the main structure of the arch could be used as a core for the gate.

The towers were built over solid rectangular platforms, several courses high, both of which were constructed of rectangular blocks, presumably taken from other buildings in the sanctuary. Because of the slope of the land in this area, the foundations of the platform of the North Tower (Tower 19) were naturally sunk deeper than those of the South Tower (Tower 1); those of the North Tower are concealed beneath the masonry of the later bastion that surrounds it on the east and north. The top surfaces of the two platforms, however, are at roughly the same level, between 32.2 and 32.5 m. above sea level. The two platforms are not exactly the same size: that of the North Tower is *ca.* 6.37 by 3.77 m., while that of the South Tower is *ca.* 6.56 by 3.50 m. In addition, the foundations of the North Tower are much more carefully constructed than those of the South Tower, which are characterized by strikingly sloppy work.[16]

Today, nearly all the superstructure of the South Tower has disappeared, leaving only the rectangular platform, while in the North Tower up to two courses of the tower walls are preserved *in situ*. Interestingly enough, the walls of the North Tower had already been robbed down to that level by 1909, as Dinsmoor's photographs of that year show (Pl. 15:c, d).

The masonry of the towers is firmly bonded to that of the Hexamilion, which approaches the gate from the west and the south, showing clearly that the Northeast Gate is contemporary with the construction of the Hexamilion. This can be seen most clearly in the South Tower, where several blocks of the east face of the Hexamilion run over blocks from the tower platform (visible on the plan, Fig. 17).

In the South Tower, where it is clearly visible, the platform is three rough courses high above a leveling course of rubble and mortar footed on hardpan. As mentioned above, the workmanship on this platform is not very careful: blocks frequently protrude unevenly from the surface of the walls,

---

[14] Lawrence, *Greek Aims*, p. 189; Pringle, *Defence* I, pp. 238–243, 325–326, pl. XLVII:a, b.

[15] Door, bolt, and reveals to secure the door when open.

[16] See Monceaux, "Fouilles," 1884, p. 282: "aspect barbare."

and many of the re-used stones have been crudely cut to make them fit the position in which they were placed.

In the North Tower the workmanship was more careful and the blocks more regularly laid. Two courses of the North Tower platform are now visible, but construction of the later bastion around the tower obscured the foundations, and it is not possible to say how much further they may have been sunk.

On the platform of the North Tower are four curving blocks with moldings (IA 2054, 2059, 2060, 2061), which formed part of the lowest course of the walls of the tower (Ill. 4, Fig. 17, Pl. 16:a). These blocks are made of typical local Corinthian building stone, and they are finished with Ionic base moldings on the outside of the curve: above a broad plinth, a fillet and inverted cyma recta with ovolo and fillet crown (Ill. 4). The moldings project *ca.* 0.16 m. from the face of the block above. The blocks form an arc with an exterior radius, at the base of the moldings, of *ca.* 3.42 m. The inner sides of two of these blocks are marked by irregular cuttings, undoubtedly designed to allow them to interlock with the interior blocks of the building from which they originally came.

These base blocks are clearly not in their original position, and they have been re-used in the tower. In fact, at either end of the arc, the moldings have been rather roughly cut away to make the blocks fit the dimensions of the platform, which is slightly smaller than the exterior circle of the curved blocks. Apparently, the width and the spacing of the piers of the Roman Arch determined the width of the platform of the tower, and the previously used curved blocks did not have exactly

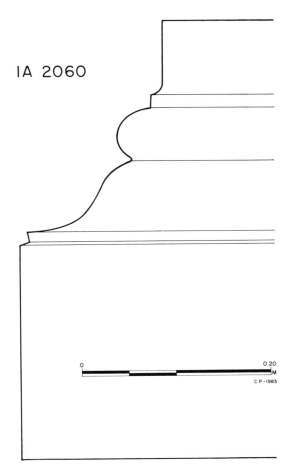

ILL. 4. North Tower, profile of base block IA 2060

the correct dimensions. Some small adjustment in the width of the platform, however, should have been possible, perhaps by widening the platform to the north. The extant remains therefore suggest either that the approach of the Hexamilion from the west had already been constructed when the platform was built or that simple errors were made in calculating the size of the platform necessary to support the series of base blocks that was to rise above it. In any case, this discrepancy was only cosmetic; it had no effect on the structural soundness of the tower.

Above the base blocks three orthostate blocks are preserved *in situ* (IA 2062, 2063, 2064). These blocks are *ca.* 0.75–0.77 m. high and about a meter long each. They fit perfectly the curved blocks beneath them, and one of the orthostates (IA 2062) and one of the base blocks (IA 2061) share identical back cuttings; it would seem that at least some of these blocks were reassembled in the tower in exactly the same position they held in the original structure. The visible upper surfaces of all these curved blocks have swallowtail-clamp cuttings (Fig. 17); the two blocks at the northwest and the southwest have traces of iron preserved in the cuttings. The clamps used in these two blocks, however, were not the swallowtail type for which the cuttings were made but rather hook clamps; perhaps these clamps were inserted in the Hexamilion period to help bond the semicircular superstructure of the tower more firmly to the rest of the fortification.

The published plans of both Monceaux[17] and Megaw[18] show a semicircular superstructure on a rectangular foundation in the South Tower as well as the North. Indeed, one of the 1909 photographs seems to show a rounded face on the northern side of the South Tower (Pl. 15:c, lower left), and Megaw's plan shows that at least two of these curved blocks were still *in situ* at the time of his investigation in 1932. All these blocks have subsequently disappeared, and almost nothing of the superstructure of the South Tower is preserved. Close examination of the top of the platform, however, shows that only the northern part of the superstructure was circular, while the southern part was rectangular in plan.[19] Evidence for this can be seen along the south side of the tower, where the rectangular wall is preserved above the level of the platform; traces of mortar along the southern part of the east face of the tower show that this section was also rectangular. It is impossible to say with certainty whether there were moldings on the blocks of the lowest course of the South Tower. Symmetry would certainly call for this, and one might assume that additional base blocks were available from the building that contributed the blocks on the North Tower. Nevertheless, the juxtaposition of circular and rectilinear forms on the South Tower destroyed any attempt at complete symmetry, and the testimony of Monceaux seems to imply that the South Tower had no moldings: "L'une de ces tours est encore décorée de moulures; l'autre est d'aspect barbare."[20] Further, although he says nothing about this in his text, Megaw's plan of the Northeast Gate seems to show moldings on the North Tower but not on the two curved blocks of the South Tower that apparently survived in 1932.[21]

Clearly, the curved blocks in the North Tower must have come from an important round building in the Sanctuary of Poseidon. It is tempting to assign them to the single fully published example of such a building, the Palaimonion.[22] The foundations identified by Broneer as those of the Palaimonion consist of a concrete core, *ca.* 8.80 by 8.00 m., onto which one should add a facing of cut blocks on all sides. The curved blocks from the Northeast Gate have an exterior diameter of

[17] Monceaux, "Fouilles," 1884, p. 283, fig. 2.
[18] Jenkins and Megaw, "Researches," p. 72, fig. 2.
[19] This was first noted by Clement, 1968, p. 139.
[20] Monceaux, "Fouilles," 1884, p. 272.
[21] Jenkins and Megaw, "Researches," p. 72, fig. 2.
[22] Broneer, *Isthmia* II, pp. 99–112.

ca. 6.84 m., and so would fit the foundations of the Palaimonion, but their form makes this identification unlikely. Broneer restored the superstructure of the Palaimonion on the basis of several coins that represent the temple.[23] These coins show the temple as monopteral, while the blocks from the Northeast Gate are from a circular wall, which rises from a base with moldings. The orthostates of this wall are preserved to a height of *ca.* 1.24 m., and the clamp cuttings on the upper surfaces show that the wall rose at least one course further. Possibly, the coins used by Broneer in the restoration of the Palaimonion simply failed to show an existing cella wall on the interior of the temple, but the restored diameter of the blocks at the Northeast Gate is in any case too large for them to have been used in an interior wall on the foundations identified as those of the Palaimonion. It is therefore necessary to suggest that the Sanctuary contained one or more other round buildings and that the blocks used in the construction of the Northeast Gate came from one of these.

The preserved walls of the North Tower are only *ca.* 0.80 m. thick, clearly not enough to support the superstructure of the tower or to defend the tower against attack. Thus, this wall must have been further thickened. On the basis of the surviving portions of the rectilinear wall of the South Tower, we have suggested a restored thickness of 1.20 m., although there is no evidence of additional masonry preserved on the upper surface of the North Tower platform (see Fig. 20).

The top of the tower platforms appears to have been the floor level of the lowest story of the towers. The so-called North Wall of the gateway (see below) overruns the northwest corner of the North Pier at the level of its fifth course for a distance of *ca.* 0.15 m., and this might suggest that the pier had been taken down to its present level when the gate was built. It is more likely, however, that the North Wall was simply "notched into" the pier at this point and that the pier itself was allowed to stand to help support the superstructure of the gate.

A similar arrangement seems to have been followed in the South Tower, where the South Pier of the Roman Arch must have been intact above the level of the ground floor of the tower. This much can be derived from the single course of blocks in the pier (*ca.* 0.43 m. high) that is still preserved *in situ* above the near-by floor level of the tower. It is impossible to know how high the South Pier was preserved when the gate was built, but it is reasonable to assume that it also stood to its full height to support the superstructure of the arch. The two side passages of the Roman Arch, narrowed on the outer side by the curved wall of the towers, provided entrances into the ground floor rooms of the towers (Ill. 5).

As mentioned above, the North Wall extended westward from the northwest corner of the North Pier, where it partially overran the masonry of the arch. This wall was constructed with ashlar masonry a single block thick, set in a hard lime mortar. The south face of the wall is straight and well finished, while the north face is very irregular and was obviously never meant to be seen. The North Wall is preserved for a distance of over 9.5 m., and its western termination apparently was robbed out. It is 0.55–0.65 m. wide and preserved to a height of eight courses, with its lowest course resting on hardpan at an elevation of 31.55 m. The wall seems to be contemporary with the first phase of the Hexamilion, both because it has been fitted into the masonry of the North Pier of the Roman Arch and because pottery of the late fourth or early fifth century was found in the fill up against its foundations (see pp. 70–74 below).

The North Wall was obviously too thin to be an outer defensive wall and its finished face was in any case turned inward toward the roadway. Probably the wall was constructed to block access to the south face of the Hexamilion and its system of stairways and fighting platforms and perhaps to form one side of a secondary gate complex. Certainly the defenders of the Fortress would not want

[23] Broneer, *Isthmia* II, pp. 110–112, pl. 73; the coins are listed on p. 110, note 14 (but note that the first coin [pl. 42:a, b] should be assigned to Commodus rather than to Caracalla).

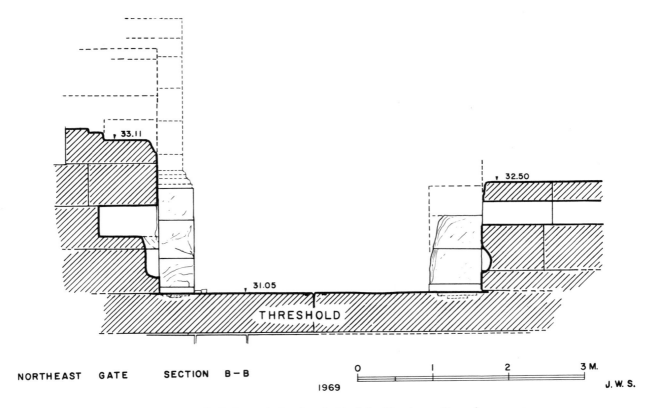

ILL. 5. Section B–B through the threshold of the Northeast Gate, from west

their positions open to easy attack if an opponent should force the main gate. In addition, the North Wall served to square off the defensive part of the roadway in an area where the fortifications were otherwise irregular. On the southern side of the roadway a similar wall, nearly parallel to the North Wall but much less well preserved, ran westward from the northwestern corner of the South Reveal. This wall apparently followed the course of the roadway as it turned slightly to the south once inside the gate (Figs. 17, 20).

The arrangement of these walls suggests the possibility of an interior gateway to the west of the primary gate. Such interior gateways were, of course, common in Greek fortifications from an early date,[24] and parallels can be found at several late Roman fortifications in the Aegean area. Thus, as we have already seen, the Istanbul Gate at Nicaea had a secondary gate behind the re-used Roman Arch, although the interior walls there were curved and formed an oval space between the two gates.[25] Likewise, in the fortifications on the citadel at Ephesus, two walls *ca.* 30 m. long, which terminated in an interior gate, framed the road through the main gateway.[26] At Isthmia, however, there is no further evidence of such an interior gate, and we must conclude there probably was none.

The actual roadway through the Northeast Gate was made entirely of white marble blocks, re-used from many buildings and monuments of the Sanctuary, and its appearance at the time of construction must have been quite spectacular (Fig. 21:b; Pls. 14:a, 16:c). Either at the time of the

---

[24] Perhaps the most famous example of such an arrangement is the Dipylon Gate at Athens: Winter (*Greek Fortifications*, pp. 217–233, fig. 211) calls this form an "enclosed court".

[25] Schneider and Karnapp (footnote 13 above, p. 55), pl. 13.

[26] *Forschungen in Ephesos* IV, iii, Vienna 1955, fig. 1, p. 23.

construction of the Northeast Gate or sometime earlier, the foundations of the central roadway were cut down to *ca.* 2.50 m. below the earlier road surface (Fig. 21:a). This excavation was deepest just in front of the actual gateway, between and immediately to the east of the piers of the Roman Arch; further east and west the foundations were not so deep. The purpose of this excavation is unclear. Perhaps it was the result of an earlier leveling of the grade of the road as it approached the Sanctuary from the northeast; alternatively, it might have been designed to deter sappers (although it is difficult to see why sappers would attempt to dig under the wall in the best-defended place) or simply to strengthen the road for the heavy military traffic it was expected to bear.

Throughout most of the length where excavation has exposed it, the roadway was constructed in three distinct levels, consisting of two foundation courses of "sub-roads" and the upper paving, although in a few places the road appears to have had only one foundation course (Fig. 21:a). The blocks in foundation courses were all local sandstone. They included columns and capitals of various sizes and at least two Doric cornices (blocks 120c and 124b) on which red-painted *viae* were still visible at the time of excavation. The lowest course of blocks was laid directly on hardpan, while an uneven layer of sand separated the paving blocks from the foundation blocks. Mortar was unevenly used in construction of the roadway: in some places the blocks were apparently laid dry, while in others large amounts of lime mortar were used, for example, in the area of the main threshold block and on some of the many column drums used in the foundations. The upper surfaces of these foundation blocks were not at all worn, which shows that they can never have been used as part of the actual paving.

A surprising feature of the roadway construction is that its foundations slightly undercut those of the central piers of the Roman Arch. Apparently, the need to sink deep foundations for the roadway was considered more important than the danger of destabilizing the piers.

As mentioned above, the actual road surface was made entirely of marble blocks, laid with their long axes perpendicular to the direction of the roadway, and many of them were hacked and chopped to make them fit their places (Fig. 21:b, Pl. 16:c). Columns were flattened on one side to allow them to serve in the road surface, and blocks with moldings were turned so that the back or a side was facing upward. This road surface is naturally much worn from the traffic that passed through the gate. Many of the blocks preserve a distinct pair of wheel grooves, the amount of wear on a particular stone obviously dependent upon its relative hardness.

The full presentation of these important items must await the completion of study now under way on both the sculpture and the architecture represented. Here, only a few examples can be cited. These include the stele set up to honor L. Kornelios Korinthos, *pythaulis*, for his many victories at most of the great competitions in Greece and Asia (roadway block 43, IΣ 69-1, Pl. 16:b).[27] Another victor's monument (block 86, IΣ 69-2) was used in the roadway along with a large number of marble entablature blocks, some of them inscribed. Thus, block 39 (used as the southern half of the threshold, IΣ 524) and block 27 (IΣ 69-5, IA 69-48) are from the same entablature series with inscribed Latin letters. Block 42 (IΣ 69-4, IA 69-42) is another finely carved Ionic entablature block with a partially preserved Latin inscription.[28] The architectural detail on all these stones is fresh and crisp except where the blocks have been hacked and chopped, showing that the buildings from which they came had been standing until a point not long before construction of the roadway.

To the east of the gateway, beyond the later rubble blocking wall (Fig. 21:a), the marble road surface has been almost completely robbed away, making it impossible to say how far the marble

[27] P. A. Clement, "L. Kornelius Korinthos of Corinth," ΦΟΡΟΣ. *Tribute to Benjamin Dean Merrit*, D. W. Bradeen and M. F. McGregor, edd., Locust Valley, N.Y. 1974, pp. 36–39.
[28] Clement, 1970, pp. 166–167.

paving continued in this direction. To the west, however, at a distance of *ca.* 9 meters from the west face of the central piers of the Roman Arch, excavation revealed the end of the marble paving. The road surface beyond that point was simply packed earth and stone (Figs. 17, 21:b). It might be thought that this surface was a rebuilding after a period of disuse and robbing of the original marble road surface. There is evidence, however (see p. 75 below), that this earth-and-stone surface was in use during the third quarter of the fifth century, and it is unlikely that the road was destroyed and rebuilt in such a short period. Thus, we should imagine the grand marble pavement coming to an end at this point, with the road surface within the Fortress continuing in a rather less spectacular fashion.

Overlying the marble pavement within the gate was another layer of hard, compacted earth and small stones *ca.* 0.26–0.38 m. thick (Fig. 21:a; Pl. 17:a). This undoubtedly represents a later road surface, perhaps even laid after the gate went out of use. This road surface was found only in the western part of the roadway; presumably it had been cut away in the east by Monceaux.

The direction of the wheel ruts in the marble roadway, the positioning of the actual road surface blocks, and the direction of the wall to the south of the road suggest that the road west of the gate did not follow the axis of the passage but rather diverged slightly to the south as it passed into the interior of the Fortress. Soundings in this direction west of the gate, however, failed to reveal any further trace of the road. Once again, this may simply have been a result of Monceaux's earlier excavation, which apparently stretched westward for a considerable distance.

The threshold of the gateway was made of two large blocks of marble set directly up against the west faces of the central piers of the Roman Arch (Ill. 5, Figs. 19, 21). The pivot holes for the great bivalve doors of the gate are visible on either end of these blocks; they are composed of an oval socket set down inside a roughly rectangular cutting. The pivot hole on the south side of the threshold is considerably larger than that on the north, and the oval socket there is oriented with its long axis north–south, while the axis of the socket to the north is oriented east–west. The doors obviously opened inward, a common arrangement that allowed the defenders to prevent the doors from opening in a time of crisis by piling huge amounts of debris behind (i.e., west of) the doors, while also allowing them to open the doors quickly to make a sortie or force an escape.[29] In the middle of the threshold are several roughly rectangular cuttings that must have been holes for vertical bolts; the best preserved of these is *ca.* 0.032 by 0.022 m. and 0.018 m. deep.

To the west of the central piers of the arch and flanking the roadway on both sides are the North and South Reveals (Fig. 18; Pl. 17:b). These were constructed after the road surface had been laid, since their lowest courses lie over the north and south edges of the road pavement. Basically, the reveals continue the line of the piers of the arch to the west, inside the gate. On the surfaces facing the roadway, however, the reveals are indented from the line of the piers to allow for the placement of the door pivots and for the valves to be recessed and out of the way when opened.

Information about the gate-closure mechanism can be gleaned from the surviving cuttings. Certainly, the vertical bolt cuttings mentioned above cannot ever have been meant to secure the gateway against attack, and they must have been used only to hold the doors closed temporarily. The primary means for closing the gate was a series of bars or beams that can be reconstructed from socket cuttings in the two reveals. The lowest set of these cuttings is *ca.* 0.78 m. above the road surface on the North Reveal and *ca.* 0.92 m. above the road on the South Reveal (Ill. 5, Fig. 21:b). On the North Reveal the cutting is roughly 0.40 m. high, 0.34 m. wide, and 0.50 m. deep, while that on the South Reveal is *ca.* 0.32 m. high and 0.34 m. wide. The latter runs completely through the reveal for a distance of *ca.* 1.63 m. and discharges into the space between the South Reveal and the

[29] See Pringle, *Defence* I, p. 160.

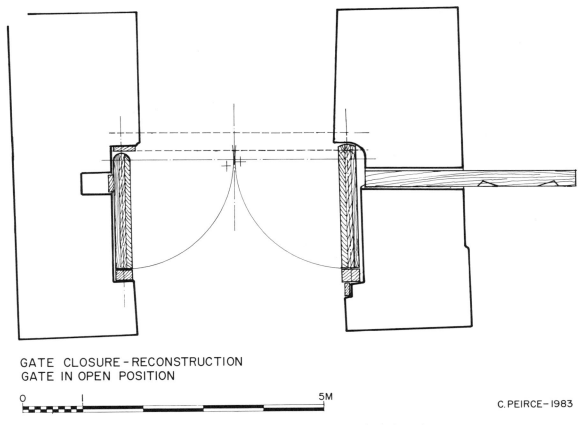

GATE CLOSURE - RECONSTRUCTION
GATE IN OPEN POSITION

0   1   5M

C. PEIRCE – 1983

ILL. 6. Gate closure of the Northeast Gate (open)

face of the Hexamilion beyond. The surface of the stone below the cutting is roughly broken on both reveals, but this is probably accidental and has no connection with the original gate mechanism. About 0.90 m. above the top of this lowest cutting another socket is preserved on the North Reveal, *ca.* 0.30 m. wide and 0.70 m. deep (visible as the longer cutting on Figure 21:b; cf. Ill. 5). The upper part of this socket has been lost, but one of the 1909 photographs (Pl. 15:c) shows it to have been roughly square in shape. Presumably, there was a matching socket on the South Reveal opposite, and there may have been yet a third hole at a point higher up. Certainly, a door of this size must have been closed with bars at more than one level.

The door may have been secured by a single beam, removed and stored elsewhere when not in use, but the surviving cuttings indicate that otherwise a single beam cannot have spanned the entire width of the gateway, since there was not enough clearance for the beam to slide free through the socket in the South Reveal: the doors were *ca.* 4.2 m. wide, while the space available for the storage of the beam in the South Reveal and beyond was only *ca.* 3.5 m. In addition, the lowest cuttings are not on exactly the same level on the two reveals, and a single beam would not have fitted properly into the two holes. This means that the bolts used in the Northeast Gate must have been broken into two sections. When the gate was opened, the larger of these would be stored in the cutting in the South Reveal, but when the gate was closed, the two pieces would be joined together and their ends fitted into the slots in both reveals. This arrangement is illustrated in the gate-closure reconstructions, Illustrations 6 and 7. The beams were probably secured by diagonal struts fitted into the returns at the west end of the reveals, as shown in Illustration 7.

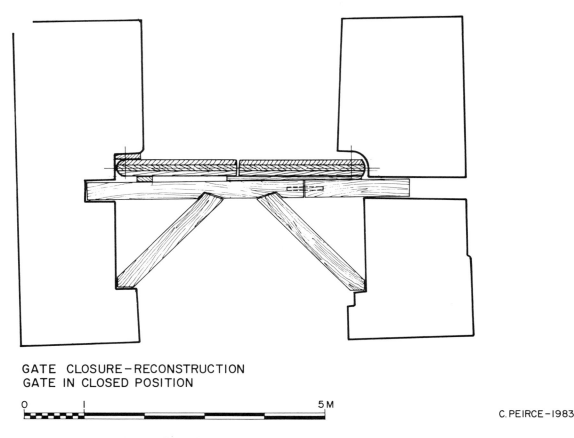

GATE CLOSURE – RECONSTRUCTION
GATE IN CLOSED POSITION

0   I   5 M

C. PEIRCE – 1983

ILL. 7. Gate closure of the Northeast Gate (closed)

At about 0.10 m. from the west end of the North Reveal there is another socket *ca.* 0.75 m. above the road surface (Fig. 21:a; cf. p. 87 below). This cutting is roughly 0.15 m. square, and it is only *ca.* 0.13 m. deep. There is no corresponding socket on the South Reveal. Perhaps there was a gateway of some kind here at one period or another, and the narrowing of the passage at this point would have made an ideal place to block the entrance. There are no pivot cuttings in the roadway, however, and it is probably best to assume that no secondary gateway existed here at the time the Fortress was built.

Construction of the two reveals and the near-by parts of the Hexamilion created at least partly enclosed spaces to the west of the two towers: the North and the South Bays (Fig. 18). As can be seen from the plans, the North Bay was considerably larger than the South Bay, since the Hexamilion intruded into the space directly west of the South Pier of the Roman Arch.

Access to the South Bay from the roadway was barred by the wall along the south side of the road, but there was no such impediment to the north. Floor level in the North Bay cannot now be determined, but presumably it was the same as that in the North Tower, that is, +32.44 m. This was more than a meter higher than the road surface at this point, and so one should reconstruct a stairway joining the roadway with the North Bay (Fig. 20). There must also have been some means to close off the interior of the towers, such as a doorway, either at the entrance to the bays or to the towers themselves. Running between the west end of the North Reveal and the North Wall was a small wall *ca.* 0.47 m. wide, made of small uneven blocks (Fig. 17). It is unlikely that this was contemporary with the construction of the Fortress (see pp. 84–85 below), but at a later period it allowed for the enclosure of the North Bay as an independent room west of the North Tower. There is, however, no evidence of a parallel wall west of the South Tower.

THE SUPERSTRUCTURE

The remains of the Northeast Gate are nowhere preserved above the lowest level. Nevertheless, several indications of the upper structure survive, and along with comparanda from better-preserved fortifications elsewhere, provide evidence for a hypothetical reconstruction of the super-structure of the gate. The two most important pieces of evidence are the springing for a vault at the preserved top of the North Wall and the two sets of stairs on the interior of the Hexamilion, one at either side of the Northeast Gate. In addition, the course of the Hexamilion veered to enclose the Roman Arch, and it is reasonable to assume that those who built the gate made as much use of the arch as possible.

The better preserved of the stairways is in the triangular space between the south face of the Hexamilion and the North Wall, about 8 meters west of the North Tower (Figs. 17, 20; Pl. 17:c). The first step of this stairway was founded directly on bedrock at an elevation of +33.07 m. This step was removed in the construction of Grave 2 (see p. 77 below), but the three preserved steps show an average rise of *ca.* 0.24 m. and a tread of 0.28 m. (Ill. 8). The stairway presumably came to an end before the beginning of the vault over the North Bay (see pp. 66–68 below), a distance of 4.76 m. Using these figures, the top of the stairway may be calculated at an elevation of +37.61 m., or 7.29 m. above the hardpan on the outside of the wall (Ill. 8). This presumably represents the level of the fighting platform at this point. The stairway to the south of the gate is much less well preserved, and none of the steps survive *in situ*. The stairway can, however, be traced in the greater width of the Hexamilion as it approaches the Northeast Gate from the southeast. It is reasonable, then, to restore a stairway of similar dimensions here, with a fighting platform at the same height, as shown on the restored elevation, Illustration 12 (see also Ill. 10).

The stairway on the northern side of the gate is *ca.* 0.70 m. wide, *ca.* 0.10 m. narrower than the normal stairs along the Hexamilion. This narrowing was apparently to facilitate passage between the stairway and the North Wall to a latrine under the stairs (Ill. 8, Fig. 20).[30] The existence of this latrine is suggested by a ceramic drain pipe running down through the triangular space between the south face of the Hexamilion and the North Wall (Pl. 18:a). This pipe was made of sections 0.45–0.46 m. long and *ca.* 0.13 m. in diameter, with an upper end that narrowed to fit into the section above it (IM 67-1 to 67-3), the reverse of the arrangement one would expect. At the bottom, the pipe emptied into a channel cut into the bedrock. The channel began in the area of the roadway, proceeded north under the proposed latrine, and then ran under the lowest course of the Hexamilion, where it emptied out to the north (cf. Fig. 17). On the north face of the Hexamilion this channel is *ca.* 0.26 m. wide and *ca.* 0.26 m. high (Pl. 18:b).

The drain may have been fitted with some sort of fixture at the top, and it would have been located in a narrow vaulted chamber tucked under the upper part of the stairway (Ill. 8). The springing for this small vault could easily have been fitted into the masonry on either side, and a block between the North Wall and the south face of the Hexamilion (shown in section in Illustration 8, elev. +33.68 m.) presumably formed the threshold of the latrine. The latrine would have been reached, at the level of the bottom of the stairway, by walking between the stairway and the

---

[30] For a rather casual attitude to the location of a latrine, see *Corinth* XVI, pp. 17–21, 129, 131. See also Richmond ([footnote 12 above, p. 55] pp. 84–85), who argues that each of the towers in the Aurelian Wall had a latrine.

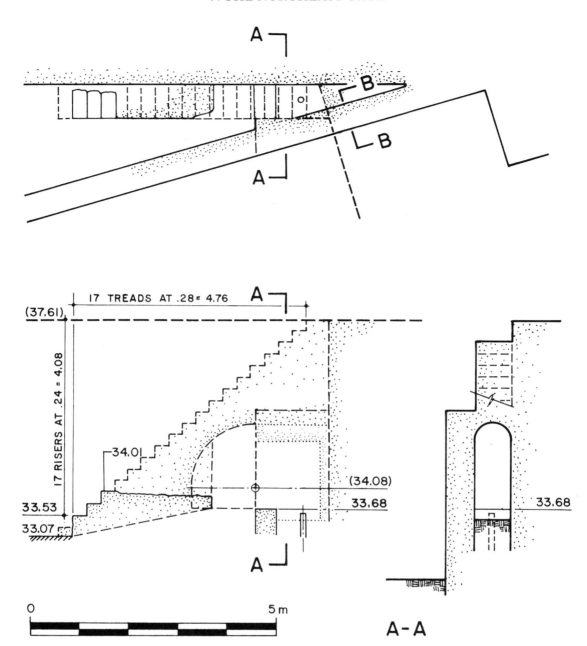

ILL. 8. Restored stairway and vaults of the Northeast Gate

North Wall and turning eastward through a half-vaulted passage under the stairs (Ill. 8). The preserved eastern end of the stairway support, which is cut back slightly at an angle toward the north, indicates the edge of this passageway.

The three blocks at the east end of the North Wall, which are all cut down by 0.05 m. to allow the springing for a vault, provide evidence for a series of vaults over the western part of the gate. Since the width of the North Bay is *ca.* 3.42 m., the interior radius of the vault was 1.71 m., centered at an elevation of +34.08 m. (Ill. 9). The vault may be restored using either bricks or stone voussoirs *ca.* 0.30 m. wide; if stone voussoirs were used, 19 would fit into the half circle. The underside of the peak of the vault would then have been at an elevation of +35.80 m. and the top at *ca.* +36.10 m., requiring approximately a meter and a half of packing below the level of the fighting platform at +37.61 m., the elevation obtained from the stairway calculations discussed above (Ill. 8).

The width between the west ends of the two reveals is almost exactly the same as that of the North Bay, and so we may reasonably restore an identical vault in the western end of the gate, over the roadway, springing from the same elevation (cf. Ills. 8, 9). The eastern part of the reveals, however, is *ca.* 0.68 m. wider than the western part, and so the vault over this section must have been *ca.* 0.34 m. higher (cf. Ill. 9). Although the tops of the two vaults must have been at approximately the

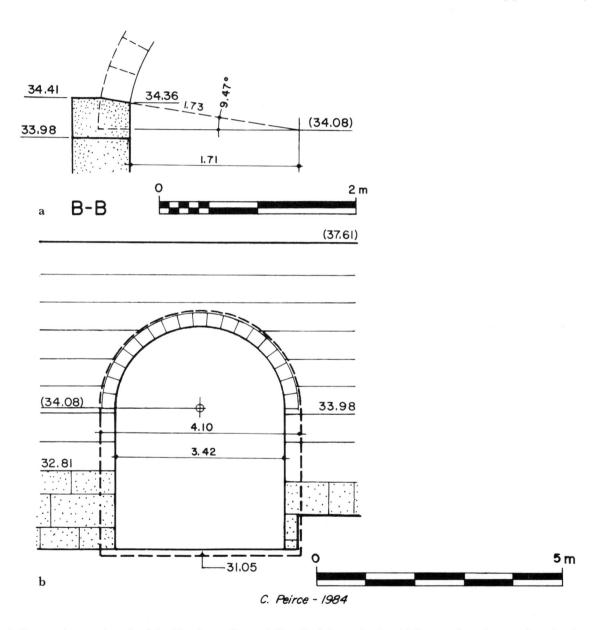

ILL. 9. Restored central vault of the Northeast Gate. a) Detail of the springing. b) Restored southwest elevation (eastern opening in dashed line)

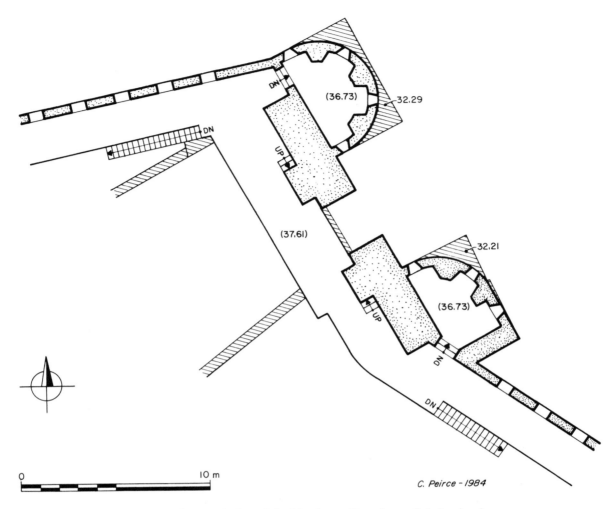

ILL. 10. Restored plan of the Northeast Gate, lower fighting level

same elevation, the road surface through the gate was considerably lower than the presumed floor of the North Bay (+31.50 m., as opposed to +32.29 m. in the North Bay), and so the clear height of the central vault was in fact somewhat greater, rising some 4.82 m. above the pavement.

The rest of the superstructure of the gate (Ills. 10, 12, 13) has been restored partly on the basis of analogy with other contemporary fortifications, especially the Land Walls of Constantinople. Thus, the spacing of the archery slits and crenellations has been restored by analogy with the outer (smaller) circuit of the Theodosian Walls in Constantinople. Likewise, the system of vaulting in the towers and the use of small groin vaults over the archery slits (see Ills. 10, 14) are suggested by contemporary practice in Constantinople and elsewhere.

The proposed restoration, however, is also based on the supposition that the Roman Arch was largely preserved within the gate structure, although military construction and the cutting away or covering of moldings to allow for the construction of stairways will have obscured much of its façade (Ills. 12, 13). Such a suggestion is supported by the near absence of fragments of the arch in the foundations of the gate construction; only three blocks from the attic geison of the arch have been identified, built into the platform of the South Tower (p. 55 above). One of these probably came from the southeast corner of the arch, and it was used in the foundations right where it may have fallen, either before or during the construction of the gate. It is possible, of course, that other parts of the arch were utilized higher up in the gate, but it is surely notable that no other fragments of it could be identified in the lower courses.

In any case, clearly the two central piers of the Roman Arch (which were preserved to nearly their full height in 1909) would have prevented the defenders of the Fortress from bringing direct fire against an enemy pressed up against the doors of the gate. This weakness is difficult to understand, since any number of measures might have been taken to correct it, but there is no evidence of them. We must simply ascribe this defect to careless military planning. It is possible, of course, that some form of machicolation was used in the gateway. This design element is recommended by Vitruvius (4.4), but there is little evidence of its implementation in late antiquity, and we have no reason to restore it here.[31]

At the level of the fighting platform on the Hexamilion (+37.61 m.), entrance into the towers can have been through doorways on either end of the Roman Arch (see Ills. 10, 12). The floors of the upper tower rooms were presumably of wood, since there was no need to support heavy equipment at this point. This reconstruction assumes that the floor of the upper fighting platform of the towers would have been at the level of the top of the Roman Arch (at +41.37 m.; see Ills. 12, 14) and that the ceilings of the upper rooms must have been vaulted to support artillery on these platforms above them. The vaulting would have seriously limited headroom in the tower, and for this reason the reconstruction has shown the first (wooden) floor of the towers down three steps from the main fighting platform, at a level of +36.73 m. Again, on the model of Constantinople, the reconstruction in Illustration 13 shows the first fighting level in the towers with three arrow slits, each of them tapering toward the outside.

A vaulted ceiling for the lower level of the towers would have required that the upper fighting level be reached by a set of stairs on the interior of the gate, and these may be hypothetically restored above the roadway, partly cut into the west façade of the Roman Arch (Ill. 12).[32] The stairs would naturally have required the partial removal of the moldings of the west façade of the arch. The reconstruction restores the stairways to the upper level as running upward from the lower fighting platform near the entrances to the lower floors of the towers (Ills. 11, 12, 14).

The floor of the upper level of the towers was presumably at the same elevation as the top of the arch. Although it is more common for the towers of a gate to rise above the curtain wall over the gateway (as for example all the gates at Resafa), the Golden Gate of Constantinople provides the best parallel for the Northeast Gate at Isthmia, and there the towers were constructed at the same level as the top of the (possibly) earlier arch.[33] Above the fighting level of the gate there was undoubtedly a parapet wall, here restored as two meters high. Some late Roman towers were, in fact, roofed,[34] but there is no reason to think that any of the towers on the Hexamilion were anything but

---

[31] S. Toy, *A History of Fortification from 3000 B.C. to A.D. 1700*, London 1955, pp. 120, 197–198; Pringle, *Defence* II, p. 441, note 9 and cf. pp. 444–445, notes 22 and 26.

[32] There are no exact parallels for this arrangement, but similar stair constructions over gates can be seen at Nikopolis, Resafa (Karnapp, *Stadtmauer*, pls. 133–134), and Constantinople (Meyer-Plath and Schneider, *Landmauer* II, pls. 4 and 10).

[33] Meyer-Plath and Schneider, *Landmauer* II, pl. 10.

[34] See Johnson, *Late Roman Fortifications*, pp. 40–43: "Rectangular towers, on the other hand, probably did have flat roofs"; Karnapp, *Stadtmauer*, pls. 52, 54, and *passim*.

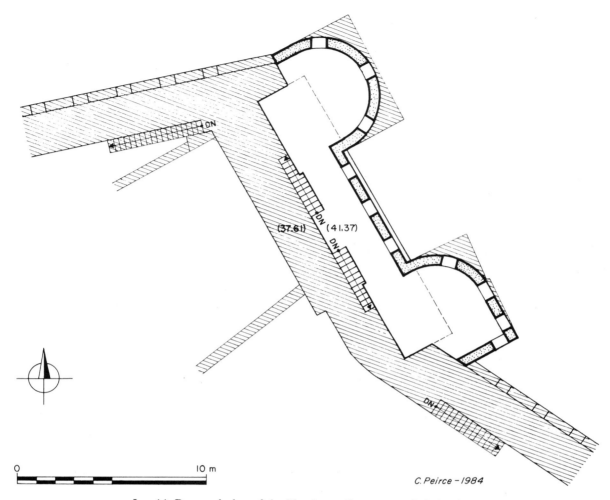

C. Peirce – 1984

ILL. 11. Restored plan of the Northeast Gate, upper fighting level

flat and open to the sky. Their primary purpose was probably to support artillery, which could be used against any attacker approaching the Fortress from the north or east.

THE CHRONOLOGY

Excavation in the area of the Northeast Gate naturally sought firm evidence for the date of its construction. The continuous use of the site throughout the Middle Ages and earlier excavations, which had partially exposed the gate, made this task especially difficult. Excavation beginning in 1967, however, cleared areas that had not previously been disturbed, and these preserved considerable evidence about the construction and use of the gate.

North Wall Foundations

Excavation in the North Bay along the south face of the North Wall revealed foundations at a level of +31.66 m. (Fig. 17). In the footing trench for these foundations were found a large basin

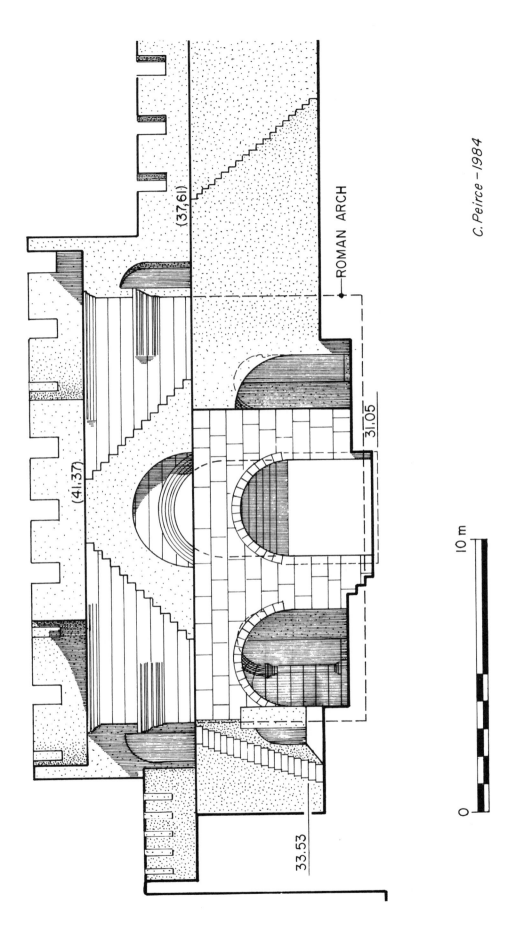

(41,37)

(37,61)

ROMAN ARCH

31.05

33.53

C. Peirce – 1984

10 m

0

ILL. 12. Restored southwest elevation of the Northeast Gate

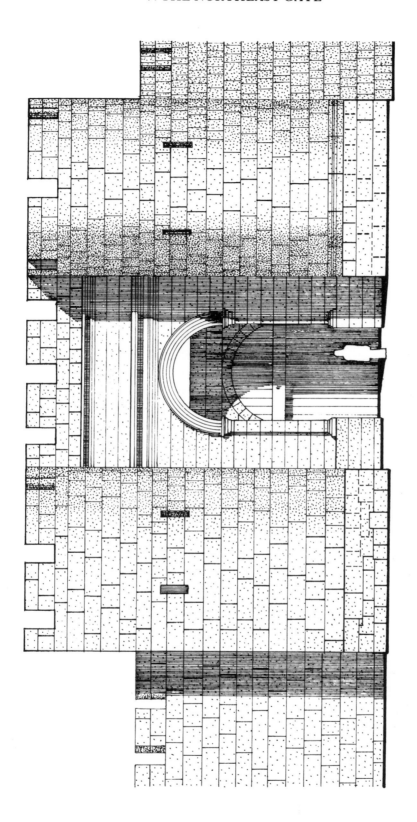

C. Peirce - 1984

ILL. 13. Restored northeast elevation of the Northeast Gate

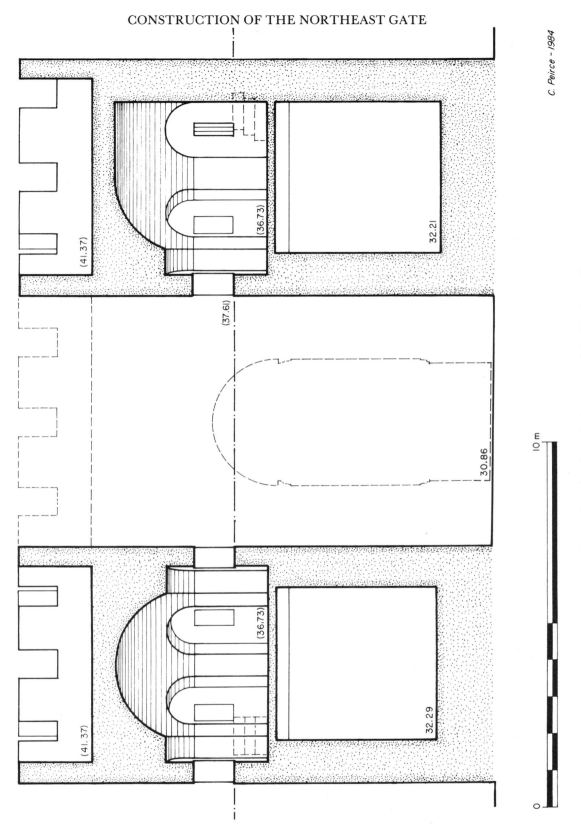

C. Peirce - 1984

10 m

ILL. 14. Restored section through the towers of the Northeast Gate

and several lamps (Pl. 18:c, d).[35] Material from this fill at the base of the North Wall provides a consistent date for construction of the wall. The basin is of a type common in late antiquity, dating from the mid-third to the early fifth century after Christ. All the lamps are Athenian, and they include late examples of glazed and early examples of post-glaze types, dating to the later years of the fourth or the first years of the fifth century.

Hexamilion Foundations

On the south side of the gate, the interior foundations of the Hexamilion were set in a fill that contained a single coin and considerable quantities of pottery.[36] This fill was apparently laid down in preparation for construction of the Hexamilion. The material in it is consistent with a date in the late fourth or early fifth century, but the coin of Arcadius provides a firm *terminus post quem* of A.D. 402–408.[37]

Roadway Coins

In 1883 Monceaux cleared the roadway down to the marble paving blocks, but there is no record that he cleaned out the clamp cuttings or any of the cracks between the blocks. These areas were carefully investigated during the 1967 and 1969 seasons, and in them were found a number of coins, all of which must have been in circulation, either when the roadway was laid or during the time it was open for use.[38] Of these coins, 18 can be confidently identified, ranging from Constantine I to Justinian I, with 4 coins from the house of Theodosius and 1 of Leo I.[39]

[35] Peppers, pp. 304–305.

a) Basin (IPR 67-1), Pl. 18:c, d: rest. H. 0.264 to 0.284 m., rest. Diam. 0.315 m. Three-fourths preserved. Hard, coarse yellowish red (5YR 5/8) clay with large inclusions. Deep basin with flat base, flaring sides, and plain, rounded, outturned rim. Wheel ridged on interior and exterior. Cf. *Agora* V, K78, K79, p. 66, pl. 13, mid-3rd century. Bibl.: Wohl, "Deposit of Lamps," p. 122, note 26; Peppers, Q 347, p. 305, fig. 98:e; Clement, 1970, p. 165, pl. 131:c.

b) Lamp (IP 3690): Athenian post glaze (early 5th century).

c) Lamp (IP 3691), Pl. 19:a: Athenian glazed (second half 4th century).

d) Lamp (IPL 67-17): Athenian glazed (second half 4th century).

e) Lamp (IPL 67-18): Athenian glazed (second half 4th century).

[36] NEG 67 CL, Baskets 21, 22; cf. Wohl, "Deposit of Lamps," p. 136, note 44.

a) Clement, 321 (IC 887), Arcadius (A.D. 402–408): CONCORDIA AVGGG, cross. Cf. *LRBC* II, no. 2221.

b) Amphora (IPR 67-30), Pl. 19:d: p.H. 0.575 m., max. Diam. 0.422 m. Restored from many fragments, bottom missing. Hard, reddish yellow clay (7.5YR 6/6) with some medium-large white inclusions, evenly fired. Large amphora with flaring sides, rounded shoulder, tapering neck, and flaring plain rounded rim; handles, oval in section, from upper part of shoulder to top of neck; deep spiral grooves over shoulder, light wheel ridges below. Cf. *Agora* V, M 272, p. 109, pl. 29 (late 4th century); *Kenchreai* IV, RC, pp. 114–115, pl. 26 (destruction debris of 375 earthquake).

c) Stamped plate fragment, Phocaean red-slip ware (IPR 67-39), Pl. 19:b: max. L. 0.064 m. Fragment. Hard, gritty, pale red clay (10R 6/4) with red slip. On floor of fragment, stamped decoration: two rows of running-leaf pattern radiating from center; in center and between leaves very small double concentric-circle motif. Cf. Hayes, Late Roman C motif no. 20, pp. 352, 355 (early in the series 440–490; for small circles, pp. 350–351, motif no. 2, 400–450). Bibl.: Clement, 1970, pp. 163–164 (incorrectly listed as being found in Grave 1); Peppers, X432, pp. 329–330, fig. 116:b.

d) Lamp (IP 3678), Pl. 19:c: Athenian glazed (second half 4th century).

[37] Five other lamp fragments were also found in this fill: IP 3684, 3693–3696. They are also probably all Broneer Type XXVIII lamps and date from the same period.

[38] Clement ("Date of the Hexamilion," pp. 159–164) first published and interpreted this material; see now his article, "Isthmian Notes," in Φίλια ἔπη εἰς Γεώργιον E. Μυλωνᾶν II, Athens 1987, pp. 380–383.

[39] a) Clement, 132 (IC 912), Constantine I (A.D. 335–337): GLORIA EXERCITUS, two soldiers. Cf. *LRBC* I, no. 1024.

b) Clement, 149 (IC 916), Constantius II (A.D. 337–361): SPES REIPUBLICAE, emperor left. Cf. *RIC* VIII, p. 461, no. 153.

Because these coins could have found their way into the archaeological record either when the road was being laid or while it was in use, the latest coin in this group will not provide a *terminus post quem* for the construction of the Fortress, as Robert L. Hohlfelder seemed to think.[40] Referring to the coin of Leo I (p. 175), he says: "This numismatic evidence from Isthmia suggests that the earlier wall of *Aed.* 4.2.27–28 was constructed sometime in the middle of the fifth century, probably late in the reign of Theodosius II." In fact, the latest coin simply indicates how long the road surface was open. The coins of Leo I and Justinian do not contribute any significant information about the construction of the gate, but they do show that the marble roadway was open until at least the middle of the sixth century. The earliest coins of the group, on the other hand, provide a rough date for construction of the gate, as long as it is remembered that coins of the fourth century were often in circulation in the fifth.[41] The preponderance of fourth-century coins and the scarcity of sixth-century coins show that a Justinianic date for the Fortress is clearly out of the question; the roadway coins prove that construction of the gate took place well before the age of Justinian. These coins cannot provide a precise date for the gate, but they are consistent with one in the early fifth century.

All these coins were found in connection with the marble roadway surface, except for the coin of Leo I (no. 366), which was found just to the west of the westernmost marble paving block. The coin was lying above the road surface of packed earth and stones that continued the road off to the west and below the later road surface which was present there (Figs. 17, 21). This coin must have fallen into place while the packed road surface was in use, which shows that the packed roadway

---

c) Clement, 160 (IC 921), Constantius II (A.D. 337–361): FEL TEMP REPARATIO, soldier spearing horseman. Cf. *LRBC* II, nos. 1681, 1684.

d) Clement, 168 (IC 910), Constantius II (A.D. 355–361): SPES REIPUBLICAE, emperor helmeted. Cf. *LRBC* II, no. 2053.

e) Clement, 169 (IC 911), Constantius II (A.D. 355–361): as preceding.

f) Clement, 170 (IC 923), Constantius II (A.D. 355–361): as preceding.

g) Clement, 188 (IC 908), Constans I (A.D. 337–350): VOT XX MULT XXX in wreath. Cf. *LRBC* II, nos. 2156, 2157.

h) Clement, 196 (IC 909), Julian Caesar (A.D. 355–361): SPES REIPUBLICAE, emperor left. Cf. *LRBC* II, nos. 1690, 1692.

i) Clement, 207 (IC 913), Jovian (A.D. 363–364): VOT V MULT X in wreath. Cf. *LRBC* II, no. 2513.

j) Clement, 215 (IC 914), Valens (A.D. 364–378): SECURITAS REIPUBLICAE, victory. Cf. *LRBC* II, nos. 1922, 1935.

k) Clement, 229 (IC 915), Valentinian II (A.D. 375–392): SALUS REIPUBLICAE, victory. Cf. *LRBC* II, no. 2406.

l) Clement, 324 (IC 920), Arcadius (A.D. 402–408): CONCORDIA AVGGG, cross. Cf. *LRBC* II, no. 2221.

m) Clement, 337 (IC 932), House of Theodosius (A.D. 395–408): CONCORDIA AVGGG, cross. Cf. *LRBC* II, nos. 2583–2585.

n) Clement, 338 (IC 917), House of Theodosius (A.D. 395–408): CONCORDIA AVGG. Cf. *LRBC* II, nos. 2594–2596.

o) Clement, 347 (IC 919), Theodosius I or II (A.D. 379–395 or 402–450): Reverse defaced.

p) Clement, 366 (IC 69-105), Leo I (A.D. 457–474): Monogram of Leo I. Cf. *LRBC* II, nos. 1882, 2262–2264, 2612.

q) Clement, 472 (IC 918), Justinian I (A.D. 548–565): Monogram of Justinian, star beneath. Carthage. Cf. *DOC* I, p. 170, no. 310.

The following coins were also found in the detailed investigation of the roadway, but they were illegible: IC 924, 933, 941, 957, 961, and 69-84.

[40] R. L. Hohlfelder, "Trans-Isthmian Walls in the Age of Justinian," *GRBS* 18, 1977, pp. 173–179.

[41] H. L. Adelson and G. L. Kustas, "A Bronze Hoard of the Period of Leo I," *American Numismatic Society Museum Notes* 9, 1960, pp. 139–188; J. A. Dengate, "Coin Hoards from the Gymnasium Area at Corinth," *Hesperia* 50, 1981, pp. 149–150, no. 6; p. 157, note 21.

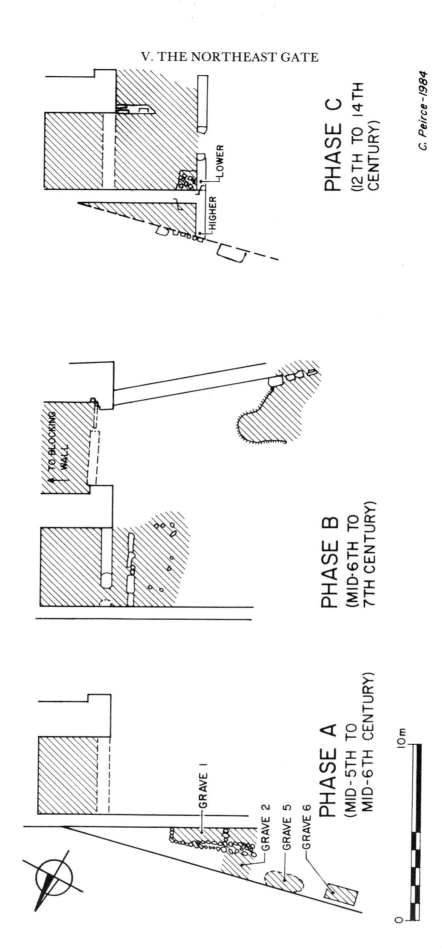

ILL. 15. Restored plans of later phases of the Northeast Gate

was probably contemporary with the marble roadway further east or, at least, that it had been constructed by the middle of the century.

Graves

Eight graves were explored in the immediate vicinity of the Northeast Gate (Fig. 17; Pl. 19:e), and these provide important information about the history of this area, both before and after the construction of the Fortress. All the graves were multiple burials, with evidence of both simultaneous interment and successive burials over a period of time. In all cases the graves were relatively simple structures, several of them merely cists cut in the hardpan and covered over with slabs. There were few grave goods, and some of the tombs contained nothing other than the bones of the dead.

Grave 1. Built between the Hexamilion and the North Wall, just south of the stairway to the lower fighting platform on the wall (Ill. 15, Fig. 17).[42] The grave was constructed up against the north face of the North Wall, which forms the south wall of the grave. The other walls were built of rubble and mortar. There are no preserved cover slabs, and the grave measures *ca.* 2.10 m. (east–west) by 0.60 m.

Contents: At least eleven skulls and bones of adults and the bones of one child, all apparently placed into the grave at the same time, one on top of the other, with heads to the west (Pl. 20:a, b). The grave goods were apparently with the uppermost skeletons and included three coins (two of Marcian, one perhaps of Leo I), a pair of bronze earrings, and a ceramic cup.[43]

Date: Mid-to-later fifth century after Christ; the coins of Marcian provide a firm *terminus post quem* of A.D. 450–457.

Grave 2. Built between the Hexamilion and the North Wall (Ill. 15, Fig. 17). The bottom step of the stairway on the interior of the Hexamilion was removed to allow construction of the east end of the grave. The south face of the Hexamilion formed the north wall of the grave, while the south wall of the grave was provided by a continuation of the north wall of Grave 1. No evidence of closure slabs preserved. The grave is *ca.* 2.20 m. (east–west) by 1.00 m.

Contents: The bones of two adults, one on top of the other, skulls to the west; around the skull of the upper burial were scattered the bones of a child.

Date: Presumably the same as Grave 1, since they share a common wall.

Grave 3. Located along the west face of the Hexamilion, west of the South Tower (Fig. 17).[44] The grave was covered by three slabs, and the Hexamilion overran the eastern part of the grave. The grave itself is *ca.* 1.75 m. (east–west) by 0.57 m. and is simply cut in the hardpan.

Contents: Two skeletons, heads to west, a lamp, and a jar.[45]

Date: Late fourth–early fifth centuries after Christ.

---

[42] Peppers, Group M, pp. 300–302.

[43] a) Clement, 360 (IC 888), Marcian (A.D. 450–457): Monogram of Marcian. Cf. *LRBC* II, no. 2468.

b) Clement, 361 (IC 889), Marcian (A.D. 450–457): as preceding.

c) Clement, 368 (IC 885), uncertain emperor, possibly Leo I (A.D. 457–474): Monogram.

d) Pair of bronze earrings (IM 3553). Bibl.: Peppers, MCon1, pp. 301–302.

e) Cup (IP 3688): H. 0.097 m., max. Diam. 0.090 m. Intact except for handle. Gritty, reddish yellow clay (5YR 6/6), flaking in layers, self-slip. Ovoid body on small disk base. Wide mouth, flaring rim; marks where vertical handle was attached. Bibl.: Peppers, M344, p. 302; no good published parallels.

[44] Peppers, Group N, pp. 302–303.

[45] a) Lamp (IPL 69-23): Athenian glazed (second half 4th century).

b) Jar (IPR 69-76): H. 0.142 m., max. Diam. 0.108 m. Intact. Rather fine red clay (2.5YR 5/8). Small fusiform, one-handled jar; grooved base and slightly flaring foot; body wheel grooved. Bibl.: Peppers, N345, pp. 303–304; cf. Clement, 1970, p. 165, pl. 135:a; *Agora* V, F42 (later 4th century), M268 (late 4th century), M295 (early 5th century).

Grave 4. Located on the west face of the Hexamilion west of the South Tower and just south of Grave 3. The grave was covered by four cover slabs, two of which were overrun by the Hexamilion. The grave is 1.75 m. (east–west) by *ca.* 0.67–0.70 m.

Contents: Five skeletons, heads to west; the lowest burial was missing from the kneecaps down. Immediately below the cover slabs were two glass vessels, one of which disintegrated.[46]

Date: Late third–early fourth centuries after Christ.

Grave 5. Located west of the North Tower on the south face of the Hexamilion, just west of Grave 2 (Ill. 15, Fig. 17).[47] The grave originally had four cover slabs, but one was disturbed before excavation; these were set above the grave in a groove cut in the face of the Hexamilion, which forms the north side of the grave. The grave is *ca.* 1.97 m. (east–west) by 0.62 m.

Contents: Three skeletons, heads to west.

Date: After the construction of the Hexamilion.

Grave 6. Located west of the North Tower on the south face of the Hexamilion, just west of Grave 5 (Ill. 15, Fig. 17). The grave was covered by one large slab and several small stones at either end. The interior face of the Hexamilion formed the north wall of the grave, but the other three sides were built of tiles laid in horizontal courses with mortar, forming a ledge on which the cover slab was laid. The grave is 1.60 m. (east–west) by *ca.* 0.49–0.54 m. At the time of a secondary burial, the east end of the grave was extended by *ca.* 0.28 m.

Contents: Two small and two large skeletons, heads to west. The two smaller skeletons were apparently an earlier burial, and the bones were scattered at the time of the later burial (Pl. 20:d). The feet of the larger skeletons were placed over the tiles in the eastern end of the grave. Associated with the skull of one of the earlier burials were two gold earrings (Pl. 21:a).[48]

Date: After construction of the Hexamilion.

Grave 7. Cut into the scarp of the *taphros* outside the Fortress enclosure, *ca.* 15 meters north of the North Tower (Fig. 22). The grave was covered with several slabs, including one piece of marble. The grave is *ca.* 2.11 m. (east–west) by 0.60 m.

Contents: Two skeletons, heads to west.

Date: Indeterminate, but probably well after construction of the Hexamilion.

Grave 8. Located along the west face of the Hexamilion, west of the South Tower and just north of Grave 3 (Fig. 17). This grave preserved several of the cover slabs over a cutting *ca.* 1.60 m. (east–west) by 0.54 m., but no burial was found. Probably it was disturbed in antiquity, perhaps even by construction of the Hexamilion.

Contents: No skeletal remains. In the upper level of the fill under the cover slabs was a lamp.[49]

Date: Late fourth–early fifth centuries after Christ.

Study of the graves further confirms a date in the first quarter of the fifth century for construction of the Northeast Gate. Thus, the Hexamilion overran Graves 3 and 4, and they must, accordingly, antedate its construction. Grave 4 contained a glass vessel of the third–fourth centuries

---

[46] Glass pitcher (IM 69-42), Pl. 20:c: H. 0.109 m., Diam. of base 0.072 m., Diam. of rim 0.054 m. Rim chipped, otherwise intact. Yellow-green, with concave bottom, globular body, sloping shoulder, short cylindrical neck, flaring into slightly thickened rounded rim; strap handle with wide, central vertical grooves. Cf. Hayes, *Roman Glass*, nos. 340, 437, 438 (all late 3rd–early 4th centuries). Bibl.: Clement, 1970, p. 166, pl. 135:b.

[47] Peppers, Group P, pp. 303–304.

[48] Gold earrings (IM 69-36, 69-37), Pl. 21:b: Diam. 0.024 m. Intact. Matched pair. Thick, heavy gold wire, twisted into a cable, forming circular hoops, twisted in section; simple clasp. Bibl.: Clement, 1970, p. 166, pl. 136:a–c.

[49] Lamp (IPL 69-79): Athenian glazed (second half 4th century).

after Christ, while Grave 3 had a lamp datable to the last quarter of the fourth century or the first decades of the fifth century after Christ. Grave 3, therefore, seems to have been used just before construction of the wall (perhaps even by the soldiers involved in the project), and it provides a *terminus post quem* for the Hexamilion.

Graves 1, 2, 5, and 6 were built in the triangle between the south face of the Hexamilion and the North Wall, making use of the walls that stood in the area. These four graves, therefore, must have been built after the gate complex. The coins in Grave 1 show that it was used in the mid- or later fifth century, as Clement noted,[50] and the other two graves are probably to be assigned to the same period. The presence of the graves suggests a period of abandonment of the Fortress, at least for military purposes, since construction of Grave 2 rendered the stairway to the fighting platform at least temporarily inoperable.[51] In late antiquity soldiers were not uncommonly buried near the walls which they defended,[52] but the burials at Isthmia were not all of soldiers, since the gold earrings in Grave 6 naturally suggest a female burial. On the other hand, some of the attested graves along the Land Walls of Constantinople are those of the wives and daughters of soldiers.[53] This evidence raises, but does not answer, tantalizing questions about the staffing and use of the Fortress in the decades after its construction: was it completely abandoned as a military installation or were *limitanei* (local militia as opposed to *comitatenses* or troops of a standing army), along with their families, established within the fortifications?

In the absence of further information and pending full examination of the skeletal material, little more can be said. The evidence of Graves 1 and 2, however, shows conclusively that the Fortress was built before the middle of the fifth century, at a date early enough for it to have fallen into disrepair during or shortly after the reign of Marcian. The other graves support such a chronology, while showing that the area of the Northeast Gate continued to be used for burial both before and after construction of the Fortress.

THE AREA NORTH OF THE GATE

Investigation north of the Northeast Gate, outside the Fortress proper (Fig. 17; Pl. 21:c, d), reveals little in the way of monumental architecture, but it does provide significant information about some of the fortification outworks.

The local hardpan in this region is a loose, sandy material, much less firm than the bedrock further south. Directly north of the face of the Hexamilion, this hardpan was cut away in antiquity to form a flat surface, undoubtedly to provide a secure footing for the wall. Northward from the wall, the hardpan descends gradually toward the ravine. Beginning about 8 meters from the wall, however, there is a double trench in the hardpan, running east and west parallel to the face of the wall. In section, this cutting resembles the letter W (Fig. 22). Later intrusions have obscured the situation considerably, but it is still possible to make out the general shape of the cutting, which must have dominated the area when it was open.

[50] "Date of the Hexamilion," pp. 163–164. There is no reason to accept Megaw's suggestion that the coins were from the strata in which the graves were dug ("Archaeology in Greece, 1967–68," *AR* 14, 1968, p. 7).

[51] Interestingly enough, the fortifications of Corinth seem also to have fallen into disrepair at an early date, and they were apparently being quarried within the 5th century; see Gregory, "Late Roman Wall," pp. 272, 280.

[52] E.g., Meyer-Plath and Schneider, *Landmauer* II, nos. 41:a, 72, 75, 77. This is also, I think, the best explanation for the burials along the ancient wall of Corinth (G. R. Davidson, "The Avar Invasion of Corinth," *Hesperia* 6, 1937, pp. 227–240).

[53] E.g., nos. 41:a, 75.

The southern part of the cutting (the one closer to the wall) is a V, *ca.* 2 meters wide at the top and *ca.* 2 meters deep. The northern part of the cutting is another V, *ca.* 4 meters wide (at the top) and nearly 3 meters deep (Pl. 22:a). Between the two cuttings, *ca.* 11 meters from the face of the wall, was a ridge, probably over a meter wide and at the original level of the hardpan (*ca.* +28.43 m.). The bottom of the southern of the two depressions was *ca.* 3.95 m. lower than the bottom of the north face of the Hexamilion; the northern cutting is *ca.* 4.25 m. lower than the bottom of the wall.

This cutting seems to have been part of the outworks designed to protect the Northeast Gate from attack along this side. It bears some resemblance to the *taphros* encountered at various places along the Hexamilion, although this is the only recorded instance of two defensive trenches outside the main wall. In addition, no evidence of an outer wall (*proteichisma*) exists in this area, although later robbing may have removed all trace.

In the area just north of the northwest buttress for the later Bastion (pp. 81–83 below), a large cutting was made in the hardpan, essentially extending the level of the bottom of the south cutting back to the North Tower foundations (Fig. 22; Pl. 22:b). This must have been done when the Bastion around the North Tower was built, to set its foundations deeper than the natural level of the hardpan. This extension of the cutting is present only in the area of the Bastion foundations, and it destroyed the original form of the W-shaped defensive trench in this region.

Another intrusion into this area was a large circular structure with interior diameter of *ca.* 3.50 m., preserved at the time of excavation to a height of *ca.* 2.50 m. (Fig. 17; Pl. 21:c, d). The structure was filled with dark earth and quantities of burned material, indicating that it was a furnace of some kind, probably a lime kiln of the sort encountered at several places along the Hexamilion. A floor of small stones to the west of the structure was probably associated with the kiln, and two stones on the east side were probably part of the entrance to the firing chamber. Presumably, this structure was once much higher than now preserved, and large quantities of stone found in the area may have come from its upper courses.

The center of the circular structure was located directly over the raised central part of the W-shaped cutting, resting partly on soil which had completely filled the cutting and leveled it off. Its position shows that the circular structure must have been built well after the construction of the Fortress, presumably when it had experienced some period of disuse and the W-shaped cutting had been allowed to fill up.

At a distance of *ca.* 15 meters north of the Hexamilion is a series of stones oriented with their long axes along a rough east–west line (Fig. 22). One of these stones was plastered on its upper side and a crude cross scratched in the plaster while it was still wet. The stone appeared to be covering a grave, but when it was lifted nothing was found under it. Just over a meter farther east several of these stones covered what was in fact a grave (Grave 7; see p. 78 above). This grave was cut down through the hardpan into the side of the northern part of the W-shaped cutting (Fig. 22). With the exception of the cuttings in hardpan associated with the Hexamilion, all the activity in the area north of the gate seems to have taken place at a later date, after the Fortress had gone out of use for military purposes.

THE SIXTH-CENTURY REBUILDING

By the early years of the fifth century after Christ, the Northeast Gate stood complete in the form described above (pp. 56–70; Ills. 12, 13). In the centuries that followed, however, many changes were made necessary, either by earthquakes[54] and the passage of time or by the changing military situation in this part of the empire. In addition, the Hexamilion clearly was abandoned during many periods and thus required repair whenever the fortifications had to be put into commission once again. Such rebuildings are evident throughout the Hexamilion, but in the Northeast Gate they can be documented and hypothetically restored, although Monceaux's earlier trenches removed much of the evidence of later mediaeval activity in the area.

In the roadway east of the central piers a Π-shaped blocking wall, 1.65–1.70 m. thick, closed the gateway completely (Fig. 18; Pls. 14:a, 22:c). On the east the Blocking Wall is nearly on a line with the east faces of the North and South Towers, while its returns run directly up to the east faces of the central piers of the Roman Arch. On the east the Blocking Wall is set directly over the marble paving of the roadway, while the returns overrun the north and south edges of the pavement (Fig. 17). The Blocking Wall was built of rubble and mortar in a rather careless style, and the whole structure bears the signs of haste. The wall was obviously designed to be permanent, however, since provisions were made for drainage of water through its bottom. The section across the roadway obviously needed to be stronger, and it was built of roughly coursed large blocks, while the north and south returns were made of small uncoursed rubble. On the east the Blocking Wall is preserved to a height of three courses, while the south return (where a later roadway ran) is preserved only in foundations. The interior corner between the main blocking wall and the south return is plastered over (Pl. 23:a), showing that at least the foundation of the entire Π-shaped structure was built in one period.

Just above the roadway surface, the Blocking Wall is pierced by two large openings that run through the thickness of the wall. The roadway slopes down considerably from west to east through the area of the Northeast Gate, and these drains must have been necessary to accommodate the large volume of water that flowed along the road surface during periodic rains. The openings are higher than they are wide, and they narrow considerably from west to east, measuring ca. 0.67–0.62 m. by 0.14 m. on the eastern face. This narrowing was undoubtedly designed to prevent an enemy from using the drains as an easy means of access into the Fortress.

On the northwest and northeast sides of the North Tower are the foundations of a large bastion (Fig. 18; Pl. 23:b, c). On the northwest the Bastion is ca. 9.5 m. long and ca. 2.65 m. wide, while on the northeast it is ca. 10.9 m. long and ca. 2.33 m. wide. A rectangular buttress projects from each of the two long sides, and there is another pair of buttresses at the north corner of the structure. At the east corner the Bastion turns southwest and runs along the south face of the North Tower for a distance of ca. 0.22 m. before it butts up against the east face of the Blocking Wall. (Plate 23:d shows the Bastion on the right and the Blocking Wall on the left.)

The Bastion and its supporting buttresses are constructed of uncoursed rubble set in a soft, crumbly mortar alternating with triple leveling courses of horizontal bricks. The corners of the Bastion are made of larger blocks, most of them re-used (including IΣ 69-3; Pl. 24:a). The triple courses of brick are ca. 0.17–0.18 m. high. As far as can be determined, the brick courses went all the way through the structure and were not restricted to the facing. Two triple courses are preserved in the Bastion, and the footing for a third appears in the mortar of the top surviving masonry of the structure. This technique is paralleled in Tower 15 of the Fortress and elsewhere in the Aegean world, most notably in the Theodosian Walls of Constantinople (both the main wall and

---

[54] Procopius (Testimonia, 3) says that the earlier wall had collapsed. This was presumably a result of the earthquakes of 522 or 551, or both.

the presumably later smaller wall), at Nikopolis, and at Thessaloniki.[55] In the Corinthia the technique is also used, for example in the Lechaion Basilica, which was completed, probably, in the second quarter of the sixth century after Christ. The use of brick leveling courses in Byzantine architecture is not restricted to a single period; at Constantinople, for example, the general technique apparently continued into late Byzantine times. The masonry of the North Tower Bastion, however, is distinctive in that it combines only roughly coursed rubble with the brick courses, while most Byzantine architecture uses cut blocks.

It is impossible now to know how high the Bastion was when it was built. It may have risen only to the top of the North Tower base, but this would have provided attackers with a foothold at the bottom of the tower and afforded them assistance in besieging the Fortress. The primary purpose of the Bastion undoubtedly was to protect the North Tower and to keep the structure from sliding down the hill into the ravine; it would also have deterred sappers who might have sought to undermine the foundations of the tower. For these purposes, the Bastion superstructure might have risen only high enough to make its top unassailable. More likely, however, the Bastion was designed to reach a considerable height and even to dominate the gate and perhaps the Fortress as a whole. At the time of excavation, considerable quantities of brick were found fallen from the remains of the Bastion (Pl. 24:b), but certainly not enough to demonstrate its original height. The presence of scaffolding holes in the preserved northeast and northwest faces of the Bastion, however, shows that the builders at least intended it to reach a substantial height.

When combined with the already existing structure of the North Tower, the Bastion would have created a rectangular tower ca. 9.50 m. by 10.90 m., a size on the same scale as the large square towers of the Theodosian Walls of Constantinople, which are approximately 10 meters on a side,[56] the larger towers of Resafa in Mesopotamia, probably built under Justinian,[57] and the towers of the West Gate at Nikopolis. Certainly, if the Bastion rose to any significant height, it would have dominated the surrounding area and made it possible for a small force to hope to hold out against a powerful attack.

From Procopius we know that Justinian (who was probably responsible for construction of the Bastion) frequently increased the size and the height of towers so that they were like forts (*phrouria*; *Aed.* 3.5.11, 4.11.16); this sounds very much like what was done at the Northeast Gate. Perhaps we should also equate the Bastion with what Procopius calls a *pyrgokastellon*, a strongly fortified tower of the sort Justinian built at Constantina in Mesopotamia (*Aed.* 2.5.8–9). Considerable scholarly debate centers on the meaning of the term *pyrgokastellon*:[58] whether it was an independent fortress, the prototype of the mediaeval donjon, or a strong point in the fortification system. The Bastion at Isthmia was certainly not an independent fortress but rather a large and strongly built tower in the over-all fortification system. If the Bastion represented what Procopius called a *pyrgokastellon*, it lends support to the latter argument.

It is clear that the Blocking Wall and the Bastion are not part of the original construction of the Hexamilion and the Fortress. Their styles of construction are similar, utilizing faces of rubble and mortar, although the Bastion is certainly much more carefully built than the Blocking Wall. There are apparent breaks in the fabric of the latter, perhaps suggesting different periods of construction, and it is difficult to believe that much energy would have been spent on the Bastion after the roadway was blocked. The precise chronological relationship between the two structures is impossible

---

[55] Meyer-Plath and Schneider, *Landmauer* II, pls. 19–21.
[56] Kirchen, *Landmauer* I, p. 6, fig. 2.
[57] Karnapp, *Stadtmauer*, figs. 13, 18, 19.
[58] Pringle, *Defence* I, p. 155.

to determine, since they butt up against each other, but it seems reasonable to assume that the Bastion was built before the Blocking Wall.

Earlier excavation in the roadway of the Northeast Gate unfortunately removed all stratigraphic evidence for the date of the Blocking Wall. Careful excavation in the northern part of the Northeast Gate, however, has provided good evidence for the absolute chronology of the Bastion. Thus, as we have seen, in the North Bay the lowest levels were associated with the period of the construction of the Fortress.

Above these levels was a floor on which sixth-century pottery was found (NEG 67 RMM, Basket 53), suggesting intensive occupation at that time; probably the occupation was still connected with the military use of the Fortress (see pp. 83–89 below). In the area north of the Northeast Gate, outside the Fortress, the cuttings made for the foundations of the Bastion disturbed the original shape of the defensive trenches, showing that the Bastion postdated the Tower. Fill dumped into the foundation cutting contained a partially preserved amphora, placed right up against the footing of the western buttress on the northwest face of the Bastion. The amphora, which presumably dates the Bastion wall, can be assigned to the early sixth century.[59]

In addition, the fill throughout the W-shaped fortification trenches can be dated to the sixth century after Christ. The fill included several lamps assigned to the early fifth century,[60] but sixth-century material was present at the very bottom of the fill,[61] suggesting that the whole area was filled and leveled in the sixth century. Why this was done is difficult to say, since the leveling process clearly put the defensive trenches out of operation. Perhaps it was felt that this additional fill would render the North Tower more stable. In any case, the defensive trenches in this part of the fortifications clearly remained operational only a little over a century.

The marble roadway was open at least until the middle of the sixth century, since a coin struck in Carthage between 548 and 565 found its way into a crack between the paving blocks (see footnote 39 above, p. 75). One of the last travelers through the gateway or one of the soldiers or workmen involved in the construction of the Bastion or Blocking Wall must have lost the coin.[62] All evidence, then, points to the mid-sixth century for the construction of the Bastion, and we may confidently associate this with Justinian's rebuilding of the Hexamilion in the years after 550. Perhaps earthquakes damaged the whole of the Hexamilion; the North Tower of the Northeast Gate would have been particularly vulnerable. Alternatively, Justinian may have been making preparations in the face of an expected attack from the Huns. In any case, the response seems to have been to enlarge the fortifications, perhaps substituting mortar for manpower. It is impossible to know when the gateway was blocked, but presumably it was done at the time of the Slavic invasions, either in the later sixth or the seventh century.

LATER NONMILITARY CONSTRUCTION

Phase A: Mid-fifth to Mid-sixth Century

The Northeast Gate, like other parts of the Fortress, was occupied for domestic purposes during various periods of nonmilitary use. The architecture of these rehabitation periods is naturally

[59] Amphora (IPR 69-240), Pl. 24:c: p.H. 0.351 m., p.Diam. 0.31–0.32 m. Partially restored from several fragments, preserving foot and part of body. Moderately coarse, hard, very pale brown (10YR 8/3) clay. False ring foot, flaring rounded sides. Exterior wheel ridges. Cf. *Agora* V, M 323 and M 326 (early 6th century); *Kenchreai* IV, RC10:a (late 4th century). Bibl.: Peppers, Q348, p. 305, fig. 98:c; Clement, 1970, p. 165, pl. 131:a (there identified as IPR 69-250).

[60] IPL 69-125 and 69-120.

[61] NEG 69, Baskets 28 and 34.

[62] Clement, "Isthmian Notes" (footnote 38 above, p. 74), p. 383.

not very distinguished, and most of the floor levels and walls were removed in the course of excavation. Only detailed study of the excavation notebooks and context pottery allows the reconstruction suggested here. Occasionally, walls and floor levels will appear on the actual-state plan of the Northeast Gate (Fig. 17), but more commonly they were already removed and can be seen only in the excavation photographs and on the plan of the successive phases (Ill. 15).[63]

The process of abandonment and re-use had already begun by the middle of the fifth century with the construction of graves against the interior face of the Hexamilion (see pp. 77–79 above). In addition, other structures can be connected with this first period of abandonment (Ill. 15). The north wall of Grave 1 was constructed of rubble and tiles set in mortar against the earlier foundations of the Hexamilion stairway. This wall continued beyond the west end of the grave into ground that is presently unexcavated. Whether it formed the wall of another grave (no burial was found inside it) or a structure with some other purpose must remain unknown for the present, but it does clearly date from the first period of abandonment of the fortifications. Pottery in this area, above Grave 1, and in the vicinity of the western extension of the wall, is consistently datable to the latter part of the fifth century.[64]

The North Bay (the western part of the North Tower) may also have been used for domestic purposes between the middle of the fifth and the middle of the sixth century. This area was probably built up during the original Hexamilion phase to bring floor level up to that of the eastern part of the tower (see p. 64 above). Sometime after the original abandonment, however, some of this leveling fill may have been removed, since there are several floor levels above the foundations of the Hexamilion (see below). This area was subject to considerable disturbance over the centuries, but there is clear evidence of several phases of habitation during this early period. Thus, the foundations of the poorly built late wall at the western end of the North Bay (Ill. 15, Phases B and C; see below) were sunk down into early fifth-century fill, and fifth- and sixth-century material was packed up against its eastern face, suggesting that the wall may have been built in the first period of abandonment. Perhaps the North Bay was used as a dwelling by some of the individuals who constructed the graves against the interior of the Hexamilion.

PHASE B: MID-SIXTH TO SEVENTH CENTURY

A well-defined strosis of hard-packed earth covered the earliest levels of the North Bay and the area farther west (Ill. 15, Phase B). In the North Bay this strosis was at an elevation of +30.94 m., while immediately west of the wall at the end of the North Bay, the strosis was at +31.35 m. Under this strosis (at least in the area west of the North Bay) was material of the early sixth century.[65]

Associated with this strosis was a wall that ran from the western end of the North Reveal to the North Wall, closing in the western end of the North Tower (visible in the right half of Plate 24:d).

[63] Of the walls discussed in this section, the following are visible on the actual-state plan (Fig. 17): the North Wall, the northwest–southeast wall at the western end of the North Bay, the wall running southwest from the northwest corner of the North Reveal, and a fragment of the northwest–southeast wall paralleling the North Reveal ca. three meters to the west.

[64] NEG 67 RMM, Basket 26, including an Athenian post-glaze lamp (IPL 67-22): 5th century.

[65] NEG 67 RMM, Baskets 71, 72, including a cooking pot (IPR 67-48): p.H. 0.102 m., p.W. 0.045 m. Single fragment preserves rim and handle. Coarse red clay (2.5YR 5/8) fired darker and burned black on exterior, with many stone inclusions. Rounded sides and vertical handle, oval in section, to midpoint on rim. See H. P. Isler, "Heraion von Samos," *Mitteilungen des deutschen archäologischen Instituts, Athenische Abteilung* 84, 1969, no. 34, for similar profile (mid-6th century). Other material from this strosis can be paralleled by (unpublished) early 6th-century pottery from Isthmia and Corinth.

The southern two-thirds of this wall survives and is shown on the actual-state plan (Fig. 17). The wall was *ca.* 0.47 m. thick, and there was a doorway *ca.* 0.70 m. wide at the northern end. At either end of the threshold were small round holes, 0.08 m. in diameter.

About one meter to the west of this wall was another, running southeast from the North Wall and preserved at the time of excavation for a distance of *ca.* 3.30 m. (Ill. 15; Pls. 24:d, 25:a). Directly under this wall were pottery and other material from the early sixth century (NEG 67 RMM, Basket 71). To the west of the wall, the strosis was at a level about 0.42 m. higher than on the east (elev. +31.67 m.), but this seems to represent the same fill. Cut into this strosis was a series of nine irregularly spaced holes, about 0.20 m. in diameter and *ca.* 0.15 deep (visible in Pls. 24:d, 25:a). Eight of these holes were located to the west of the wall (Ill. 15, Phase B), while one was to the east. These were presumably post holes, but since they form no recognizable pattern, their purpose must remain uncertain.

On the basis of the surviving evidence, this phase might be associated with the Justinianic rebuilding of the Hexamilion, but it is more likely that it represents a later phase of "squatter" occupation, perhaps connected with the Slavic invasion and the flight of individuals to potential places of security. Overlying this strosis was a large quantity of material apparently dating from the later sixth and the seventh centuries and perhaps representing the period of use for this phase.[66]

Thus, we seem to have a series of walls constructed about the mid-sixth century, with intensive use probably continuing well into the seventh century. There was no indication of a destruction level in this debris; while in the North Bay this level is only *ca.* 0.27 m. thick, in the area to the west it is as much as a meter deep. All this suggests that the deposit in the western area was the result of a cleaning and leveling operation at a later date.

Remarkable among the finds in this level inside the North Bay were fragments of a cooking pot of what has been identified elsewhere as Slavic or Avaro-Slavic pottery.[67] In southern Greece "Slavic" pottery has already been identified at Corinth,[68] Olympia,[69] and Argos.[70] This pottery has been generally associated with the Avaro-Slavic invasions of Greece at the end of the sixth and throughout the seventh century. Indeed, for Argos Aupert argued that the Slavs devastated the city in 585 and rapidly withdrew, leaving a few of their pots behind.

[66] NEG 67 RMM, Baskets 25, 33, 34, 37, 53, 54, 65:

a) Clement, 488 (IC 934), Justin II and Sophia (A.D. 565–578): mint and year uncertain.

b) Belt buckle (IM 3546), Pl. 25:b: 6th–7th centuries.

c) Cooking pot (IPR 67-47), Pl. 25:c: p.H. 0.182 m., Diam. of rim 0.155 m. Partially restored from many fragments, preserving part of bottom, sides, and rim. Coarse red clay (2.5YR 5/8) with many large white inclusions and voids, fired darker and burned unevenly black on exterior. Rounded bottom, slightly piriform shape, rounded shoulder, and plain slightly outturned rim. No handle preserved, although more than half of rim is present.

d) Lamp (IPL 67-5): North African imitation (6th century, probably later part).

[67] Cooking pot (IPR 67-49), Pl. 25:d: p.H. *ca.* 0.103 m., est. Diam. of rim 0.18 m. Two fragments preserve shoulder, one handle, *ca.* 1/3 of rim. Very coarse red clay (2.5YR 5/6) fired or burned black over most of vessel, with many rectangular voids and large pieces of quartz. Rounded sides and outturned plain rim; vertical handle from shoulder to upper part of rim, oval in section. Either handmade or made on a slow wheel; there are many finger depressions where the clay was smoothed or formed. Combing over all the exterior, either oblique vertical incisions or vertical marks made by pressing the points of the comb into the clay. Cf. Aupert, "Céramique slave," pp. 373–394. This piece is not paralleled exactly by any of those from Argos: it has a handle (none of those from Argos do), and there is no trace of horizontal lines; in addition, the decoration made by pressing the comb into the clay is apparently not present at Argos. The decoration is like Aupert's Argos, nos. 31–34, and the profile, as far as it is preserved, is most like Form 1.

[68] G. D. Weinberg, "A Wandering Soldier's Grave in Corinth," *Hesperia* 43, 1974, pp. 514–515.

[69] N. Ialouris, Δελτ 16, 1960 [1962], pp. 125–126; 17, 1961–1962, Β' [1963], p. 107, pl. 117; 19, 1964, Β' 2 [1966], p. 176; 20, 1965, Β' 2 [1967], p. 209; 21, 1966, Β' 1 [1968], p. 170.

[70] Aupert, "Céramique slave," pp. 373–394.

While at first sight the importation of such poorly made pottery must seem unlikely, undoubtedly the plentiful material from Argos and the pot described above closely resemble Slavic or Avaro-Slavic pottery from sites in Hungary, Czechoslovakia, Romania, and elsewhere.[71] Scholars have not always noted, however, that, in form, this "Slavic" pottery closely resembles Roman cooking pots of similar date; some Roman influence on wares manufactured further north is not inconceivable. Further, one need not assume that these "Slavic" pots were all manufactured in the north; rather, immigrants from the north (whether Slavic or not) may have continued to make their pottery in Greece using materials and techniques with which they were familiar. In fact, the "Slavic" pottery from Isthmia displays considerably more variation than what has been published at Argos, and the preference for vessels with handles, exhibited at Isthmia but lacking at Argos and uncommon in Hungary and elsewhere north of the Danube, shows that more study of this pottery is necessary before firm historical conclusions can be drawn from it.

More examples of this "Slavic" pottery were found on the south side of the Northeast Gate, in an area without any clear floor levels or associated architecture. In this fill, however, was a coin of Constans II, which can presumably be used to date the pottery.[72] The coin shows that "Slavic" pottery found in Greece can date to the middle of the seventh century, but great caution should be observed in using the pottery to date the Northeast Gate. There is no reason to assume that Phase B ended at the time of the first wave of Slavic invasions in the 580's or even that this period ended in violent destruction.[73] Occupation may well have continued within the structures associated with the Fortress far into the seventh century. Certainly, there were several waves of Slavic invasions in the sixth and seventh centuries, and there is evidence of a Bulgarian attack on Corinth in the 640's.[74] All historical considerations suggest that Corinth remained in Byzantine hands throughout this period, and the Fortress at Isthmia may well have provided a place of refuge for survivors of the invasions.

---

[71] V. Popović, "Les Sklavinies macédoniennes," *Compte rendus de l'Académie des Inscriptions et Belles-Lettres* 1980, pp. 233–239; *Cemeteries of the Avar Period (567–829) in Hungary*, I. Korvig, ed., 2 vols., Budapest 1977; Aupert, "Céramique slave," pp. 389–392.

[72] From NEG 67 CL, Basket 11; other sherds of the same ware in NEG 67 CL, Basket 12.

a) Clement, 496 (IC 896), Constans II (A.D. 655/6): Follis, long cross, *Corinth* VI, 70, no. 70.

b) Cooking pot (IPR 67-51), Pl. 26:a: p.H. *ca.* 0.068 m., p.W. 0.077 m. Three fragments preserve part of the rim and side. Coarse red clay (2.5YR 5/8) fired gray on surfaces, with many stone inclusions and small pieces of quartz (fabric lacks the large voids and large pieces of quartz of IPR 67-49 [footnote 67 above, p. 85]). Rounded tapering sides and plain outturned rim. Combed decoration of alternating wave pattern and horizontal bands. On interior, faint wheel marks (thus, vessel made on a wheel). Under rim, a small hole presumably for suspending the vessel. For decoration cf. Aupert, "Céramique slave," nos. 1–21.

c) Cooking pot (IPR 67-52): p.H. *ca.* 0.044 m., p.W. 0.052 m. Single fragment preserves part of rim and upper handle attachment. Very coarse red clay (2.5YR 5/6) fired or burned black on exterior, with many rectangular voids and large pieces of quartz (same fabric as IPR 67-49 [footnote 67 above, p. 85]). Rounded sides and outturned plain rim; vertical handle to just under rim. No evidence of decoration on exterior or wheel marks on interior.

There are several other uninventoried fragments from similar vessels in this fill.

[73] Note, however, the hoard of 270 Byzantine coins from the Temple of Poseidon, the latest of which was struck in the second year of Maurice (583/4): Broneer, "Corinthian Isthmus," p. 88; Broneer, 1955, pp. 116–117, 123, 126; MacDowall, "Byzantine Coin Hoard," pp. 264–276; D. M. Metcalf, "The Slavonic Threat to Greece circa 580: Some Evidence from Athens," *Hesperia* 31, 1962, p. 136, note 5. The literature on the "Slavic" invasions of Greece is enormous. See especially P. A. Yannopoulos, "Le pénétration slave en Argolide," *Études argiènnes* (*BCH*, Suppl. 6) 1980, pp. 323–371; M. W. Weithmann, *Die slawische Bevölkerung auf der griechischen Halbinsel*, Munich 1978.

[74] K. M. Setton, "The Bulgars in the Balkans and the Occupation of Corinth in the Seventh Century," *Speculum* 25, 1950, pp. 502–542; Davidson (footnote 52 above, p. 79), pp. 227–240. See also P. Charanis, "On the Capture of Corinth by the Onogurs and Its Recapture by the Byzantines," *Speculum* 27, 1952, pp. 343–350, and K. M. Setton's reply, "The Emperor Constans II and the Capture of Corinth by the Onogur Bulgars," *Speculum* 27, 1952, pp. 351–362.

Further, while there is no specific record that the troops of Constans II occupied the Hexamilion and the Fortress, that emperor's activity at Athens and Corinth makes such a situation likely.[75]

After the construction of the Blocking Wall, the roadway through the Northeast Gate would naturally have gone out of use, and the space between the central piers and the two reveals would have been ideally suited for domestic quarters. This probably explains a door closure at the western end of the reveals in the Northeast Gate. The evidence for this closure is a rectangular cutting in the northern face of the South Reveal immediately east of the jamb (Pl. 26:c). This cutting, which was probably designed for the door bolt, is *ca.* 0.30 m. deep, *ca.* 0.16 m. wide, and 0.20 m. high. Just slightly to the west of this cutting is a roughly circular hole in the surface of the marble pavement (Pl. 26:b), which was probably a socket for a door opening inward toward the east. On the southeast face of the North Reveal, just opposite these cuttings, there is a rough hole that might once have been more rectangular (see p. 64 above), but there is no corresponding cutting for a door post in the pavement. It is probably better to assume that the opening between the two reveals was narrowed, and this will explain the absence of clear door cuttings in the North Reveal. Monceaux's excavation in 1883 would presumably have removed all trace of such a partial blocking of the western end of the gate.

Probably also connected with this phase of reoccupation is the roadway of hard-packed dirt and stones laid down over at least the western end of the marble roadway through the gate (see p. 62 above). Only a small patch of this road surface, some 0.31 m. thick, was discovered at the far western extremity of the excavated area. It is likely, however, that this road surface continued farther to the east but was removed by Monceaux. It must have been laid down after the closure of the Northeast Gate with the Blocking Wall, and so it presumably led to the domestic structures built inside and around the gate after that time.

The small wall running along the southern side of the later roadway presumably also should be assigned to this phase. Four blocks of this wall are preserved, for a distance of *ca.* 2.10 m., before it runs off into unexcavated ground.

There is no indication when this post-Justinianic phase of occupation came to an end: habitation may have continued through to the end of the seventh and into the eighth century. After that time, however, there is a gap until the eleventh or twelfth century.[76]

PHASE C: TWELFTH TO FOURTEENTH CENTURY

Immediately above these levels from latest antiquity are several floors and walls representing the reoccupation of this area in the middle and late Byzantine periods. Floors at three separate elevations can be identified, all apparently contemporary, stepping down sharply from the ruins of the Hexamilion to the interior of the North Bay. Thus, the floor level in the North Bay was at +31.21 m., while in the area to the west it rose to +32.68 m. and +34.05 m. just to the north of that, up against the south face of the Hexamilion (see Ill. 15, Phase C).

The wall closing off the western end of the North Bay does not survive from this period; the wall shown on the actual-state plan must belong to the sixth century, since its top surface was

[75] Constans spent the winter of 662 in Athens; cf. M. Thompson, *The Athenian Agora*, II, *Coins from the Roman through the Venetian Period*, Princeton 1954, pp. 3–4. On Constans in the Corinthia, see J. H. Kent, "A Byzantine Statue Base at Corinth," *Speculum* 25, 1950, pp. 544–546 and *Corinth* VIII, iii, no. 510, p. 169; and the articles by Setton and Charanis cited above (footnote 74 above, p. 86).

[76] It is significant that no examples of the characteristic white wares produced in Constantinople and popular in Corinth from the 8th century onward were discovered in the excavation of this area.

overrun by sixth- and seventh-century debris. But that such a wall must have existed in Phase C is shown by the different floor levels that meet where the wall would have been; presumably, this later wall was removed at the time of Monceaux's excavation. Some 3.10 m. west of this wall is another one parallel, set into the floor at +32.68 m. It is *ca.* 0.50 m. thick and preserved to a distance of *ca.* 5.23 m. southeast of the south face of the North Wall. At the time of excavation, this wall was preserved to a height of *ca.* 0.77 m. Another wall, 0.40 m. wide, running westward from the west face of the North Reveal for a distance of *ca.* 1.60 m., presumably joined it to form a room of a larger structure.

The earlier walls from Phase B were covered by the deep fill placed over them (see p. 84 above), although some wall probably existed between the North Wall and the North Reveal in this period. The depth of this fill, however, and the extension of the parallel (northwest–southeast) wall toward the south suggest that the old roadway to the Northeast Gate was now totally out of service and covered with debris (although this had naturally all been removed by Monceaux).

The northwest–southeast wall in this area was originally constructed of small stones and bricks laid in fairly regular courses (Pls. 26:d, 27:a: note that the northern part of this wall was removed in the course of excavation, and so only its southern extension is shown on the actual-state plan, Figure 17). At a distance of *ca.* 1.49 m. from the face of the North Wall was a doorway 0.88 m. wide, whose jambs were two large blocks *ca.* 0.90 m. high (Ill. 15). No threshold or cuttings for a door mechanism were present. At a later time the upper part of this wall was rebuilt in a less careful style, using small stones and dark earth laid on top of the earlier construction and filling in the doorway completely (Pl. 27:b). In the northwest corner of the room formed by this wall there was an area, less than a meter square, that was paved with tiles and clay (Pl. 27:c, also visible in Pl. 27:a), but the rest of the paving in the room was hard-packed earth and stones.

To the north of this area was another floor at an elevation of +34.05 m. This was defined toward the west by a wall, *ca.* 0.45 m. wide and 0.57 m. high at the time of excavation (Ill. 15). The facing blocks of the interior of the Hexamilion had already been robbed away before this wall was constructed, and the wall was butted up against the Hexamilion's rubble core. From this point, the wall extended southward for *ca.* 2.43 m. (along the same line as the northwest–southeast wall discussed above) and then turned eastward along the preserved top of the North Wall for a distance of 1.85 m. The North Wall thus formed a common boundary for the two structures west of the North Bay. Nothing else of this complex to the north can now be recovered, but it shows that in the Middle Ages the robbing of the facing blocks of the Hexamilion had already progressed quite far and that structures in this area were constructed on at least three levels and over a considerable space. The appearance of this complex must have resembled that of traditional Greek villages, with slightly ramshackle houses climbing up and down hills in apparent disarray.

Despite the preservation of these walls and evidence for reconstruction of one of them, there is no record of stratigraphic differentiation preserved within the structures. Given our present knowledge of late Byzantine ceramics, the pottery above the floors cannot be closely dated. It ranges, however, from the twelfth to the early fourteenth century, and we may suggest that habitation spanned that period.[77] Two coins from this area confirm this chronology. One of these was not

---

[77] a) Ring foot, sgraffito (IPB 67-10), Pl. 27:d: p.H. 0.022 m., p.W. 0.072 m. Single fragment preserves foot and part of body. Coarse red clay (2.5YR 5/8) fired buff at surfaces, with many small inclusions and voids and some quartz. Plain, low ring foot and flaring sides. White slip on interior and very thinly on exterior. On interior, yellow glaze with thin uneven splotch of green; sgraffito circle in center. Cf. *Corinth* XI, nos. 1416, 1418, pp. 142–144: Late Byzantine Painted Sgraffito, Group II, second half 13th–early 14th centuries.

b) Jug (IPB 67-8), Pl. 27:e: p.L. 0.132 m., p.W. 0.112 m., Th. 0.004 m. Single sherd preserves part of shoulder and neck. Yellow clay (10YR 7/6) fired reddish yellow (5YR 6.6) on exterior, with many small inclusions and voids.

found in close association with the pottery, but the other came from within the wall of the upper-most structure, set against the core of the Hexamilion.[78]

It is perhaps significant that no pottery or coins datable after the fourteenth century were dis-covered in this area. At the time of the final restoration of the Fortress and its military use in the fif-teenth century, these domestic structures were presumably abandoned.

Rounded shoulder and cylindrical neck. Wheel marks on interior; wheel ridges around neck. Exterior preserves part of a graffito. Cf. MacKay, "More Byzantine Pottery," nos. 59, 76, pls. 66, 67 (12th century).

c) Jug (IPB 67-9), Pl. 28:a: p.H. 0.065 m., Diam. mouth 0.029 m. Restored from two fragments, preserving part of body and mouth. Coarse reddish yellow clay (5YR 6/6) with many small to large brown stone inclusions. Small, unglazed jug with rounded sides, straight neck, and slightly outturned, plain rim; vertical handle, oval in section, from shoulder to middle of neck. Single groove at shoulder. Cf. *Corinth* XI, nos. 275–277, fig. 42:e, pp. 58–60 (12th century).

d) Cooking pot (IPB 67-11), Pl. 28:b: p.H. 0.127 m., est. Diam. mouth 0.13 m. Two fragments preserve upper part of body, one handle, and mouth. Hard, coarse red clay (2.5YR 5.8), fired darker and burned black on exterior, with many stone inclusions. Rounded sides and shoulder with a broad ridge below a plain vertical rim; vertical handle, oval in section, from point of maximum diameter to just below ridge. Several drops of brown glaze on exterior of rim. Cf. MacKay, "More Byzantine Pottery," no. 127, fig. 5, for similar profile (later 13th and early 14th centuries).

[78] a) Clement, 533 (IC 893), Manuel I Comnenus (A.D. 1143–1180).

b) Clement, 560 (IC 903), Corinth, Geoffrey Villehardouin (1218–1245 or 1245–1250). *Corinth* VI, p. 152, no. 2.

VI

THE SOUTH GATE

THE SOUTH GATE provided a monumental entrance to the Fortress for travelers approaching from the south (Fig. 23; Pl. 28:c. In Figure 8, it is indicated by Towers 8 and 9). In splendor and size, it matched the Northeast Gate. It is now much the better preserved, the two towers each standing to a height of *ca.* four meters. In terms of strategy and siting, of course, the South Gate was much less important, since it opened onto territory that was already within the circuit of the Hexamilion, but it was originally the only other gateway into the Fortress and provided a fitting balance for the Northeast Gate.

The absence of any really reliable stratigraphic evidence made investigation of the South Gate difficult. The gate was first excavated by Monceaux (p. 2 above); he cleared the area down to hardpan, five meters below the surface, and backfilled much of his trench, making any further stratigraphic excavation all but impossible.[1] In 1932 Megaw briefly explored the South Gate.[2] Demetrios Pallas, in Oscar Broneer's campaigns of 1956 and 1958, carried out further clearing.[3]

Monceaux thought that the original structure of the South Gate was "Hellenic" but that it was disfigured "à une basse epoque" by the enlargement of the wall and the partial rebuilding of the gate.[4] Megaw was the first to realize that the gate was constructed in one period, and he provided solid evidence to that effect: the use of mortar, the identity of all the tool work on the visible surfaces of the faces, and the absence of any earlier wall behind the admittedly Byzantine outer face of the gate.[5]

To the east of the South Gate, the South Fortress wall is approximately 2.30 m. wide, but within the gate itself and to the west of the gate, the Fortress wall is *ca.* 3.65 m. wide. Megaw thought that the "abutment of internal buildings at this point" might explain this widening.[6] While this explanation is possible, and we have seen several examples of this phenomenon, it is probably more likely that the widening was the result of a desire to strengthen the Fortress wall in the area of the South Gate. There is no good evidence as to whether the Fortress wall maintained the greater width all the way to Tower 10, but it is clear that the exterior (south) face ran in a straight line between Towers 9 and 10. In the area of the gate, both faces of the Fortress wall are constructed with large, well-laid ashlar blocks.

Two octagonal towers, Tower 8 on the east and Tower 9 on the west, flanked the gateway, each positioned with its outermost face approximately parallel to the line of the Fortress wall. This arrangement contrasts with the recommendation of Philo of Byzantium (1.6), who said that hexagonal towers should be used at gateways, with their faces arranged so that a point projected toward an attacker. For example, Tower 1 of the Land Walls of Constantinople, which stood beside a small gateway, conforms to this dictum; other towers at Constantinople (e.g. Tower 50), however, reproduce the arrangement at Isthmia. The interior of Tower 9 is octagonal, while that of Tower 8 is circular.

These are the only octagonal towers at Isthmia, either along the Hexamilion or in the Fortress. The shape, however, is common on the Land Walls of Constantinople, where along much of the

---

[1] Monceaux, "Fouilles," 1884, pp. 277–279.
[2] Jenkins and Megaw, "Researches," pp. 73–74.
[3] Broneer, 1959, pp. 320–321.
[4] Monceaux, "Fouilles," 1884, p. 279.
[5] Jenkins and Megaw, "Researches," p. 74.
[6] Jenkins and Megaw, "Researches," p. 73.

inner wall octagonal towers alternate with rectangular examples. At Constantinople all the octagonal towers have circular interiors, and they stand out from the curtain more than do those at Isthmia.[7]
Those at Constantinople have seven freestanding sides, while, as high as they are preserved, those at
Isthmia have only five; only a short return defines the innermost angles. At ground level, however, the
towers at Constantinople allowed fire only from three sides. At the level of the fighting platform, the
towers at the South Gate are likely to have had seven sides available for fire, while at the uppermost
level they were presumably completely freestanding, allowing fire in any direction.

Good parallels for the arrangement of the South Gate are the Silivri Kapi (Pege Gate) and the
Edirne Kapi (Charisios Gate) at Constantinople, both of which have octagonal towers flanking the
gateway.[8] The proportions and size of the South Gate more closely resemble those of the Silivri
Kapi, since the towers of the Edirne Kapi project approximately 14 meters from the face of the
curtain wall; the Silivri Kapi towers project *ca.* 10 meters, while the projection at Isthmia is less
than 6 meters.[9]

At the South Gate, both octagonal towers are built on roughly rectangular foundations reminiscent of those of the Northeast Gate. The sides of the foundations range from 5.62 to 9.26 m. in
length. They are constructed of two courses of roughly cut blocks, *ca.* 0.88 m. high, set on a thin
bedding of mortar and rubble. The foundations apparently were not solid platforms that continued
all the way under the towers (as they did at the Northeast Gate), since excavation of the tower
interior discovered no trace of them. They were thus apparently simply built as foundations for the
tower walls and extended somewhat on the outside of the towers, to give them additional strength
and discourage sapping (Fig. 23).

The towers themselves are constructed with two faces of large blocks, with an interior filling of
rubble and mortar. Especially in the lower courses, the facing blocks are frequently set up as orthostates. The exterior blocks of the towers are very well cut and well fitted together; the joints are
generally filled with mortar that is smoothed off on the exterior. Most of the material in the towers
was apparently re-used. In Tower 8 the individual blocks were curved to form the circular interior
wall; some of these blocks are also curved on the face set into the rubble-and-mortar core, but some
are simply rectangular on this buried surface. In Tower 9 several of the blocks on the interior have
been recut to form the angles of the interior octagon.

Tower 8 is generally better constructed than Tower 9; it is built with large blocks carefully
fitted together with few spaces between them, while the blocks of Tower 9 are generally smaller and
much less carefully joined. Somewhat surprisingly, Monceaux said little about Tower 8 (which he
called "round") but described Tower 9 as "d'un joli travail et peut être attribuée à l'époque hellénique."[10] The exterior faces of Tower 8 are all approximately 2.85 m. wide, and the diameter of
the interior is *ca.* 3.05 m. Holes in the interior surface are filled with a brown plaster, similar to that
used at Tower 15. The exterior faces of Tower 9, by contrast, range from 2.66 to 3.14 m. in width,
and the faces of the interior octagon vary widely, from 1.45 to 1.95 m. Today both towers are
preserved to a maximum height of eight courses above the top of the foundations (3.07 m. above the
top of the foundations in Tower 8 and 4.00 m. in Tower 9). There is no entrance into either of the
towers from ground level (a doorway through the southwest face of Tower 8 is a modern intrusion).

[7] Meyer-Plath and Schneider, *Landmauer* II, pls. 8, 9.

[8] Meyer-Plath and Schneider, *Landmauer* II, pp. 64, 70–71, pls. 31:d, 33. Both gates have been so substantially
rebuilt "dass nur noch wenige ursprüngliche Reste an den Tortürmern sichtbar sind" (p. 71).

[9] Meyer-Plath and Schneider, *Landmauer* II, pls. 1, 3.

[10] Monceaux, "Fouilles," 1884, p. 279. There can be little doubt of the attribution, since he says that the "round"
tower was on the right and the polygonal tower on the left. Megaw (Jenkins and Megaw, "Researches," p. 74) seems to
have been unaware of this inaccuracy in Monceaux's account.

In Tower 9 the traces of a stairway rise clockwise along the interior face toward the fighting platform. This stairway is indicated by two well-preserved steps, *ca.* 0.40 m. wide, the upper one rising from an elevation of +44.92 m. to +45.33 m. This gives a tread of 0.40 m. and a rise of 0.41 m. for the stairway. Fragments of three other steps can be seen below these two examples, but they do not have a preserved upper surface. There is no trace of a stairway in Tower 8, and its lowest level must have been entered by a ladder from above.

The supports for the top of the stairway of Tower 9 may be discerned about 1.2 m. east of the top preserved step. This would have allowed two further risers, reaching a restored elevation of +46.15 m., 3.95 m. above the top of the foundations. This is certainly too low for the fighting platform of the Fortress wall and the upper room of the tower, but no further direct evidence exists on which to base a restoration. Presumably, either the stairway doubled back through the thickness of the Fortress wall (a good reason for its extraordinary width here), or it rose over a vault to reach the level of the fighting platform. By comparison with the towers in the Northeast Gate, we should expect the level of the fighting platform to be approximately 7 meters above ground level outside the Fortress, or at an elevation of *ca.* +49.0 m.; the top level of the tower would then have been *ca.* 3.8 m. higher, or at an elevation of +52.8 m.

Because there are no arrangements for stairs in Tower 8, the floor of the upper room must have been wooden, supported either by beams or posts. The corresponding floor in Tower 9 may have been either wooden or vaulted, but the top level of both towers was probably vaulted. As the surviving remains show, there were no arrow slits in the lower rooms of the towers, and they cannot have been used for defense. The upper rooms of the towers were probably equipped with arrow slits on five of the faces. Two of these slits would have offered enfilading fire directly in front of the gate, while two others provided fire along the face of the wall to the east and the west. The top level was undoubtedly a crenellated fighting platform.

The actual passageway through the South Gate is *ca.* 3.20–3.40 m. wide (Pl. 28:d), almost exactly the same width as the passageway through the Northeast Gate. This similarity shows, interestingly enough, that there was apparently a standard width for gateways, perhaps based on the normal width of contemporary wagons; it had not changed appreciably since construction of the Roman Arch some three centuries earlier. A blocking wall across the gateway obscures the passageway in the South Gate. The construction apparently resulted in the dismantling of some of the wall facing as well as covering the whole of the south end of the passageway with later masonry. In addition, there is virtually nothing of the original paving of the roadway left *in situ*. A block at the lowest level of the blocking wall, in the center of the south face (Pl. 28:d), may be one of the original roadway blocks, but otherwise nothing remains.

Today there is a large cutting in the hardpan, approximately the width of the gateway and extending both north and south of the gate. This cutting is probably the trench that Monceaux dug through the gate in 1883, and it has no connection with the ancient structures in the area. It also, unfortunately, removed all stratigraphic evidence in the middle of the gate. The trench extends below what must have been the level of the road surface in late Roman times, and so we have no firm datum on which to base a reconstruction of the gate. The foundations of the towers, however, are unlikely originally to have been fully exposed, and so we may assume that their tops (+41.88–42.20 m.) represent approximately the level of the ancient road surface.

The south face of the Fortress wall on either side of the passageway was not excavated down to the foundation level. To the east this face is preserved in six courses to +44.79 m., 2.59 m. above the presumed ancient road surface. On the west only five courses are preserved, to an elevation of +44.48 m. (Pl. 28:c). This section of the Fortress wall is constructed of large, well-cut ashlar blocks, alternatively laid as headers and stretchers. On either side, the first blocks in the lowest two courses were robbed away before construction of the blocking wall.

On the south face of the gateway the two jambs, 0.43–0.48 m. wide, project 0.22 m. into the passage. In the upper courses, where they are not obscured by the blocking wall, these jambs are cut from the single piece of stone that forms the face of the Fortress wall, a technique identical to that used in the Hexamilion Gate west of Tower 15 (see p. 99 below). Behind (north of) the jamb, the wall of the passageway on the east is straight, while on the west after *ca.* 0.80 m. there is a further set-back of *ca.* 0.20 m., making the passageway *ca.* 3.40 m. wide at the northern end.

Construction of the blocking wall obscured all trace of the gate mechanism, although it must have been located in the area immediately north of the jambs. Since there are no projecting jambs at the north end of the passageway, we must conclude, first, that the opened leaves of the door cannot have been recessed, as in the Northeast Gate, and, second, that the means of bolting the doors was different from that used in the other gate. The absence of projecting inner jambs means that the door could not be anchored with transverse struts. The bolt must have been simply fastened to the door leaves by means of metal rings or straps of some sort, a slightly weaker system than that employed in the Northeast Gate, but one that was probably thought sufficient for the lesser vulnerability here.

In terms of over-all arrangement and strategic location, the placement of the gate mechanism is also significantly different from that in the Northeast Gate. In the latter, it will be remembered, the central piers of the Roman Arch formed a kind of jamb, and the gate mechanism was located behind them, making it impossible for soldiers in the towers to bring enfilading fire directly against the gate front. In the South Gate, by contrast, the small jambs did not obscure the south face of the gate, and it would have been possible to fire directly against it from the flanking towers.

On either side of the gateway are crosses with equilateral flaring arms in raised relief (Pl. 29:a, b).[11] On the east the cross is located in the fourth course above the lowest one visible, on a block immediately beside the gateway. On the west side the cross is in the fifth course, on a block one removed from the edge of the gateway. Each cross is inscribed in a circle 0.37–0.40 m. in diameter and is raised *ca.* 0.035 m. from the surface of the block. The crosses have arms of equal length that flare broadly to a maximum width of *ca.* 0.14–0.15 m. A stone with a cross of identical shape and size and executed in the same style was found in the fill between the two towers, and it must have come from the superstructure of the South Gate.[12] This block, however, was curved (i.e., convex) on its external surface. It is difficult to know exactly where it might have been placed.

A cutting *ca.* 0.22 m. wide and *ca.* 0.07–0.11 m. deep runs roughly east–west along the south side of the top two preserved blocks of the east pier of the gateway (visible at P in Fig. 23), at an elevation of *ca.* +45.31 m., over 3 meters above what we suppose was the level of the roadway. Presumably, this cutting held the lintel across the gateway, above which we should probably restore an arch.

The blocking wall across the south end of the gateway is *ca.* 1.99 m. wide at the east and *ca.* 1.68 m. wide at the west (Pls. 28:d, 29:c). It is constructed of two faces of large, roughly coursed blocks with a rubble-and-masonry core. On the south face the lowest course of the blocking wall is considerably higher than that of the surrounding masonry of the gate. This suggests that the blocking wall was laid directly on the road surface, which has been subsequently robbed away, leaving the blocking wall apparently suspended in space. On the south the blocking wall is preserved in two or three courses below the rubble core, while on the north the wall is in much better repair and is

---

[11] Jenkins and Megaw, "Researches," pp. 73–74, fig. 3. For a similar cross, see Karnapp, *Stadtmauer*, p. 49, pls. 61, 259, located above the entrances to tower 12 at Resafa.

[12] Demetrios Pallas found this block in 1956 (notebook D.P., p. 41), but it cannot now be located.

preserved to a total of eight courses. There is naturally no stratigraphic evidence to date the blocking wall, but in construction techniques as well as function it resembles that at the Northeast Gate, and it is presumably to be assigned to the same period, that is, to the late sixth–eighth centuries.

Just outside the gateway, at its southeast corner, is a single block *ca.* 1.36 m. by 0.52 m., laid with its long axis along the east side of the roadway through the gate (Fig. 23). This block is bonded into the south face of the blocking wall, which shows that it must have been in position when the latter was constructed. Its function, however, cannot now be determined. Running off to the south from this block is a wall *ca.* 0.60–0.66 m. wide and traceable for *ca.* 5.72 m.; it is constructed of roughly faced rubble, lies under but not aligned with the large block mentioned above, and is therefore presumably earlier, before construction of the Hexamilion. Excavation in this area unfortunately produced no helpful stratigraphic information, although clearly structures of Roman imperial date existed in the vicinity.

North of the gate is another series of rubble walls. These represent a number of small structures built up against the gate, certainly after the gate was blocked. One of these, in fact, was built directly in the northern part of the gateway, with the blocking wall as its south wall. In the center of this space is a wellhead, some 1.2 m. in diameter, with its top constructed in stone.

No secure chronology can be derived from the area of the South Gate, largely because of the disturbances of earlier excavation. The pottery, however, appears to fall into several distinct periods, ranging from Roman imperial to thirteenth or fourteenth century. Fifteen coins were found in the area of the South Gate, both within the towers and immediately to north and south. These provide at least a general indication of the occupation and use of the gate, although few have a secure stratigraphic context.[13]

It is noteworthy that the vast majority of these coins date to the second half of the twelfth century and the first half of the thirteenth. They were found even at the lowest levels of the excavation (IC 774, for example, comes from the bottom fill of Tower 9), which suggests that the towers may have been cleaned out for use at this time and the debris from earlier occupation dumped elsewhere. Large quantities of sgraffito pottery associated with the structures north of the gate suggest that the blocking wall across the gateway was in place by the middle of the twelfth century and that the gate cannot then have served as a passageway into the Fortress. Instead, Towers 8 and 9 were probably used as domestic quarters or for storage. The large proportion of Latin coins among this group (as well as, remarkably, one English coin) strongly suggests that the inhabitants of the gate (after A.D. 1205) were "Franks", the Crusaders who were given fiefs throughout Greece in the aftermath of the Fourth Crusade and the capture of Constantinople (A.D. 1204). The powerful masonry of the South Gate was certainly still standing to a considerable height at that time, and occupying it would have been easier than constructing the typical tower and fortified manor house that characterized the period. Small structures around the South Gate might have been outbuildings of the central dwelling or perhaps houses for the peasants who worked the land in the vicinity of the Fortress.

---

[13] The University of Chicago Excavations at Isthmia are now studying these coins. Full information on them will be available when they are published.
    a) IC 398 Corinth under Hadrian (A.D. 117–138)
    b) IC 328, 330 Anonymous Byzantine (A.D. 976–1034)
    c) IC 395, 703, 774 Manuel I (A.D. 1143–1180)
    d) IC 776 English (A.D. 1180–1247)
    e) IC 325, 783 Latin imitative, Constantinople (A.D. 1204–1261)
    f) IC 771, 781 Latin imitative, Thessalonica (A.D. 1204–1261)
    g) IC 327, 784 Latin imitative, Thessalonica (?; A.D. 1204–1261)
    h) IC 781 Latin imitative (?; A.D. 1204–1261)
    i) IC 777 Venetian Colonial (A.D. 1361–1501)

VII

FORTRESS TOWERS 15 AND 14

EXPLORATION OF TOWERS 15 AND 14 involved excavation of both towers and most of the area immediately around and between them. This work revealed not only information about these military constructions but also significant activity in earlier and later eras.

TOWER 15

Tower 15 is located at the northwestern corner of the Fortress, at the point where the West Fortress Wall and the Hexamilion meet (Fig. 24). Below the tower to the north, the land drops away steeply into the ravine, while on the west there was a more gradual but nonetheless significant drop in ground level, considerably greater in antiquity than it is today. The tower therefore dominated the surrounding unfortified land and stood guard over a corner of the Fortress and the gate through the Hexamilion that is just 1.50 m. to the west.

Investigation in this area involved the tower itself, the surrounding wall structures (both the Fortress wall and the Hexamilion), the gateway through the Hexamilion, and a number of structures later built in this area.[1] Excavation down to hardpan in most places revealed no significant traces of walls earlier than late Roman in date, although they encountered large quantities of early Roman pottery and rooftiles throughout the area at lower levels. No traces were found of the long Roman building discovered west of Tower 14 (see pp. 107–108 below), although the structure must have terminated somewhere in the vicinity. There certainly was early Roman activity in the area around Tower 15, but the absence of any large-scale architecture from this period suggests that considerable destruction and probably much leveling took place before the construction of the Hexamilion in this area. In fact, only two stretches of wall of Roman date can be identified. One is a section of rubble running east–west on exactly the same line as one of the walls in the North Drain (p. 47 above); the other is a small stretch of rubble discovered under the floor of Tower 15. This wall, however, does not line up with any other known structure, and the size, shape, and original function of the building it represents remain uncertain.

Tower 15 displays certain features that are peculiar to it. Thus, for example, the superstructure of the tower is relatively well preserved, and it shows traces of considerable rebuilding. The exterior of the tower is made of very large ashlar blocks, one of them a cornice from an Ionic building and another with a swallowtail-clamp cutting. Tile chinking is common. Imperfections in the stones and the spaces between them are filled with mortar, commonly with a smoothed, plastered face. On the western face of the tower wall, particularly near the northwest corner, where travelers would have waited for admittance through the gate in the Hexamilion, several crosses are scratched on a number of the facing blocks. Six of these crosses can still be seen (Pl. 29:d); they are deeply but simply incised, and they frequently have arms that are terminated by perpendicular lines. Whether these were meant as apotropaic devices or were simply cut by individuals idling at the gate is impossible to say.

A vaulted passageway that led westward through the West Fortress Wall and then turned north gave access to the interior of the tower (Figs. 24, 25; Pl. 30:a). The passage was approached

---

[1] Clement, 1969, pp. 118–119.

by a step, *ca.* 0.33 m. wide, made of flat stones and mortar, rising to a passageway, whose floor was also constructed of flat stones set in mortar. A half vault covered the entrance of the passageway on the south (Fig. 25; Pl. 30:a, b). Two large header blocks supported the vault. They were set vertically and separated by one horizontal block that tied the passage construction into the east facing of the West Fortress Wall. The half vault was constructed of two series of voussoir blocks, originally seven in number, which rose from a springing on the Fortress wall and rested against the south face of the tower. On the north wall of the passageway is a small cross, closely resembling those on the outside of the tower. Also in the interior of the passageway, built into its western wall, is a large limestone Ionic column drum (IA 68-3), originally from the orchestra of the Theater at Isthmia (Pl. 30:b).[2]

At this point the passageway turns sharply to the north and crosses a threshold block as it passes through the south wall of the tower. A deep cutting on the threshold block and other cuttings on the side walls suggest the arrangement for a door, but the details of how it worked are not at all clear. From this point the passageway is *ca.* 3.00 m. long, 2.05 m. high, with its top sloping steeply up from west to east. The ceiling of the passageway is a series of five unfluted column drums laid horizontally side by side, the interstices between the rounded sides of the columns and the flat blocks above and below filled with a packing of small stones, mortar, and pieces of tile (Fig. 25; Pl. 30:c).[3] At the north end of the passageway is another threshold block, and *ca.* 0.30 m. below that is a step down to the tower floor, this step made of four stones of irregular shape set on a loose fill without any trace of mortar.

Inside the passage, just *ca.* 0.10 m. north of the threshold block, two sixth-century coins were discovered, undoubtedly lost while the passage into the tower was open.[4] These coins show that the passage into the tower and presumably the tower itself were open and in use at least until the 570's; it is not unreasonable to connect this use with the defense of the Hexamilion against the Slavs in the late 570's and 580's.

The interior of Tower 15 reflects the irregularities already noted on the exterior (Figs. 25, 26; Pl. 30:d). At least the upper portions of the preserved walls were rebuilt several times, and they were hacked into at various places during one or another of the periods in which the tower was occupied. No two of the interior walls are of the same length, and the south wall does not bond with either the east or the west wall of the tower. In addition, these interior faces are constructed in a technique not encountered in any of the surviving parts of the towers of the Fortress. The interior face of the south wall was built of rough masonry throughout, with small stones set in uneven courses. The other three sides were all built alike but in a very different style: their foundations, explored only along the western side, are made of simple rubble-and-mortar construction. Above the foundations are several courses of large, well-cut blocks laid in reasonably level courses occasionally chinked with tiles. At a height of *ca.* 1.81 m. above the top of the foundations is a leveling course, *ca.* 0.19 m. high, made of three courses of bricks set in mortar. This lowest leveling course did not continue into the interior of the walls but was confined to the surface. Small, rectangular holes were let into the tile courses, and since these are not regularly placed and are nowhere aligned, they must have supported the scaffolding used in construction of the tower.

---

[2] Clement, 1968, p. 141, plan 2; Clement, 1969, p. 118; Gebhard, *Theater*, pp. 93–99, fig. 49. Other fragments of these two columns were discovered in the excavation of the Northeast Gate.

[3] The use of column drums as the ceiling of a passageway is well attested, as for example in the Carmadino Gate of the Castle of the Knights on Kos, constructed in 1478.

[4] a) Clement, 468 (IC 68-78), Justinian I (A.D. 539/40): follis. *DOC* I, pp. 83, 85, no. 38:c, 1–4

b) Clement, 476 (IC 68-79), Justin II (A.D. 570/1): follis. *DOC* I, p. 207, no. 28:d, 1–3.

Above this triple brick course is a section of masonry, *ca.* 0.98 m. high, that combines large, well-cut blocks with smaller, less carefully worked stones. At the top of this section is a series of irregular rectangular cuttings; three large cuttings survive in the eastern and western walls and two smaller cuttings in the wall on the north. These cuttings are at approximately the same level, and those on the east and west sides probably supported a wooden floor within the tower. The southern wall has no cuttings of this kind, and the cuttings in the northern wall may have been used for an opening in the floor for ladder access to the upper story.

Above this layer of masonry was another leveling course, now only poorly preserved. The course was originally three bricks high (*ca.* 0.17 m.), and it continued all the way through the thickness of the walls and was visible on the outside as well as the inside of the tower. In most places, however, this course has been broken away; it is fully preserved only in the southeastern and southwestern corners of the tower. Above the bricks, and often replacing them, is a section of rough rubble-and-mortar masonry, completely uncoursed and very different from the construction lower down in the tower. The interior face of this section is reasonably smooth and well finished, but the exterior face has completely fallen away, making it impossible to know exactly how the exterior was finished. In the southwestern corner of the tower, this section of masonry is preserved to a height of 0.75 m. above the top of the upper brick leveling course.

Clearly, then, the interior of Tower 15 represents at least two and more likely three periods of construction, the last of which consisted in the rebuilding of the upper part of the tower, above the upper brick leveling course, in rough rubble-and-mortar construction. It is impossible to say whether the central portion of the surviving walls, with the two tile courses, represents the original Hexamilion construction phase of the tower. On the basis of comparison with other parts of the Fortress, and even with the south interior wall face of the tower, probably it does not but should rather be seen as a rebuilding and strengthening of the tower at a later date. The use of tile courses is paralleled in the bastion at the North Tower of the Northeast Gate, dated to the mid-sixth century, and we should probably attribute to Justinian the partial rebuilding Tower 15 as well. The upper rubble-and-mortar reconstruction would then be later, and we might reasonably assign it to one of the fifteenth-century rebuildings of the Hexamilion.

The top of the foundations and the step that leads from the passageway into the tower indicate the original floor level of Tower 15. In the southwest corner, this level is *ca.* 2.8 m. below the cuttings for the upper-level floor joists. It is uncertain whether the ground floor of the tower was originally paved; the excavators encountered a row of stones along the south wall and an uncertain construction in the northeast corner, perhaps the flooring for a built-in cupboard. In any case, there was a confusing sequence of use levels in the tower, some of which had apparently been disturbed in antiquity. These were characterized by much burning, bones, glass, rooftiles, and large quantities of broken, coarse pottery.

Above the uppermost floor level was considerable debris and broken pottery, most of it Late Roman in date but clearly from a mixed context, since it contained Classical Greek and later Byzantine material as well. Below this layer of loosely packed debris were at least three separate floor levels, each with considerable evidence of burning, especially in the southeast corner. The two later stroses were impossible to distinguish chronologically since they contained the same kind of material (Tower 15, Boxes 102, 107). Both contained fragments of late sixth- or early seventh-century combed amphoras of the type found in the Yassi Ada wreck and at Halieis and Kenchreai.[5] This

---

[5] *Yassi Ada*, pp. 157–160; W. W. Rudolf, "Excavations at Porto Cheli and Vicinity Preliminary Report V: The Early Byzantine Remains," *Hesperia* 48, 1979, pp. 301–302, 305–309, nos. 1–9, 11–12; Aupert, "Objets," nos. 325, 325:a, pp. 440–441.

period of use appears to have been particularly intense. Associated with it were two coins, as well as an iron knife, an ivory ring, and several other coins that broke in cleaning.[6] Both the coins and the pottery connect this period not with the emperor Justinian and his restoration of the Fortress but with the time of the Slavic invasions of the later sixth and seventh centuries.

The pottery from the earliest floor level in the tower (Box 108) can be dated to the fifth and sixth centuries, and it is probably connected with the use of the tower during the earliest phase of the Hexamilion. Below this level the excavators encountered one other stratum (Box 109), with pottery of Roman imperial date and large quantities of glass, much of it from windows like the fragments found in quantity in the Roman Bath. The only foundation that may be associated with this earlier level is the small wall, mentioned above, which runs northwest–southeast in the middle of the western side of the tower. This wall is of poor rubble construction, and it cannot be connected with any other known structure in the area.

Inside and outside the tower, in the area of the gate, and on the west face of the Fortress wall many of the joints between blocks were filled with smoothed mortar, and lines were frequently scratched in the wet mortar to show the divisions, in much the same way that modern Greek builders delineate their rough masonry walls. This technique occurs also in the area of the National Highway and the Roman Bath (pp. 32, 35, and 40 above) and was used to draw two graffiti on the walls. On the north wall, near the northeast corner, is a fish (Fig. 26; Pl. 31:a), *ca.* 0.42 m. long and 0.13 m. wide, with its nose pointing upward toward the west.[7] Another graffito, *ca.* 0.30 m. high and *ca.* 0.30 m. wide, is on the east wall near the northeast corner; it is broken at the top but seems to resemble either a cross or a bow of some sort (perhaps a crossbow, Fig. 26; Pl. 31:b). Other graffiti are inscribed in plaster outside the tower (p. 100 below).

Investigation of Tower 15 naturally involved a close examination of how the tower was attached to the Hexamilion and to the West Fortress Wall. The east face of the east wall of the tower butts up against the northern face of the Hexamilion.[8] The east wall, however, continues through the Hexamilion, and it is plastered and finished on its east face. This wall also bonds with the southern face of the Hexamilion, showing that the tower and the Hexamilion were built at the same time.

On the western side of the tower, the situation is more complicated, partly because the entrance to the tower obscures the meeting of the walls, while the Hexamilion changes direction at just this point. Thus, west of Tower 15 are two sections of masonry representing the south face of the Hexamilion. One, preserved in a section that steps down steeply from east to west, maintains the northeast–southwest line that the Hexamilion follows east of Tower 15 (Fig. 24; Pl. 31:c). Exactly at the point where the West Fortress Wall leaves the tower, however, another face is visible, going almost due west. This, in fact, represents a change in the direction of the Hexamilion to the course that it follows westward toward the Roman Bath. It is peculiar, however, that surviving masonry on the Hexamilion west of Tower 15 preserves clear traces of both directions of the wall and that the West Fortress Wall is not bonded to any of the faces of the Hexamilion or the tower west wall.

One should not, however, conclude from this any lack of contemporaneity in the various parts of the fortification. The masonry technique used in at least the lower stretches of all the elements is exactly the same, and, as we have seen, the southern face of the Hexamilion is bonded to the east wall of the tower. Furthermore, the entrance into the tower, into the West Fortress Wall and through the

[6] a) Clement, 474 (IC 68-72), Justin II (A.D. 568/9): follis. *DOC* I, p. 206, nos. 25:b, 1, 2.

b) Clement, 494 (IC 68-76), Maurice (A.D. 587/8): follis. Cf. *DOC* I, p. 324, no. 96.

[7] Graffiti of fish are fairly common in the Corinthia in late antiquity: see O. Broneer, *Corinth*, I, iv, *The South Stoa*, Princeton 1954, p. 139, pl. 43:2, and the references cited there.

[8] It will be remembered that the east and west interior walls do not bond with the south wall (i.e., with the northern face of the Hexamilion).

Hexamilion, must have been built in the fortification's earliest phase. The entrance ties all three elements closely together; its sides are carefully finished rather than hacked, while the column drum from the Theater (p. 96 above) suggests contemporaneity of this section with that of the Hexamilion southeast of the Northeast Gate, where other sections of the same columns were used.

To the west of Tower 15 the direction of the Hexamilion appears to have been determined by a pre-existing structure (or structures) on which the fortification was built (p. 44 above), while to the east the Hexamilion had to follow the slightly irregular edge of the Great Ravine. The gate through the Hexamilion west of Tower 15 was an appropriate place to change the direction of the wall and to allow a certain overlap to act as a kind of buttress in the area behind the gate and the tower. In addition, the surviving ruins suggest that three teams were working in this general area simultaneously, one on the Hexamilion east of the tower, a second on the tower itself, and a third on the gateway west of the tower. In such an arrangement, the crew that built the tower continued its work on the Hexamilion to the west, perhaps building this section before the crew on the gate began to work. The gate was obviously built to continue the line of the Hexamilion west of the Fortress, and a part of the Hexamilion already built by the crew in the tower apparently had to be partially dismantled.

This important gateway through the Hexamilion is located 1.50 m. west of Tower 15. It allowed traffic to pass through the Hexamilion under the watchful eye of defenders in the tower and without entering the Fortress itself (Fig. 24). The gateposts, set nearly flush with the north face of the Hexamilion, were *ca.* 0.45 m. wide (north–south through the gate); behind the posts the reveals were set back *ca.* 0.25 m. The posts used a series of interlocking blocks laid in alternating horizontal and vertical courses with large vertical blocks in the first course on the north face (Pl. 32:a, b). These blocks were beveled on the exterior (north) corners facing the roadway; at a height of *ca.* 2.30 m. above the road surface, a pair of console blocks projected over the gateway to receive the lintel blocks.[9] The blocks of the east post were found *in situ*, while only a single vertical block survived on the north face of the west post. The console block for this post, however, was found a short distance to the north. The gate clearly faced northward, and the interior sides of all the post blocks were cut away at right angles to form the reveals and allow the doors to open flush against them. This meant, of course, that the doors opened inward, as they did on the gates in the Fortress.

The gate is 1.56 m. wide between the posts and *ca.* 2.40 m. between the reveals. Two pivot holes are cut in the threshold block behind the posts; both were equipped with iron fittings for the door pivots. The west cutting is square and *ca.* 0.15 m. on a side, while the east cutting is more rounded, with an uneven rectangular extension to the east. In the reveals immediately behind the gateposts and at a height of 1.20 m. above the threshold are square cuttings for the bolt, *ca.* 0.25 m. square. On the east reveal the bolt hole is *ca.* 0.27 m. deep, while on the west it is 2.60 m. deep; this depth would have allowed the full withdrawal of the bolt into the western reveal when the doors were opened, avoiding the complicated arrangements that were used in the Northeast Gate. We should thus restore a single bolt in this gate. At some time the builders made two vertical cuttings, *ca.* 0.019 m. wide on the east and 0.07 m. wide on the west, downward from the bolt holes. What these were to accomplish is not at all clear. In any case, both were filled in with small stones and tile and plastered over at some time before the gateway was closed and filled with debris.[10]

---

[9] The use of console blocks or corbels to support the lintel is common in early Byzantine fortifications. In Constantinople the outer wall of the Rhegion Gate (Kirchen, *Landmauer* I, pls. 4, 37; II, p. 65, fig. 19) and the Siliviri Kapi (Meyer-Plath and Schneider, *Landmauer* II, pl. 31:d) use this technique. For a later use, see the Carmadino Gate (see footnote 3 above, p. 96).

[10] The plaster covering these cuttings seems to be the same as that from the original phase of the Hexamilion. This apparent inconsistency is difficult to resolve.

The roadway through the gate was paved with roughly square blocks, *ca.* 0.70 m. on a side. This paving extended over the whole area outside the gate, from the west wall of Tower 15 at least to the later wall that ran off to the north some 8.30 m. to the west (Fig. 24). Inside the gate, the paving was less grand, with smaller, irregular stones used, but of course some of this paving may represent later repairs of the road surface. Above the paving in the gateway itself was a hard-packed layer of dirt containing at least ten iron nails, which may once have been from the doors. The pottery in this layer was mostly nondistinct Roman and late Roman coarse ware, but one fragment of Byzantine pottery suggests that the gateway was kept open until at least the thirteenth century.[11]

At some time, however, the gate was blocked by a rough wall of rubble faced with larger blocks and carelessly set into position at the north end of the gateway. The north face of the wall was more or less flush with the northern face of the Hexamilion (Pl. 32:c). This blocking is, of course, reminiscent of the similar closures of the Northeast and South Gates of the Fortress, but the technique here is very different and less careful than the work at the other gates. The fill under the blocking wall contained several pieces of Byzantine brown-glazed pottery of the eleventh or twelfth century. One piece of later pottery provides a *terminus post quem* in the fourteenth century for construction of the wall,[12] showing that the late blocking wall cannot have been constructed until the fourteenth or fifteenth century at the earliest. Probably, it is to be connected with the refortification of the Hexamilion, either in 1415 or later in the century.[13]

In the area of the gate a number of graffiti were scratched in the plaster between blocks while it was still wet. Two are on the west face of the east reveal; both are very difficult now to read. One is a series of letters ending in a cross; they perhaps read ISTHMIA. The other is a circle surmounted by a cross, perhaps representing a crown. Another series of graffiti, fortunately better preserved, is on the south face of the Hexamilion immediately west of the gate. It represents three ships, all sailing toward the west (Ill. 16). The first two ships are obviously galleys, since a series of oars extends down from the deck. The third (easternmost) ship has a rounded keel, sails, and no oars; it is undoubtedly meant to represent a different kind of vessel. A ladderlike device extends in front of this round-bottomed ship; it is uncertain whether this is part of the rigging or an indication that one of the last two ships has boarded the other. To the west of the three ships is another figure: it may be one more ship, or it may represent a standing figure with a full skirt. Graffiti of ships are very common in Byzantine times, but they are notoriously difficult to date.[14]

With its outer courtyard, ornamental consoles, and beveled gateposts, the gate through the Hexamilion presented a monumental face to the north, and the looming presence of Tower 15 by the entrance must have impressed any barbarian who thought to force the doors. The gateway,

---

[11] Glazed body sherd (IPB 68-39): p.L. 0.038 m., p.W. 0.023 m. Coarse red clay (2.5YR 5/8) with many large voids, fired brown at surfaces. Body sherd preserving floor, probably of a large plate or bowl, including beginning of foot. On interior pale green glaze probably over light slip; on exterior traces of grayish slip. Cf. *Corinth* XI, nos. 282–284, 286–292, fig. 44, 13th century.

[12] Sgraffito bowl (IPB 68-38), Pl. 32:d: p.H. 0.041 m., p.W. 0.073 m. Body sherd. Reddish yellow clay (5YR 6/6) with a few large white inclusions and many voids. White slip and light-green glaze on interior. Series of concentric sgraffito circles and brown painted design in center. Cf. *Corinth* XI, nos. 1416–1418, p. 144, 14th century.

[13] Cleaning west of Tower 15 revealed a late roadway across the Hexamilion between the original gate and the North Drain. This road simply crossed over the top of the preserved masonry of the Hexamilion. Presumably it replaced the road through the gate sometime after the latter was blocked.

[14] R. L. Scranton, *Corinth*, XVI, *Mediaeval Architecture in the Central Area of Corinth*, Princeton 1957, pp. 137–139, figs. 14, 15, show both a round-bottomed ship and a galley (dated later than 12th century). See also the graffiti of ships on the stairway to the Baths of Aphrodite, *Corinth* III, ii, pp. 270–271, fig. 221, dated to the Venetian or Turkish periods; M. Goudas, «Μεσαιωνικὰ χαράγματα πλοίων ἐπὶ τοῦ Θησείου», Βυζαντινίς 2, 1911–1912, pp. 329–357; A. K. Orlandos, Τὰ χαράγματα τοῦ Παρθενῶνος, Athens 1973, esp. nos. 107, 112, pp. 93, 95.

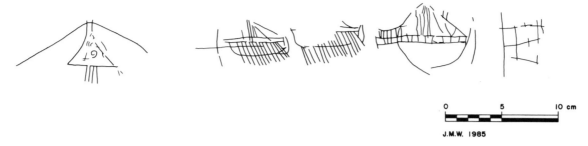

ILL. 16. Graffiti near the gate beside Tower 15

however, was relatively narrow, almost a meter narrower than the passageway through the Northeast Gate, certainly not wide enough for two carts to pass abreast, and its appearance from the Peloponnesian side was less impressive. The threshold block was not very worn, although there are wheel marks on the western post where drivers apparently cut the corner short. Nevertheless, there must have been some reason for the construction of this gate so close to the Fortress wall. Presumably, the gate allowed traffic passing north and south through the Hexamilion to be routed around the Fortress and thus avoid the passage through the Northeast and the South Gates. These latter gateways were clearly more grand, and the main traffic through the Hexamilion presumably passed through them, but there might be military reasons to divert traffic around the Fortress to the passageway below Tower 15.

The northern face of the Hexamilion west of the gate seems to have been built following an earlier wall (see p. 44 above; Pl. 33:a). The southern face of the Hexamilion here is full of problems, and it seems to be marked by several periods of construction. Immediately to the west of the gateway, the Hexamilion is ca. 2.35 m. wide, with a south face made primarily of roughly coursed rubble and mortar. This probably represents the earliest Hexamilion phase of the fortification, although a facing of cut blocks might originally have been placed against the rubble-and-mortar core, bringing the width to what is more normal for the Hexamilion. That the line of this south face was the original interior of the Hexamilion, however, is suggested by the finished south face immediately west of the gate, built of ashlar blocks (Pl. 32:b), and by the alternative line of the Hexamilion east of the gate, which is roughly the same width as to the west. We might also note that 2.35 m. is approximately the normal width of the Fortress wall. Perhaps the builders responsible for this section of the Hexamilion were working from plans drawn up for that wall.

Built up against the rubble and mortar of the south face is a large pier or bastion, some 10.32 m. long (Fig. 24). It rests directly upon sandy soil, in most cases without any apparent foundations, and it survives to a maximum height of 3.80 m. The bastion is nowhere bonded to the Hexamilion but is built directly up against the masonry that stood at the time of its construction. In the center the bastion overruns the core of the Hexamilion, showing that the Hexamilion facing walls had fallen to this level when the bastion was constructed. At the northwest corner of the bastion are six courses of cut blocks resting on a foundation course (Pl. 31:c), but it is not certain whether the six courses belong to the bastion or to the earlier Hexamilion construction. The bastion may originally have been faced with cut blocks, but no trace of them survives; all that is left is the roughly rectangular mass of rubble and mortar. Presumably, the bastion was constructed to protect this vulnerable section of wall and to provide greater firepower to defend the gateway than could be massed from Tower 15 alone. In the absence of stratigraphic evidence, we can only note that the bastion is later than the construction of the Hexamilion and that some time must have elapsed for the partial collapse of the walls here. In view of the massiveness of the construction, the bastion might reasonably be assigned to the reign of Justinian.

Just to the south of this bastion is a circular structure, *ca.* 2.19 m. in diameter and preserved to a height of *ca.* 2.10 m. above its floor (Pl. 33:b). The interior is faced with alternating courses of bricks and small stones, but above the doorway it is built of smooth, slightly curved stones and tiles whose interior faces have vitrified because of intense heat. The structure was undoubtedly a lime kiln, and its entrance was from the west, through a vaulted passage *ca.* 0.80 m. long, 1.45 m. high, and 0.80 m. wide. The floor of the kiln was of packed earth overlaid with lime, which had turned into mortar, but no marble, burned or otherwise, was found in the interior, nor was anything precisely datable uncovered. It is not impossible, however, that the kiln was built as part of the construction works for the Hexamilion, which certainly needed tremendous quantities of mortar. It should nevertheless be remembered that at least two of the other lime kilns discovered near the Hexamilion (one west of the Roman Bath and one north of the Northeast Gate; pp. 38 and 79–80 above) must be assigned to a late period. Northeast of the kiln was a smaller (*ca.* 0.70 × 0.80 m.), mortar-lined pit. This was apparently also used in the manufacture or use of mortar, again possibly for the construction of the defense or one of its repairs.

Immediately west of the lime kiln are two parallel east–west walls running roughly in the same direction as the Hexamilion and *ca.* 5.7 m. south of its north face. The northern of these two walls was built in rubble and mortar and is relatively well preserved, while the other is represented only by a thin layer of stones laid in a deep footing trench cut in the hardpan. The purpose and date of these two walls remain elusive, but it is tantalizing to note that the southern of the two is exactly on a line (see Fig. 24) with a heavy east–west wall encountered in the North Drain complex, some 37.5 m. to the west (see p. 47 above).

In the area of Tower 15 two structures of late date were discovered. One was built into the angle made by the West Fortress Wall and the Hexamilion just outside the entrance to the tower, while the other lay to the south of the lime kiln. There is no evidence to date the latter, but some conclusions can be drawn about the former. The two rubble walls that closed off the angle just south of the tower were apparently built on hardpan, and the deep fill inside the room contained pottery dating from Roman times until the fifteenth century.[15] Within the fill were two coins of the eleventh century.[16]

The area just outside the entrance to the tower obviously had to be kept open as long as the tower was in use, which probably explains why Byzantine pottery and coins were found right down to hardpan here; the room formed by the south wall of the tower, the West Fortress Wall, and the two rubble walls was obviously periodically cleaned out. Besides the two coins found in this room, 13 other Anonymous Byzantine coins were found in the general vicinity of Tower 15. These coins, quite common in excavations elsewhere in the Aegean, are rather rare at Isthmia, and the large number around Tower 15 testifies to considerable activity in the late tenth and eleventh centuries in the area. One cannot, of course, date the rubble walls, since they could have been erected at any time from the early fifth century to the time the dump of Byzantine material was deposited within the room, effectively blocking access to the tower through the original entrance. From the numismatic evidence (p. 98 above), the passage into the tower was still open at least as late as the 570's.

---

[15] Although Roman pottery was more common toward the bottom of this fill, 13th-century wares were found at the very bottom of the deposit. Three pieces of "Slavic" pottery were in the fill (Box 51); cf. Box 54, from the area immediately outside the gate, which has considerable quantities of this ware.

[16] a) Clement, 517 (IC 68-42), Byzantine Anonymous, Class D: *ca.* A.D. 1050–*ca.* 1060. *DOC* III, ii, pp. 685–687.

 b) Clement, 519 (IC 68-54), Byzantine Anonymous, Class D: same as preceding.

Evidence from the fill in the room outside shows that the passage was probably open through Late Byzantine times: the pottery in the fill dates as late as the fourteenth century. The material was presumably dumped into the room in a general clean-up of the area, perhaps at the time the gateway outside was closed and possibly as part of the effort to block the fortifications altogether.

TOWER 14

Tower 14 is located *ca.* 54 meters south of Tower 15 along the West Fortress Wall (Figs. 8, 27, Pl. 33:c, d). Excavators first explored this area in 1967, when the exterior of the tower was investigated, while further exploration was carried out south of the tower in 1969.[17] At Tower 14 the West Fortress Wall is 2.20 m. thick; it is constructed with cut blocks on each face and a rubble-and-mortar core. The tower walls are built in the same style and are 1.62–1.67 m. thick; the tower forms an irregular rectangle, 4.61 m. and 4.92 m. on the north and south and 6.77 m. on the west (making the tower almost a perfect square if one counts the thickness of the Fortress wall in the length of the north and south walls).

The blocks of the interior of the tower were blackened by fire and many have inscribed crosses, similar to those found at Tower 15 (p. 95 above). Large numbers of voussoir blocks found in the tower and in the vicinity suggest that the upper level of the tower was originally vaulted; many of the voussoirs show traces of burning only on their lower curved surface, indicating that the vaulting may still have been intact at a time when heavy burning occurred within the tower. A floor level in the tower was revealed at an elevation of +39.71 m., 2.18 m. below the highest preserved masonry on the tower walls. This was presumably not the original tower floor, but excavation was not continued below it. The fill inside the tower unfortunately was completely mixed, and no chronological conclusions can be derived from it. In addition, the relatively low level of the preserved masonry of the tower does not allow any further speculation about its original height or arrangement.

Doorways were cut in both the east and the west faces of the tower, but these were clearly not part of the original plan. The doorway in the east wall is cut through the West Fortress Wall and gave access to the ground floor of the tower from the Fortress (Pl. 34:a). It is near the center of the east wall, with its north side *ca.* 1.90 m. south of the interior face of the north tower wall; it is roughly 1.00 m. wide and 1.55 m. high on the west. Its top is formed by a false corbeled arch: the opening was simply created by the removal of the wall blocks. The floor of the passageway is the second course of blocks above the foundations. The doorway in the west wall, leading from the interior of Tower 14 into the undefended land beyond, is near the southwest corner of the tower; it is 1.00 m. wide and of uncertain height. A block *ca.* 0.23 m. above floor level was recut as a threshold block, and there is a cutting which may have been used as a pivot. On the sides of the doorway are other cuttings which may have been used to secure a bolt.

Some 1.44 m. north of the tower, another passageway runs east and west through the West Fortress Wall (Pl. 34:b, c). This is the so-called West Gate of the Fortress. It is unevenly 1.56 m. to 2.02 m. wide, and the sides of the passageway were simply hacked through the facing and the core of the Fortress wall. Well-worn threshold blocks survive on either end of the passageway, suggesting that the gateway once accommodated considerable traffic. On the west face of the gate, a single block of the north door jamb is preserved, and there is a circular pivot hole cut in the threshold block behind the jamb (Pl. 34:b). The jamb and pivot hole show that, at least in one period, doors stood at the west face of the gate and that the doors opened inward, allowing the gate to close off access to the Fortress.

[17] Clement, 1968, p. 142; Clement, 1970, pp. 163–164.

Oscar Broneer suggested that one of the main routes through the Isthmus in Roman (and possibly earlier) times passed over the hill that was marked by the Roman monumental arch and then divided somewhere in the area that was to become the Fortress. One branch of the road passed to the Temple of Poseidon, while the other went toward the Theater and the buildings that lay north of it.[18] The latter road must have passed very close to Tower 14. Indeed, earlier observers thought that the West Gate was one of the original entrances to the Fortress (which, it should be remembered, they thought was the temenos of the Sanctuary).[19] The principal gates of the Fortress were blocked at a relatively early date (pp. 83 and 93–94 above), and some means must have been found to allow the passage of traffic. The West Gate at least partially filled this need, although it is not located in a place that would allow communication with the north and east. Further, the West Gate pierces the Fortress wall rather than the Hexamilion. Perhaps traffic from the north and east had to cross the Hexamilion at the gate west of Tower 15 and then enter the Fortress through the West Gate (although the gate in the Hexamilion was itself blocked at a late date; p. 100 above).

In any case, it is important to know when the West Gate was built. A coin of the early fourteenth century was found in the gateway at the bottom of one of the threshold blocks.[20] This coin must have found its way into the roadway either when the passageway was cut through the Fortress wall or while the roadway was open. The coin does not tell us unequivocally when the passageway was made, but it may be significant that no earlier material was found in the roadway fill; it is unlikely that the gate was constructed long before the fourteenth century. The coin also shows clearly that the roadway was already in use in the early fourteenth century, a century earlier than Manuel II's rebuilding of the fortifications. Probably, the West Gate was constructed in the twelfth or thirteenth century, when heavy activity in the Fortress seems to have resumed.

In the area of Tower 14 there are walls of several buildings of late medieval date which seem to have no connection with the military function of the Fortress. The only building for which all the walls are preserved is a rectangular structure built up against the south face of Tower 14, making use of the south tower wall and the west face of the Fortress wall (Fig. 27). The other walls are constructed of rubble and mortar, 0.48–0.55 m. wide. The south wall is 6.68 m. long, the west wall is 4.95 m., and the north wall extends 1.92 m. beyond the southwest corner of the tower. In the northwest corner of the building there was a doorway ca. 1.62 m. wide. An enormous amount of debris from its final destruction covered the floor of the building; among the debris were fourteen coins,[21] and large quantities of pottery also came from this level.[22]

---

[18] *Isthmia* II, pp. 18–22, 87–89.

[19] Monceaux ("Fouilles," 1884, pp. 276–277, pl. 38) thought he had found a triple entrance into the "temenos", and he placed it *south* of Tower 14; this error was repeated by Fowler and Stillwell (*Corinth* I, i, pp. 62–63, fig. 26) and corrected by Jenkins and Megaw ("Researches," pp. 74–75).

[20] Clement, 568 (IC 904), Philip of Savoy (A.D. 1301–1307), Pl. 34:d, e: Clarenza. Cf. *Corinth* VI, p. 153, no. 17.

[21] a) Clement, 133 (IC 873), Crispus (A.D. 317–320): PROVIDEN-TIAECAESS. *RIC* VII, p. 604, no. 31.

    b) Clement, 501 (IC 897), Anonymous Byzantine, Class A1 (A.D. 970–976?). *DOC* III, ii, pp. 648–649.

    c) Clement, 567 (IC 907), Isabelle de Villehardouin (A.D. 1297–1302): Clarenza. *Corinth* VI, p. 153, no. 13.

    d) Clement 591 (IC 846), 594 (IC 850), 595 (IC 852), 596 (IC 853), 597 (IC 858), 598 (IC 862), Antonio Venerio (A.D. 1382–1400): Cross and Lion of St. Mark. *Corinth* VI, p. 159, no. 55.

    e) Clement, 613 (IC 856), Michele Steno (A.D. 1400–1413), Pl. 35:a, b: Cross and Lion of St. Mark. *Corinth* VI, p. 159, no. 56.

    f) Clement, 625 (IC 864), Venetian colonial, uncertain.

    g) Clement, 628 (IC 868), as preceding, although perhaps a forgery.

    h) Clement, 629 (IC 935), 631 (IC 948), Venetian colonial, uncertain.

    Besides the 11 Venetian coins found in this structure, another 14 were found in the area of Tower 14. This should be contrasted with other areas, for example, Tower 15 (where 1 Venetian coin was found), Northeast Gate (6), and Tower 2 (7).

[22] The following are representative of the pottery from this level:

With the exception of the two earlier coins (Clement, 133, 501), all this material is from the fourteenth and early fifteenth centuries, probably representing the period of occupation of the building. The structure, it will be remembered, lay just outside the Fortress and was built up against the exterior wall, undoubtedly when the Fortress was not being used for military purposes. It is probably significant that the coin series from the building comes to an abrupt end with an issue of Michele Steno (1400–1413), which may have been struck just before Manuel II rebuilt the Hexamilion in 1415. This building would then have been a threat to the security of the Fortress, and it was probably abandoned and perhaps demolished as part of the fortification project.

The other late buildings in the area of Tower 14 are not so easy to comprehend, and none of them have been excavated in their entirety. On the west side of the Fortress wall at least one other structure north of the West Gate must have existed, represented by a rubble-and-mortar wall 3.90 m. long and 0.52 m. wide (Fig. 27). This was undoubtedly the south wall of a building that fronted on the roadway through the Fortress wall, but none of its other walls have been excavated. Some 21 meters south of the south face of Tower 14 another late rubble wall butts up against the West Fortress Wall. It is *ca.* 0.55 m. wide and continues roughly west for *ca.* 6.74 m. before it turns south for another 1.62 m. (Fig. 27).

On the east side of the Fortress wall at least two other structures must have existed, on either side of the roadway through the wall. The building to the north is represented by a single rubble-and-mortar wall, 0.50 m. wide, which runs off from the west face of the Fortress wall at an oblique angle for a distance of 3.95 m. and then turns north for 0.55 m. before it disappears into unexcavated ground. This wall has a window or doorway, 1.38 m. wide, facing out into the roadway, 1.20 m. east of the east face of the West Fortress Wall. The building to the south is defined by two roughly parallel rubble-and-masonry walls, *ca.* 0.60–0.65 m. wide and 8.20–8.60 m. long. The northern of the two walls has a window facing onto the roadway, 0.74 m. east of the east face of the

---

a) Sgraffito bowl (IPB 69-40), Pl. 35:c: H. 0.117 m., Diam. 0.266 m., Diam. of foot 0.117 m. Restored in plaster from many pieces. Coarse red clay (2.5YR 5/6) with some large white inclusions, fired buff on exterior. Large bowl with string-cut disk foot and straight, flaring sides. Vertical rim with two deep, wide grooves on exterior, cut back sharply on interior. White slip and brown glaze on interior and just over rim. Design of *ca.* 10 incised concentric circles under rim, under which is a series of incised pendant triangles, each of which contains a careless sgraffito spiral design in another pendant triangle; under the triangles is a series of 2–3 concentric circles; central medallion: incised zigzag motif with filling ornament of sgraffito spirals surrounded by sgraffito lines, the whole surrounded by incised concentric circles. On floor: marks of three triangular kiln supports; extraneous pieces of clay adhere to interior. See discussion in *Corinth* XI, pp. 138–140 (but with no good parallels); MacKay, "More Byzantine Pottery," p. 264: "These bowls . . . do not appear until the later thirteenth century."

b) Sgraffito bowl (IPB 69-43), Pl. 35:d: H. 0.071 m., Diam. 0.152 m., Diam. of foot 0.060 m. Restored in plaster from many fragments. Hard, coarse red clay (2.5YR 5/6), evenly fired with many large white inclusions and some quartz. Small bowl with small, low, slightly flaring ring foot; plain vertical rim. White slip and yellow glaze on interior and over rim; green glaze on rim and in splotches on floor. Series of incised concentric circles under rim, between two of which is a series of incised pendant triangles. Inside these triangles is a series of smaller pendant sgraffito triangles with filling device of sgraffito spiral. Central medallion surrounded by two incised circles: four roughly parallel, incised lines on crosshatched sgraffito ground. Cf. *Corinth* XI, pp. 159–161 (mid-13th to early 14th century, but with no good numismatic evidence), and IPB 69-42, from same deposit, for identical shape.

c) Cooking pot (IPB 67-4), Pl. 35:e: rest. H. 0.195 m., rest. Diam. 0.146 m. Restored in plaster from many fragments. Hard, coarse red clay (2.5YR 5/8) with many inclusions. Tall cooking pot with round bottom, slightly rounded nearly vertical sides, flaring rim, triangular in section; vertical handles from below midpoint on body to bottom of rim. Two concentric grooves under upper handle attachment and on upper surface of rim. Brown glaze on interior and over rim. Cf. MacKay, "More Byzantine Pottery," nos. 127–133, pp. 299–300, fig. 5, pl. 69; no exact parallels, but these resemble IPB 67-4 in general form (later 13th and early 14th centuries); cf. also IPB 67-3 (from same deposit) for same shape in slightly smaller size.

In the same deposit is the following pottery: IP 3660, 3692, IPB 67-1, 67-2, 67-3, 67-5, 67-6, 69-41, 69-42, 69-44. All this material will be presented fully in the Isthmia volume on Byzantine pottery.

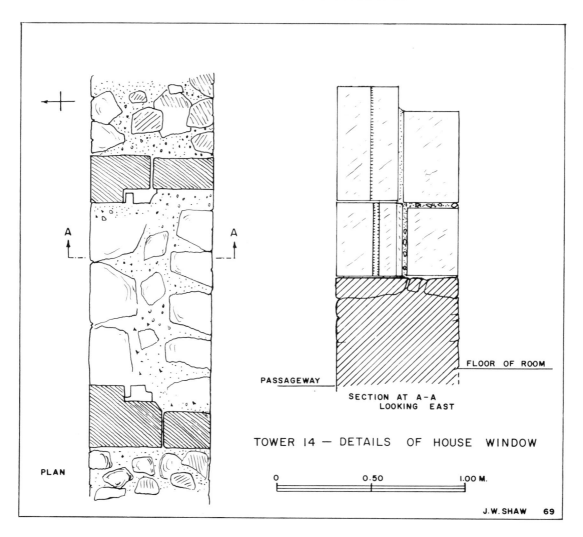

ILL. 17. Details of the window east of Tower 14

Fortress wall and *ca.* one meter wide. The bottom of the window is 0.50 m. above the paved floor of the room and 0.59 m. above the paved roadway outside; it is fitted with slots to allow the insertion of a grill or some other device, presumably to protect the building from passersby on the street (Ill. 17; Pl. 36:a). The upper part of the window jambs was cut back to allow a frame to be placed flush against the back of the window, while the lower block (0.40 m. high) has vertical slots, *ca.* 0.03 m. wide, into which a grill device could be lowered to close off the bottom part of the window. How this window worked is not completely clear, but the basis was the division of the window into two parts, an upper and a lower section. The slot in the lower part does not seem wide enough to accommodate two window frames, so the arrangement must have been designed primarily to open and close the lower section. Perhaps the easiest explanation is to imagine shutters or other closures on the window, divided horizontally in the center, in the manner of a "Dutch door"; a grill in the lower part would allow air and light to enter the room but maintain security when that section was open.

The southernmost of the pair of walls on the east side of the Fortress wall has a doorway 0.91 m. wide. Further south, in the area of the stairways (pp. 108–109 below), there must have been at least two other structures on the east side of the Fortress wall. On the east face of the Fortress wall, just south of Tower 14, are the remains of a vaulted oven or kiln with an interior diameter of *ca.* 1.34 m., preserved to a height of 0.70 m. above the tiled floor of the room associated with it. Another oven was found in upper levels along the west face of the tower, but it was removed in the course of the exploration. Presumably, it dates to the period after the final abandonment of the Hexamilion.

This complex of structures, most of which were probably contemporary with the building just south of Tower 14, must have continued all the way to Tower 13. This is shown by a late doorway, *ca.* 0.74 m. wide, cut through the north face of Tower 13 in a manner similar to the late doorways in Tower 14.[23] There is no good dating evidence for these other buildings; those to the west of the Fortress wall were not fully excavated, while those to the east did not contain any evident destruction level such as that in the building to the south of Tower 14. A coin of Tomaso Mocenigo (Clement, 623 [IC 861], A.D. 1414–1423) found in the roadway east of the West Fortress Wall suggests that the gate remained open after Manuel II's rebuilding. The houses inside the Fortress may not have been destroyed in 1415, since they provided no threat to the defenses.

Excavation in deep levels west of Tower 14 revealed the so-called Long Wall running approximately northwest–southeast for over fifty meters (Fig. 27; Pl. 36:b [where its southern terminus is visible at the lower left], c). It is *ca.* 0.76 m. wide and set on a rubble foundation 1.13 m. wide. The wall is constructed of large, well-cut blocks, but only a single course is preserved. The Long Wall stretches northward almost to the Hexamilion west of Tower 15, although no definite traces of its northern terminus were found, probably owing to later disturbances (see p. 95 above and Fig. 24 [dashed line]). In the south the wall comes to an abrupt end *ca.* 14.50 m. south of Tower 14.

This wall and its chronology present many complexities that cannot be fully discussed here.[24] The area seems to have been subject to considerable leveling before the earliest construction, presumably because the land originally sloped down precipitously to the west. The Long Wall was set in a broad footing trench, cut down deeper on the west than on the east. A similar footing trench, 1.0 m. wide and 2.80 m. east of the Long Wall, was completely robbed out, but it suggests another wall parallel to the Long Wall to the east. The footing trenches were filled with a reddish brown soil, which contained five coins[25] and considerable amounts of pottery, the latter already studied by Jeanne Marty Peppers.[26]

The pottery confirms a date in the third quarter of the first century after Christ for this material, and this presumably dates construction of the Long Wall.[27] It is known that there was considerable building activity in the Sanctuary in connection with Nero's visit to the site in A.D. 66 or 67[28] and presumably again after the earthquake of A.D. 77.[29] It is significant that nothing earlier than the first century was found in this area; apparently the Roman imperial period witnessed the first construction in this part of the Sanctuary.

The blocks of this Long Wall are evenly set on the western face but not along the east; this, together with the packing along the eastern face of the wall, suggests that the interior of the building was to the east, and the footing for a parallel wall 2.80 m. to the east supports this view. No returns

[23] In 1952 and 1954, Oscar Broneer (1953, p. 185; 1955, p. 124, pl. 48:c) excavated the area around Tower 13.

[24] See Peppers, pp. 136–214.

[25] a) Clement, 44 (IC 69-49), Corinth under Caligula (A.D. 37–41): Duoviri. *Corinth* VI, p. 20, no. 45.

b) Clement, 47 (IC 69-52), Corinth under Claudius (A.D. 49/50 or 50/51): Duoviri. *Corinth* VI, pp. 7, 21, no. 51.

c) Clement, 48 (IC 69-53), 50 (IC 871), 52 (IC 871), Corinth under Nero (A.D. 51/52?): Duoviri. *Corinth* VI, pp. 7, 22, no. 54.

[26] Peppers, fig. 5:d, p. 352; see discussion pp. 211–212, note 5.

[27] Peppers, Group A, pp. 142–210.

[28] Gebhard, *Theater*, pp. 86–87.

[29] See A. B. West, *Corinth*, VIII, ii, *Latin Inscriptions, 1896–1926*, Cambridge, Mass. 1931, no. 20, pp. 18–19; Gregory and Mills, "Roman Arch," pp. 424–426.

or any perpendicular walls connected with the structure have been found, however, testimony to the thoroughness with which the building was cannibalized when the Hexamilion was constructed. The Roman structure, nevertheless, must have been an important one.

Exactly at the point where the Long Wall breaks off in the south another wall begins, running somewhat southeast in a line parallel to the line of the Long Wall but offset slightly to the east (Fig. 27; Pl. 36:b, c). This wall is *ca.* 0.33–0.48 m. wide; the blocks are laid evenly along their western face but unevenly along the east (in the same fashion as the Long Wall). There is likewise a packing against the east face of this wall. After 5.22 m., this wall butts up against another, which runs westward at right angles, presumably part of the same structure or complex. The east–west wall forms the lowest course of a three-stepped construction which ascends to the south, rising 0.31 m. in the first step and 0.24 m. in the second. The three-stepped construction is slightly more carefully built than the smaller northwest–southeast wall, but it too disappears after a distance of *ca.* 5.41 m. The same packing as that found to the east was encountered south of the three-stepped construction, along with a rubble-and-mortar foundation of indeterminate size, which seems to have run off to the east where it was later built over by the West Fortress Wall.

The building sequence in this area is very complex, and ancient construction connected with the Hexamilion has disturbed the stratigraphy. Certainly, the building represented by the Long Wall was the earliest on the site, probably datable to the last third of the first century after Christ. At some point, perhaps after the destruction of this earlier building, the structure represented by the small northwest–southeast wall and the three-stepped construction was built, cutting through the Long Wall at its southern end. The date for this phase is uncertain, but it must have been after the construction of the Long Wall and before that of the Hexamilion. Late pottery mixed in with the earlier debris and a coin of Diocletian suggest a possible date at the end of the third or the early fourth century.[30]

Above the two phases of Roman walls is a burned layer and above that, late Roman sherds. The burned layer may be further testimony to Alaric's visit to the Isthmus (A.D. 396). When the Hexamilion was constructed in response to that event, all but the lowest courses of the earlier Roman buildings were removed and used to construct the Fortress.

South of Tower 14, between it and Tower 13, are traces of stairways used to reach the fighting level of the Fortress wall (Fig. 27). Thus, south of Tower 14 for a distance of approximately 7 meters, the Fortress wall is *ca.* 2.32 m. wide. From this point southward for a distance of *ca.* 28.22 m., the wall widens to 3.38–3.48 m. to support two stairways. The stairways were "opposed" to each other in that the northern stairway rose to the south, while the southern stairway rose toward the north.

The foundation of the northern stairway is a small construction of several courses *ca.* 0.90 m. high, butted up against the east face of the Fortress wall and resting on hardpan at a level of +39.42 m. (Pl. 37:a). A layer of clay *ca.* 0.50 m. above the hardpan probably represents ground level at the time of the construction of the Fortress. Above the foundation are six steps, bonded into the east face of the Fortress wall. The lower four steps are broken on the east and preserved only to a width of *ca.* 0.25–0.30 m., but the two uppermost preserved steps are 0.74 m. wide, *ca.* 0.18 m. of which is bonded into the wall. The width of the stairway must originally have covered the whole of the widened part of the wall, that is, more than one meter. These stairs have a mean rise of 0.32 m. and a mean tread of 0.36 m. At about the same level as the fifth step (i.e., at *ca.* +41.94 m.) is a

---

[30] Clement, 114 (IC 69-50), Diocletian (A.D. 295/6 to 297/8): CONCORDIAMILITVM. *RIC* VI, pp. 531, 532, nos. 13, 21.

Note also Clement, 115 (IC 69-19), another issue of Diocletian found in the area of Tower 14.

rubble wall, *ca.* 0.70 m. wide, butted up against the east face of the Fortress wall (Fig. 27). This is certainly the wall of a later structure, similar to the small buildings discovered further north, but no floor or any dating evidence was found.

The stairway on the south rises toward the north, and five steps are preserved, bonded into the east face of the Fortress wall (Fig. 27, Pl. 37:b). These steps are apparently of similar size and rise as those on the north, but they are much less well preserved because a circular oven was constructed up against the stairway, and much of the east face of the Fortress wall was cut away.

The upper parts of these stairways are not preserved, and it is impossible to restore them with certainty. It is significant, however, that these stairs did not converge toward either Tower 13 or Tower 14 but rather to a point midway between the two towers. This is a different arrangement from what we see at the Northeast Gate and Tower 2.[31] Access into the upper room of the towers must simply have been from the fighting platform at the top of the stairs. Access into the third level of the towers, however, cannot have been by these stairways. If the top floors were supported on wooden beams, the ascent can simply have been made by a ladder. Alternatively, masonry stairs may have run up over a vault (as suggested for Tower 6 and the towers of the South Gate)[32] or have doubled back in the opposite direction from the lower flights, running up to the top of the tower behind a protective parapet wall. This latter system can be seen on tower 50 in the Land Walls of Constantinople.[33]

Several floor levels were identified in the area of the stairs, one of them probably connected with the oven south of the south stairway, and a rubble wall which runs eastward from the Fortress wall just south of the oven. Another wall and another floor may antedate construction of the Hexamilion, but not enough material was found to allow any more specific chronological indications.

South of the more southern stairway, the Fortress wall is again *ca.* 2.42 m. wide for a distance of *ca.* 7.33 m. After this, it once again widens to *ca.* 2.74 m. and turns slightly to the west as it approaches Tower 13. The widened area continues for a further *ca.* 2.30 m. This area was not investigated, but it is likely that there was a single stairway here rising to the fighting platform just north of Tower 13.

Three graves were discovered south of Tower 14 and west of the West Fortress Wall (Fig. 27). These were all oriented east–west, with the skeletons' heads at the west, and so they are presumably Christian. There were no chronologically diagnostic finds in the graves, but all of them were at a relatively high level and so are presumably rather late. Grave 2 (Fig. 27) was built in the robbed-out line of the north wall of the building located *ca.* 21 meters south of Tower 14 (p. 105 above). If we assume that this building, like the others in the area, was destroyed at the time of the reconstruction of the Hexamilion in 1415, the grave must be dated sometime after that.

---

[31] Compare the normal arrangement at Constantinople (Kirchen, *Landmauer* I, pl. 4, wall near tower 47), and Resafa (Karnapp, *Stadtmauer*, pls. 44, 67, and *passim*), also Nikopolis (T. E. Gregory, "The Early Byzantine Fortifications of Nikopolis in Comparative Perspective," in *Nikopolis I. Proceedings of the First International Symposium on Nikopolis*, Preveza 1987, pp. 253–261).

[32] Compare the arrangement for towers 39 and 40 at Resafa (Karnapp, *Stadtmauer*, pl. 223).

[33] Meyer-Plath and Schneider, *Landmauer* II, pl. 9.

VIII
FORTRESS TOWER 2

TOWER 2 is located at the northeast corner of the Fortress at the point where the East Fortress Wall joins the Hexamilion (Figs. 8, 28, Pl. 37:c).[1] The ground below the tower drops off steeply on the east and, when the Hexamilion was constructed, on the south as well. The tower was thus strategically placed overlooking a double defile. To the north is the Great Ravine that runs across the eastern part of the Isthmus and curves around from the north side of the Fortress. To the southeast was a smaller ravine that ran from the area of the New Stadium to empty into the Great Ravine just below the tower. Today this ravine is hardly visible below the East Fortress Wall, and the highway between Kyras Vrysi and Epidauros runs through part of it. The modern landscape, however, is the result of alluviation southwest of the Hexamilion caused by blocking of the sluices between Tower 2 and S-1 (see pp. 9 and 48 above). Originally, the slope immediately southeast of the Fortress was much steeper than it is now, and as a result Tower 2 stood as a powerful bastion strengthened by its natural position.

There has been considerable destruction in the area of Tower 2, not least because of the steep declivity of the land in this area, and by the time excavation began, soil had washed up against the inside faces of the walls, covering them almost completely. Most of the northeast face of the tower had tumbled into the ravine, and a modern cart road passed over its walls, leaving only the lowest courses of the tower available for investigation.

Although Tower 2 was functionally part of the Fortress, it was actually constructed against the Hexamilion outside (i.e., to the southeast of) the Fortress proper. In this respect Tower 2 is to be contrasted with Tower 15, its counterpart in the northwest corner of the Fortress, where the West Fortress Wall meets the Hexamilion. Tower 15 was built against the Hexamilion just inside the Fortress, while Tower 2 was built outside. This different arrangement has no chronological or strategic significance but is simply another indication of the lack of consistency that characterizes the construction of the Hexamilion.

The exterior of Tower 2 is slightly irregular, its walls measuring 5.07 m. long on the north, 4.80 m. on the east, and 4.17 m. on the south. The walls are *ca.* 1.20 m. thick, constructed of two parallel rows of blocks, without any rubble-and-mortar core; the blocks on the exterior face of the tower are notably larger than those on the interior face (Pl. 37:c). Most of these blocks were apparently taken from the older buildings of the Sanctuary, and the surface of one of these was covered with plaster painted with three vertical bands of red and blue-black; the plastered face of this re-used block was turned toward the interior of the tower wall where it would have been invisible.

Several of the blocks in Tower 2 have swallowtail-clamp cuttings, and two of these in the northwest tower wall adjoin, showing that these blocks were re-used in the tower in exactly the same arrangement as in their original position (Pl. 38:a). The southeasternmost block of the southeast tower wall has such cuttings, and it is bonded to the Hexamilion, showing clearly that the Hexamilion and Tower 2 were constructed at the same time. The northwest tower wall simply butts into the Hexamilion, but given the bonding in the southeast wall of the tower, this can have no chronological or structural significance; it is simply another example of the builders' general indifference to consistent bonding.

[1] Excavation of Tower 2 was carried out in 1968. See Clement, 1969, pp. 116–118. Note that the East Fortress Wall actually runs southwest–northeast for more than half its length.

At first sight there might appear to be a difference in construction in the Hexamilion north and south of the tower: it is *ca.* 3.12 m. wide northwest of the tower and *ca.* 3.19 m. wide southeast of it, and the wall makes a noticeable jog eastward at the point of the tower attachment. As noted, however, the northwest wall of Tower 2 is clearly bonded to the Hexamilion, while the tower extends well beyond the Fortress to the southeast, showing that this section of the Hexamilion must be contemporary with the section to the north.

This leaves unexamined only the relationship between the Hexamilion and the East Fortress Wall, which is *ca.* 2.30 m. in width, nearly a meter narrower than the Hexamilion at this point. Careful examination of the join between the inner faces of the two walls (Pl. 38:b) shows that there is no bonding but that the East Fortress Wall simply butts up against the Hexamilion, which was apparently finished and plastered at this point. The rubble-and-mortar cores of the two walls similarly do not bond, although there is no facing visible on the interior (southwest) side of the Hexamilion as it butts up against the masonry of the Fortress wall. This suggests at least some chronological priority for the Hexamilion. The two walls also display some difference in construction techniques, such as the use of cut blocks in the foundations of the interior face of the Hexamilion and their almost complete absence from the foundations of the interior face of the East Fortress Wall (Pl. 38:c). At least eighteen unfluted column drums (most *ca.* 0.60 m. in diameter) were re-used in the fabric of the Hexamilion in this area, while none appear in the East Fortress Wall. In the foundations of the Fortress wall, however, there was a limestone Doric capital and cornice that may have come from the same building as at least some of the columns (Pl. 39:a); if so, this would indicate that no great interval of time elapsed between construction of the two walls.

Central to a discussion of the relationship between the Hexamilion and the East Fortress Wall is a series of "steps" discovered on the exterior of the latter as it abuts the Hexamilion (Pl. 38:c). At one time, it was thought that these were part of a passageway leading through the Hexamilion into the tower, thus indicating a phase before the construction of the East Fortress Wall.[2] It is clear now that these are not steps at all but a powerful buttress designed to strengthen this corner of the Fortress and, in fact, serving to tie the Fortress wall and the Hexamilion together.

The lowest block of this construction rests on bedrock at an elevation of +28.74 m., and three blocks rise from southwest to northeast to an elevation of +29.74 m. (Fig. 28). The blocks vary from 1.08 m. to 1.63 m. in width, and mortar from the Fortress wall overlaps the second block, showing that the wall was built after the block was in place.

A proper understanding of this structure can be gleaned from a consideration of ground level at the time the various walls were built. Bedrock in this area is relatively high, and most of the walls are footed directly on it. There was, however, obviously some overburden in antiquity. Here, as elsewhere throughout the fortifications, the level of the rough foundation courses can be taken as an indication of ground level at the time the walls were constructed (Pl. 39:b). In the interior of the Fortress, where the two walls join, this is fairly easy to determine, as the top of the foundation course of the Fortress wall is at an elevation of *ca.* +30.16–30.26 m., some 0.80–0.90 m. above bedrock at this point. As one might expect, there is a similar arrangement on the outside of the East Fortress Wall, and although the soil has now all washed away, the top of the first course of masonry there is at *ca.* +30.00 m., some 1.06 m. above bedrock. This bottom course had some cut blocks, such as the capital and cornice mentioned above, but it was faced partly in rubble, something that is unparalleled elsewhere in the visible remains of the fortifications. Thus, the lowest course of masonry on the exterior was a foundation and the ancient ground level in this area was at approximately +30.00 m.

[2] Clement, 1969, p. 116.

A confirmation of this conclusion can be found in the drain through the East Fortress Wall (p. 116 below), whose exterior bottom is at a level of +29.70 m., corresponding to the top of the lowest course of the foundations in that area. Naturally, the drain would have emptied out approximately at ground level, which would have been found at just that point.

This identification of ancient ground level is of crucial importance for a proper understanding of the buttress, since the top of its lower block is at an elevation of +29.15 m., almost a meter below ancient ground level: soil would, in fact, have covered all three surviving blocks, which cannot therefore have been part of a stairway construction. Thus, the buttress should be seen as a construction designed to strengthen the defenses at a topographically and strategically important point. As mentioned above, the ground drops off precipitously at Tower 2, and a buttress might have been thought necessary to help anchor the walls and keep them from sliding into the ravine. The preserved blocks of the buttress would have been completely underground, but it is possible that the construction was carried higher, perhaps even to the level of the fighting platform, allowing the defenders additional space to maneuver. The buttress thus formed an integral part of the Fortress, whose east wall must have been envisioned when it was built. This is a significant piece of evidence to argue the contemporaneity of the Hexamilion and the East Fortress Wall. They must have been perceived as a strategic unit, and the time lapse between the construction of the two walls would have been insignificant.

The well-preserved section of the southeast face of the Fortress wall allows close examination of a large stretch of masonry (Pl. 39:c). The mortar used here is hard and white, with large quantities of crushed tile, closely resembling that used in Tower W-22 at the Kyras Vrysi Ravine. There are well-defined horizontal lines in the rubble-and-mortar core, showing that the masonry was laid in horizontal courses *ca.* 0.68–0.80 m. high with well-defined upper surfaces and with the mortar on the exterior (i.e., southeast) surface smooth where it ran up against the now-missing ashlar facing blocks. This clearly demonstrates the construction technique used in the fortification. The whole process was carried out course by course: the ashlar faces were laid first, then the rubble-and-mortar core was laid in the space between, and the whole left to harden. Then the next course was laid, and construction continued thus to the top of the wall.

At a point 5.17 m. northwest of the East Fortress Wall, three blocks preserve the beginning of a stairway attached to the interior face of the Hexamilion (Fig. 28). As elsewhere, the wall widens to accommodate the stairway, from *ca.* 3.12 m. to *ca.* 3.90 m. (Pl. 39:d). The bottom step of the stairway is set on a concrete-and-rubble footing that itself rests directly on bedrock (Ill. 18). The lower two steps are poorly preserved, but the third has a clear upper surface and allows the calculations shown on Illustration 18. Thus, the stairs rose at approximately a 45-degree angle with risers averaging 0.343 m. and treads of the same size. Presumably, the stairway ran all the way to the junction with the east wall of the Fortress, since the Hexamilion is widened to support the stairway throughout that distance. Using these figures, we can project a total of sixteen steps, which would rise to the fighting platform at a level of +35.64 m., some 6.48 m. above the level of the hardpan on the northeast side of the Hexamilion.

There is no secure evidence for the superstructure of Tower 2, but it is reasonable to restore the floor of the upper room of the tower at the level of the fighting platform of the Hexamilion (i.e., at +35.64 m.). In addition, it seems reasonable to suggest that the solid foundations of the buttress discussed above would be used as a fighting platform, and this would presumably have been vaulted over and provided with arrow slots on two faces. This arrangement would allow flanking fire against an enemy who had penetrated the Hexamilion and attacked the East Fortress Wall between Towers 2 and 3.

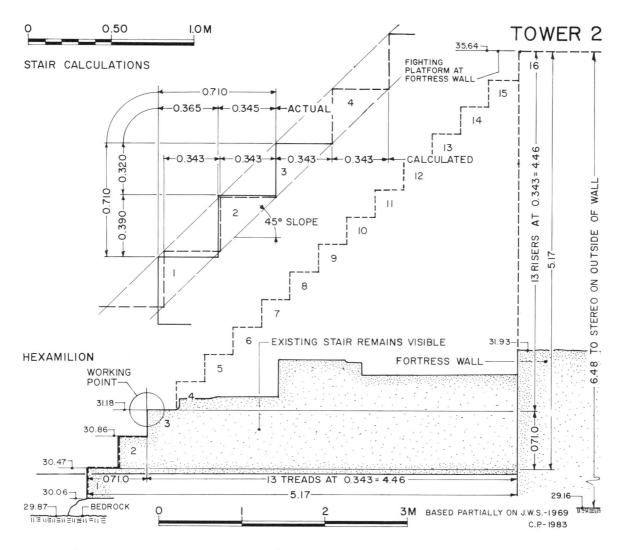

ILL. 18. Stairway calculations for Tower 2

At least the tower itself must have had an upper fighting platform, and, on analogy with the towers of the Northeast Gate, this may be restored at an elevation of approximately +39.40 m., some 10.24 m. above hardpan on the northeast face of the Hexamilion.

Just as at Tower 15, there are graffiti scratched in the plaster of the joints between the blocks at Tower 2. Four such graffiti can still be clearly read, three of them located close to the junction between the walls and one above the footing of the stairway. All the graffiti are similar: a vertical line crossed by V-shaped lines (Pl. 40:a). These may have been intended as crosses, but the best-preserved examples have three separate Vs and resemble a crude version of a menorah. Is it possible that these graffiti represent mute testimony to a Jewish presence among the crews responsible for the construction of the fortifications, parallel to the crosses and fish scratched on the walls at other points?

Although the topsoil is relatively thin in the area of Tower 2, excavation revealed important stratigraphic contexts, particularly at the interior of the junction of the two walls, where the soil was not all washed away into the ravines on either side of the tower (Pl. 40:b). At an elevation of

+29.56 m., immediately below the junction of the inside faces of the Hexamilion and the East Fortress Wall, there is the top of a grave (Grave 3; Fig. 28). The grave was cut directly into the conglomerate bedrock, measuring 1.97 m. (northwest–southeast) by 1.03 m., and *ca.* 0.97 m. deep. The grave was covered with three rectangular stone slabs set in mortar (Pl. 40:c). The slab at the northwest end did not fully cover the northeastern side of the grave. When the Hexamilion was constructed above the grave, the inner face of the Hexamilion foundations was placed up against this slab, while the foundations overran the other two cover slabs. Even so, the slab at the southeast end did not fully cover the southeast part of the tomb but left the end exposed. Two skeletons, in rather poor condition, were found in the grave, with heads to the northwest and lying on a bed of 12 tiles, most of which were 0.54 m. square and *ca.* 0.06 m. thick. There were no finds associated with the grave, but the northwest–southeast orientation of the burial and the tile floor place it sometime in the Roman imperial period.

Directly over bedrock in the area between the two walls was a fill containing characteristic pottery of the late fourth and early fifth centuries after Christ.[3] Probably associated with this fill was a coin, unfortunately much worn, but still roughly datable to the 360's or 370's.[4]

This fill must certainly represent either the earth in which the foundations of the fortifications were sunk or fill placed up against the walls at the time of original construction. This fill was consistent throughout the area between the walls, a further indication that the East Fortress Wall and the Hexamilion must have been built at approximately the same time, since they are founded in the same fill. The fill is dated by the pottery and the coin to the late fourth or the early fifth century. Since the coin was much worn at the time of its deposit and must have been in circulation for some time, a date in the early years of the fifth century seems likely.

Immediately above this level, close to the walls (but resting directly on bedrock a short distance away), is another distinct layer of debris mixed with mortar. This fill covered a wide area and contained many fragments of pottery from the mid- to later sixth century.[5]

[3] a) Phocaean red-slip bowl (IPR 68-36): Rim: p.H. 0.027 m., p.W. 0.038 m., est. Diam. of rim 0.24 m. Ring foot: p.H. 0.059 m., p.W. 0.061 m. Two nonjoining fragments preserve profile of rim and ring foot. Red clay (10R 4/8) with a few small lime inclusions and a few flecks of mica. Red slip on interior and over rim. Hayes Form 1A or B, similar to no. 3, Agora P 27170, end of 4th century; Type B dated early to third quarter 5th century (pp. 325–327).

b) Amphora (IPR 68-37): p.H. 0.098 m., p.W. 0.072 m. Single fragment preserves handle and part of shoulder. Red clay (2.5YR 5/6) fired buff at the surface with many large white inclusions and small flecks of mica. Large spherical amphora with vertical handles and spiral grooves on shoulder.

[4] Clement, 245 (IC 68-36), House of Valentinian (A.D. 364–379): SECURITAS REIPUBLICAE. Cf. *LRBC* II, pp. 79–81.

[5] a) African red-slip bowl (IPR 68-38): p.H. 0.029 m., p.W. 0.033 m., est. Diam. of rim 0.24 m. Single fragment preserves profile of rim. Red clay (2.5 YR 5/6) with slip over all, thicker on inside and over rim. Hayes Form 99, probably C (pp. 152–155). Cf. no. 22, Agora P 14882, and no. 23, Corinth C-56-15, both from *ca.* A.D. 600 (p. 154).

b) Amphora (IPR 68-39): Neck: p.H. 0.082 m., p.W. 0.163 m., est. Diam. of bottom of neck 0.013 m. Shoulder: p.H. 0.112 m.; p.W. 0.130 m. Two nonjoining fragments, preserving neck, upper handle attachment, shoulder, and fragment of body. Reddish brown clay (2.5YR 4/4) fired buff at surface; many large lime inclusions, some of which erupt at the surface. Combing on the shoulder. Cf. G. Bass, "Underwater Excavations at Yassi Ada: A Byzantine Shipwreck," *Archäologischer Anzeiger* (*Jahrbuch des deutschen Instituts* 77) 1962, p. 546, fig. 6:a; *Kenchreai* IV, RC14, pp. 114–115; F. Felter and W. W. Wurster, *Alt Ägina*, I, ii, *Die spätrömische Akropolis-Mauer*, Mainz 1975, no. 108; Aupert, "Objets," no. 325, p. 440, fig. 46. All late 6th century.

c) Beehive (IPR 68-40), Pl. 40:d: p.H. 0.062 m., p.W. 0.144 m., est. Diam. of rim 0.34 m. Rim mended from two fragments. Pink clay (7.5YR 7/4) with many inclusions and voids, and considerable mica. Plain horizontal rim with slight thickening at the edge; straight vertical walls. Inside scored with vertical and horizontal combing. Beehive ware. Cf. E. Crane, *The Archaeology of Beekeeping*, London 1983, pp. 45–51; J. E. Jones, "Hives and Honey of Hymettus: Beekeeping in Ancient Greece," *Archaeology* 29, fasc. 2, 1976, pp. 80–91; Broneer, 1959, no. 17, p. 337, a beehive from Tower 7.

d) Large basin (IPR 68-41): p.H. 0.046 m., p.W. 0.048 m., est. Diam. of interior of rim 0.31 m. Single fragment

In this same fill nine coins were discovered.[6] All the coins were found in context with the pottery, and three of them were very close together (Clement, 477, 479, 480). The coins do not, technically, constitute a hoard, although the small range of dates suggests that the coins may once have been hidden together.[7] Both the numismatic and the ceramic evidence point to considerable activity in the area of Tower 2 during the later years of the sixth century, and the termination of the coin series in 580/1 is particularly suggestive. Probably this level represents an occupation of the tower area at the time of the beginning of the Slavic incursions into Greece, otherwise well attested in the Corinthia (see pp. 85–86 and 97–98 above). It may be significant that there was no evidence of fire or other destruction associated with this material, although the loss of the coins, especially if they were originally part of a hoard, suggests considerable disturbance.

Above this late sixth-century debris were several levels of middle and late Byzantine date in the corner of the Fortress near Tower 2. These consisted of floors of packed earth or tiles, without, however, any surviving evidence of walls or other architectural detail. Large amounts of pottery and several coins were associated with these levels, the earliest of which seems to be dated by a coin of Constantine VII.[8] Above this there appear to be levels of the twelfth or early thirteenth century.[9] Finally, above a tile floor there was considerable material of the fourteenth and fifteenth centuries.[10]

---

preserves rim and part of wall. Red clay (10R 5/6) fired buff at the surface. Many inclusions including lime particles. Plain, straight vertical sides; plain horizontal rim, slightly tapering at the extremity.

e) Cooking pot (IPR 68-42): p.H. 0.022 m., p.W. 0.072 m., est. Diam. of rim 0.13 m. Single fragment preserves rim and part of one handle. Red clay (10R 4/6) fired dark gray at the surface. Very gritty fabric with many small stone inclusions. Plain vertical rim, nearly triangular in section; vertical handle, ovoid in section, from top of rim. Cf. Aupert, "Objets," no. 269, p. 433, fig. 43, dated to 585.

f) Lid (IPR 68-43): H. 0.025 m., Diam. ca. 0.059 m. Intact. Coarse, very pale brown clay (10YR 7/3), with many large inclusions, including lime. Small lid with slightly concave upper surface and vertically projecting circular handle in the center.

[6] a) Clement, 469 (IC 68-25), Justinian I (A.D. 542/3): pentanummium. *DOC* I, p. 89, no. 41:e, 1–3.

b) Clement, 481 (IC 68-28), Justin II (A.D. 566/7): half-follis. *DOC* I, p. 220, no. 62, 1–4.

c) Clement, 485 (IC 68-31), Justin II (A.D. 569/70): follis. *DOC* I, pp. 221–222, no. 66, 1–3.

d) Clement, 479 (IC 68-19), Justin II (A.D. 571/2): follis. *DOC* I, p. 228, no. 97:c, 1, 2.

e) Clement, 477 (IC 68-20), Justin II (A.D. 572/3): follis. *DOC* I, p. 210, no. 35:a.

f) Clement, 480 (IC 68-23), Justin II (A.D. 572/3), Pl. 41:a, b: follis. *DOC* I, p. 229, no. 98:d, 1, 2.

g) Clement, 486 (IC 68-26), Justin II (A.D. 573/4): follis. *DOC* I, p. 223, no. 76.

h) Clement, 489 (IC 68-34), Justin II (A.D. 565–578): pentanummium. *DOC* I, p. 218, no. 60:a, 1–5.

i) Clement, 491 (IC 68-27), Tiberius II (A.D. 580/1), Pl. 41:c, d: half-follis. *DOC* I, p. 277, no. 25, 103.

[7] Cf. Broneer, 1955, p. 117; MacDowall, "Byzantine Coin Hoard," for a hoard of similar date.

[8] Clement, 499 (IC 68-29), Constantine VII (A.D. 945–ca. 950): follis. *DOC* III, ii, pp. 562, 565, Class 4, and pp. 565–567, Class 5.

[9] a) Clement, 552 (IC 68-17), Uncertain Byzantine (12th–mid-14th centuries): concave.

b) Bowl (IPB 68-7), Pl. 41:e: p.H. 0.51 m., p.W. 0.64 m. Fragment of bottom and ring foot preserved. Coarse red clay (10R 5/6), fired unevenly gray, with many large white inclusions. Large bowl with ring foot. White slip inside and out; on interior pale yellow glaze over crude wave-shaped sgraffito design within border of two concentric circles; at center, a circle of incised lines. Colorless glaze on exterior and greenish brown glaze on underside of ring foot. Cf. *Corinth* XI, Medallion Style, no. 1436, pp. 149, 308, fig. 125 (mid-12th century).

c) Bowl or plate (IPB 68-15), Pl. 41:f: p.L. 0.071 m., p.W. 0.032 m., Th. 0.006 m. Single body sherd. Coarse, soft light red clay (2.5YR 6/6) with some medium-large inclusions, fired buff on exterior. White slip and yellow glaze on interior; sgraffito design, probably of spirals within a circular line. Cf. *Corinth* XI, Spiral Style, pp. 120–123, fig. 96, pl. XLI (first half 12th century).

[10] a) Clement, 571 (IC 68-22), Venetian Colonial, Andrea, Contarini (A.D. 1368–1382): Cross and Lion of St. Mark. Cf. *Corinth* VI, no. 53, p. 159.

b) Bowl or plate (IPB 68-8), Pl. 41:g: p.W. 0.074 m., p.H. 0.027. Two fragments preserve ring foot. Light-red clay (2.5YR 6/8), fired unevenly gray, with many medium-large voids. Plain ring foot. White slip and light-green glaze on interior, with crude sgraffito decoration of concentric circles. For decoration, cf. MacKay, "More Byzantine Pottery," no. 17, p. 256, fig. 1, pl. 63.

All these layers are inside the Fortress and not in the tower itself, where no good stratigraphy was preserved, and we cannot be certain whether they were associated with military activity on the Hexamilion or merely with habitation in the area, although the former seems more likely, at least for some of the periods represented. The coin of Constantine VII may be particularly significant, since it suggests habitation at a time that is otherwise poorly attested at Isthmia.

At a distance of *ca.* 2.65 m. southwest of the Hexamilion and *ca.* 0.80 m. northwest of the Fortress wall is a stone-built grave, its cover slabs resting at an elevation of +30.35 m. (Grave 1; Fig. 28, Pl. 42:a). The grave was constructed of limestone blocks of various sizes, leveled at the top with smaller slabs set horizontally. The floor is of hard-packed earth, and it is covered with four limestone slabs, the easternmost of which is triangular. The grave is oriented northeast–southwest, and at its southwest end it had what appears to have been a headstone, originally covered with plaster but without any surviving markings. The tomb contained a single skeleton, 1.62 m. long, oriented with its head to the southwest but without any grave offerings or remains of ornament.

Another grave is located 6.70 m. southwest of the Hexamilion and 1.50 m. northwest of the Fortress wall, with its cover slabs at an elevation of +29.70 m. (Grave 2; Fig. 28, Pl. 42:a). Its construction is similar to that of Grave 1, and it had, apparently, both a headstone and a footstone. Like Grave 1, this tomb contained only a single skeleton, 1.85 m. long.

There is no solid evidence to date these two graves, since nothing other than the skeletons was found in them. They were both cut down through sixth-century levels, but they cannot have been buried too deeply if the stones found with them were indeed grave markers that were meant to be seen. It is reasonable to assign the graves to the Middle Byzantine period or later; they are perhaps even early modern in date.

At a distance of *ca.* 14.96 m. southwest of the intersection between the two walls, a drain pierces the East Fortress Wall from northwest to southeast, designed to allow the passage of water running off along the natural slope inside the Fortress. On the inside (northwest), face the entrance to the drain is a narrow slit, 0.04 m. wide at the top and 0.10 m. wide at the bottom, purposely small to prevent any infiltration of the defenses here. The drain slopes down slightly through the interior of the wall and emerges on the southeast face through an opening 0.41 m. high and 0.30 m. wide (Pl. 42:b). The technique used in the construction of this drain, widening out through the passage through the wall, is rather unusual and is directly the opposite of that used in the two drains through the blocking wall in the Northeast Gate (p. 81 above). On the exterior (southeast) face, the bottom of the drain, at +29.70 m., is at the level of the bottom of the first course of masonry, just above the foundations of the east wall; as mentioned previously, this must indicate ground level at the time the Fortress was constructed.

The bedrock outside the East Fortress Wall drops away precipitously toward the south. At a distance of *ca.* 2.00 m. southeast of the face of the wall there is a deep cutting in the bedrock, *ca.* 0.74 m. to 0.84 m. wide, running roughly parallel to the Fortress wall from a point just under the southwest face of the Hexamilion to a terminus *ca.* 4.75 m. to the southwest. At the western end of the cutting its bottom is at an elevation of +26.68 m., and the bottom descends in several steps to an elevation of +25.67 m. at the east. This area was used as a quarry, and a cutting where five blocks were removed was visible along its bottom at the time of excavation. These cuttings are between 0.71 m. and 0.80 m. long, making them roughly the same size as many of the preserved facing blocks of the Hexamilion. Within the fill in the quarry were several fragments of amphoras (Tower 2, Box 40) similar to examples from the Athenian Agora (*Agora* V, M237) dated to the fourth century after Christ. This shows that the quarry was open when the fortifications were constructed and that some of the stones were quarried at this spot for the purpose.

The practice of opening impromptu quarries was, of course, common in antiquity, but it is interesting to see that despite the availability of spolia in the Sanctuary, newly quarried stones still had to be used in this area. On the other hand, this cutting will also have had the effect of making the approach to the East Fortress Wall steeper, thus increasing the effectiveness of the defense. It is also noteworthy that the quarry was not only laid out parallel to the East Fortress Wall but that on the east it came to an end just before the southwest face of the Hexamilion. Apparently, some planning went into the layout of the quarry and its relationship to the projected walls.

IX
OTHER FORTRESS TOWERS

EXCAVATION IN THE FORTRESS at Isthmia was most intensive in the areas of the two gates and those of the two northern corner towers. Nonetheless, exploration was also carried out in several of the other Fortress towers and their vicinities. Thus, Towers 2 and 15 (see pp. 110–117 and 95–103 above) were corner towers of the Fortress, designed to guard the junction of the Hexamilion with the Fortress wall (Fig. 8). As a result, these two were the most important single towers in the complex. Towers 6 and 10, by contrast, protected the southern corners of the Fortress. The three remaining ones, Towers 17, 5, and 7, lie along relatively straight stretches of the curtain wall.

SOUTHERN CORNER TOWERS 6 AND 10

In terms of siting and construction, as well as strategic importance, Towers 6 and 10 are distinguished from the other towers of the Fortress. They were not exposed, like Towers 2 and 15, in the first line of defense, but they were critical points of resistance against any enemy that penetrated the Hexamilion and attacked the Fortress from within the defenses. The walls of Towers 6 and 10, like those of Towers 2 and 15, projected outward from the front face of the Fortress wall, so that arrow slits in their side walls would allow a field of fire along the two walls they were expected to protect.

TOWER 6

Tower 6 is located at the southeast corner of the Fortress, at a high point that still dominates the roadway and the surrounding area (Pl. 43:a).[1] The tower is oriented at an oblique angle to the section of the South Fortress Wall that runs between the tower and the South Gate, while it is slightly offset from, but on approximately the same orientation as, the East Fortress Wall (Fig. 29). This arrangement would allow the tower to offer enfilading fire toward both Tower 7 and Tower 5. The exterior of the east side of the tower has not been excavated, and it is still encased in fallen debris from the collapse of the Fortress. It is reasonable, however, to restore the tower as a square, measuring roughly 7 meters on a side.

The tower is built upon a foundation of cut blocks, which projects out slightly from the tower walls. This foundation was apparently not a solid platform, like those at the Northeast Gate, but ran only under the walls of the tower. This is seen in the interior of the tower, where the excavated floor level (at *ca.* +35.48 m.) is well below the top of the foundations (*ca.* +35.65 m.; see Fig. 29). The walls of Tower 6 are between 1.30 m. and 1.92 m. thick, and they are constructed of large, well-cut rectangular blocks laid in alternating high and low courses (Ill. 19), commonly in header-and-stretcher technique, with a fill of rubble and mortar between the finished faces.

The tower has a partially preserved stairway which gave access to the interior of the tower from the fighting platform of the Fortress wall (Fig. 29; Pl. 43:b, c). The stairway was constructed within the thickness of the tower's west wall, between the two finished faces, so that a defender using the stairs would be completely shielded from enemy fire. This stairway does not descend all

[1] In May of 1958 Demetrios Pallas excavated the interior and exterior of Tower 6. See Broneer, 1959, pp. 320–321.

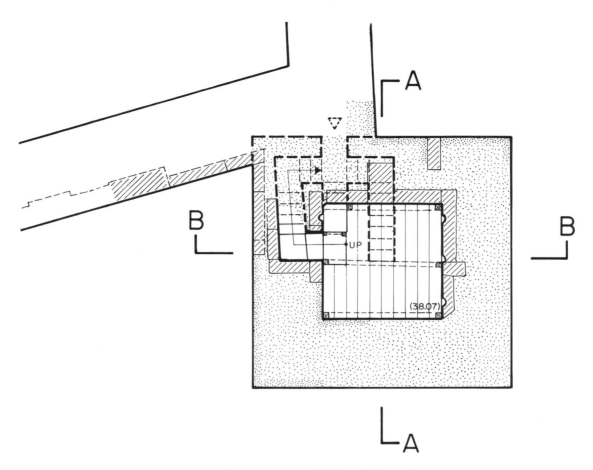

ILL. 19. Schematic restored plan of Tower 6

the way to the bottom of the tower: the bottom step is at an elevation of *ca.* +38.70 m. There are no cuttings for floor joists in the walls of the tower, and so one must suppose the floors to have been made of wood and supported by braces. The reconstruction shown in Illustrations 20–22 is an indication, *exempli gratia*, of what the upper rooms of the tower may have been like. The shallow cuttings on the walls (Ill. 21) may have been designed to hold lamps, since the interior of the tower must have been very dark.

Two steps of the stone-cut stairway are preserved running upward toward the west; the stairway then turns north, and a further two steps are preserved within the thickness of the west tower wall. North of the highest preserved step is a footing for others higher up. The rest of the stairway must be reconstructed, bearing in mind the constricted space available and the necessity to keep the stairway shielded from fire from several directions. It seems reasonable to restore the stairway completely within the thickness of the tower walls, always allowing enough space on the exterior to guard against attack. The surviving steps preserve an average rise of *ca.* 0.31 m. per step, and so we may reconstruct a stairway running northward for six steps to a second landing, then turning east for three more before reaching the level of the fighting platform at a restored elevation of *ca.* +41.52 m. (Ills. 21, 22). This would put the fighting platform 5.87 m. above the top of the tower foundations, a level which approximates ground level outside the tower.

No evidence for the upper story of Tower 6 survives, but the simplest solution is that the upper part of the tower was supported on a vault, such as we have restored at the Northeast and South

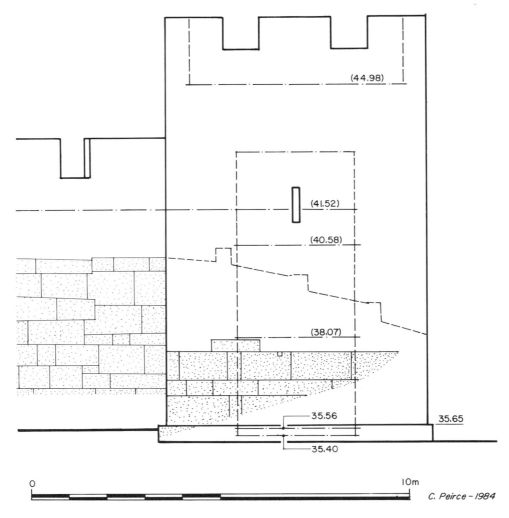

ILL. 20. Restored south elevation of Tower 6

Gates. This would allow the construction of a stairway within the thickness of the tower and up over the top of the vault (Ills. 20, 21). In 11 steps the stairway would reach the top of the vault in the center of the tower, at a restored elevation of *ca.* +44.98 m., which may be suggested as the level of the fighting platform of the top of Tower 6 (Ill. 22).

There were no significant ceramic finds within the tower, but a coin of the tenth–eleventh centuries was discovered in the upper levels.[2] On an interior wall of the tower is a graffito probably to be read as K(ύρι)ε β(οηθ)ῆ, "Lord, help (your servant)."

TOWER 10

Tower 10 is located at the southwest corner of the Fortress, some 24.30 m. west of Tower 9 in the South Gate (Fig. 30; Pl. 44:a).[3] Like Tower 2, Tower 10 projects outward from the corner of the Fortress wall so that the latter is joined to it only at the northeast corner of the tower. The

[2] IC 397, Anonymous Byzantine (A.D. 976–*ca.* 1030/35).

[3] The interior of Tower 10 and the field lying immediately to the south of it were excavated in 1972 (Clement, 1973, p. 149); the area outside and further south (Loukos area) was excavated in 1969 (Clement, 1970, p. 163).

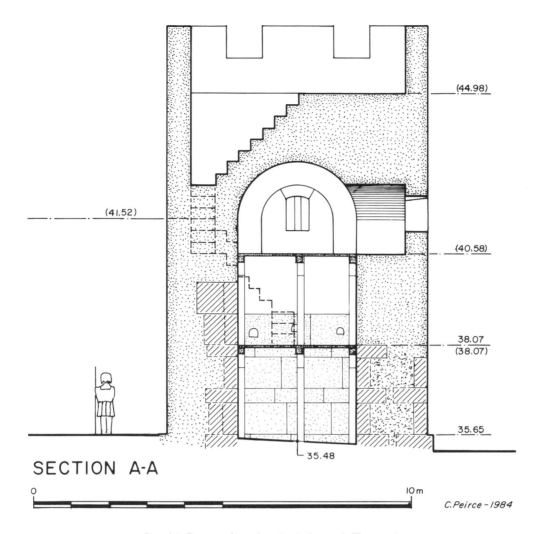

ILL. 21. Restored section A–A through Tower 6

Fortress wall makes a right-angle turn at this point, and the walls of Tower 10 are arranged to allow the defense to enfilade the west and the south walls of the Fortress. In form, the tower is rectangular, its outer walls roughly 6.2 m. long north–south and 5.0 m. east–west.

The interior of Tower 10 was excavated to a depth of 3.14 m. below its highest preserved masonry, and the exterior is preserved to a height of five courses. The interior and exterior walls of the tower are very irregular: the walls are not at all even, and large gaps between the blocks are filled with mortar and tile (Pl. 44:c, d). All this suggests that the walls of the tower were substantially repaired, from the foundations up, at some undetermined time.

Most of the fill in the tower was the result of the abandonment of the Fortress and its final destruction. The highest floor level was encountered at a level of +43.88 m., and above this floor was pottery of the thirteenth and fourteenth centuries.[4]

[4] Fortress Towers 1972, Baskets 2–5, including IPL 72-3 (Byzantine lamp stand) and IPB 72-3 (Byzantine cooking pot):

a) Bowl (IPB 72-1), Pl. 45:a: p.H. 0.092 m., max. W. 0.142 m., est. Diam. rim 0.28 m. Five fragments preserve complete profile. Red clay (10R 5/8) with some small inclusions and voids, evenly fired. Low ring foot, flaring straight sides, and slightly thickened, pointed rim. White slip on interior and over rim; clear glaze on interior and over rim;

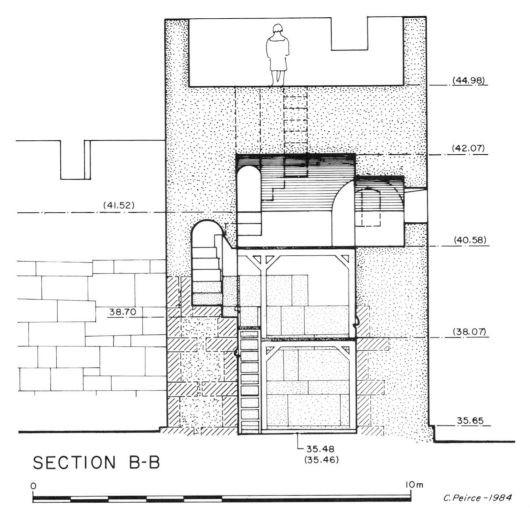

(44.98)

(42.07)

(41.52)

(40.58)

38.70

(38.07)

35.65

35.48
(35.46)

SECTION B-B

0   10m

C. Peirce -1984

ILL. 22. Restored section B–B through Tower 6

In the interior of Tower 10 excavation below the top floor level revealed a second floor, at an elevation of +43.38 m. The pottery above this floor was not particularly diagnostic, but it seems to date as late as the latter part of the sixth century after Christ.[5] There was no excavation under this floor level, and so the original occupation levels of the tower were not exposed. This material suggests that Tower 10 was used during the sixth century (and probably earlier) and that a primary period of occupation was the Frankish period.

Investigation in the area immediately outside (i.e., to the south of) Tower 10 produced further interesting information (Fig. 30). The soil above bedrock in this vicinity was quite shallow, and

---

splotches of green glaze on and just under rim. No exact parallel at Corinth or Athens, but for profile cf. *Corinth* XI, no. 778, fig. 79:c (13th century).

b) Jug or amphora, matt-painted ware (IPB 72-2), Pl. 45:b: p.H. 0.55 m., est. Diam. base *ca*. 0.12 m. Two fragments preserve flat bottom and part of wall. Very pale brown clay (10YR 8/3) with many dark and light inclusions. Closed vessel with flat bottom and flaring sides. Wheel marks inside and out; on bottom matt-painted design of geometric and stylized floral (?) pattern. MacKay, "More Byzantine Pottery," nos. 79–84, pl. 68 (late 12th–early 14th centuries).

[5] Fortress Towers 1972, Basket 9.

more extensive excavation will be necessary for a full understanding of habitation and use. Nevertheless, there were considerable quantities of pottery of Roman imperial date.[6] It seems that walls of Roman times underlie Tower 10 and the South Fortress Wall, but these have not been fully explored, and no firm conclusions can be drawn about them. Of particular interest is a fragmentary cooking pot, found in mixed fill just south of the South Fortress Wall.[7] This piece of so-called Slavic pottery suggests that there was habitation in this part of the Fortress area during the Byzantine Dark Ages of the late sixth and seventh centuries.

Running eastward from the southeast corner of Tower 10 is a rubble wall *ca.* 0.62 m. wide that continues to the end of the excavated area *ca.* 10.5 m. away (Pl. 44:b). This wall formed the southern boundary for a series of rooms that were backed up against the exterior face of the South Fortress Wall. Three such rooms are visible on the plan (Fig. 30); the middle room has a preserved doorway. This building or complex of buildings was certainly very large, and it runs off into unexcavated ground. Associated with this complex was a series of roughly circular pits that lay to the south of the rubble wall. These pits, which were nearly all more than a meter in diameter, were sunk into the hardpan, and most of them were covered with a layer of small stones. The purpose of these pits is uncertain, although the stone covering suggests that they may ultimately have been used simply for refuse.

The stratigraphic record in this area was not well preserved, but some finds inside the rooms defined by the east–west rubble wall suggest occupation in the Middle Byzantine and Frankish periods.[8] The pits contained pottery that ranged from Roman imperial through the thirteenth century after Christ, including several examples from the eleventh and twelfth centuries, among which is an example of Byzantine Imitation Lustre Ware.[9] The mediaeval coins from this area, although rarely from good stratigraphic contexts, confirm the occupation of the area during the eleventh century through the thirteenth.[10]

[6] Peppers, Group I, pp. 278–287; Clement, 1970, p. 163.

[7] Cooking pot (Slavic) (IPR 69-246), Pl. 45:c: p.H. *ca.* 0.062 m., p.W. 0.082 m. Single fragment preserves shoulder and rim. Very coarse, red clay (2.5YR 5/6), fired or burned black over most of the fragment; many large stone inclusions and voids, with some quartz. Rounded shoulder and plain outturned rim. Vessel either handmade or made on a slow wheel; there are many finger depressions on the interior where the vessel was formed. On the exterior under the rim is a series of oblique combed incisions above a faint horizontal band. In uninventoried pottery from this basket are two other sherds of the same fabric, including part of a flat bottom. Cf. Aupert, "Céramique slave," pp. 373–394. Decoration is similar to nos. 23–30. Cf. also IPR 67-49, 67-51, and 67-52 from the Northeast Gate (pp. 85–86 above).

[8] Glaze-painted bowl (IPB 69-5), Pl. 45:d: H. *ca.* 0.67 m., Diam. 0.162 m. Restored from many fragments. Coarse, red clay (2.5YR 5/6) with many small inclusions, poorly turned. Low, slightly flaring ring foot and round sides to plain rim. White slip on interior, and over rim; on interior, clear glaze over design of crude spirals in green glaze. Cf. *Corinth* XI, nos. 508–547 (13th century).

[9] Imitation lustre-ware bowl (IPB 69-24), Pl. 45:e: p.L. 0.142 m., est. Diam. 0.236 m. Several fragments preserve rim and upper part of body. Hard, red clay (2.5YR 5/8) with many small inclusions and voids. Steep rounded sides and bluntly pointed rim. White slip on interior and exterior; on interior, good-quality, highly vitreous light-green glaze; on exterior, dark green mottled glaze. Under rim, wide band of mixed spiral and kufesque pattern in deep brown color. Cf. *Corinth* XI, nos. 577–639: for profile cf. no. 620, fig. 65:e, for design no. 592, pl. XXV (second half 11th century, perhaps close to 1100).

[10] a) Clement, 502 (IC 69-65), Anonymous Byzantine. Class A2 (A.D. 976–1030/35).

b) Clement, 523 (IC 69-18), Nicephorus III (A.D. 1078–1081). *DOC* III, ii, pp. 831–832.

c) Clement, 524 (IC 69-55), Alexius I (A.D. 1081–1118). *BMC* II, p. 680, Type 4.

d) Clement, 527 (IC 69-57), Alexius I (A.D. 1081–1118). *BMC* II, p. 74, no. 1887.

e) Clement, 531 (IC 69-71), John II (A.D. 1118–1143). Cf. *BMC* II, p. 698, AE 01-05.

f) Clement, 532 (IC 69-107), John II (A.D. 1118–1143). *BMC* II, p. 699, Type 2.

g) Clement, 537 (IC 69-2), 538 (IC 69-3), 539 (IC 69-59), 543 (IC 69-39), 544 (IC 69-106), Manuel I (A.D. 1143–1180). *BMC* II, p. 712, Type 2.

h) Clement, 542 (IC 69-72), Manuel I (A.D. 1143–1180). *BMC* II, p. 720, Type 1.

As might be expected, the evidence for the settlement history of the area of Tower 10 very much resembles that of the South Gate. The indication of activity during the eleventh through the thirteenth centuries is particularly noteworthy, since this period is otherwise poorly documented in the Fortress.

TOWERS 17, 5, AND 7

Three remaining towers have been systematically investigated, Towers 17, 5, and 7, along the curtain wall of the Fortress.

TOWER 17

Tower 17 is located on the Hexamilion, looking northward out over the Great Ravine, midway between Tower 15 and the Northeast Gate.[11] Only the tower and the exterior face of the Hexamilion have been investigated; the interior of the Hexamilion and its southern face were not exposed. The tower forms a rough rectangle 5.68 m. long on its north side, with west and east sides of 4.49 m. and 4.28 m., respectively. The bedrock in this area slopes off steeply toward the north, and so the foundations of the tower had to be set at least a meter more deeply on the north than they were on the south. The lower parts of the tower walls are uneven, and they project into the interior of the tower, showing that they were foundation courses not meant to be seen. Many channels were discovered cut in the hardpan on the interior of the tower, but these seem to have no connection with the tower; presumably they are to be associated with earlier building activity in the area. The south tower wall, which represents the outer face of the Hexamilion in this area, is founded upon another wall, ca. 1.02 m. high and of indeterminate width (Pl. 46:a). This wall, in contrast to the Hexamilion and its foundations in Tower 17, is made of uncoursed, small stones carefully set in mortar. It was undoubtedly part of an earlier structure of unknown size and date, used as the foundation of the Hexamilion here.

In the middle of the south wall of the tower is a door, ca. 0.95 m. wide, preserved to a height of 1.51 m., with its upper part broken away (Pl. 46:b). The doorway is now filled with debris, but its sides are made of cut blocks. Presumably, it is part of the original structure of the Hexamilion, giving access to the upper story of the tower from the interior of the Fortress.

Material in the tower was almost completely jumbled, suggesting that the tower was cleaned out one or more times during its period of use and then mixed fill dumped in at the time of a final clean-up of the area. Thus, pottery of Roman imperial date was indiscriminately mixed with pottery of the fifth and sixth centuries in all levels. Among the Roman material was a fragment of a Corinthian moldmade bowl (IPR 72-67) which joined with a piece found in the excavation of the East Field.[12] Stones or dump from the East Field were probably used in the construction of this part of the Hexamilion, and the sherd found its way into the fill in Tower 17 in this way. Among the late Roman material was a single coin of Justin II, dated to the last third of the sixth century.[13]

---

i) Clement, 542 (IC 69-29), Guillaume de Villehardouin (A.D. 1245–1250). *Corinth* VI, no. 4, p. 152.

j) Clement, 569 (IC 69-38), Guillaume de la Roche (A.D. 1280–1287). *Corinth* VI, no. 23, p. 154.

[11] Tower 17 was investigated in 1972 (Clement, 1973, p. 149).

[12] The East Field was a residential area in the Roman period; it is located east of the southeast corner of the temenos of Poseidon (Fig. 8). Peppers, X546, pp. 335–336, fig. 118:e; Clement, 1973, p. 149, pl. 132:g.

[13] Clement, 483 (IC 72-26), Justin II (A.D. 568/9): Justin and Sophia enthroned, half-follis, Thessalonica. *DOC* I, p. 221, no. 65:1.

A plastered floor was encountered in the tower at a level slightly below the threshold of the doorway, and this provided the only real stratigraphic indication. Since the floor was not at the same level as the threshold of the door, it was probably not contemporary but may have been laid after the doorway was blocked with rubble; it would therefore represent a floor level of some later period of the tower. Both the Roman bowl and the coin of Justin II were sealed below this floor level, apparently as part of debris that was dumped into the bottom of the tower at some period of refurbishment. Since the doorway was apparently part of the original construction of the tower, there must have been an earlier floor at the level of the threshold, either made of wood or laid over debris piled up in the manner of the later floor. Unfortunately, no stratification was preserved above the later floor, and it is impossible to say anything about this period of occupation.

Tower 5

Tower 5 is located along the east wall of the Fortress, not far north of the southeast corner (Fig. 8).[14] The tower is 6.35 m. wide, and the north and south walls are 4.88 m. and 4.68 m. long, respectively. The walls are preserved to a maximum height of *ca.* 4.04 m. in six courses. Although the workmanship on the tower is careful and the coursing even, the walls nowhere bond to the face of the Fortress wall.

Excavation on the interior of the tower was carried down to a concrete floor, in which is a hole *ca.* 0.35 m. in diameter cut down into the bedrock to a depth of *ca.* 0.80 m. On the eastern side of the tower, at approximately the level of the concrete floor, is a square channel that runs under the east tower wall and presumably emptied into the area outside the Fortress. These are probably the remains of a latrine in the lowest room of the tower. On the east interior wall are several graffiti depicting crosses (Ill. 23).

Material immediately above the concrete floor was predominantly Late Roman and included a small amphora.[15] Above this layer of Late Roman material, no trace of a later floor survives but rather a fill, nearly four meters deep, without any significant stratigraphy and material that is nearly all consistent. Within this fill were five coins and enormous quantities of pottery.[16]

This upper fill in Tower 5 contained nearly twenty other inventoried pieces of Byzantine pottery, none of them otherwise precisely datable. The whole fill, however, is homogeneous, and it is dated by the four coins of Antonio Venerio to the last years of the fourteenth or the early years of the fifteenth century. The material has all the characteristics of a dump, and we should probably

---

[14] Tower 5 was investigated in 1972 (Clement, 1973, p. 149).

[15] Amphora (IPB 72-8), Pl. 46:c: p.H. 0.38 m., p. Diam. 0.30 m. Restored from many pieces, upper portion missing. Coarse, very pale brown clay (10YR 8/3) with many medium light and white inclusions. Small amphora with pointed toe and cylindrical body, rounded shoulder, and vertical neck. Light vertical gouges or scrapes on exterior, heavy wheel marks on interior. Cf. Hayes, *DOP* 22, 1968, p. 215, Type 7 (late 6th–early 7th centuries); *idem*, "Excavations at Saraçhane in Istanbul: A Seventh-Century Pottery Group," in *Histria* I, Bucharest 1954, pp. 460–461, fig. 388 (late 6th century); *Yassi Ada*, nos. 66–68, p. 181, figs. 9–11 (mid-7th century). Pallas found a similar amphora (IP 2142) in Tower 7.

[16] a) Clement, 586 (IC 72-17), 587 (IC 72-18), 588 (IC 72-19), 589 (IC 72-22), Venetian Colonial, Antonio Venerio (A.D. 1382–1400): Cross and Lion of St. Mark. *Corinth* VI, no. 55, p. 159.

b) Clement, 624 (IC 72-20), Venetian Colonial: Uncertain Doge (A.D. 1342–1457).

c) Cooking pot (IPB 72-12), Pl. 46:d: rest. H. 0202 m., Diam. mouth 0.169 m. Restored from many pieces, bottom not perserved. Coarse, reddish yellow clay (5YR 6/8) with many large inclusions and voids, fired unevenly gray. Rounded sides, offset shoulder, flanged, nearly vertical plain rim. Vertical strap handles from body to bottom of rim. Broad wheel marks on interior. For good parallel cf. MacKay, "More Byzantine Pottery," no. 132, p. 299, pl. 69, fig. 5 (later 13th–14th centuries).

J.M.W. 1985

ILL. 23. Graffiti in Tower 5

assume that the fill was placed in the tower as part of a cleaning operation, probably in connection with Manuel II's repair of the Fortress in 1415.

TOWER 7

Tower 7 is located along the South Fortress Wall, midway between the South Gate and Tower 6 (Fig. 8).[17] It is nearly square in shape, with a southeast wall of 5.23 m. in length and northeast and southwest walls of 4.95 m. and 4.91 m. These shorter walls of the tower are bonded to the south face of the South Fortress Wall. Excavation in the interior of the tower revealed large quantities of Late Roman pottery, including various sixth-century amphoras, two Type XXXI lamps,[18] and four large, Late Roman beehives.[19] This material, however, does not appear to have been stratified, and Middle Byzantine material, an early Roman lamp, and Late Roman pottery were all encountered in the lowest level of the tower.[20] The examples of nearly complete sixth-century vessels appear to have been scattered throughout the fill, from top to bottom, and so it is unlikely that the amphoras and beehives were used in the tower. Rather, they must have been dumped into the tower at some later date, perhaps even in the fourteenth or fifteenth century. The only coin from the tower came from the uppermost level, and it offers little assistance in chronology.[21]

[17] Tower 7 and the area in front of it were investigated for Oscar Broneer by Demetrios Pallas in 1958 (Broneer, 1959, pp. 320–321).

[18] Broneer, *Isthmia* III, no. 3146 (IP 1927), p. 81, pl. 35; no. 3149 (IP 1928), p. 81, pls. 10, 35.

[19] Broneer, 1959, no. 17, p. 337, cf. nos. 15 and 16; Jones (footnote 5:c above, p. 114), pp. 80–91, esp. 83–84.

[20] Pallas notebook for May 23, 1958, lower fill; cf. May 22, 1958, lower fill, which is much more consistently 6th century.

[21] IC 394, Anonymous Byzantine (A.D. 970/76–1030/35): Class A1 or A2. Cf. *DOC* III, ii, pp. 648–675.

X

OBSERVATIONS

STRATEGY AND SITING

The Hexamilion as a Barrier Wall

Typologically and in terms of function, the Hexamilion may be classified as a "barrier wall" (διατείχισμα).[1] Originally the term was used to describe a "partition wall" within a circuit, but in late antiquity a διατείχισμα meant a fortification that sought to close off an entire region to an enemy by blocking the means of access. Construction of a barrier wall obviously assumes that an attack is expected from a certain direction, and it requires that the defensive power control all the territory behind the wall. Barrier walls are also normally quite long, and they thus also require considerable resources, both for construction and for their adequate defense.[2] Such walls were obviously most effective at a pass or an isthmus that an enemy could not easily circumvent. In Greek antiquity, such barrier walls were constructed across the neck of the Thracian Chersonese (Herodotos, 6.36), at the Dema gap in Attica,[3] and perhaps in various parts of the Isthmus of Corinth (pp. 4–6 above). In some cases, these barrier walls were made of solid, permanent masonry (e.g., the Dema wall), but in other cases, they must have been constructed of mounds of earth, wooden stakes, and the like. The Roman use of barrier walls is, of course, best known from examples such as Hadrian's Wall in northern Britain.

This type of defense was again very popular during early Byzantine times. Procopius uses the word *diateichisma*, certainly a technical term for this kind of linear fortification.[4] The best-known example is the so-called Long Wall in Thrace, which was the outlying defense of Constantinople and protected the sources of the aqueducts for the capital.[5] Other examples of the genre are a long wall in the Dobrudgia,[6] the 100-mile-long Abkhazian wall in southern Russia,[7] and, of course, the wall at Thermopylai attributed by Procopius to Justinian.[8]

[1] Lawrence, *Greek Aims*, pp. 167–172.

[2] Cf. Wiseman, *Land*, p. 59.

[3] C. W. J. Eliot, "Tὸ Δέμα. A Survey of the Aigaleos-Parnes Wall," *BSA* 52, 1957, pp. 157–189; M. H. Munn, *Studies on the Territorial Defenses of Fourth-century Athens* (diss. University of Pennsylvania 1983), pp. 178–313.

[4] Cf. *Aed.* 4.9.6–13; *Vand.* 7.40.43.

[5] R. M. Harrison, "Tὸ μάκρον τεῖχος, The Long Wall in Thrace," in *Transactions of the Eighth International Congress of Frontier Studies*, E. Birley and B. Dobson, edd., Cardiff 1974, pp. 244–248; idem, "The Long Wall in Thrace," *Archaeologia Aeliana* 47, 1969, pp. 33–38; B. Croke, "The Date of the 'Anastasian Long Wall' in Thrace," *GRBS* 23, 1982, pp. 59–78.

[6] C. Chuchhardt, "Die Anastasius-Mauer bei Konstantinopel und die Dobrudscha-Wälle," *Jahrbuch des deutschen archäologischen Institut* 16, 1901, pp. 107–115; but see E. Condurachi, I. Barnea, and P. Diaconu, "Nouvelle recherches sur le *Limes* byzantin du Bas-Danube aux Xe–XIe siècles," in *Proceedings of the XIIIth International Congress of Byzantine Studies*, Oxford 1967, pp. 317–333.

[7] T. B. Mitford, "Survey of the Euphrates Limes," *Anatolian Studies* 17, 1967, pp. 13–14; compare Harrison's suggestion ([footnote 5 above] p. 247) that a wall discovered by Pierre MacKay near Komotini in northern Greece ("A Turkish Traveller in Northern Greece" [lecture, Toronto 1968], abstract in *AJA* 73, 1969, pp. 242–243) may date from this period.

[8] *Aed.* 4.2.1–15; cf. *Anekdota* 26.31–32; P. A. MacKay, "Medieval Walls at Thermopylae" (lecture, New York, 1961), abstract in *AJA* 66, 1962, p. 198; idem, "Procopius' De Aedificiis and the Topography of Thermopylae," *AJA* 67, 1963 (pp. 241–255), p. 250; W. Cherf, "Carbon-14 Chronology for the Late-Roman Fortifications of the Thermopylai Frontier," *Journal of Roman Archaeology* 5, 1992, pp. 261–264; J. Rosser, "The Role of the Great Isthmus Corridor in the Slavonic Invasions of Greece," *Byzantinische Forschungen* 9, 1985, pp. 245–253 (referring to the "corridor" at Thermopylai). See also *Aed.* 3.7.5, for a διατείχισμα in Lazica, and 4.10.5–17, for the early Byzantine wall across the Thracian Chersonese.

SITING

Throughout its length, the Hexamilion was built to take advantage of the natural lay of the land. Indeed, it is difficult to see how the military engineers could have chosen a better course for the wall to follow. As Dodwell was the first in modern times to note, the walls of the Hexamilion were "not built in a straight line across the Isthmus, but follow the sinuosities of the ground" (see Testamonia, 27). On both the east and west, a stretch of wall that ran along a height just above the sea guarded the approach of the Hexamilion to the sea, so that if an enemy should try to force these vulnerable, low-lying points, he would be exposed to fire from two sides. Wherever possible, the Hexamilion ran along a natural ridge, allowing the defenders the advantage of height, while the wall made a transition from one ridge to another at appropriate breaks in the landscape, frequently gully crossings. Given these principles, the Hexamilion follows the shortest course possible across the Isthmus. It does not retreat into the interior to find the greater heights in the south: at Acrocorinth, the Agios Demetrios ridge, or Mt. Oneion.

Corinth and Acrocorinth were, of course, already fortified, and they could serve as places of last refuge if the Hexamilion did not hold. But the builders of the Hexamilion must have considered the needs of defense and understood that the manpower necessary to guard a wall such as this was its weakest aspect, and so they made its course as short as possible. This required that the Hexamilion pass over relatively level land in several places, especially in the area of the National Highway and in the region where the western end of the Great Ravine approaches the Hexamilion (W-13 to W-22). Another factor that affected the course of the Hexamilion was the tendency to make use of pre-existing walls wherever possible. This can obviously be documented only where excavation has taken place, but it is clear, especially in the area of the Roman Bath, where the north wall of the Bath was strengthened and used as the north face of the Hexamilion.

ARCHITECTURAL ELEMENTS

FORTRESSES

As Procopius tells us, a number of fortresses strengthened the Hexamilion (φρούρια, *Aed.* 4.12.28). One of these was the Fortress at Isthmia. Its purpose was two-fold: (1) to house the garrison and officers who manned the Hexamilion and (2) to provide a strong point and place of last refuge in the defense of the fortifications. The Fortress at Isthmia forms an uneven "pork-chop" shape, roughly 210 meters north–south, 100 meters east–west at the south, and 200 meters east–west at the north. The lay of the land largely determined the shape of the Fortress, and walls were placed along the slopes of natural declivities: the North Fortress Wall above the Great Ravine, the South Fortress Wall along the ravine that ran through the Later Stadium, and the West Fortress Wall along the small gully that ran between Tower 15 and the North Drain. Another factor that affected the layout of the Fortress was the Roman Arch and the road that ran through it from the port at Schoinos. The Hexamilion and the Northeast Gate were arranged so as to incorporate the arch, and this helps to explain the extension of the Fortress toward the northeast. The towers of the Northeast Gate were, on the other hand, at an ideal forward position in the fortifications, and they provided an admirable look-out over the Great Ravine and toward the low-lying land to the east.

Jenkins and Megaw found that the area of the Fortress had been leveled before construction of the Hexamilion.[9] Thus, the land originally sloped down, at least in the southern part, from west to east, but fill was brought in to level the whole area. For that reason, virgin soil is only *ca.* 1.6–2.0 m.

[9] Jenkins and Megaw, "Researches," pp. 79–82.

below the early Byzantine surface in most of the Fortress, but close to the East Fortress Wall it is
4.5 m. below the surface. This had the added effect of making the South Fortress Wall higher than
it would otherwise have been on the exterior. From this evidence, however, it is clear that the
builders of the Hexamilion had plans to make use of the whole of the Fortress interior, since they
took the trouble to level all of it.

The Fortress has an area of *ca.* 27,100 sq. m. (2.71 ha.), making it a fortification of considerable size. Scholars have distinguished *forts* from *fortresses* on the basis of size. Pringle, for example, in his study of North Africa, proposed a figure of 1.75 ha. as the division between forts and
larger fortresses.[10] Compared with 65 North African sites that could be ranked on the basis of size,
the Fortress at Isthmia would hold the twenty-second place.[11] This observation, however, is probably misleading, since most of the sites larger than Isthmia were cities, such as Carthage (390 ha.),
Caesarea (370 ha.), and Lepcis Magna (44 ha.). Two of the African sites termed forts by Procopius, rather than cities, are Diana Veteranorum and Thugga, with enclosures of 0.29 and 0.28 ha.,
respectively.[12]

The layout of the walls shows that the Fortress at Isthmia must have been intentionally large.
As we have seen, the northern limit of the Fortress was determined by the side of the Great Ravine,
but, had they wanted to, the builders could easily have decreased the size of the Fortress by shorten-
ing its extension to the south. This suggests, then, that the Fortress must have been designed to hold
a large garrison.

No concerted excavation has been carried out within the area of the Fortress itself, and we
cannot therefore be sure what buildings were located there. Monceaux, however, identified what he
called "soubassements byzantins," three Byzantine chapels, and a Byzantine wall.[13] Staïs mentioned nine buildings of Byzantine date, although he failed to supply a plan of them.[14] Megaw
excavated parts of some Byzantine buildings, and his plan of the Fortress included those buildings
standing above ground in 1933.[15]

Monceaux clearly was wrong about the identification of the Byzantine chapels, since the buildings are not oriented correctly. It is also difficult to know how to date Megaw's Byzantine buildings,
although his association of combed ware with the "upper or Byzantine stratum" shows that he at
least thought that these buildings were contemporary with construction of the Fortress. Near the
church of St. John inside the Fortress are two large and one small broken, unfluted monolithic
columns. One of these is limestone and *ca.* 0.60 m. in diameter; perhaps it belonged to the series of
columns built into the Hexamilion near Tower 2. Another column, however, is of mottled purple
and yellow marble, with a bottom diameter of *ca.* 0.65 m. The base diameter of the third marble
column is *ca.* 0.24 m. The origin of these columns is unknown, and they may not originally have
come from the Fortress at all, but it is nevertheless tempting to associate them with a large building
or buildings still awaiting investigation within the Fortress. We should, of course, expect the Fortress to have had barracks and possibly stables,[16] a command post, warehouses, and probably a
church. But in the absence of further exploration within the Fortress, none of these buildings can be
documented at Isthmia.

[10] Pringle, *Defence* I, p. 145.
[11] Pringle, *Defence* I, pp. 126–127.
[12] Pringle, *Defence* I, pp. 123, 126.
[13] Monceaux, "Fouilles," 1884, pl. 38.
[14] E. Staïs, Πρακτικά 1903, p. 16.
[15] Jenkins and Megaw, "Researches," pp. 79–83, fig. 7.
[16] Pringle, *Defence* I, pp. 164–166.

In first- and second-century Britain, a fortress the size of Isthmia could have held a cohort of *ca.* 800 men,[17] but by the fifth century the situation is likely to have changed considerably. Pringle made a tentative attempt to determine the size of Byzantine garrisons from the area enclosed within a fortress wall. He points out the difficulties in doing this, but at Isthmia those difficulties may be minimized by the following considerations: (1) since Corinth was fortified at the time the Hexamilion was built and Acrocorinth was also probably available, there was no need to provide a large area for civilian refugees in the Fortress, and (2) although there must have been some mounted soldiers stationed at Isthmia, both the terrain and nature of the barbarian enemy suggest that the majority of the troops were infantry.

Using Pringle's calculations from Thamugadi and his very rough "rule of thumb", we might estimate that the Fortress at Isthmia could accommodate a force of some 2,000 men.[18] That a figure of 2,000 soldiers is not completely unreasonable is indicated by Procopius' statement (*Aed.* 4.2.14) that Justinian established a garrison of 2,000 soldiers at Thermopylai. The fortifications at Thermopylai may be slightly more difficult to defend than those on the Isthmus, although they are of roughly similar scale, and most of the soldiers defending the Hexamilion may have been stationed at the Fortress. It is not unreasonable then to think of a total garrison for the Hexamilion of up to 2,000 soldiers, of whom most might have been maintained at the Fortress. Soldiers were, of course, often stationed in early Byzantine cities, and one might expect some of them to have lived in Corinth and Acrocorinth. It is, however, probably significant that of all the many Christian epitaphs from Corinth, only three are of soldiers or military officials, and all of these refer to *excubitores*, who were members of the imperial guard in Constantinople; presumably, they simply retired to Corinth.[19]

The anonymous sixth-century *De re strategica* says that a *tagma* was made up of four units of 64 men, for a total of 256 soldiers.[20] On the basis of this evidence, the Fortress at Isthmia may be thought to have been designed to accommodate eight *tagmata* of infantry. Relying more on fourth- and fifth-century evidence, Jones argued that a legion had approximately a thousand men, while smaller units (*numeri* or *arithmoi*) had about half that number, and so the Fortress may have held two legions or their equivalent.[21]

In fact, it is unlikely that the Hexamilion was ever designed to be manned continuously. In the fifth century, barbarian attacks were, after all, relatively infrequent, and it would have been unreasonable to maintain a permanent garrison there. The *Notitia dignitatum*, moreover, which was compiled about the time the Hexamilion was constructed, has no information about any military units stationed in Greece, and it was traditional for the proconsul of Achaia to be a civilian official with no troops at his disposal. Probably, the Hexamilion was designed to be occupied and defended by an expeditionary force such as that commanded by Stilicho in 396 during the invasion of Alaric.

---

[17] R. G. Collingwood and I. A. Richmond, *The Archaeology of Roman Britain*, 3rd ed., London 1969, pp. 25–26.

[18] Pringle, *Defence* I, pp. 83–89. Thamugadi has an area of 0.75 ha. Using the size of the stables as a guide, Pringle estimated that the fort would accommodate approximately 300 cavalry or twice that number of infantry. The fortress at Isthmia is 2.71 ha., or 3.6 times larger than that at Thamugadi. Using Pringle's "rule of thumb", the corresponding number of infantry would be 2,160, but the few cavalry that were certainly present would undoubtedly have reduced the number somewhat.

[19] *Corinth* VIII, iii, nos. 541, 558. Cf., however, no. 553; Bees, *Inschriften*, pp. 11–12, no. 3. The latter inscription was first published by Monceaux ("Fouilles," 1885, p. 410), and Bees implied that it was excavated in the area of the Fortress ("Die Inschrift wurde in der Umgebung des Isthmos ausgegraben"), which might be of considerable significance for the Hexamilion. Monceaux, however, clearly says ("Fouilles," 1885, p. 409) that the tombstone was found west of Corinth along the road to Sikyon.

[20] *De re strategica*, pp. 1–209, 311–355.

[21] A. H. M. Jones, *The Later Roman Empire*, Oxford 1964, pp. 681–682.

Alternatively, local residents may have been pressed into service to defend their homes by manning the Hexamilion.[22]

Procopius says that before Justinian, the fortifications at Thermopylai were not guarded by regular soldiers, but that when the enemy arrived, some local farmers (ἀγροικικῶν ἐπιχωρίων τινες) guarded the walls. Not surprisingly, Procopius notes that these makeshift soldiers were not very successful in holding the line and that Justinian replaced them with regular troops.[23] The situation on the Hexamilion is likely to have been similar.

There were probably other forts or fortresses along the course of the Hexamilion. Bastions were certainly placed at either end, overlooking the Corinthian and the Saronic Gulfs, and there may have been fortresses above the Kyras Vrysi Ravine and at the top of Mytikas (see pp. 36 and 49 above).

TOWERS

All the towers of the Hexamilion were rectangular, except for the four towers of the two gates of the Fortress. Those of the Northeast Gate were, individually, half-round and quarter-round, while those of the South Gate were externally octagonal. (Details of tower construction are discussed in "Construction Technique," pp. 136–140 below.) The preference for rectangular towers is typical of Byzantine fortifications of the fifth and sixth centuries, as seen, for example, at Constantinople, Thessaloniki, Resafa, and Nikopolis. In the western part of the empire, round, half-round, and even fan-shaped towers enjoyed considerable popularity,[24] but in the eastern part of the empire, Hellenistic models prevailed.[25] In terms of fortification techniques, there can be no doubt that the Hexamilion falls clearly in the world of Byzantium.[26]

The towers normally had no entrance from ground level (exceptions are Tower 15, some of those recently excavated east of the National Highway, S-3 and S-4), and access into the towers was from the fighting platform. Descent to ground level inside the towers must normally have been by means of a ladder, showing incidentally that floors at the lower fighting level must have been of wood, although in Tower 6 there was a stairway partly built into the masonry of the tower wall. Most of the towers must have had a second story above the level of the fighting platform, although there is little direct evidence for it, and this was probably carried on vaults to support artillery, and left open to the sky.[27]

The purpose of the tower was twofold: (1) to provide a solid and elevated platform for the deployment of artillery and (2) to allow enfilading fire along the line of the wall.[28] Arrangements were probably always made to allow enfilading fire wherever the lay of the land or turns in the Hexamilion made this important. As we have seen, for example, the bastion at Tower 2 was probably extended to fighting-platform level to allow fire from the tower in four separate directions.

[22] Again, we have no evidence, either literary or epigraphic, of the presence of *limitanei* in the province of Achaia. See *ibid.*, pp. 607–686.

[23] *Aed.* 4.2.15; cf. *Anekdota* 26.31–33, where the same story is told, but Justinian's motives are described very differently. Cf. also Procopius' note (*Aed.* 4.10.9) that when the enemy (the Huns?) attacked the διατείχισμα across the Thracian Chersonese, the defenders simply ran away.

[24] Johnson, *Late Roman Fortifications*, pp. 38–41.

[25] Note the comments of Winter (*Greek Fortifications*, p. 203).

[26] R. Krautheimer, *Early Christian and Byzantine Architecture*, 3rd ed., Harmondsworth 1979, pp. 108–114, 141, 375.

[27] See pp. 69–70 above; compare, however, evidence for roofing elsewhere, in Johnson, *Late Roman Fortifications*, pp. 40–43.

[28] Winter, *Greek Fortifications*, pp. 152–203; E. W. Marsden, *Greek and Roman Artillery: Historical Development*, Oxford 1969, pp. 116–163.

The placement of towers seems commonly to have been determined by the steepness of the land immediately below the Hexamilion; in general, towers were located only in places where access to the Hexamilion was relatively easy. This observation assumes that the original spacing of the towers is more or less what is visible now, and this requires a consideration of the literary evidence for the towers. Procopius speaks of *phrouria* and *phylakteria* (fortresses and guard-stations), and it seems reasonable to identify the latter with the towers. Procopius, however, gives no evidence about the number of towers. Pseudo-Phrantzes, perhaps following the Short Chronicle 35 (Testimonia, 8), says that the Hexamilion was originally constructed (by Justinian) with 153 towers. We have been able to identify 68 towers, which suggests, if the literary evidence is correct, that over half the towers have not been found. Indeed, we may have failed to identify a number of towers in the eastern section of the Hexamilion, between W-2 and W-5, and it is of course impossible to locate any towers southeast of S-21. Nevertheless, long sections of the Hexamilion are relatively well preserved, and these have been carefully investigated; it is, for example, very unlikely that any towers have been missed between the Kyras Vrysi Ravine and the top of Mytikas. Recent excavations east of the National Highway resulted in the discovery of one tower beyond those that we had previously noted, and this is a good indication of what might be expected if the whole wall were exposed. In such a situation, one may reasonably question the number given by our literary sources. These may, of course, have counted certain strong points (such as the corners of the Roman Bath) as towers, but a simpler solution is to conclude that they are plainly wrong in saying that the Hexamilion had 153 towers. As will be argued below, they may have based the total not on observation or an official account but on a simple formula.

It may be concluded, in any case, that the towers were generally located where the danger of access to the Hexamilion was great, in other words, where the land to the north was not steep. Thus, towers are concentrated at either end of the Hexamilion, protecting the sea bastions (W-2, S-17 to S-21). Other points of danger were in the flat land near the modern National Highway (W-5 to W-10), in the area where the Great Ravine would have funneled an attacking enemy toward relatively flat land, and at the crossing at the Kyras Vrysi Ravine (W-13 to W-26). The entire section of the Hexamilion southeast of the Fortress may be regarded as an especially crucial part of the fortification since an enemy coming from Attica or central Greece would have been expected to turn the Hexamilion along the eastern flank. This probably explains the presence of towers not only in relatively low-lying land (S-2 to S-6 and S-18 to S-21) but also along the slopes of Mytikas (S-7 to S-17).

The strategy envisioned for the Hexamilion must have been to turn an attack away from the naturally weak eastern section inward toward the west. As the enemy passed westward along the Great Ravine, their army would be subject to heavy fire from the Fortress and the towers of the southeast. If an enemy passed beyond this difficulty, the maximum range of catapults (*ca.* 400 meters) and the steepness of the ascent would make any massed attack on the Hexamilion impossible until W-26, and this, of course, is the area where the towers begin once again.

The discussion above suggests that we should not expect any rigidly regular spacing of the towers; spacing will depend on the lay of the land and the accompanying threat to the Hexamilion. Nevertheless, is it possible to determine an ideal tower spacing in those areas where towers exist? The "normal" spacing seems to be somewhere in the neighborhood of 40–50 meters, or sometimes double that distance (see Appendix). This suggests that the builders may have been using a quarter-stade of *ca.* 45.97 m. as their basic linear distance (assuming a stade of 625 feet and a foot of 0.2942 m. = a stade of 183.875 m.). Even the larger distances between towers may have been calculated in this way, since some of the larger spacings fall close to a multiple of a stade. Thus the distance between W-3 and W-4 is 360 meters, that between W-26 and T-15 is 377 meters, while two stades would be 368 meters. Even a large distance such as the 1,694 meters between W-2 and W-3 comes close to the 1,656 meters of nine stades.

Several late Byzantine sources give the length of the Hexamilion in stades or *ourgiai*, one one-hundreth of a stade; thus, Chalkokondyles says that the length of the Hexamilion was 42 stades, while the Short Chronicle and Pseudo-Phrantzes give 3,800 *ourgiai* = 38 stades. These calculations are remarkably close to the actual length, given the distances involved, 7,728 meters for Chalkokondyles and 6,992 meters for the Short Chronicle and Pseudo-Phrantzes.[29] Interestingly, if we assume that the latter authors knew or were able to infer that the "normal" tower spacing was a quarter of a stade, they would easily have been able to calculate the number of towers along the Hexamilion (but naturally not along the Fortress walls). The figure obtained would be exactly the 153 given by the two authors (i.e., 38 stades × 4 = 152 spaces between towers, with a total number of 153 towers). It is difficult to think this is entirely coincidental: their figure for the number of towers may have been based on a formula rather than on observation.

PROTEICHISMA AND TAPHROS

Hellenistic and Byzantine manuals on fortification called for the addition of a forward wall (προτείχισμα) and ditch or moat (τάφρος) in front of the main defensive wall.[30] Both *proteichisma* and *taphros* have previously been identified on the Hexamilion,[31] and abundant literary evidence survives to show that Manuel II excavated defensive trenches along the Hexamilion. The wall that Megaw identified as a *proteichisma*, however (p. 45 above), was part of an earlier building and had no connection with the Hexamilion. No other evidence of a *proteichisma* exists in any other part of the fortifications, and we may conclude there was none.[32]

There is much better evidence for the *taphros*. In the area of the Northeast Gate, the *taphros* can be shown to belong to the original phase of the Hexamilion (p. 80 above). It was, in fact, filled in when the bastion was built in the middle of the sixth century. There is, however, no other evidence of a *taphros* in other parts of the Fortress, presumably because of the natural declivity of the land in nearly every direction.

Along the course of the Hexamilion, the *taphros* can be detected at a number of places, usually in concert with a string of towers (e.g. between 0 + 2,400 m. and the National Highway, between 0 + 4,600 m. and the Roman Bath, and on the slopes of Mytikas). In the absence of excavation and close observation of ancient ground level, it is difficult to form an impression of the width and depth of the *taphros* of the Hexamilion, and the situation is obviously complicated by successive re-exposure of the ditch.[33] It is clear that at least the bottom of the *taphros* was often cut directly into the bedrock in front of the Hexamilion, and blocks removed from the ditch must have been used in the wall. The *taphros* seems generally to have been 8–10 meters in front of the Hexamilion. This is considerably less than the almost 18 meters from the face of the inner wall at Constantinople to the

[29] Compare the observations and calculations of Lambros («Tὰ τείχη», 1905, p. 450), where he uses a stade of 184.98 m.

[30] *De re strategica* 12.5–7; the principles were already in place in the work of Philo of Byzantium, e.g., 1.69–74.

[31] See Pringle, *Defence* I, pp. 147–148; compare the rather peculiar comments of Lawrence ("Skeletal History," pp. 185–186), who makes a "massive" *protechisma* an indication of mid-5th-century date.

[32] Jenkins and Megaw, "Researches," pp. 77–79, fig. 5; cf. *Corinth* I, i, pp. 52–53, fig. 24, following Frazer.

[33] The situation with the *taphros* exactly reverses that of the Hexamilion itself; in the case of the latter, rebuildings normally affected only the superstructure and left the lower part of the wall largely untouched, while later excavation in the *taphros* may affect the size of the original ditch.

taphros[34] and the 21–36 meters at Resafa.[35] The cuttings in bedrock vary from 2.50 to 4.50 m. wide, but this may represent only the bottom of the cutting. A depression *ca.* 9 meters wide, visible west of the National Highway and southeast of the Fortress, probably gives a better indication of the width of the *taphros*. It should be noted, however, that the *De re strategica* advocates a width of 18.74 m. for the *taphros*, and the trenches at both Constantinople and Carthage closely approach this size.[36]

DIMENSIONS AND STAIRWAYS

The normal width of the Hexamilion is *ca.* 2.94 m., equaling ten Roman feet of 0.294 m. each. This strongly supports a pre-Justinianic date for the whole of the fortifications, since by the early sixth century the size of the foot had increased to *ca.* 0.315 m.[37] The Fortress wall was thinner, regularly about 2.30 m. wide, which may represent eight Roman feet (= 2.34 m.) or the five cubits (also 2.34 m.) recommended by the author of the *De re strategica* (12.1).

Unfortunately, the Hexamilion is nowhere preserved to the fighting platform, and so observations about the height of the wall must be based on restoration or analogy. In addition, the height of the Hexamilion may have varied from place to place. At the Northeast Gate the fighting platform has been restored at an elevation of *ca.* 7.29 m. above the ground outside the Fortress, and at Tower 2 it is restored at a level of 6.48 m. above the ground; at the Roman Bath, however, we have suggested a height of 5.36 m. To these levels should be added a parapet wall of *ca.* two meters. These figures may be compared to the height of 20 cubits (9.37 m. in the sixth century) recommended by both Philo and the *De re strategica*.[38] If Procopius is to be relied upon, fifth- and early sixth-century fortification walls were considerably lower than their Justinianic successors, and the Hexamilion seems to fit nicely into this scheme.[39] There are of course, very few securely dated fifth-century walls that preserve their original height, which makes comparison with the Hexamilion difficult. The larger wall at Constantinople was 11 meters high, but this represents a special case, and the smaller wall at Constantinople, which was 4.80 m. high on the interior and perhaps twice that high on the exterior where it faced on the *taphros*, presents a closer parallel with the Hexamilion. By contrast, the wall at Resafa is 11.70 m. high,[40] Amida varied from 8 to 12 meters,[41] and the original wall of Dara was higher than the 30 feet (*ca.* 9 meters) described by Procopius.[42]

[34] This assumes that the original *taphros* on the Land Walls was directly in front of the smaller wall.

[35] The considerable distance between the main wall and outworks elsewhere, both along the Hexamilion and at other sites, is further reason to doubt the reality of Megaw's *taphros* and *proteichisma*, which lie even closer to the outer face of the Hexamilion.

[36] 12.6–7; on Carthage, see Pringle, *Defence* I, p. 149.

[37] See P. A. Underwood, "Principles of Measure in the Architecture of the Period of Justinian," *Cahiers archéologiques* 3, 1948, pp. 64–74; E. Schilbach, *Byzantinische Metrologie* (*Handbuch der Altertumswissenshaft* XII, iv), Munich 1970, pp. 13–16, 20–21. The width of the wall at Resafa varies from 2.80 to 3.10 m. (Karnapp, *Stadtmauer*, p. 9).

[38] Philo, 1.12; *De re strategica* 12.1.

[39] E.g., *Aed.* 2.1.16 (Dara); 2.5.2–5 (Constantina, where the earlier walls were supposedly so low they could be scaled with a ladder); 2.9.18–20 (Zeugma and Neocaesarea); 3.2.10 (Martyropolis, where the walls were supposedly so low the enemy could just climb over them; they were only 20 feet high); 3.5.6–12 (Theodosiopolis); 4.10.5 (the *diateichisma* on the Thracian Chersonese, which Procopius compares to the wall around a garden, surmountable with a ladder); 4.9.16 (Toperus in Rhodope). Note, however, the cautionary comments of Brian Croke and James Crow, "Procopius and Dara," *JRS* 73, 1983, pp. 143–159.

[40] Karnapp, *Stadtmauer*, p. 17; this is the level of the upper fighting platform; the level of the lower fighting platform is 5.90 m.

[41] A. Gabriel, *Voyages archéologiques dans la Turkie orientale*, Paris 1940, pp. 96–113.

[42] Croke and Crow (footnote 39 above), p. 155.

There is relatively good evidence for stairways within the Fortress but very little for the rest of the Hexamilion.[43] The absence of ground-level doorways in most of the towers, however, shows that the system of stairways along the Hexamilion must have been similar to that within the Fortress. In all known cases, the stairways were built on foundations that widened the Hexamilion or the Fortress wall on the interior by *ca.* 0.70 m. The stairs are *ca.* 1.00 m. wide and bonded into the interior face of the wall, a system that precluded the necessity of narrowing the fighting platform to accommodate the stairways. The stairs have treads that vary from *ca.* 0.28 m. to 0.36 m., and a rise of from *ca.* 0.24 m. to *ca.* 0.34 m., but the angle of ascent is always very close to 45 degrees.

In most cases, the stairways ascend toward a tower, and we may imagine that nearly every tower had such an ascent, from which entrance would be made into the upper story. At the Northeast Gate we can identify two stairways converging on the gate complex, replicating a system that is common in early Byzantine fortifications elsewhere.[44] Between Towers 13 and 14, however, the stairs simply converge toward each other and do not ascend toward the towers.[45] Entrance into the second story of the towers must have simply been through doorways at the level of the fighting platform. Arrangements for the ascent to the third story of the towers may have varied. In the absence of direct evidence, we have suggested three possibilities: (1) in the case where the third floor was wooden, a simple ladder may have been used, (2) stairs may have risen from the fighting platform on the wall outside the tower, necessitating a protective parapet along the stairs,[46] or (3) a stairway may have been concealed within the masonry of the tower, possibly rising over the vaulted ceiling of the second level.[47]

CONSTRUCTION TECHNIQUE

The Hexamilion was normally constructed of two faces of ashlar masonry with a core of mortar and rubble.[48] Header blocks, not uncommonly sections of columns, bind the facing to the core and prevent the faces from simply becoming detached and falling off. This technique is apparently what Vitruvius (2.8.7) called *emplekton* (ἔμπλεκτον).[49] The key element of *emplekton* technique is the use of header-and-stretcher construction, and Vitruvius advised Italian architects to take advantage of the greater strength that it allowed. Originally, of course, the core of the *emplekton* wall was simply dry rubble, but by the early fifth century, mortar was commonly added both to the rubble core and to the facing walls. This addition allowed the wall to rise to a greater height than it could otherwise attain,[50] and it is to be contrasted with other masonry techniques, such as the *opus mixtum* used extensively in western Asia Minor, Constantinople, and the Balkans. *Emplekton* technique, in fact, seems to reflect Hellenistic rather than Roman influence,[51] and it can be seen at

---

[43] On systems of stairways, see Lawrence, *Greek Aims*, pp. 345–347.

[44] E.g., Karnapp, *Stadtmauer*, pls. 133, 134; Meyer-Plath and Schneider, *Landmauer* II, pl. 4.

[45] Cf. Kirchen, *Landmauer* I, pl. 4, stairs near tower 47 at Constantinople.

[46] Kirchen, *Landmauer* I, pls. 6, 11; Meyer-Plath and Schneider, *Landmauer* II, pl. 9.

[47] Meyer-Plath and Schneider, *Landmauer* II, pl. 9.

[48] In general, see J. B. Ward Perkins, "Notes on the Structure and Building Materials of Early Byzantine Architecture," in *The Great Palace of the Byzantine Emperors*, 2nd report, D. Talbot Rice, ed., Edinburgh 1958, pp. 53–104, and W. L. MacDonald, "Some Implications of Later Roman Construction," *Journal of the Society of Architectural Historians* 17, 1958, pp. 2–8.

[49] R. A. Tomlinson, "Emplekton Masonry and 'Greek Struktura,'" *JHS* 81, 1961, pp. 133–140; L. W. Daly, "Echinos and Justinian's Fortifications in Greece," *AJA* 46, 1942, pp. 500–508; see also Pringle, *Defence* I, pp. 138–139, 428–429.

[50] Pringle, *Defence* I, p. 138.

[51] Cf. Winter, *Greek Fortifications*, pp. 69–100, 203.

various sites in Greece, notably at near-by Corinth, Sparta, Epidauros, and Aigina, all of whose walls may date to the fifth century. Significantly, the Late Roman fortification at Athens, securely dated to the late third century, has a core that may not have been bonded with mortar.[52]

The mortar used in the Hexamilion naturally varies considerably from place to place, but normally it is very white and quite hard, with many small and medium-sized river stones mixed in. Commonly, there are large quantities of crushed tiles, but in some places these are absent.

The Hexamilion was normally constructed over shallow foundations of mortar poured into a cutting dug into the soil or cut into bedrock.[53] The foundations are usually wider than the wall by 0.10–0.25 m. Not uncommonly, the natural slope of the landscape was made even steeper by a substantial excavation in bedrock directly in front of the Hexamilion, thus leaving a vertical rock face upon which the Hexamilion could be built. Two different techniques seem to have been used in this connection: one placed the blocks of the outer face at the top of the ledge cut in bedrock, while in other places these facing blocks were laid up against the vertical cutting.

The faces and the core of the Hexamilion were built together in courses. The rubble of the core was not simply dumped into the interstices, but the small irregular stones were actually laid and cemented into courses.[54] The facing walls were naturally laid first, and where the facing blocks have fallen away, the core preserves the impression of their interior faces, often forming a flat surface that looks almost finished. Once a section of the facing walls had been laid, and presumably allowed to set for a time, the rubble-and-mortar core was laid until it reached the top of the highest course of the facing walls. The masonry was then allowed to set before the next course of facing walls and core were added. The height of the coursing of the core was naturally determined by the height of the blocks used in the facing walls. The technique has frequently left horizontal lines in the core where the facing blocks have fallen away; this is most clearly visible in the East Fortress Wall southwest of Tower 2 (Pl. 39:c).

The facing walls are normally made of large rectangular blocks of local Corinthian sandstone, most of them originally taken from the quarries between Isthmia and Ancient Corinth.[55] The blocks are naturally of different sizes, but they are commonly ca. 1.2–1.6 m. long, 0.4–0.7 m. high, and 0.6 m. thick; header blocks, of course, are placed with their greatest length within the interior of the wall (Ills. 24, 25). The blocks are commonly worked with a clawtooth chisel, which has left characteristic marks on the stone.

The rectangular blocks were normally laid in level courses, although the height of the courses varies considerably from place to place, and in some areas (Towers 6 and 8, for example) orthostate courses alternate with the more normal horizontal technique (Ill. 24). Likewise, the vertical joints between blocks are sometimes so well fitted that it is obvious that the blocks were cut to be placed together, either in the Hexamilion or in some earlier structure that was cannibalized for construction of the latter. Tiles and mortar are frequently used as chinking to level the courses when the

[52] Gregory, "Fortified Cities." Monica B. Fullerton, who is preparing a dissertation on the 3rd-century fortifications of Greece, informs me that the notebooks of the Agora Excavations clearly indicate that the core of the Late Roman fortification in Athens originally contained mortar. This has presumably been washed away. See now John Travlos in *Agora* XXIV, p. 126: "The spaces between the stones were filled with small chips of architectural members . . . all bonded together by lime mortar of a poor consistency and not very strong."

[53] See Philo (1.1), who recommends plastered foundations already in Hellenistic times.

[54] Cf. Ward Perkins (footnote 48 above, p. 136), p. 66: "[In the Theodosian Walls of Constantinople] the normal practice seems to have been to distinguish between the part [of the core] lying immediately behind the facing, which was solidly built of coursed and mortared rubble to a depth of 1–1.3 m., and the heart of the wall, which consisted of two or more layers of angular rubble, loosely tipped in between two faces and sealed in place by the next band of brickwork. Very little mortar was used in this core, in many places only a capping between one and the next."

[55] Freyberg, *Geologie*, "Korinthischer Bausandstein," pl. 31.

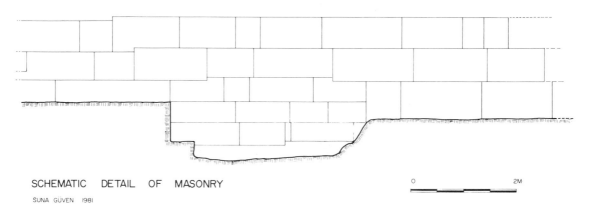

SCHEMATIC   DETAIL   OF   MASONRY

SUNA GÜVEN 1981

0 _____ 2M

ILL. 24. Detail of wall construction west of the Northeast Gate

blocks were not all of equal height; this is done quite neatly in some parts of the Hexamilion and much more crudely elsewhere. In at least three places, however (Tower 15, the Northeast Gate bastion, and Tower S-9), there are leveling courses of mortar and brick, such as one sees, for example, on the Land Walls of Constantinople and elsewhere in the Aegean. In at least two of these cases, the brick courses are clearly additions to the Hexamilion, probably of Justinianic date, and no certain evidence exists that brick courses were ever used in the original construction of the Hexamilion.

So far as can be determined, the exterior face of the Hexamilion was always built of ashlar masonry. The inner face, however, displays considerably more variation. In the immediate area of the Fortress, it seems always to have been built in ashlar style, but in the Roman Bath, for example, it is constructed of small stones set in mortar, in a style that is more reminiscent of the core than of the normal outer face. There can, however, be no doubt that this was the original inner face of the Hexamilion here, and it does not, in fact, have the horizontal coursing lines that mark normal core construction. Inside the Roman Bath, although small uncoursed stones are used, the inner face of the Hexamilion is carefully finished with troweled mortar. A similar technique is used on the inner face of the Hexamilion in the area of the National Highway.

Throughout the Hexamilion, the builders clearly were not concerned about careful bonding. Thus, many of the tower walls do not bond with the curtain wall, but this was not done, as some of the military manuals suggest, to prevent the towers from falling if the curtain wall were to fall, for we see at Tower 2 that one tower wall is bonded while the other is not. Presumably, the builders were simply indifferent to the issue of bonding.

The construction of the tower walls also shows considerable variation. As can be seen in the Appendix, many of the towers are longer than they are wide, while others are wider than they are long. In addition, some of the tower walls are built exactly like typical Hexamilion construction, with two faces of ashlar blocks and a rubble-and-mortar core, while others are built of two facing walls without a core. These differences seem to have no chronological significance but are probably the result of different construction crews working along the course of the Hexamilion.[56] We have already suggested such an arrangement in the area of Tower 15. Further evidence of this may be sought in the grouping of tower proportions in the Appendix. Thus, if we divide "long" towers (e.g.,

[56] Cf. Ward Perkins (footnote 48 above, p. 136), p. 66: "With so many hands at work at the same time there was inevitably considerable variation of detail [in Constantinople]."

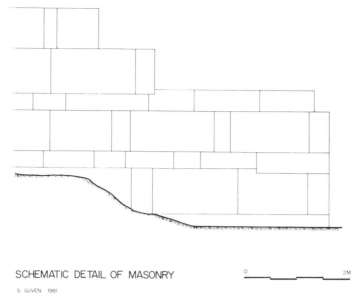

SCHEMATIC DETAIL OF MASONRY   0 _____ 2M

S. GUVEN 1981

ILL. 25. Detail of wall construction west of Tower 6

those whose projection is greater than their width) from "wide" towers, there is a clear tendency for towers of the same type to group together along the course of the Hexamilion.

Also characteristic of Hexamilion construction is the use of spolia from the near-by Sanctuary of Poseidon and from other ancient buildings in the area. Some blocks clearly were quarried for construction of the Hexamilion, for example, from the small quarry near Tower 2, but it must be admitted that a large quantity of the ashlar facing of the Hexamilion must have come from ancient buildings.[57] Such a practice, it might be noted, was encouraged both by Vitruvius (1.5.8) and the anonymous author of the *De re strategica* (10.3). Even column drums from the classical Temple of Poseidon were not exempt from this treatment, and they were frequently cut into three sections to serve as facing blocks.[58] Nonrectangular blocks, however, were more commonly used in the core of the Hexamilion and in the foundations. Two columns from the orchestra of the Theater were incorporated into the Hexamilion, one drum built into the entrance into Tower 15 and other fragments in the area between the Northeast Gate and Tower 2. Inscribed entablature blocks with moldings were built into the roadway through the Northeast Gate, and two victor's monuments found their way there as well, turned with their faces down and the back of the blocks used for paving. Column drums were used as header blocks in the facing of the interior of the Hexamilion in the area of Tower 2 and just north of the Roman Bath.

Spolia were not only incorporated in the Hexamilion in the immediate vicinity of the sanctuary. As we have seen, there are columns built into Tower S-9 on the slopes of Mytikas, ancient blocks in the area just east of the Kyras Vrysi Ravine, in the area near the National Highway, and in the Sea Bastion. In the present state of our knowledge, it is impossible to know whether these

[57] See Wiseman's comment (*Land*, p. 77, note 97): "It is possible that the ruins of the Isthmian Sanctuary afforded such a copious amount of building material that the builders of late imperial times chose the shorter route of the Wall of Justinian chiefly for that reason."

[58] See Broneer, 1953, pp. 184–185, fig. 65:a, lower right.

blocks were brought to these locations for a specific decorative purpose or whether there had been older buildings near by that were available for use when the Hexamilion was built.

Blocks with swallowtail-clamp cuttings are common in the Hexamilion, especially in the area from the Roman Bath to the Fortress.[59] In some cases, the blocks were probably reassembled by the builders of the Hexamilion in exactly the same relationship they had in the original structure, but in other cases, it seems that the Hexamilion simply followed the walls of pre-existing buildings, and this can be seen most clearly in the area of the Roman Bath and probably also in some parts of the Fortress (the Roman Arch, of course, but also probably in the areas of Towers 17 and 10). This apparent eagerness to make use of pre-existing walls is, in fact, one of the primary features of the Hexamilion.

The use of spolia, however, was not only a practical expedient; re-used ancient blocks were also attractive in their own right, and they were incorporated for decorative as well as economic purposes.[60] In fact, as Pringle has pointed out, the use of spolia is not a "sign of decadence or evidence for a decline in building skill."[61] Thus, the greatest use of spolia was to incorporate the Roman Arch within the fabric of the Northeast Gate in such a way that the central arch was still visible from the east and much of the superstructure could be seen on the west. The use of the curved blocks with moldings on the North Tower is another example of the same phenomenon, where a decorative effect was obviously intended. The superstructure of the Hexamilion is not preserved high enough to allow us to know if other ancient blocks were used for the same purpose, but it certainly seems likely.

Indeed, it is clear that aesthetic considerations often played a role in the construction of the Hexamilion. Again, the use of the Roman Arch is a case in point, as are the crosses that decorated the South Gate. Certainly, the better sections of wall construction, for example, between Towers 6 and 8 and west of the Northeast Gate, are impressive and beautiful in their own right; the technique was such as to lead Monceaux and many later scholars to consider them examples of the finest classical Greek work. Clearly, the early Byzantine mind could consider fortification walls as beautiful and more than merely utilitarian. Procopius, for example, expressed such an attitude when he described the wall at Meletine as a thing of beauty (ἐγκαλλόπισμα), something to be proud of, and when he said that Justinian made the walls of Bosporus and Cherson "beautiful" (καλοί).[62] The same can be seen even more strikingly in the ruins of early Byzantine fortifications that are better preserved than those at Isthmia. Perhaps the best example is the North Gate at Resafa, presumably a Justinianic construction, where the triple entrance is decorated with an engaged arcade with deeply carved capitals and architrave.[63]

[59] Pp. 46–47 above. For a discussion of such clamp cuttings and whether they ever had clamps, see Gregory and Mills, "Roman Arch," p. 413.

[60] Gregory, "Fortified Cities," pp. 16, 20.

[61] Pringle, *Defence* I, p. 133.

[62] *Aed.* 3.4.20; 3.7.10.

[63] Karnapp, *Stadtmauer*, pls. 173–211.

XI
THE HISTORY OF THE HEXAMILION

AS INDICATED IN THE INTRODUCTION, temporary or permanent defenses across the Isthmus may have been built before construction of the Hexamilion, although it is difficult to connect any known remains with a single line of defense. No "Valerian" Hexamilion, however, or any other defense along the line of the Hexamilion existed until the early years of the fifth century. Zosimus' account of these years (Testimonia, 1) merely reveals one of the many occasions in which the Isthmus of Corinth was seen as a natural point of defense for the Peloponnesos.

Paul Clement repeatedly pointed out that construction of the Hexamilion is surely to be connected with the aftermath of Alaric's devastation of Greece and Italy.[1] It is, of course, rather fashionable today to minimize the effect of the barbarian invasions, and these certainly cannot be held, in themselves, as the primary cause of the demise of ancient civilization. Nevertheless, several invasions were of unusual severity, and they had the effect, at least, of drawing attention to the problems of military weakness that characterized the world of late antiquity. The invasions of Alaric and the Visigoths certainly had such an effect.[2]

In the military vacuum caused by the death of Theodosius the Great in 395, Alaric's Visigoths found themselves deprived of both government support and active Roman control. Unable to move directly against Constantinople, Alaric turned south into Greece, where he devastated the Peloponnesos, apparently remaining in the countryside for a year or so.[3] Zosimus says specifically that Megara, Corinth, Argos, and Sparta were taken by the barbarian, while Claudian paints a picture of enslaved women and despoiled sanctuaries.[4] No literary source directly mentions Alaric at Isthmia, but the archaeological evidence is clear.[5] Alaric's depredations were certainly aided by the rivalry between Stilicho, master of the West, and his enemy Rufinus, the primary adviser of the young emperor Arcadius, but the devastation had a significant impact on Greek society, including the attitudes of the aristocrats who were still attached to traditional paganism. This latter point is not often noted, but it is clearly shown by the reaction of Eunapius, one of the strongest supporters of the "old system" in Greece. Zosimus' account of these events (Testimonia, 2) comes directly from Eunapius' now lost *Universal History*, and Zosimus' interest in and hostility toward Alaric are certainly derived from that source. Also from Eunapius is Zosimus' thinly veiled disdain for the cowardice or complicity of the imperial official Gerontius, who allegedly allowed Alaric passage through Thermopylai and the Isthmus. In his *Vitae sophistorum*, Eunapius has even more telling evidence about the effect the invasion had on him and his fellow pagan aristocrats: the "crime" of choosing an Eleusinian hierophant from outside the traditional Athenian families was a prelude to and a cause of the devastation and destruction of the temples of Greece at the hands of the Visigoths.[6]

---

[1] Clement, "Date of the Hexamilion"; Clement, "Alaric," pp. 135–137; Beaton and Clement, "Date of Destruction."

[2] J. B. Bury, *History of the Later Roman Empire from the Death of Theodosius I to the Death of Justinian (395–565)*, 2nd ed., I, London 1923, pp. 110–112, 174–185; Stein, *Histoire* I, pp. 321, 355–361; *Agora* XXIV, pp. 49–56. On the effect of invasions on the fabric of late Roman society, see the thoughtful comments of Alexander Kazhdan and Anthony Cutler, "Continuity and Discontinuity in Byzantine History," *Byzantion* 52, 1982, pp. 429–478, esp. pp. 440–441.

[3] Zosimus, 5.6.

[4] *In Rufinum* 2.187–191 (p. 37, Hall); *In Eutropium* 2.200–201 (p. 174, Hall).

[5] A. E. Beaton and P. A. Clement, "The Destruction of the Sanctuary of Poseidon on the Isthmus of Corinth," *Hesperia* 45, 1976, pp. 267–279; cf. Broneer, *Isthmia* III, p. 3, note 9.

[6] *Vitae sophistorum*, pp. 436–438, 482 (Loeb).

Alaric was, of course, finally driven from Greece, but within a few years he attacked Italy, and in 410 the unthinkable happened: Rome fell to the invaders and was sacked.[7] This event, which may not have been of immediate political or military significance, exacerbated the conflict between Christians and pagans and led St. Augustine to write the *City of God*. It is within this context, and as a reaction to the invasion of Alaric, that we should place construction of the Hexamilion. The Land Walls of Constantinople were begun in 413, and the city walls of Corinth were probably built in the first two decades of the fifth century, along with other fortifications throughout the diocese of Illyricum.[8] On the basis of historical evidence, it is reasonable to connect the Hexamilion with these other fortification projects.

The archaeological record is unequivocal that the Hexamilion, the Fortress, and certainly the bulk of the towers were constructed at essentially the same time. Evidence from all parts of the excavations suggests a date in the early years of the fifth century for the Hexamilion, but it is possible to be a little more precise. The coins from the cracks and clamp cuttings in the roadway of the Northeast Gate (see pp. 74–75 above) included a single issue of Arcadius (A.D. 402–408), and this may be taken as a *terminus post quem* for construction of the Hexamilion. Probably more conclusive are the coins from Grave 1 at the Northeast Gate. This grave was built at a time when the Fortress was out of use: construction of the neighboring grave (Grave 2) required the removal of the lowest step of the stairway to the fighting platform (p. 77 above). Within Grave 1 were three datable coins, two of Marcian (A.D. 450–457) and one possibly of Leo I (A.D. 457–474). These present a clear *terminus ante quem* for construction of the Hexamilion: it must have been built early enough so that by the time these graves were used, the fortifications had already fallen into disuse and decay. Nearly as significant as the numismatic evidence is the ceramic material discovered in foundation trenches for the Hexamilion and in fill apparently piled up against the wall at the time of construction. In place after place, these levels regularly contain Athenian pre-glaze lamps and pottery of the very late fourth and early fifth centuries.[9] For all these reasons, it is difficult to think that the Hexamilion was built later than A.D. 420, and it is probably best to assign its construction to the second decade of the century.[10]

In the absence of literary evidence, the length of time required for construction of the Hexamilion cannot be known. Comparison with other contemporary fortification projects is suggestive but provides little certain information. Thus, if the Golden Gate in Constantinople is to be assigned to Theodosius II in commemoration of his victory over the usurper Johannes in 423, then the Land Walls were being built over a period of at least ten years (since construction began in 413). In 447 a great earthquake struck Constantinople, and some fifty-seven towers of the Land Walls collapsed, and this in the face of an expected attack from the Huns. The people of the capital were enlisted for the task of restoration, and the wall was repaired in 60 days, an indication of how quickly a work of

[7] Bury (footnote 2 above, p. 141), pp. 174–185; Stein, *Histoire* I, pp. 355–361.

[8] Gregory, "Late Roman Wall," pp. 269–272; Gregory, "Fortified Cities," pp. 18–21. *CTh* 11.17.4 (A.D. 408 or 412); 15.1.34 (A.D. 396). The walls of Thessaloniki are probably to be dated to the middle of the 5th century. See M. Vickers, "The Late Roman Walls of Thessalonica," in *Transactions of the Eighth International Congress of Frontier Studies*, E. Birley, B. Dobson, and M. Jarrett, edd., Cardiff 1974, pp. 245–248; J. A. S. Evans, "The Walls of Thessalonica," *Byzantion* 47, 1977, pp. 361–362; and J. M. Speiser, *Thessalonique et ses monuments du IVᵉ au VIᵉ siècle* (*Bibliothèque des Écoles françaises d'Athènes et de Rome* 254), Paris 1984, pp. 25–80, esp. pp. 66–67.

[9] See Wohl, "Deposit of Lamps," p. 140.

[10] Robert Hohlfelder ("Trans-Isthmian Walls in the Age of Justinian," *GRBS* 18, 1977, pp. 173–179) proposed a date in the middle of the 5th century, but this was based on a misreading of the numismatic evidence. See the detailed discussion, p. 74 above.

such magnitude could be carried out.[11] In 1971 staff members of the Archaeological Exploration of Sardis calculated the time required for construction of the late antique wall there and concluded that "it could have been completed in as little as 5½ weeks."[12] This figure, however, assumed a construction team of 4,100 workmen, and given the tremendous scope of the variables, such an estimate is of little practical value. Probably more indicative are two Athenian inscriptions that complain amusingly about the ease with which Amphion, the legendary founder of Thebes, built fortifications by charming the stones into place with the music of his lyre! Obviously, the task of wall building in the early Byzantine era was much more difficult.[13]

We are on slightly better ground in considering who built the Hexamilion. Basically, there are two choices: the central government in Constantinople or the cities of the Peloponnesos acting in concert, which is to say their aristocracies. It is clear that wealthy individuals often contributed lavishly to the fortification of their cities, even in early Byzantine times, and the cases of Athens and Side are especially well documented.[14] Nevertheless, it is inconceivable that a project as enormous as the Hexamilion can have been undertaken by private individuals, or even whole cities, and we should certainly see the central government as the dominant force in its construction.

Procopius, of course, provides considerable information regarding imperial building projects. Even if we regard the *De aedificiis* as panegyric, there is still a grain of truth in his account, and especially reliable are the references to fortifications built by Justinian's predecessor Anastasius. Ammianus also preserves many accounts of fortification carried out directly by the emperor on campaign.[15] In most cases, soldiers clearly did the work (e.g., Ammianus, 18.2.3), but occasionally the emperor delegated the work to civilians. Thus, as we have seen, the people of Constantinople (including the Circus Factions) took part in rebuilding the Land Walls in 447. Furthermore, the early Byzantine government frequently resorted to forced contributions from private citizens, and these must have provided much of the material and labor required for fortifications. This policy can be seen most clearly in a law (*CTh* 11.17.4) of 408 or 412 which requires that "all persons, regardless of privilege, shall be compelled to provide for the construction of the walls as well as for purchase and transport of supplies in kind. . . . Everyone, high and low, shall contribute according to the assessment."[16]

The codes make clear that the *praefectus praetorio* was responsible for the over-all supervision of public works projects, including the construction of fortifications, and the praetorian prefect of Illyricum must have supervised building of the Hexamilion. It is even possible to suggest that the official responsible for construction of the Hexamilion was Herculius, praetorian prefect from 408 to 412.[17] Herculius was especially interested in Greece, and he must have made substantial benefactions to the Athenian Academy, leading to the erection of two statues in his honor, one in the

---

[11] P. Speck, "Der Mauerbau in 60 Tagen," *Studien zur Frühgeschichte Konstantinopels* (*Miscellanea Byzantina Monacensia* 14), Munich 1973, pp. 135–178.

[12] D. van Zanten, "Report 1," in *A Survey of Sardis and the Major Monuments outside the City Walls, Archaeological Exploration of Sardis*, G. M. A. Hanfmann and J. C. Waldbaum, edd., Cambridge, Mass. 1975, pp. 41, 176, note 28.

[13] *IG* II², 5199, 5200.

[14] H. A. Thompson, "Athenian Twilight, A.D. 267–600," *JRS* 49, 1959, pp. 61–72, esp. 63–65; cf. A. Frantz, "The Date of the Phaidros Bema in the Theater of Dionysos" (*Hesperia*, Supplement XX), Princeton 1982, pp. 34–39; C. Foss, "Atticus Philippus and the Walls of Side," *ZPE* 26, 1977, pp. 172–180.

[15] For example, 16.11.10 (Julian restores the fortifications at Tres Tabernae), 17.1.11–12 (Julian rebuilds a Trajanic fort), 18.7.6 (Constantius II fortifies the right bank of the Euphrates), 18.9.1 (Constantius fortifies Amida).

[16] Cf. *CTh* 15.1.34 (A.D. 396), which says much the same thing.

[17] Martindale, *Prosopography*, p. 545.

Library of Hadrian and the other on the Akropolis, "beside the Statue of Athena Promachos."[18] The law addressed to him (*CTh* 11.17.4; see p. 143 above) documents Herculius' involvement in wall construction elsewhere in the prefecture. In addition, an epigram from Megara suggests that Herculius fortified that city.[19]

It might be objected that Herculius was a pagan, or at least sympathetic to paganism,[20] while construction of the Hexamilion involved the brutal demolition of the buildings of the Sanctuary of Poseidon at Isthmia. Herculius may simply have been a realist, or he may have been influenced by the law (*CTh* 1.36 [A.D. 397]) that called for the use of material from demolished temples in public works. In addition, we should remember the horror with which Eunapius viewed the depredations of Alaric (p. 141 above), which struck particularly hard at the physical structure of paganism. If Eunapius is to be taken as a good representative of pagan thought (and he probably is), a pagan official would have been particularly concerned to see to the defenses of Greece, even if this meant the sacrifice of buildings that had been previously destroyed (and probably abandoned in any case in the decades before Alaric's descent).

The coins in Grave 1 of the Northeast Gate show that the Hexamilion and Fortress probably ceased to be used for military purposes by the mid-fifth century. Squatters may have found shelter inside the walls and towers, and jewelry and physical remains show that women were buried inside the Fortress. Earthquakes in 522 and 551 probably weakened the Hexamilion, and Procopius says specifically that the wall at Corinth, built at the same time as the Hexamilion, was rendered indefensible by the earthquakes.[21]

Justinian carried out his work of restoration sometime between 548 and 560 (see Testimonia, 3–5), and this involved strengthening the Northeast Gate (pp. 80–83 above). Victorinus, probably praetorian prefect of Illyricum, supervised the project. The purpose of these modifications was probably to strengthen the fortifications weakened by time and earthquakes and to allow the defense of the Isthmus by fewer troops. Masonry and elevated towers replaced soldiers in the emperor's planning.

During the latter part of the sixth century and at least the first two-thirds of the seventh the Fortress continued to be inhabited; we cannot be certain whether this was a military or a civilian presence or whether the habitation was continuous or sporadic. The evidence suggests that Towers 2 and 15, at the corners of the Fortress, may have been manned for the defense of the Isthmus at the

---

[18] *IG* II², 4224, 4225: A. Frantz, "From Paganism to Christianity in the Temples of Athens," *DOP* 19, 1965, pp. 190, 192–193; *eadem*, "Herculius in Athens: Pagan or Christian?" (*Akten des VII Internationalen Kongress für christliche Archäologie*), Trier 1965, pp. 527–530.

[19] *IG* VII, 93: ʽΕρκόλιον τὸν ἔπαρχον ἀνέστησαν Μεγαρῆ[ες]
παντοίω[ν νή]σω[ν] καὶ πόλεων φύλακα.
τείχεα δείμα[τ]ο [κ]αὶ [πόρ]ον ἔμπεδον ὦπα[σ]ε Νύμφ[αις],
ἄστεα καὶ βουλὰς πλ[ῆ]σε βροτῶν σοφίῃ.

But see L. Robert (*Hellenica* 4, 1948, p. 60), who argues that the epigram should not be taken literally. Yet, it is hard to ignore the reference to τείχεα. The second line describes Herculius as παντοί[. . .]ω[.] καὶ πόλεων φύλακα. The missing word has been restored by various editors as νήσων, ἐθνῶν, and ἔργων. It is probably significant that Herculius restored the wall of Megara, since that city had been devastated by Alaric but lay ouside the new defenses of the Hexamilion.

[20] See footnote 18 above.

[21] On the 6th-century earthquakes in the Corinthia, see A. Bon, *Le péloponnèse byzantin jusqu'en 1204*, Paris 1952, p. 15. It is true that Procopius (*Vand.* 8.25.16–22) and Evagrius (*Historia ecclesiastica* 4.23) do not speak specifically of the Corinthia when discussing these earthquakes, but they report that the devastation extended from the Malaic Gulf in the north to Patras in the south, and they mention that the area around the Gulf of Corinth was especially badly shaken. An earthquake centered in the Gulf of Corinth, such as that of February 1981, would certainly have affected the Corinthia.

time of the earliest Slavic invasions. It is significant that excavation revealed no destruction level anywhere in the Fortress that can be equated with a conquest in this period. In addition, it is clear that houses or other small buildings were erected at least in the area northwest of the Northeast Gate at this time. The presence of so-called Slavic pottery in at least four parts of the site might be taken to suggest that the fortifications were overrun by the Slavs during one of their raids into the Peloponnesos in the late sixth and seventh centuries. The pottery, however, should not be seen, in any simple way, as confirmation of a Slavic conquest of the Isthmus; what is significant is that the pottery provides proof of activity at Isthmia well into the seventh century. Evidence from this crucial period of transformation is rare at other sites in Greece, in part because the pottery and other material of the age are not well known.[22] It is hoped that this evidence from Isthmia will encourage excavators at other sites to pay careful attention to similar material and thus shed important new light on the period.

As discussed above, we cannot be certain when the gates of the Fortress were blocked, but it is reasonable to assign this action to the sixth or, more likely, seventh century. Construction of the Blocking Wall at the Northeast Gate naturally raises the question of how access into the Fortress was arranged, especially since the so-called West Gate was apparently not cut through the Fortress wall until the Middle Byzantine period. The answer to this question must, unfortunately, remain unknown. It seems improbable that there was a gate in the unexcavated stretches of the Fortress wall, since a gate would certainly have left some trace. The locations of three gates have been known since the earliest investigations of the site, and archaeologists of the caliber of Peter Megaw, Oscar Broneer, and Demetrios Pallas sought in vain for another entrance. An unknown gate could lie concealed beneath the rubble, but despite the considerable inconvenience it must have occasioned, there may have been no regular gateway to the Fortress for several centuries, and entrance must have been by means of ladders or other movable devices. A similar situation is attested at a number of towers and small fortresses in late antique North Africa.[23] This mode of access would probably have prevented the sheltering of horses in the Fortress and made the use of artillery difficult. One can only wonder at the fear that must have given rise to this response.

In any case, no certain evidence exists for habitation at Isthmia from the late seventh to the eleventh or twelfth century after Christ.[24] At Corinth and elsewhere in Greece the ninth century brought political and economic recovery,[25] but Isthmia does not seem to have shared immediately in this improvement, perhaps because of the difficulty of access to the interior of the Fortress. By the eleventh century, the term "Hexamilion" appears to have been in use for the wall across the Isthmus. This usage is suggested by the appearance of an imperial official named Georgios Hexamilites,[26] who is probably to be identified with a Georgios Korinthios, mentioned by Kekaumenos.[27]

---

[22] For a convenient summary of current thought on the period, see D. A. Zakythinos, "La grand brèche dans la tradition historique de l'Hellénisme du septième au neuvième siècle," in Χαριστήριον εἰς ᾿Αναστάσιον Κ. ᾿Ορλάνδον, Athens 1966, III, pp. 300–327 and Kazhdan and Cutler (footnote 2 above, p. 141).

[23] Pringle, *Defence* I, pp. 163–189 (Culama), 197 (Cululis Theodoriana), 235 (Thamugadi), 244 (Thubursicu Bure).

[24] See the comments of P. A. Clement, *Isthmia* (forthcoming volume on coins).

[25] In general, see P. Charanis, "Nicephorus I, The Savior of Greece from the Slavs (810 A.D.)," *Byzantina-Metabyzantina* 1, 1946, pp. 75–92, reprinted in *Studies on the Demography of the Byzantine Empire*, London 1972; on Corinth, D. M. Metcalf, "Corinth in the Ninth Century: The Numismatic Evidence," *Hesperia* 44, 1973, pp. 180–203.

[26] H. Glykatzi-Ahrweiler, "Recherches sur l'administration de l'Empire byzantin au IXᵉ–XIᵉ siècles," *BCH* 84, 1960, p. 84, note 8.

[27] *Strategicon*, p. 66, line 26, p. 72, lines 25–26. Wiseman (*Land*, p. 72, note 132) seems to think that Georgios was in charge of the Hexamilion, while he was in fact the governor of the Armeniakon theme. See also Lambros («Τὰ

By the twelfth century, squatters seem to have established themselves again in small houses inside and outside the Fortress, commonly making use of the Hexamilion or Fortress wall as one of the sides of their dwellings. Evidence exists for considerable activity in the thirteenth century in the southern area of the Fortress, and we have suggested that the South Gate may even have become part of an estate of this period (p. 94 above). The West Gate was presumably cut through the Fortress wall sometime in the twelfth or thirteenth century.

From the Middle Byzantine period, little evidence exists that the Hexamilion and Fortress were used to defend the Peloponnesos against an attack from the north. Bulgars, Magyars, and other enemies periodically ravaged central Greece, and in 881 or 883 the *droungarios* Nikitas Ooryphas (᾽Ωορύφας) transported his fleet overland, from the Saronic to the Corinthian Gulf, to defend the western Peloponnesos from Arab pirates who had penetrated as far as the Gulf of Corinth.[28]

Sometime after 923, Symeon of Bulgaria apparently entered the Peloponnesos, and the hoards of coins from that time have been taken as indication of the devastation he wrought and, thus, of the ineffectiveness of the Hexamilion as a defense.[29] Toward the end of the tenth century, the Bulgarian tsar Samuel again threatened southern Greece. In 996 Samuel took Thessaly, Boiotia, and Attica, and according to the *Life* of Nikon the Metanoeite, the *strategos* Basileios Apokaukos fortified the Isthmus in preparation for a Bulgarian attack on the Peloponnesos.[30] Worried by Samuel's success, Apokaukos sought the assistance of Nikon, the famous missionary from Sparta; Nikon came to Corinth, "despite the difficulty of the journey," and prophesied to Apokaukos that the Bulgarians would be destroyed.[31] At first sight this seems to imply that the Hexamilion protected the Peloponnesos against a Bulgarian invasion, since the *Life* is unlikely to report a prophecy that failed. Nevertheless, Skylitzes says specifically that the barbarians "invaded the Peloponnesos through the Corinthian Isthmus and destroyed and plundered everything there."[32] Presumably, the prophecy was "fulfilled" by Basil II's famous destruction of the Bulgarians at the Battle of Belasica in 1014, even though the *Life* clearly places the prophecy in the context of Apokaukos' defense of the Isthmus. It is in any case probably more significant that this refortification of the Hexamilion was connected (as it was in several later periods) with a vision of the revival of Greece. In this case, the defense of the Isthmus should be seen in context with the cults of Hosios Loukas and St. Nikon, both of which were important as much for their political and military aspects as for their religious significance.

By the late fourteenth century, however, the Ottoman Turks were in control of much of the Balkans, and they threatened the Christian powers of the Peloponnesos, prompting cooperation among the Venetians, the Byzantines, and the Knights of Rhodes. The despots of the Morea, from

τείχη», 1905, p. 439, note 1), who says that neither Basil Hexamilites nor an anonymous bishop of Hexamilion in Thrace has any connection with the Isthmus.

[28] On Ooryphas, see Theophanes Continuatus, pp. 300–301 (ed. Bonn); Kedrenos, II, pp. 227–228 (ed. Bonn); Skylitzes, pp. 153–154 (Thurn); Zonaras, 15.24 (Dindorf III, p. 399). Ooryphas had landed at Kenchreai but learned that the Arabs were despoiling "Methone, Pylos, Patras καὶ τὰ προσεχῆ Κορίνθῳ χωρία." He presumably used the route of the ancient Diolkos, and according to the sources, he transported the whole fleet in a single night.

[29] Bon (footnote 21 above, p. 144), p. 80; Metcalf (footnote 25 above, p. 145), p. 185.

[30] Skylitzes, p. 341 (Thurn); S. P. Lambros, «῾Ο βίος Νίκωνος τοῦ Μετανοεῖτε», Νέος ῾Ελληνομνήμων 3, 1906, pp. 174–175; for the date, see S. Runciman, *A History of the First Bulgarian Empire*, London 1930, p. 229, note 3. According to the *Life*, Apokaukos ἐφρούρει τὸν ἐκεῖσε ἰσθμὸν τῆς Βουλγαρικῆς ἕνεκα ἐφόδου.

[31] Lambros, *op. cit.*, p. 175: «ἀλλὰ καὶ τῆς τῶν Βουλγάρων φροντίδος ἀπελύετο ὁ ᾽Απόκαυκος, προμηνύσαντος αὐτῷ τοῦ μακαρίου τὴν ἐκείνων καταστροφήν».

[32] Skylitzes, p. 341 (Thurn): [Samuel] «εἰσβάλοντα τε καὶ ἐν Πελοποννήσῳ διὰ τοῦ ἐν Κορίνθῳ ἰσθμοῦ, καὶ πάντα ταῦτα δηοῦντα καὶ ληζόμενον. . . .». J. M. Shelley ("The Christian Basilica Near the Cenchrean Gate at Corinth," *Hesperia* 12, 1943 [pp. 166–189], pp. 184, 189) noted that the Kranion Basilica (near the Kenchrean Gate in Corinth) was burned toward the end of the 10th century, and he connected this with the Bulgarian incursion.

their capital at Mistra, were most directly involved, and in 1396 the Despot Theodore I was apparently the first to plan a rebuilding of the Hexamilion as a barrier against the Turks.[33] He was, however, unable to carry out the project, and in 1397 the Turks invaded the Peloponnesos (although they subsequently withdrew).[34]

Negotiations continued among the Christian powers, and in 1401 the Venetian Senate promised to cooperate with Manuel II in rebuilding the Hexamilion.[35] In 1402, Tamerlane's defeat of the Turks at the Battle of Ankara gave the Christians a respite, and Manuel II used the opportunity to plan reconstruction of the Hexamilion and to visit Western Europe in search of military aid.[36] The emperor returned to his capital disillusioned, but peace with the Sultan Mehmet I in 1413 allowed him to strengthen the empire against the Turkish assault that was sure to come.

Key to Manuel's policy was the rebuilding of the Hexamilion (Testimonia, 6–10). The emperor decided to supervise construction himself, and he arrived at the Isthmus on March 29, 1415, after an intermediate stop at Thasos where he put down a rebellion. Work was begun on the Hexamilion on April 8.[37] Manuel had assisted the Sultan Mehmet in his struggle to secure the throne, and the Turks were persuaded to acquiesce in the reconstruction, apparently assuming that it could not be quickly accomplished (Testimonia, 9, 10). According to Mazaris (Testimonia, 10), however, the reconstruction was accomplished in 25 days. It involved rebuilding the wall and the fortresses at either end (on the Saronic and the Corinthian Gulfs) and the re-excavation of the *taphros*. According to a local chronicle (Testimonia, 8), the rebuilt wall had 153 towers.

Manuel apparently introduced a new tax (perhaps the so-called *floriatikon*), and he forced the Peloponnesian nobility into helping with the project.[38] During reconstruction of the Hexamilion, Manuel faced a revolt of these nobles. Presumably, the revolt was a result of the taxation and the contributions that he forced upon them, but Mazaris and Manuel himself (Testimonia, 8–10) suggest other motives which cannot be easily understood at this distance. Both indicate that the nobles opposed reconstruction because they felt that the renewed Hexamilion would strengthen the power of the despot (and thus presumably the emperor in Constantinople). How this was to happen is not entirely clear. In any case, the poorer subjects of the empire, and especially the Albanians settled in the Peloponnesos, warmly supported the project. When work was nearly done, Manuel sailed to the southern part of the Morea and captured the Castle of Mandinia (in Messenia) on July 15, 1415, which put an effective end to the revolt.[39]

The reconstruction of the Hexamilion was a feat that impressed contemporaries, Byzantines and foreigners alike. Perhaps the most important reaction was that of Georgios Gemistos Plethon, who was inspired to write two treatises, one to Manuel and one to the Despot Theodore. These suggested the complete reorganization of the society and economy of the Morea, now made safe by the defenses of the Hexamilion. Plethon, perhaps the first "modern" Greek, saw the fortification of

---

[33] Lambros, «Tὰ τείχη», 1905, pp. 440–441; F. Thiriet, *La romanie vénitienne au moyen age* (*Bibliothèque des Écoles françaises d'Athènes et de Rome* 193), Paris 1959, p. 365; Barker, *Manuel II*, p. 277, note 136; Zakythinos, *Despotat*, p. 143.

[34] Zakythinos, *Despotat*, p. 156.

[35] Thiriet, *Régestes* II, no. 1017, p. 18.

[36] Barker, *Manuel II*, pp. 167–289 (p. 273, note 130, for a plan of 1408 to rebuild the Hexamilion).

[37] Barker, "Chronology," pp. 39–55.

[38] On the tax see Lambros, «Tὰ τείχη», 1905, pp. 456–460. The demands connected with construction of Hexamilion caused some of Manuel's subjects to flee to Venetian territory, and this exodus continued to be a problem for years to come. See Barker, *Manuel II*, pp. 314–315. A resolution of the Venetian Senate (Thiriet, *Régestes* II, no. 1697, p. 165) describes the tax as the ἀγγαρείαι.

[39] Barker, "Chronology," p. 48; Barker, *Manuel II*, pp. 316–317; the resolution of the Venetian Senate dated June 11, 1414 (probably a mistake for 1415), sending troops to Coron and Modon "because of the troubles," was perhaps connected with this uprising (Sathas, *Documents inédits*, III, no. 664, p. 113).

the Isthmus as allowing the revival of Hellenic civilization.[40] Even the Serbian Konstantin the Philosopher referred admiringly to Manuel's reconstruction.[41]

On June 26, 1415, Manuel proudly announced his achievement in a letter to the Venetian Senate. On July 23 the Senate responded with proper congratulations and promised the support of their governors in the Peloponnesos if the Turks should attempt to destroy the fortifications.[42] Shortly thereafter, Manuel confessed the heavy burdens he had laid on his subjects and sought Venetian support to help defray the cost of the undertaking. On September 23 the Senate agreed to return imperial subjects who had fled to Venetian territory in order to escape the financial burdens imposed by the emperor,[43] but in a resolution of February 8, 1416, the senators refused to send financial assistance, saying that the outfitting of the fleet had exhausted the treasury.[44] Manuel continued to seek western subvention for the Hexamilion. In 1417 his ambassador was successful in persuading the new Pope Martin V to grant an indulgence to Catholics who contributed to the defense of the Hexamilion.[45] The Venetians, however, remained intransigent, and a resolution of June 11, 1418, reaffirmed an unwillingness to provide financial assistance, while allowing the governors of Coron and Modon to return fugitives from Manuel's taxation to the despotate.[46]

In 1421 Manuel supported the losing side in the struggle for the Ottoman throne, and the new sultan, Murad II, began to take action against Byzantium. In 1422, as the Turks threatened the Morea, the Venetians finally became concerned about the defense of the Hexamilion, and they indicated a willingness to bear some of the expenses.[47] Hasty discussions were held among all the Christian powers of the Morea: the despot Theodore II dispatched Manuel Kavakes as an ambassador to Venice, while Dolfino Venier represented Venetian interests in the Peloponnesos. The Venetians, it seemed, hoped to use the situation to extend their territories in Greece.[48] On February 23, 1423, the Senate agreed to send troops to defend the Hexamilion but only on very harsh terms: the nobles of the Morea were to make financial payments to Venice, according to their individual wealth, and the despotate was to cede the city of Corinth.[49]

This arrangement was never finalized, and in May of 1423 the Turks, under the command of Turahan, descended on the Peloponnesos (Testimonia, 11). The Byzantine defenders of the Hexamilion apparently fled, and the Turks took the fortifications without opposition.[50] Part of the Turkish expedition remained behind to destroy the Hexamilion, while the main body ravaged the Morea, taking as many as 7,200 prisoners, most of them Greeks.[51] Turahan ultimately withdrew from the Morea, but the Florentine duke of Athens, Antonio Acciaiuoli, profited from the Byzantine discomfiture and may temporarily have seized Corinth.[52] Despite the destruction of 1423, the Hexamilion was apparently still regarded as defensible, and in 1425 the despot Theodore II again

---

[40] The texts are edited by Lambros, Παλαιολόγεια, III, pp. 246–265; IV, pp. 113–134.

[41] Cited by Barker, *Manuel II*, p. 313, note 21.

[42] Thiriet, *Régestes* II, no. 1583, p. 136; Sathas, *Documents inédits*, III, no. 668, p. 116; Lambros, «Τὰ τείχη», 1905, pp. 461–462, 466–467; Barker, *Manuel II*, p. 314.

[43] Thiriet, *Régestes* II, no. 1592, p. 138 (not in Sathas, *Documents inédits*).

[44] Thiriet, *Régestes* II, no. 1599, p. 140. The Byzantine ambassador was Nicholas Eudaimonoioannes (Nicholao de Monoiani).

[45] Barker, *Manuel II*, pp. 325–326.

[46] Thiriet, *Régestes* II, no. 1697, pp. 164–165.

[47] Thiriet, *Régestes* II, no. 1849, p. 196.

[48] Zakythinos, *Despotat*, pp. 192–196.

[49] Thiriet, *Régestes* II, no. 1870, p. 200; Barker, *Manuel II*, p. 315, note 26.

[50] Iorga, *Notes* I, pp. 344–345.

[51] Zakythinos, *Despotat*, pp. 196–198.

[52] Zakythinos, *Despotat*, pp. 198–199.

sought Venetian financial assistance in connection with the Hexamilion, but this appeal was once again turned down by the Senate.[53]

As late as 1431 the fortifications were apparently still defensible, but in that year Turahan again descended on the Isthmus and "totally destroyed the Hexamilion" (Testimonia, 12). For the next few years it lay in ruins (Testimonia, 14). During this time there was apparently some hope for a reconstruction of the Hexamilion, reflected in the so-called Pythian Oracle, the original form of which presumably dates to the period between 1431 and 1443 (Testimonia, 15). In 1443 these hopes were realized when the despot (and future emperor) Constantine rebuilt the Hexamilion (Testimonia, 16, 17). With the support of his brother Thomas, Constantine followed the precedent of Manuel II by forcing the nobles of the Morea to help in the work of reconstruction. According to one of the "Lamentations on the Fall of Constantinople," Constantine's task occupied 30 days but required great effort.[54] This feat encouraged Cardinal Bessarion[55] to write to Constantine, praising the fortification and urging the political and economic restructuring of the Morea, much as Plethon had done after Manuel's rebuilding nearly thirty years earlier.[56]

With the Isthmus secure and using the Hexamilion as a base of operations, the despot Constantine began a more aggressive policy, attacking Attica and Boiotia with considerable success. Nerio II Acciaiuoli, the duke of Athens was, however, an ally of the Ottomans, and he called on Murad II for support.[57] In the winter of 1446 the sultan appeared in person at the head of his troops and marched against the despots Constantine and Thomas (Testimonia, 18–20).[58] Some of the Greek sources say the Turkish army was enormous (50,000–60,000 men), but Chalkokondyles is probably more realistic in placing their number at 6,000. On November 27 the Turks drew up before the Hexamilion, and Constantine attempted negotiations with Murad, discussions in which the father of Laonikos Chalkokondyles was an ambassador. The sultan, however, refused any terms and demanded the destruction of the Hexamilion, which was apparently still a serious impediment to the Turks. Murad waited a few days and began the attack on December 10, using ladders, sapping operations, and artillery. The defense offered by the despots was spirited, but the Hexamilion was never meant to withstand artillery bombardment. The sultan, along with his picked troops, attacked the central part of the Hexamilion (κατὰ τὸ μέσον τοῦ Ἰσθμοῦ), presumably in the area where the modern National Highway crosses the Hexamilion, and the artillery proved ultimately too much for the defenders. A Serb in the service of the sultan was first over the wall, and the Ottoman troops followed, massacring the defenders and devastating the Peloponnesos.[59] In fact, the historian Ducas

[53] Thiriet, *Régestes* II, no. 2005, p. 232 (October 2, 1425). Again in 1428, the issue of Venetian support for the defense of the Hexamilion seems to have come up, but the Venetian ambassador to the Morea was instructed to report that he had no authority to treat on the matter (Thiriet, *Régestes* II, no. 2107, pp. 252–253).

[54] Lambros, «Τὰ τείχη», 1905, p. 472.

[55] The famous scholar and churchman of Greek origin who made his home in Italy after 1439 and supported the union of Eastern and Western churches.

[56] Lambros, Παλαιολόγεια IV, pp. 32–45.

[57] Zakythinos, *Despotat*, pp. 230–231.

[58] G. Finlay, *A History of Greece from Its Conquest by the Romans to the Present Time, B.C. 146 to A.D. 1864*, IV, London 1877, pp. 248–251.

[59] Lambros, «Τὰ τείχη», 1905, pp. 479–486, quoting these lines from one of the "Lamentations":

Ὦ Κόρινθος πολύθλιβος, πολὺ κακὸν τὸ εἶδες
Τότες ὅταν ἐχάλασαν οἱ Τοῦρκοι τὸ Ἑξαμίλι
ὅλος ὁ κόσμος ἔγεμεν ἄρματα καὶ δοξάρια,
σαγίτταις χρυσοπτέρυγαις, σπαθία κοσμημένα
κεφαλαὶ, χέρια, σώματα 'ς τὸν κάμπον ὁπῦδες,
καὶ σύ, ἀνδρειωμένε βασιλεῦ, κακὸν ῥιζικὸν ὁποῦκες.

and George Scholarios, the future patriarch of Constantinople, blamed the Albanians and the Greek defenders of the Hexamilion for the disaster, alleging that they deserted the despots.[60]

Despite this great victory, the Turks again withdrew, the Morea still remained largely in Greek hands, and the Hexamilion was still apparently defensible. The new sultan, Mehmet II, had designs on Constantinople from the beginning of his reign, and in 1452 he dispatched the general Turahan to the Peloponnesos in order to neutralize the despots Demetrios and Thomas and prevent them from aiding their brother Constantine, who had now become emperor in Byzantium. The Greeks apparently offered a spirited defense of the Hexamilion (Testimonia, 21), but once again the Turks were victorious. This was, so far as we can tell, the last defense of the Hexamilion by the Byzantines.

After the fall of Constantinople the despotate of the Morea was nominally tributary to the sultan, and the Turks may have been willing to leave the situation thus. The Albanians of the Morea, however, rose against the despots and offered to ally themselves with the Venetians, whom the Turks correctly viewed as a serious threat to their power in Greece, thus forcing them to act. In 1458 Mehmet II set out to conquer the Morea in his own name. He seized central Greece without difficulty, and in May he reached the Hexamilion. The despots apparently offered no resistance, and Mehmet crossed without opposition and occupied most of the Peloponnesos (Testimonia, 22).

Four years later, in 1462, the Venetians attempted to drive the Turks from the Peloponnesos. From their base in the Argolid (Nauplion and Argos), they moved into the Corinthia and hurriedly rebuilt the Hexamilion as a defense against the Turks (Testimonia, 23). Their effort shows that the fortifications were still seen as the basis of control of the Peloponnesos and were still capable of being refurbished. In October of 1463 the Venetian Senate ordered the dispatch of troops to guard the Hexamilion, but by November 20 it had abandoned the effort.[61]

At the end of the seventeenth century, during their brief reoccupation of the Morea, the Venetians again planned the restoration of the Hexamilion.[62] In 1696 the famous military engineers Giusto Milio and Sigismondo Aberghetti arrived at the Isthmus, and within a year they had produced the *Descrizione istorica dell' Isthmo di Morea*. This text is still unpublished, although it provides much detail about the topography of the Isthmus at that time. The report was forwarded to Venice in 1698, along with a favorable recommendation by Alessandro Molin, the Capitan General, but the Senate refused to take action, presumably for economic reasons.[63]

The Venetians failed to hold the Isthmus, as others had before them, and they ultimately withdrew, leaving the Hexamilion a picturesque ruin and a symbol of a military technology so fine in conception but so weak in execution. In all, the Hexamilion had stood for something over a millennium. During those years we know of several attempts to defend the Peloponnesos at the Hexamilion, and in no case were the defenders successful. There may, of course, have been moments of success, lost to the historical record, and the Hexamilion probably discouraged countless small groups of barbarians from crossing into the Morea at one time or another. Nonetheless, we have no single clear record of the Hexamilion denying a powerful enemy access to the Peloponnesos. This is not to say that the idea of such a massive fortification was wrong. Given adequate means of manning the fortifications, and maintaining naval superiority in both gulfs, the Hexamilion might have been a powerful and nearly impenetrable shield for the Byzantines. In fact, however, the theory of great

---

[60] Ducas, p. 223 (ed. Bonn); Scholarios in Lambros, Παλαιολόγεια II, p. 7.

[61] Thiriet, *Régestes* III, nos. 3190, 3194, pp. 251–252.

[62] C. Maltezou, Βενετσιανικὲς ἐκθέσεις γιὰ τὴν ὀχυρώση τοῦ ᾿Ισθμοῦ τῆς Κορίνθου στὰ τέλη τοῦ 17ου αἰώνα (*Acts of the First International Congress of Peloponnesian Studies* 3), Athens 1978, pp. 269–276.

[63] *Ibid.*, p. 275.

barrier walls was an impossible one, given the Byzantines' inability to man and provision such an extended line. From the sixth century on, the defenders apparently put their hope in superior technology and massive towering walls, while the barbarians simple bade their time and crossed the fortifications when and where they were poorly manned.[64] There is, probably, a lesson to be learned here, one that might have profited the French on the Maginot Line or others in search of a technologically perfect defensive scheme.

[64] The Turks, of course, took the wall using superior technology in the form of cannon.

APPENDIX
TOWER MEASUREMENTS

These measurements were made in the expectation that they would reveal information about the norms intended for such things as tower size and spacing. Measurement was made on the ground, from actual survey, as far as possible. The nature of the remains and the terrain make some of the measurements less accurate than one would like, and in some cases the measurement of individual tower walls was impossible. Measurements between towers are from the approximate center of each tower, and so the distances should correspond to those shown on Figures 3–11. The work of measuring each tower was long, tedious, and hot. I was aided in the arduous task by numerous individuals; I would especially like to thank Mark Berghold and Marianne Urse.

TOWER SPACING

A. WEST OF FORTRESS

W-1 to W-2	93 m.
W-2 to W-3	1964 m.
W-3 to W-4	360 m.
W-4 to W-5	666 m.
W-5 to W-6	74 m.
W-6 to W-6A	61 m.
W-6A to W-7	63 m.
W-7 to W-8	34 m.
W-8 to W-9	52 m.
W-9 to W-10	60 m.
W-10 to W-11	397 m.
W-11 to W-12	143 m.
W-12 to W-13	476 m.
W-13 to W-14	74 m.
W-14 to W-14A	152 m.
W-14A to W-15	44 m.
W-15 to W-16	43 m.
W-16 to W-17	126 m.
W-17 to W-18	96 m.
W-18 to W-19	44 m.
W-19 to W-20	42 m.
W-20 to W-21	46 m.
W-21 to W-22	106 m.
W-22 to W-23	62 m.
W-23 to W-24	103 m.
W-24 to W-25	44 m.
W-25 to W-26	74 m.
W-26 to T-15	409 m.

B. FORTRESS

T-15 to T-16	37 m.	
T-16 to T-17	48 m.	
T-17 to T-18	40 m.	
T-18 to T-19	36 m.	
T-19 to T-1	7 m.	(Northeast Gate)
T-1 to T-2	42 m.	
T-2 to T-3	65 m.	
T-3 to T-4	48 m.	
T-4 to T-5	46 m.	
T-5 to T-6	58 m.	
T-6 to T-7	30 m.	
T-7 to T-8	30 m.	
T-8 to T-9	7 m.	(South Gate)
T-9 to T-10	29 m.	
T-10 to T-11	36 m.	
T-11 to T-12	40 m.	
T-12 to T-13	37 m.	
T-13 to T-14	52 m.	
T-14 to T-15	58 m.	

C. SOUTHEAST OF FORTRESS

T-2 to S-1	47 m.		S-11 to S-12	60 m.
S-1 to S-2	32 m.		S-12 to S-13	130 m.
S-2 to S-3	40 m.		S-13 to S-14	38 m.
S-3 to S-4	44 m.		S-14 to S-15	112 m.
S-4 to S-5	48 m.		S-15 to S-16	41 m.
S-5 to S-6	48 m.		S-16 to S-17	92 m.
S-6 to S-7	48 m.		S-17 to S-18	67 m.
S-7 to S-8	46 m.		S-18 to S-19	64 m.
S-8 to S-9	46 m.		S-19 to S-20	45 m.
S-9 to S-10	44 m.		S-20 to S-21	45 m.
S-10 to S-11	47 m.			

TOWER MEASUREMENTS*

A. WEST OF FORTRESS

Tower	Hexamilion/FW	Projection	Width	Thickness
W-1	2.94	10.70	10.20	?
W-2	no measurements possible			
W-3	2.95	?	?	?
W-4	2.97	?	?	?
W-6	2.95	3.45–3.75	5.35	0.58
W-6A	2.95	5.95	4.30	?
W-7	?	4.92–5.20	6.20	1.50–1.64
W-8	2.85	6.20	4.65	0.72–0.92
W-9	2.85	5.90	4.54	0.97–1.30–1.31
W-10	2.90	6.07	4.55	0.95–1.38–1.42
W-11	4.45	4.90	5.80	0.90
W-12	?	3.05	4.05	?
W-12A	?	6.70–6.75	5.20	?
W-13	?	6.05	?	?
W-14	no measurements possible			
W-14A	no measurements possible			
W-15	2.85	5.10	5.70	?
W-16	no measurements possible			
W-17	?	5.60	6.50	?
W-18	?	4.65	4.10	?
W-19	?	3.95	5.10	?
W-20	no measurements possible			
W-21	?	4.60	4.33	?
W-22	no measurements possible			
W-23	location hypothetical; no measurements possible			
W-24	?	?	4.30	1.35
W-25	?	?	4.14	1.30
W-26	?	4.35	4.13	?

* In some cases the condition of the tower prevented any measurements from being taken; in this case a notice of "no measurements possible" is indicated. In other cases only some of the walls of a tower could be measured; in these instances the other dimensions are marked with "?".

B. Fortress

Tower	Hexamilion/FW	Projection	Width	Thickness
T-2	3.86–2.26	4.17–5.07	4.80	1.19–1.23–1.25
T-3	2.23	4.46–4.82	6.60	1.65–1.68
T-4	2.23	4.46–4.83	6.38	1.58–1.60–1.67
T-5	?	?	?	?
T-6	?	?	?	?
T-7	2.30	4.91–4.95	5.23	1.60–1.63–1.75
T-8	2.39–3.69	5.62–9.26	7.49	?
T-9	3.54–3.59	5.67	?	?
T-10	3.10	2.68–6.21	4.98–3.88	1.30–1.54–1.56
T-11	2.20	6.20–5.75	5.70	1.22
T-12	?	4.70–4.90	6.32	1.52
T-13	2.35	5.42–5.60	6.47	1.15
T-14	2.20	4.61–4.92	6.77	1.62–1.64–1.67
T-15	2.90	5.13–5.50	7.01	1.54–1.59–1.60
T-16	?	5.20–5.91	6.87	1.25–1.30–1.35
T-17	?	4.28–4.49	5.68	1.23–1.25–1.28
T-18	?	3.40–4.53	5.12	1.50–1.52–1.58
T-19	?	?	?	?

C. South of the Fortress

Tower	Hexamilion/FW	Projection	Width	Thickness
S-1	?	4.74–5.15	6.50	1.80
S-2	?	5.60	6.20	1.60
S-3	2.95	6.20–6.75	5.40	?
S-4	3.10	4.00–4.35	5.60	1.58
S-5	?	5.17–5.38	4.38	?
S-6	?	5.69–5.75	3.67	?
S-7	?	5.58	3.95	?
S-8	?	4.40–4.45	4.96	1.20
S-9	2.95	5.40–5.51	4.98	1.54–1.50
S-10	?	5.19	4.12	?
S-11	no measurements possible			
S-12	?	3.15–3.48	4.37	?

INDEX

FIGURES

FIGURE 1

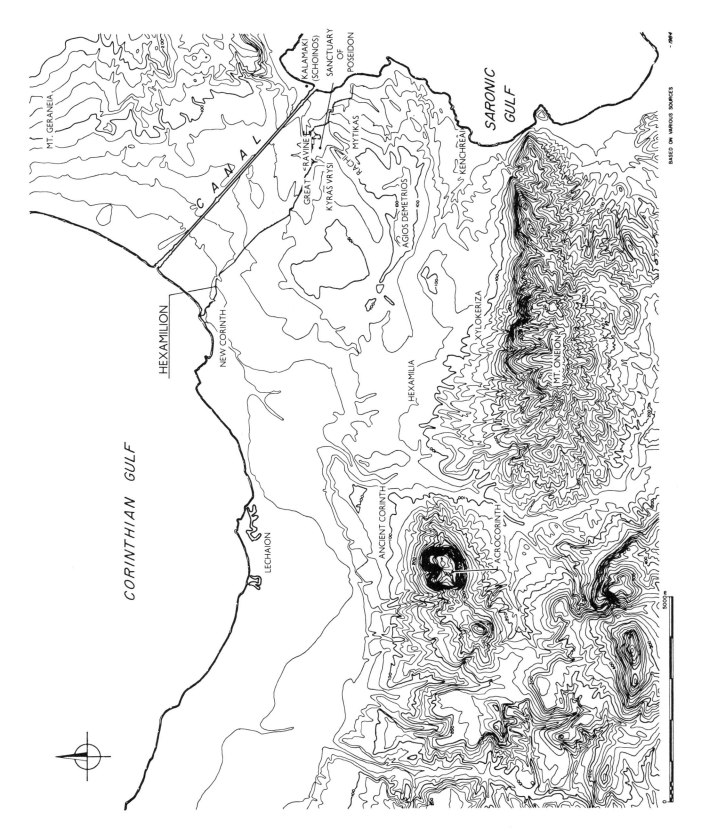

Map of the Isthmus of Corinth

FIGURE 2

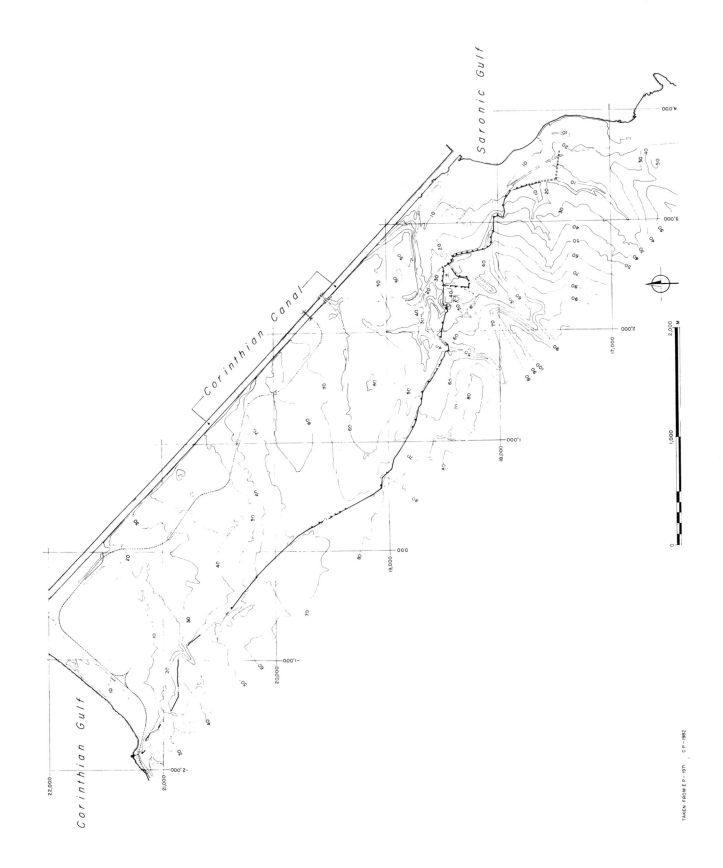

Map of the Hexamilion across the Isthmus

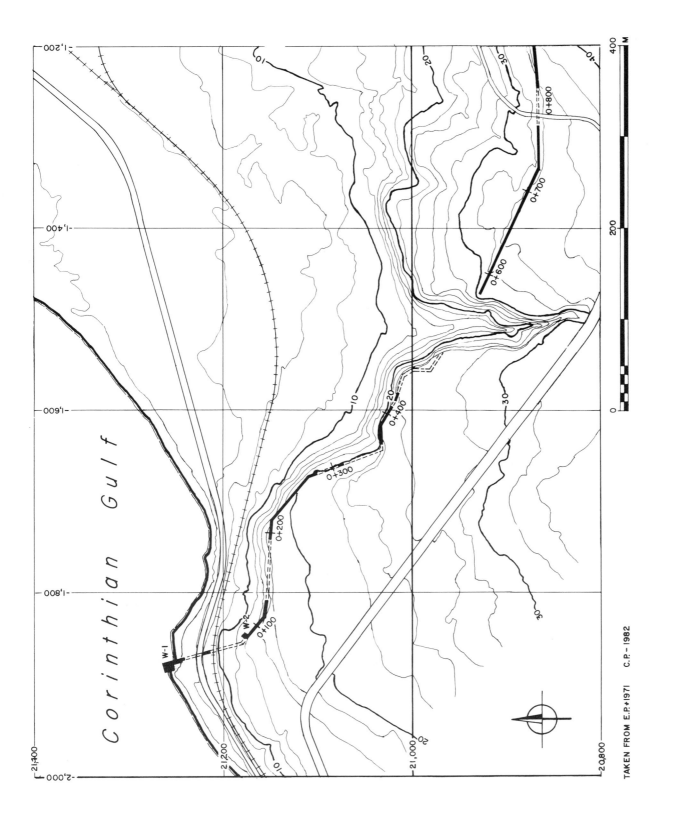

FIGURE 3

Detail map of the Hexamilion: 0 to 0+900 m.

FIGURE 4

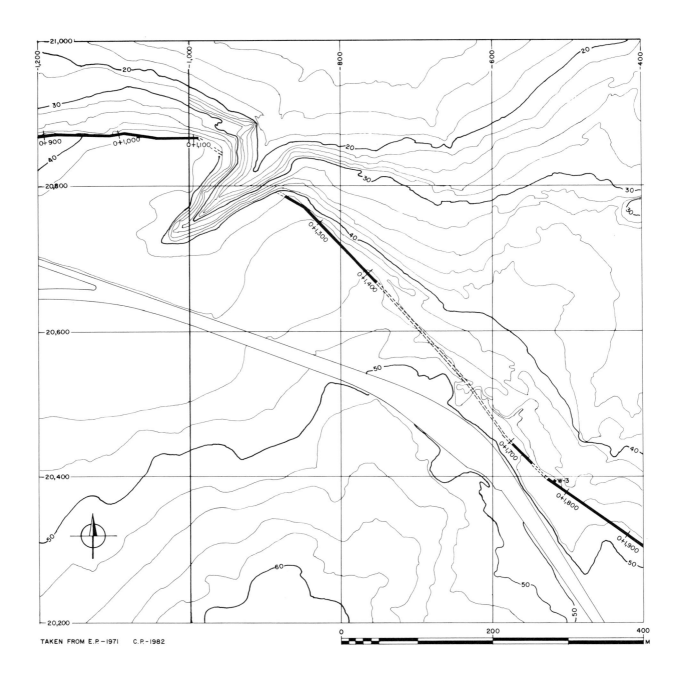

Detail map of the Hexamilion: 0+900 to 0+1900 m.

TAKEN FROM E.P.–1971   C.P.–1982

FIGURE 5

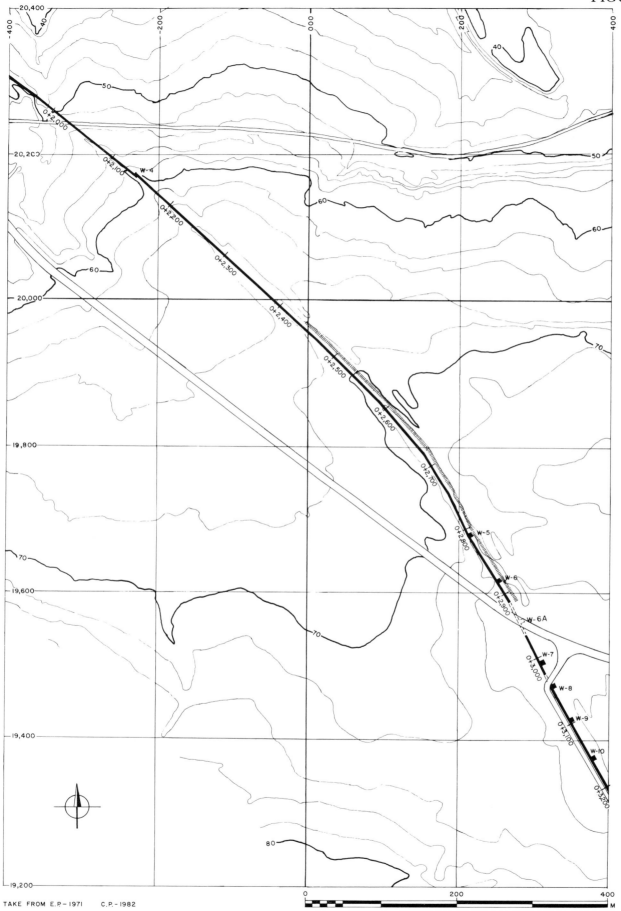

TAKE FROM E.P.-1971   C.P.-1982

Detail map of the Hexamilion: 0+1900 to 0+3200 m.

FIGURE 6

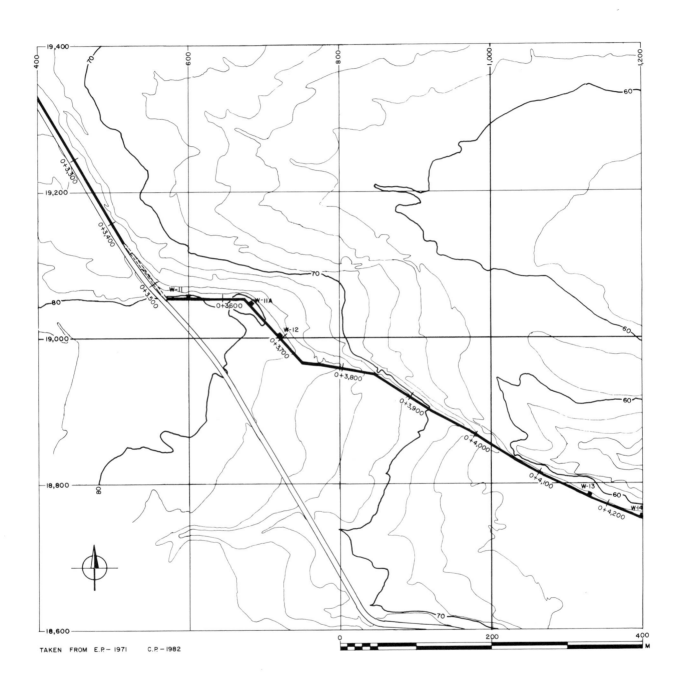

Detail map of the Hexamilion: 0+3200 to 0+4200 m.

FIGURE 7

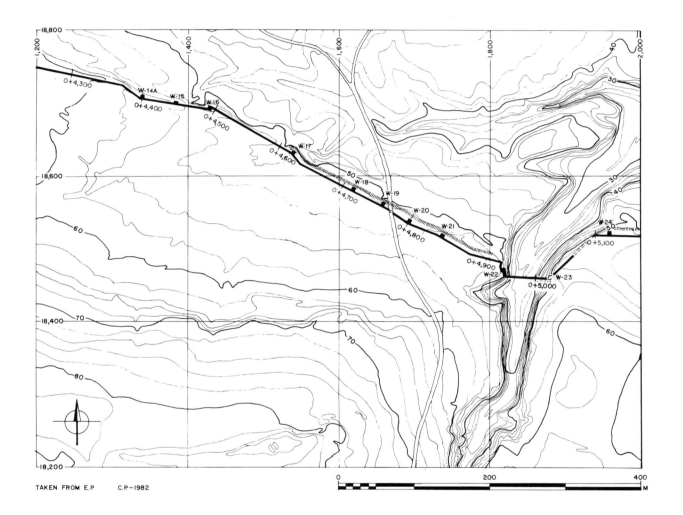

Detail map of the Hexamilion: 0+4300 to 0+5100 m.

FIGURE 8

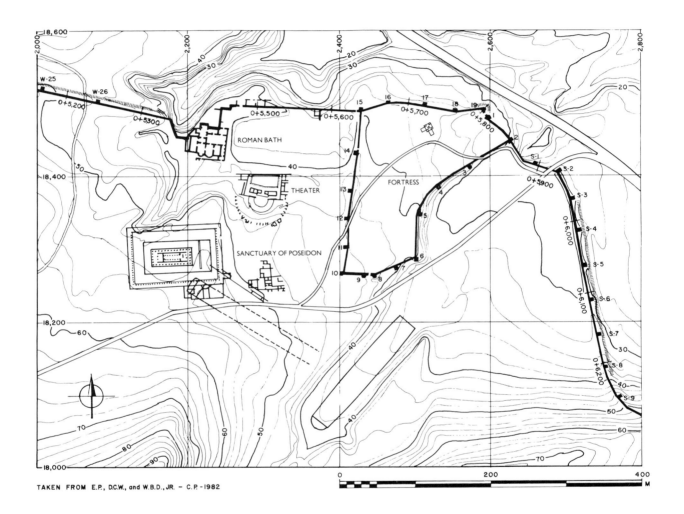

Detail map of the Hexamilion: 0+5200 to 0+6200 m.

FIGURE 9

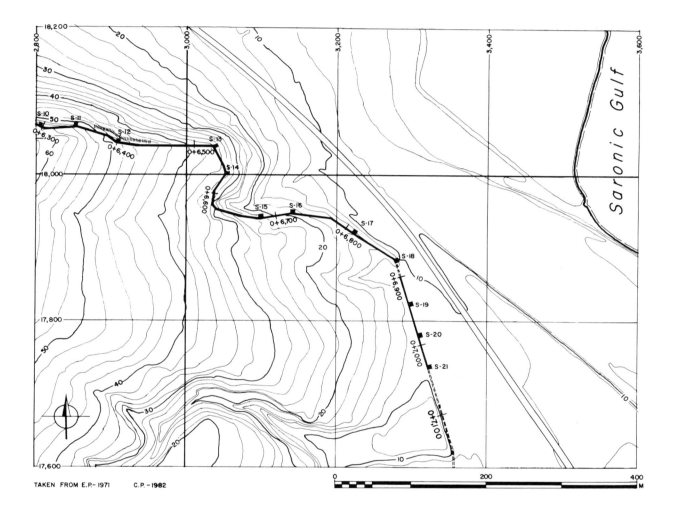

Detail map of the Hexamilion: 0+6300 to 0+7100 m.

FIGURE 10

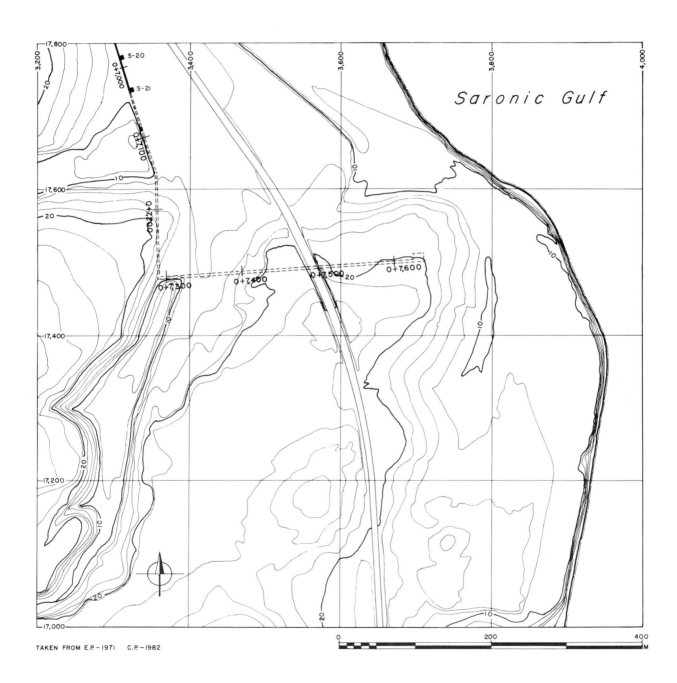

Detail map of the Hexamilion: 0+7000 to 0+7600 m.

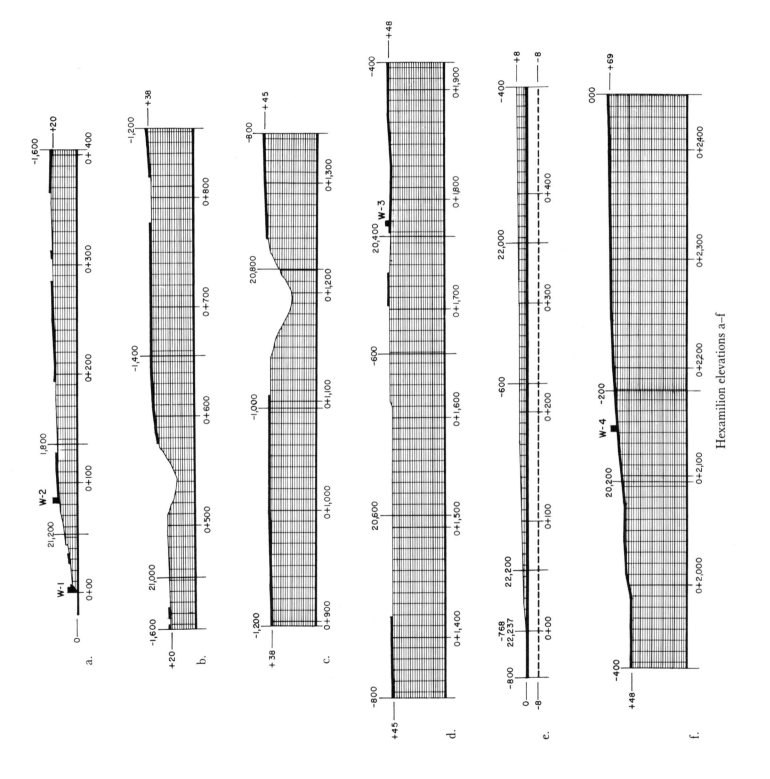

Hexamilion elevations a–f

FIGURE 11g–k

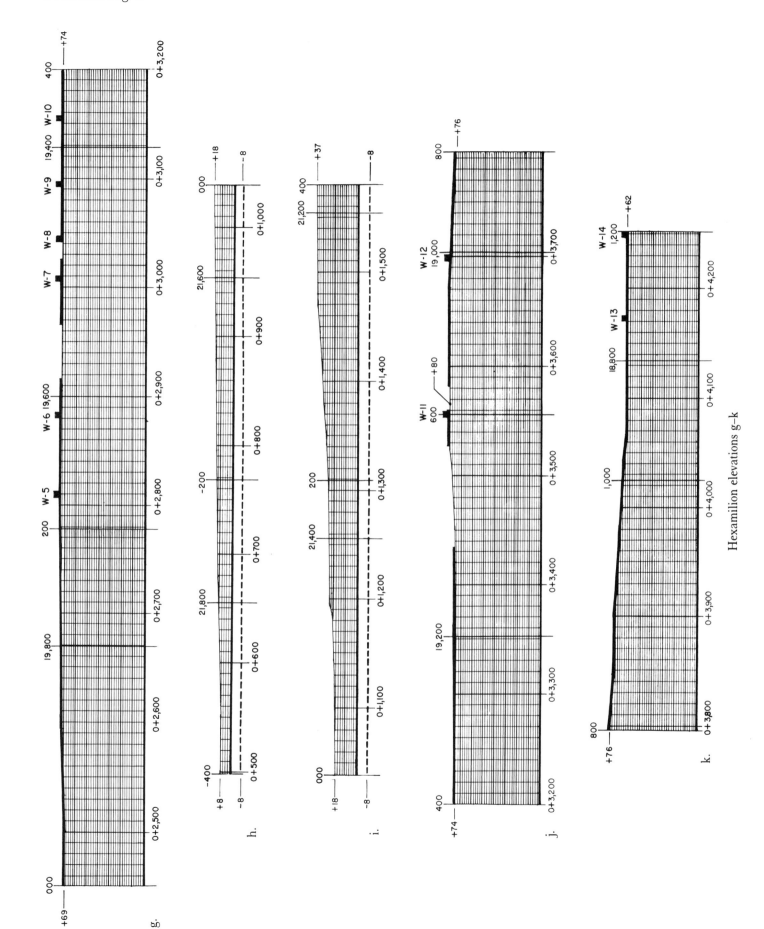

Hexamilion elevations g–k

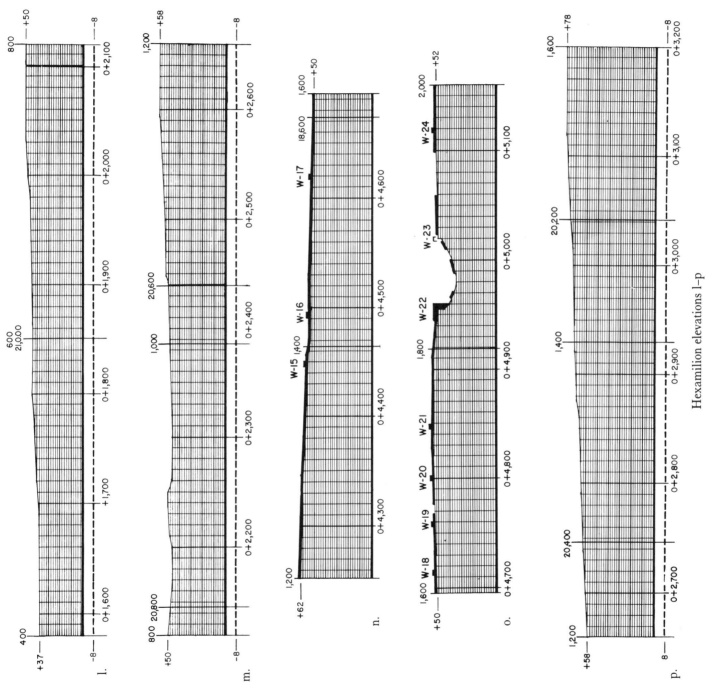

Hexamilion elevations l–p

FIGURE 11q–t

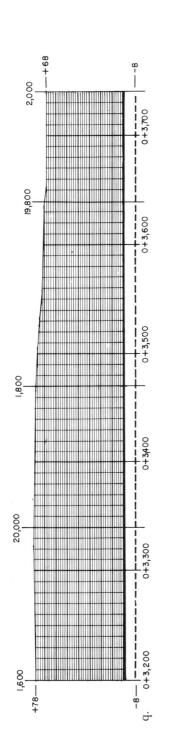

q.

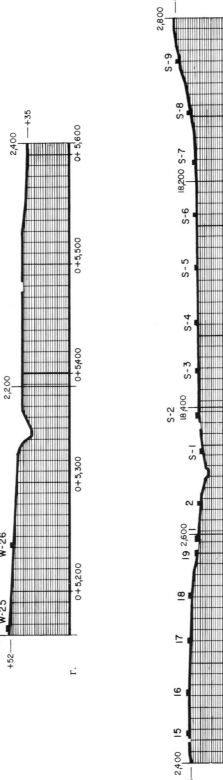

r.

s.

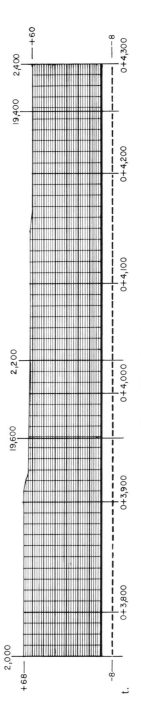

t.

Hexamilion elevations q–t

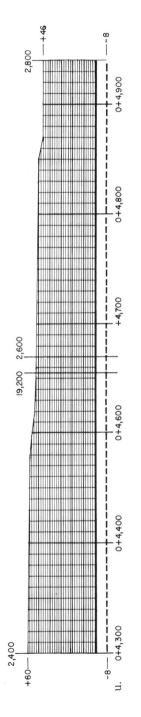

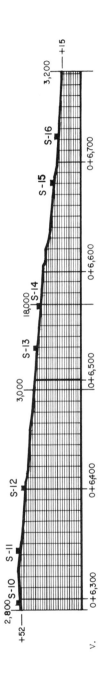

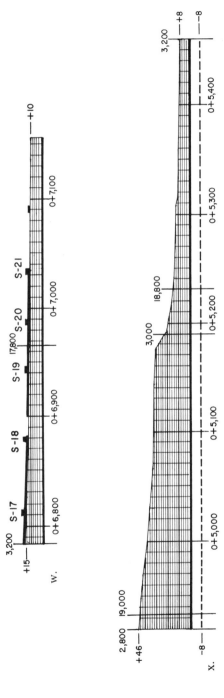

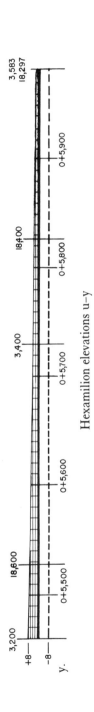

Hexamilion elevations u–y

FIGURE 12

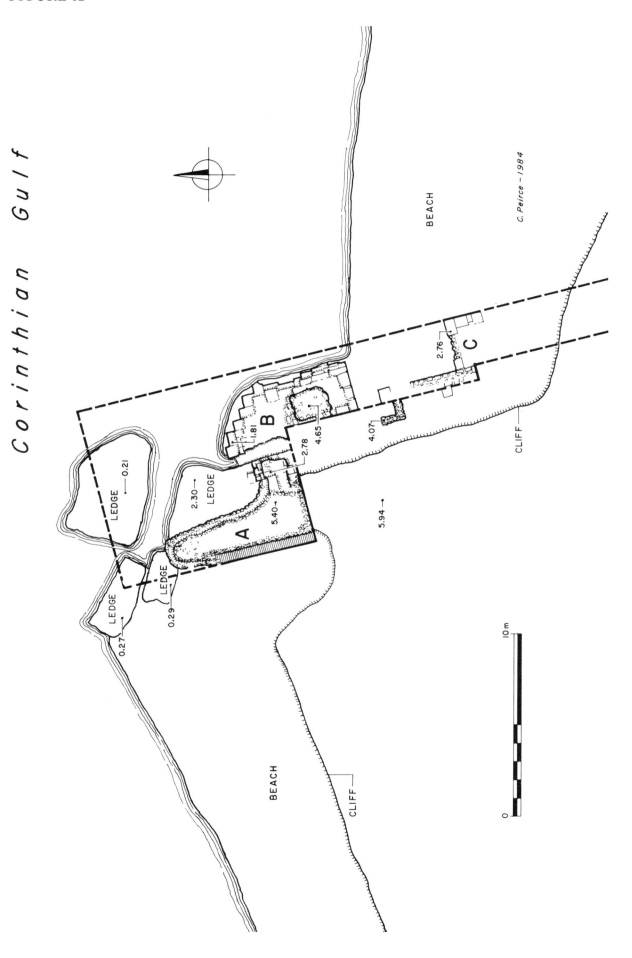

Actual-state plan of the Sea Bastion (W-1)

FIGURE 13

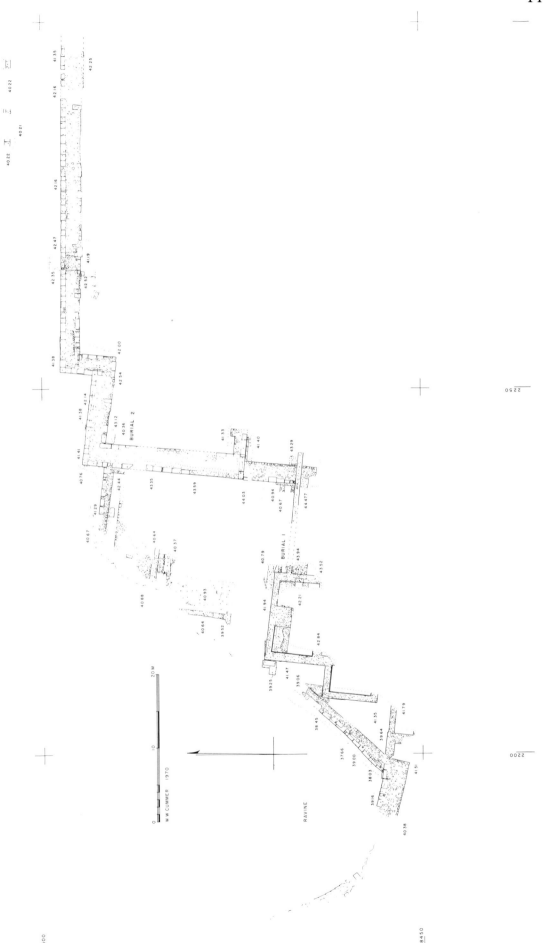

Actual-state plan of the Hexamilion at the Roman Bath

FIGURE 14

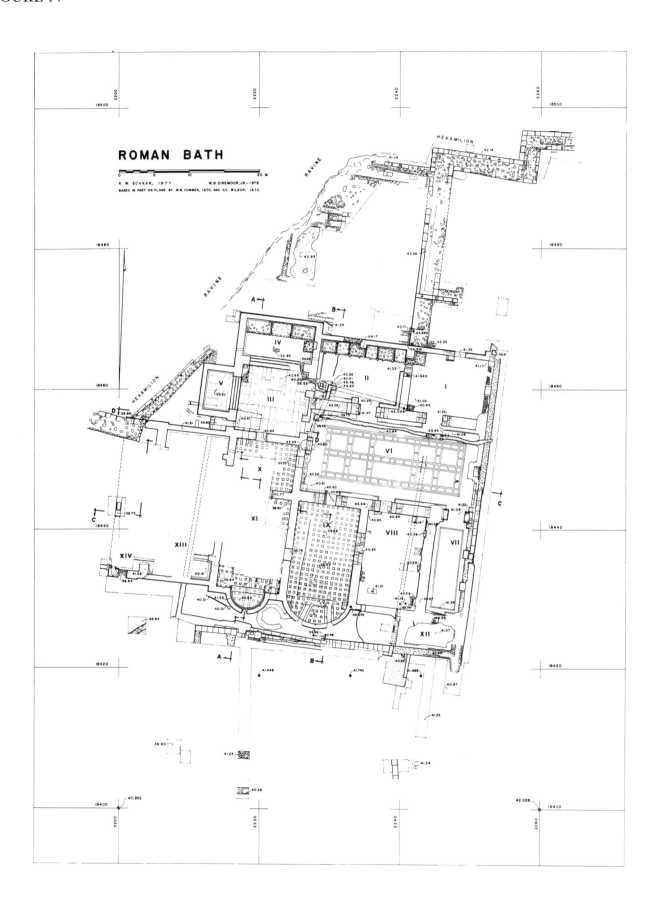

Actual-state plan of the Roman Bath

FIGURE 15

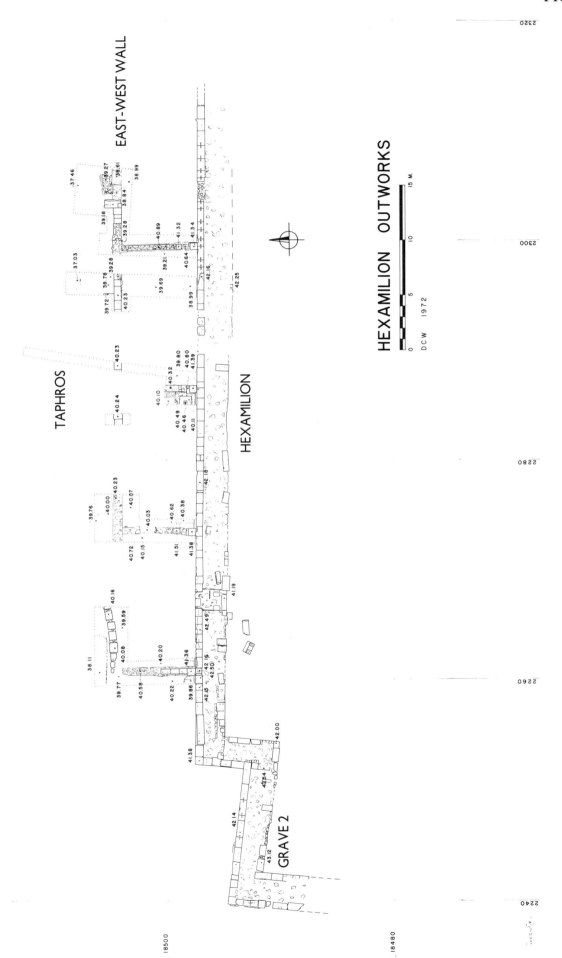

Actual-state plan of the Hexamilion Outworks

FIGURE 16

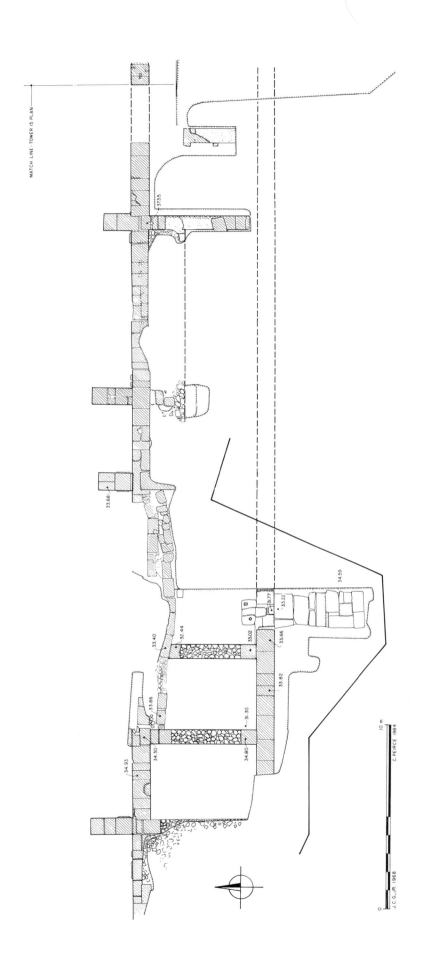

MATCH LINE- TOWER 15 PLAN

37.55

33.68

34.93

34.30

33.86

32.44

33.40

31.30

34.80

33.82

33.42

33.77

33.66

33.22

34.59

10 m

J.C.G., JR. 1968

C. PEIRCE 1984

Actual-state plan of the North Drain

FIGURE 17

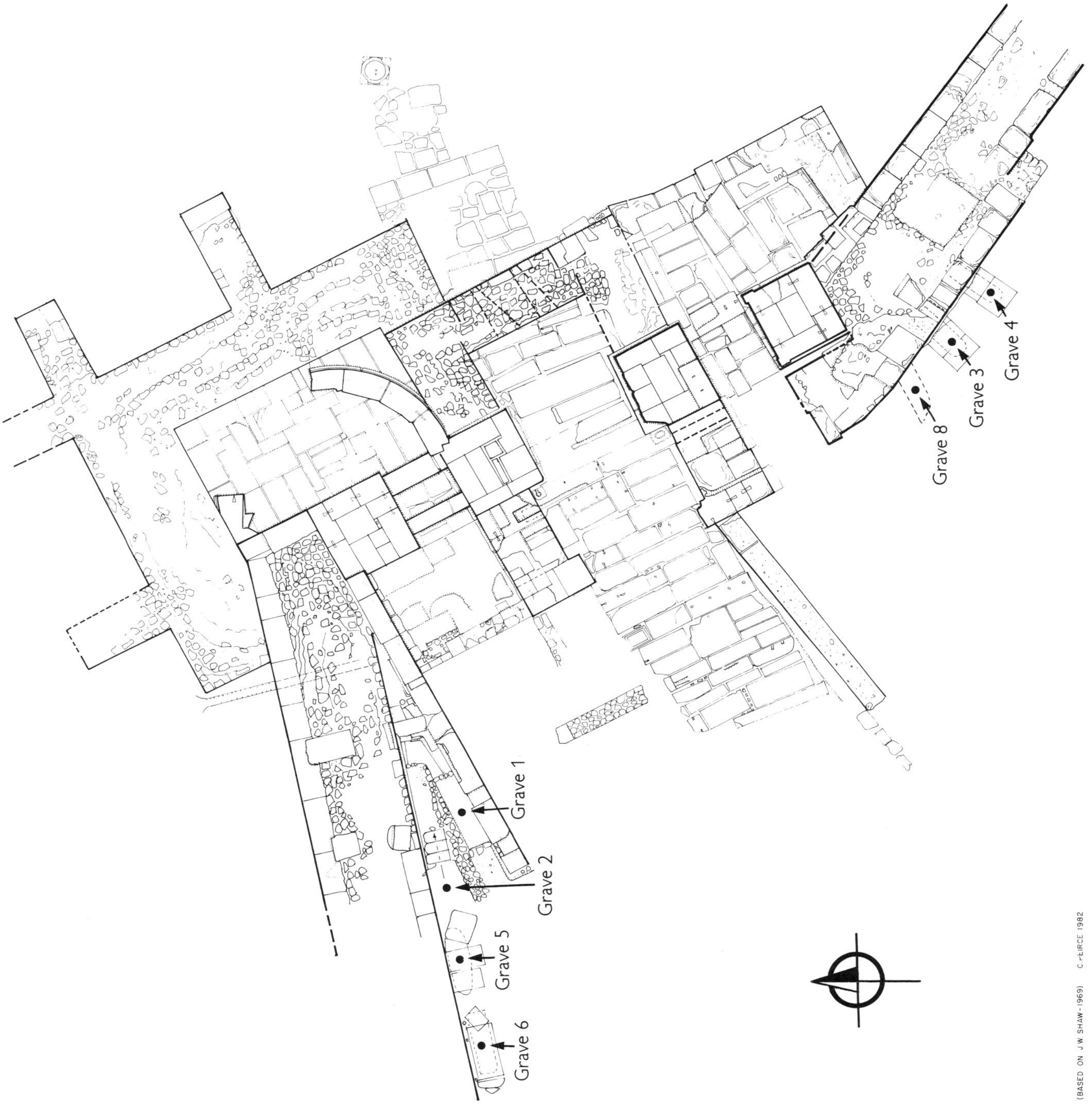

Actual-state plan of the Northeast Gate

Grave 1
Grave 2
Grave 5
Grave 6
Grave 8
Grave 3
Grave 4

(BASED ON J.W. SHAW - 1969)   C. rt.IRCE 1982

FIGURE 18

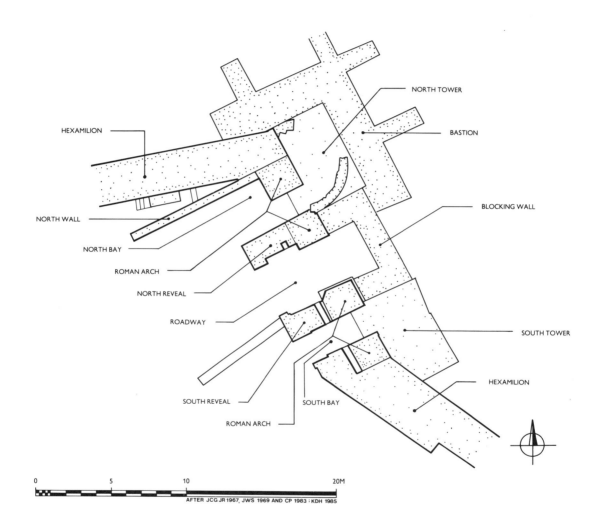

HEXAMILION

NORTH WALL

NORTH BAY

ROMAN ARCH

NORTH REVEAL

ROADWAY

SOUTH REVEAL

SOUTH BAY

ROMAN ARCH

NORTH TOWER

BASTION

BLOCKING WALL

SOUTH TOWER

HEXAMILION

0   5   10   20M

AFTER JCG JR 1967, JWS 1969 AND CP 1983 : KDH 1985

Northeast Gate, schematic plan of the existing remains

FIGURE 19

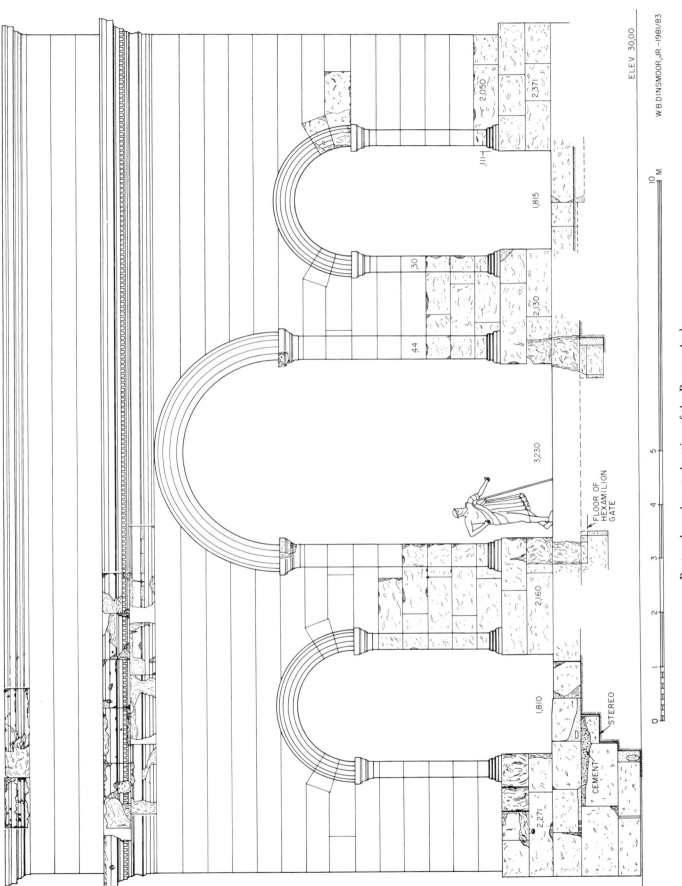

2,050

2,371

1,11'

1,815

,30

2,130

,44

3,230

2,160

FLOOR OF
HEXAMILION
GATE

1,810

STEREO

CEMENT

2,271

ELEV 30,00

W.B.DINSMOOR,JR.-1981/83

0   1   2   3   4   5   10 M.

Restored southwest elevation of the Roman Arch

FIGURE 20

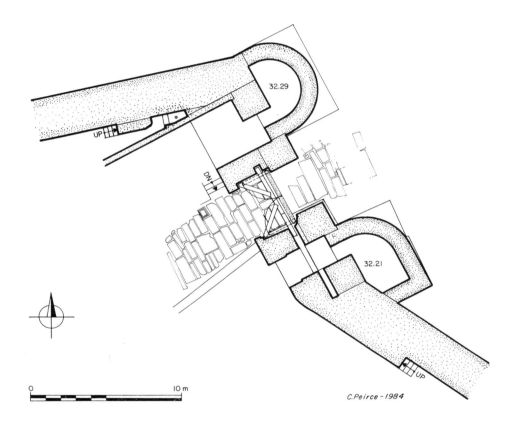

32.29

DN

UP

32.21

UP

0   10 m

C.Peirce - 1984

Restored plan of the Northeast Gate, ground level

FIGURE 21

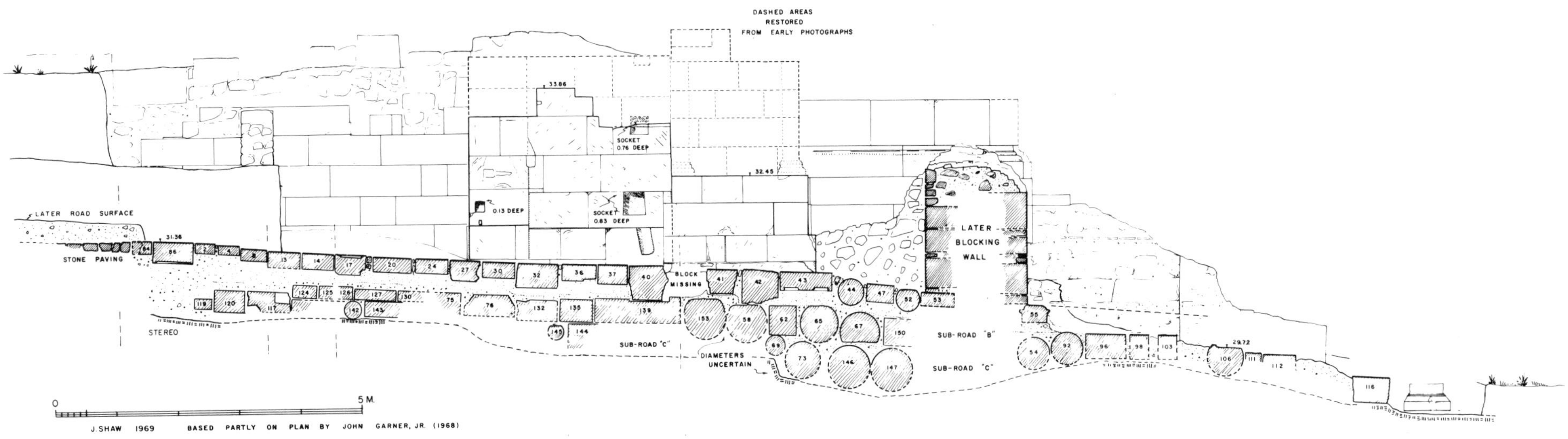

a. Section A–A through the roadway at the Northeast Gate

NORTHEAST GATE

ACTUAL STATE PLAN OF ROADWAY

J.C. GARNER JR 1968, J.W. SHAW 1969, W.W.C. 1970

b. Actual-state plan of the roadway at the Northeast Gate

FIGURE 22

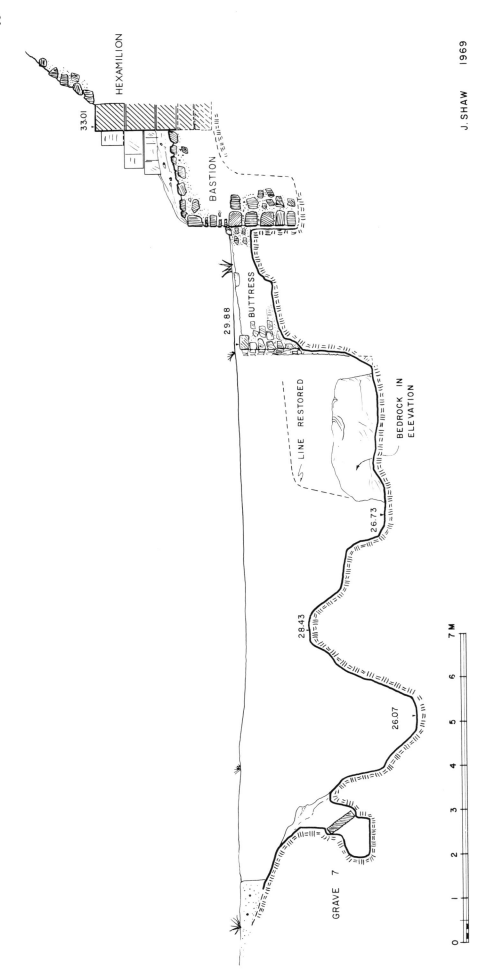

HEXAMILION

33.01

BASTION

29.88

BUTTRESS

LINE RESTORED

BEDROCK IN ELEVATION

26.73

28.43

26.07

GRAVE 7

0 1 2 3 4 5 6 7 M

J. SHAW   1969

Section through area north of the Northeast Gate

FIGURE 23

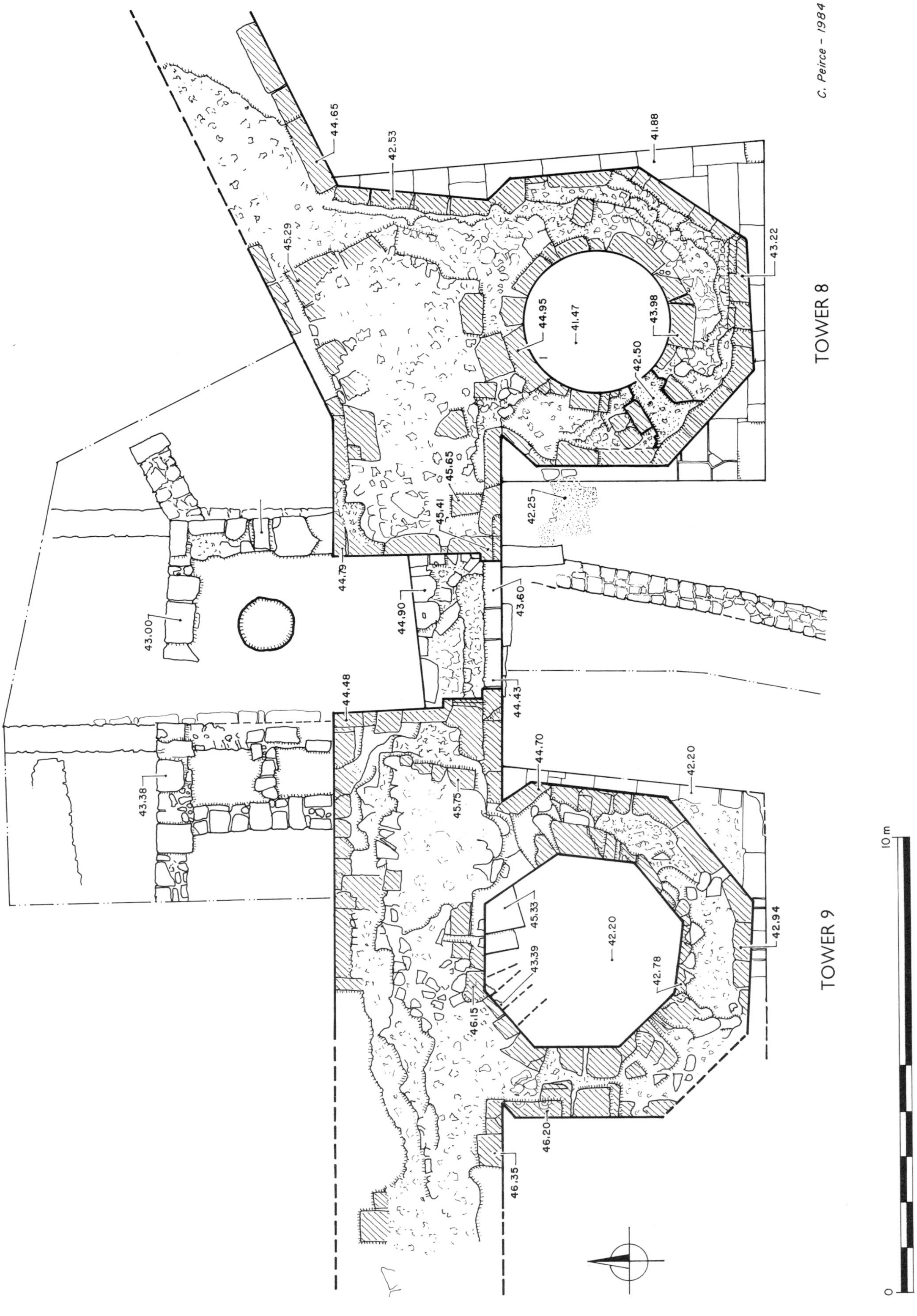

TOWER 8

TOWER 9

44.65
42.53
45.29
45.65
45.41
44.79
44.90
43.60
43.00
43.38
44.48
44.43
44.70
45.75
42.20
45.33
43.39
42.20
42.78
46.15
42.94
46.20
46.35
41.88
43.22
44.95
41.47
43.98
42.50
42.25

C. Peirce – 1984

Actual-state plan of the South Gate

10 m

0

FIGURE 24

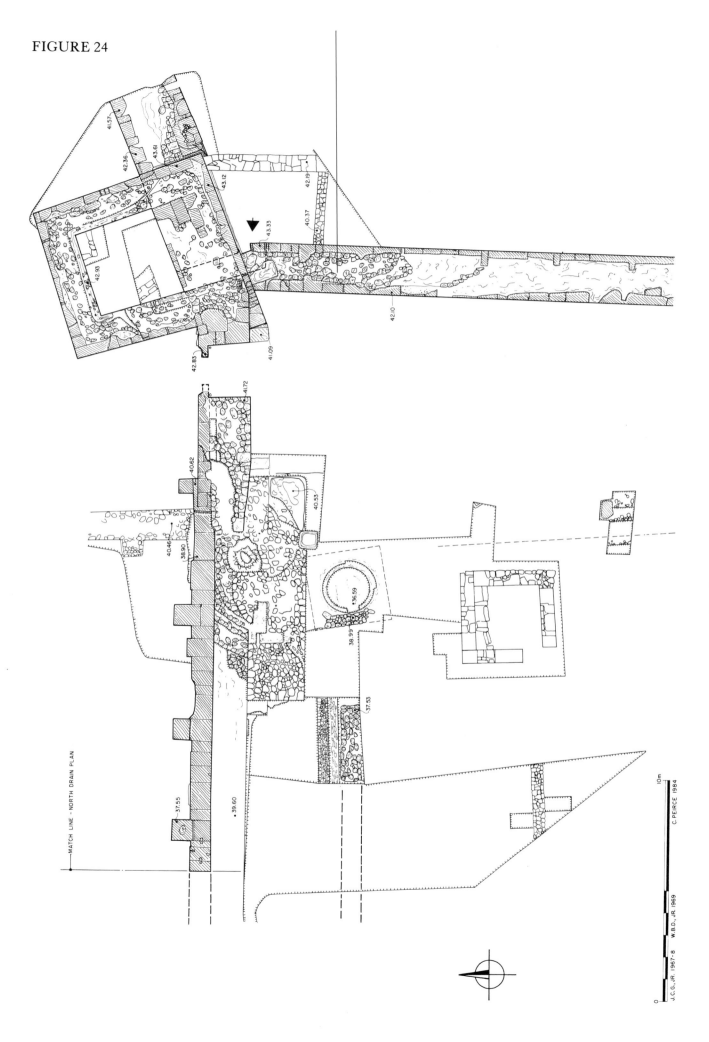

Actual-state plan of Tower 15

MATCH LINE - NORTH DRAIN PLAN

J.C.G., JR. 1967-8   W.B.D., JR. 1969

C. PEIRCE 1984

41.57

43.61

42.36

43.12

42.19

42.93

40.37

43.33

42.83

41.09

42.10

41.72

40.62

40.53

40.46

38.90

36.59

38.99

37.53

37.55

39.60

10m

0

FIGURE 25

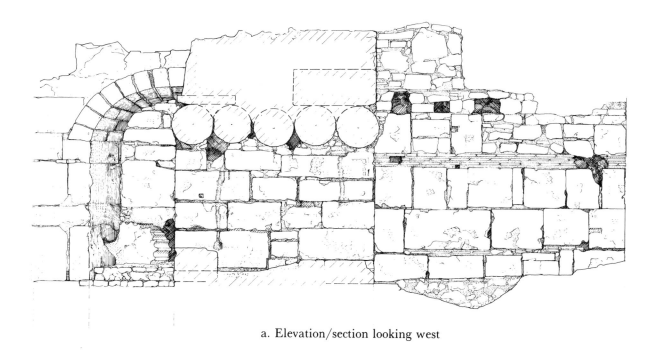

a. Elevation/section looking west

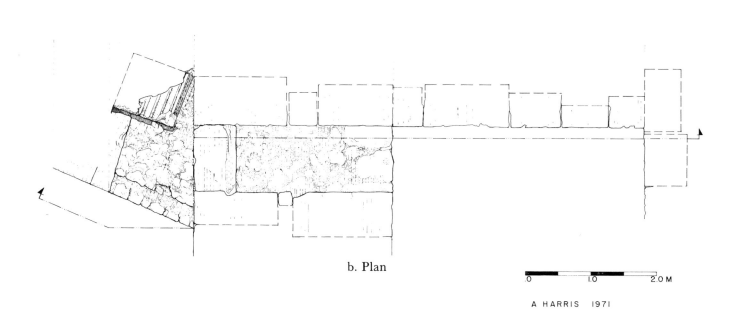

b. Plan

A HARRIS 1971

Entrance to Tower 15

FIGURE 26

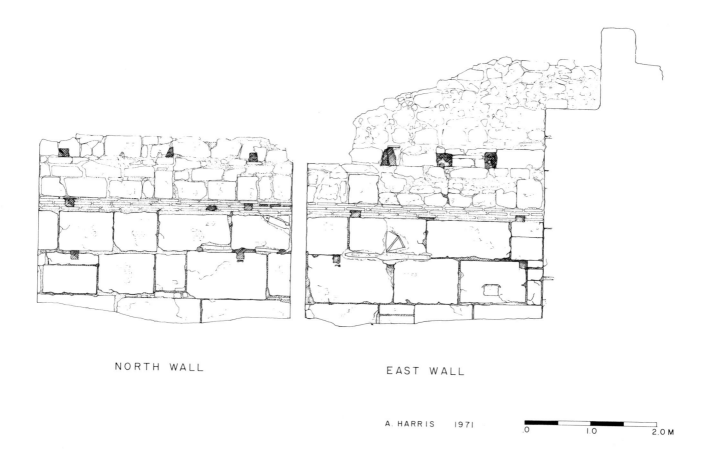

NORTH WALL

EAST WALL

A. HARRIS   1971

.0   1.0   2.0 M

Interior elevations of Tower 15

FIGURE 27

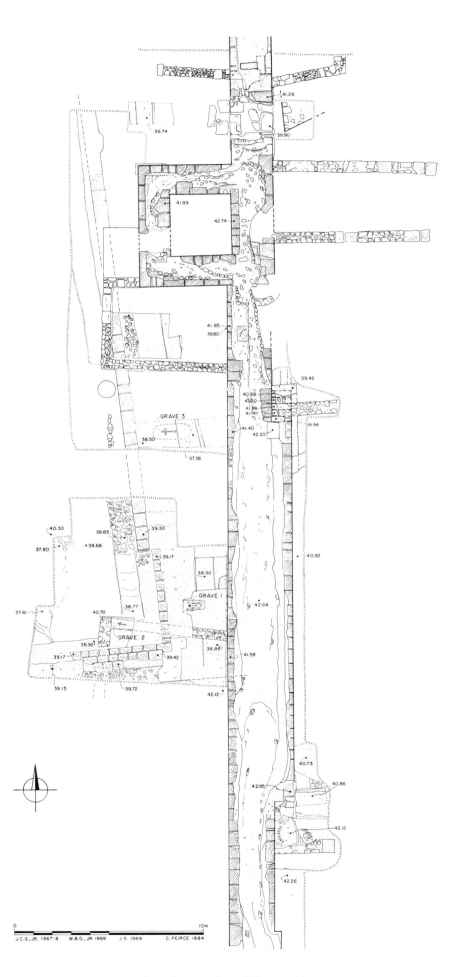

Actual-state plan of Tower 14

FIGURE 28

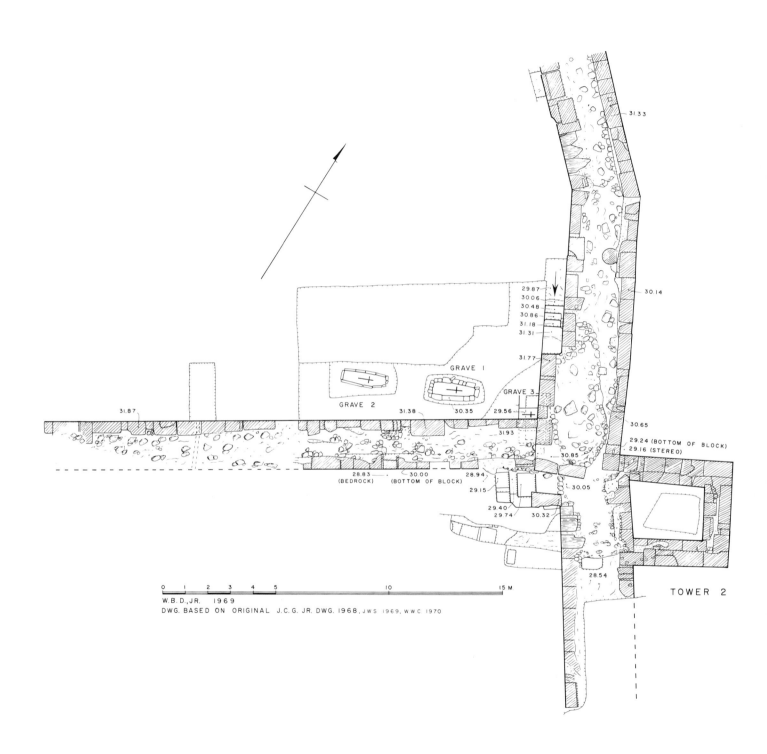

31.33

29.87
30.06
30.48
30.86
31.18
31.31

30.14

31.77

GRAVE 1

GRAVE 3

GRAVE 2

31.38

30.35

29.56

30.65

31.87

31.93

29.24 (BOTTOM OF BLOCK)
29.16 (STEREO)

28.83
(BEDROCK)

30.00
(BOTTOM OF BLOCK)

28.94

30.85

29.15

30.05

29.40
29.74

30.32

28.54

TOWER 2

0   1   2   3   4   5   10   15 M

W.B.D.,JR.   1969
DWG. BASED ON ORIGINAL J.C.G. JR. DWG. 1968, JWS 1969, WWC 1970

Actual-state plan of Tower 2

FIGURE 29

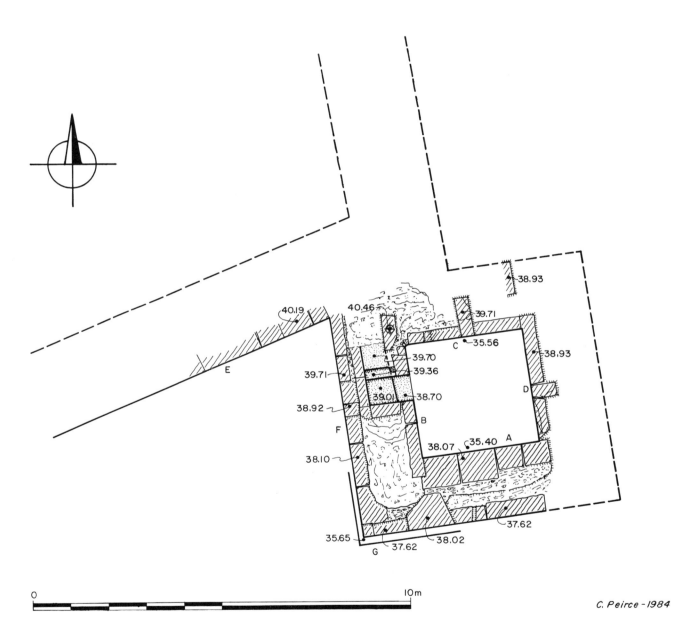

40.19

40.46

38.93

39.71

C 35.56

38.93

39.70

39.71

39.36

D

39.01 38.70

38.92

B

F

38.07 35.40 A

38.10

37.62

35.65 37.62 38.02

G 37.62

E

0 10m

C. Peirce - 1984

Actual-state plan of Tower 6

FIGURE 30

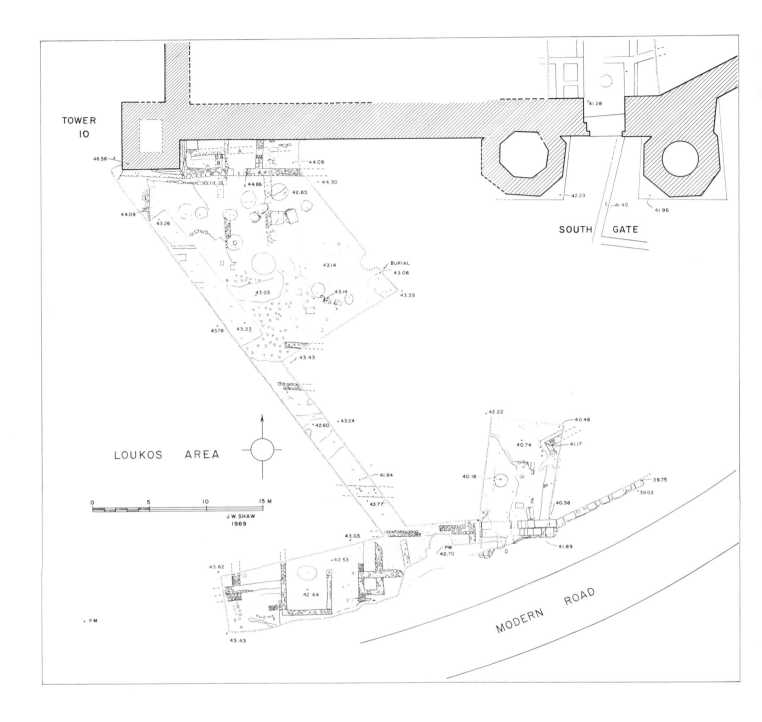

Actual-state plan of Tower 10 and the Loukos Area

PLATES

PLATE 1

a. *IG* IV, 204 (Corinth Museum)

b. Sea Bastion (Tower W-1) from northwest

c. Sea Bastion (Tower W-1) from northeast

d. Sea Bastion (Tower W-1) from west

PLATE 2

c. Tower W-2 from east

a. Hexamilion south of the Sea Bastion in 1970 (section now destroyed)

b. Sea Bastion, east face of Section B, blocks with moldings from east

PLATE 3

b. IΣ 70-3

d. Hexamilion outer face near 0+800 m., from northwest

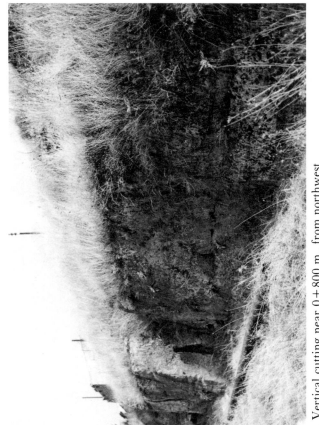

a. Hexamilion near the church of Agios Spyridon, from northwest

c. Vertical cutting near 0+800 m., from northwest

PLATE 4

c. Hexamilion inner face northwest of the National Highway, from southeast

a. Hexamilion outer face northwest of the National Highway, from northeast

b. Hexamilion inner face northwest of the National Highway, from southwest

PLATE 5

a. Detail of the Hexamilion inner face northwest of the National Highway

c. Gate wall between Towers W-6 and W-6A, from east

b. Tower W-5, entrance from east

d. Outer face of the Hexamilion northwest of the National Highway: spolia, from northeast

PLATE 6

c. Hexamilion in the gully west of Tower W-13, from southwest

a. Tower W-11 from north

b. Tower W-11 from southwest

PLATE 7

b. Hexamilion and Tower W-17 from east (cutting on right is the *taphros*)

c. *Taphros* north of Tower W-17, from west

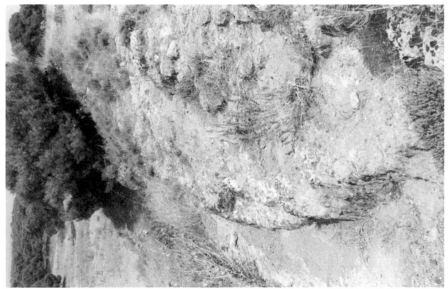

a. Hexamilion between Towers W-15 and W-16, from west

PLATE 8

b. Cutting in bedrock in the area of Tower W-22, from west

d. Hexamilion on the northwest side of the Roman Bath, from southwest

a. Tower W-22 and the Kyras Vrysi Ravine, from east

c. Area of Tower W-22, from north

PLATE 9

c. Footing trench of the Hexamilion in Roman Bath Room I

a. North wall of the Roman Bath, from south

b. North wall of Roman Bath Room II, from south

PLATE 10

a. North wall of the Roman Bath and north–south wall north of Rooms I and II, from west

b. Hexamilion Outworks, easternmost north–south wall from south

c. Hexamilion Outworks, easternmost north–south wall from north

PLATE 11

b. Hexamilion west of the North Drain, from west

d. Hexamilion south of Fortress Tower 2 in 1909, from east

a. North Drain from east

c. Hexamilion south of Fortress Tower 2 in 1970, from east

PLATE 12

b. Hexamilion, looking north from Tower S-9

a. Tower S-4, doorway from west

d. Cut bedrock south of Tower S-14

c. View north from Tower S-13

PLATE 13

b. Modern house over Tower S-16

d. Ravine south of Tower S-21, from northwest

a. Hexamilion on the south side of the ravine south of Tower S-14, from northwest

c. Tower S-20 from east

PLATE 14

a. Northeast Gate from southwest

b. Northeast Gate from west

PLATE 15

b. Northeast Gate in 1967, from west

d. Northeast Gate, north central pier of the Roman Arch and the North Tower in 1909, from south

a. Northeast Gate in 1967, before excavation, from east

c. Roman Arch, the central piers in 1909, from southeast

PLATE 16

a. Northeast Gate, North Tower from south

b. Honorary stele for
L. Kornelios
Korinthos (IΣ 69-1)

c. Northeast Gate, marble roadway from north

PLATE 17

c. Northeast Gate, North Wall stairway from west

a. Northeast Gate, west end of the marble roadway, from north

b. Northeast Gate, North Reveal from south

PLATE 18

a. Northeast Gate, vertical latrine drain from northeast

b. Northeast Gate, drain outlet on the north face of the Hexamilion, from north

c. Basin IPR 67-1 *in situ*

d. Basin IPR 67-1

PLATE 19

a. Lamp IP 3691

b. Stamped plate IPR 67-39

c. Lamp IP 3678

d. Amphora IP 67-30

e. Northeast Gate, Graves 3 and 4 from southeast

PLATE 20

a. Northeast Gate, Grave 1 from east

b. Northeast Gate, Grave 1: grave goods

c. Glass pitcher IM 69-42

d. Northeast Gate, Grave 6 from east

PLATE 21

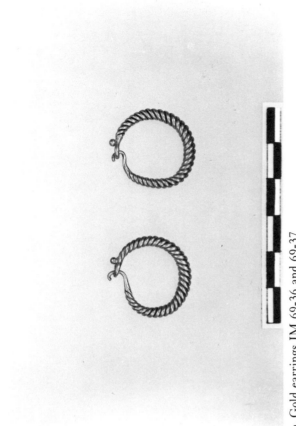

b. Gold earrings IM 69-36 and 69-37

a. Northeast Gate, Grave 6: skull with earrings

d. Area north of the Northeast Gate, from south

c. Area north of the Northeast Gate, from north

PLATE 22

a. Northeast Gate, W-shaped cutting from north

b. Northeast Gate, later cutting into the W-shaped cutting, from north

c. Northeast Gate, Blocking Wall from northeast

PLATE 23

b. Northeast Gate Bastion from northeast

d. Northeast Gate, join between the Bastion and the Blocking Wall, from north

a. Northeast Gate, southern interior corner of the Blocking Wall, from north

c. Northeast Gate Bastion from east

PLATE 24

b. Northeast Gate, brick debris east of the Blocking Wall, from south

d. Northeast Gate, area west of the North Bay, from south

a. ΙΣ 69-3 *in situ* in the foundations of the east face of the Northeast Gate Bastion

c. Amphora IPR 69-240

PLATE 25

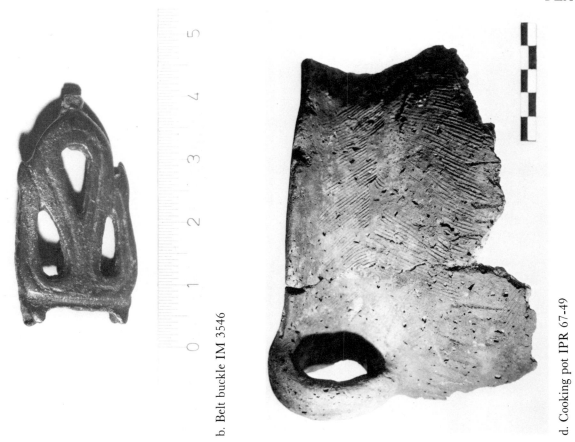

b. Belt buckle IM 3546

d. Cooking pot IPR 67-49

a. Northeast Gate, area west of the North Bay, from east

c. Cooking pot IPR 67-47

PLATE 26

c. Northeast Gate, north face of the South Reveal

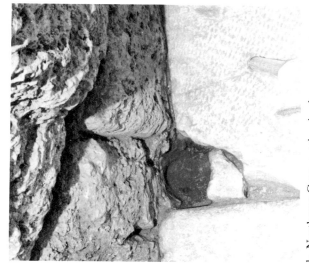

b. Northeast Gate, cutting in the pavement near the South Reveal

d. Northeast Gate, late wall west of the North Bay, from southwest

a. Cooking pot IPR 67-51

PLATE 27

a. Northeast Gate, late wall west of the North Bay, from east

b. Northeast Gate, blocked doorway in the late wall west of the North Bay, from east

c. Northeast Gate, west of the North Bay, tile floor of a late phase, from south

d. Ring foot IPB 67-10

e. Jug IPB 67-8

PLATE 28

b. Cooking pot IPB 67-11

a. Jug IPB 67-9

d. South Gate, gateway from south

c. South Gate from south

PLATE 29

a. South Gate: cross on the west jamb

c. South Gate, late walls and the blocking wall, from northwest

b. South Gate: cross on the east jamb

d. Fortress Tower 15: crosses on the west face

PLATE 30

a. Fortress Tower 15, entrance from east

b. Fortress Tower 15, entrance, column from the Theater

c. Fortress Tower 15, passageway, from north

d. Fortress Tower 15, interior from northwest

PLATE 31

a. Fortress Tower 15, graffito of fish

b. Fortress Tower 15, graffito of crossbow(?)

c. Fortress Tower 15, join between the Hexamilion interior face and the outer face
of the West Fortress Wall west of the tower, from southwest

PLATE 32

b. Gateway west of Fortress Tower 15, interior, from south

d. Body sherd of sgraffito bowl IPB 68-38

a. Gateway west of Fortress Tower 15, exterior, from north

c. Gateway west of Fortress Tower 15, blocking wall, from north

PLATE 33

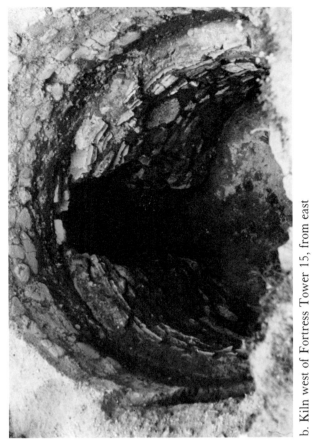

b. Kiln west of Fortress Tower 15, from east

d. Fortress Tower 14 from north

a. Hexamilion west of Fortress Tower 15, from east

c. Fortress Tower 14 from northwest

PLATE 34

b. West Gate from south

d, e. Coin Clement, 568 (IC 904)

a. Fortress Tower 14 from northeast

c. West Gate from west

PLATE 35

a, b. Coin Clement, 613 (IC 856)

c. Sgraffito bowl IPB 69-40

d. Sgraffito bowl IPB 69-43

e. Cooking pot IPB 67-4

PLATE 36

b. Long Wall from northwest

c. Long Wall from southeast

a. Fortress Tower 14, window of building east of tower, from northwest

PLATE 37

b. West Fortress Wall, south of Tower 14, from south

c. Fortress Tower 2 from north

a. Fortress Tower 14, south end of the stairway ramp
south of the tower, from south

PLATE 38

a. Fortress Tower 2, north wall from west

b. Fortress Tower 2, join between the Hexamilion and the East Fortress Wall, from south

c. Fortress Tower 2 from southwest

PLATE 39

b. East Fortress Wall from south

d. Fortress Tower 2, stairway from west

a. Spolia from the south face of the East Fortress Wall west of Fortress Tower 2

c. Core of the East Fortress Wall, from south

PLATE 40

a. Fortress Tower 2: graffiti

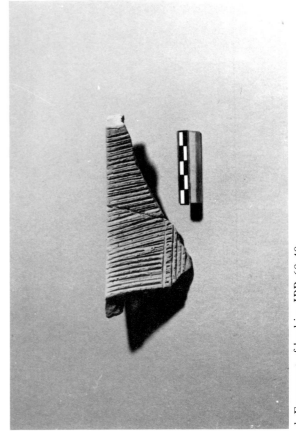

b. Fortress Tower 2, juncture between the Hexamilion and the East Fortress Wall, from west

c. Fortress Tower 2, Grave 3 from west

d. Fragment of beehive IPR 68-40

PLATE 41

a, b. Coin Clement, 480 (IC 68-23)

c, d. Coin Clement, 491 (IC 68-27)

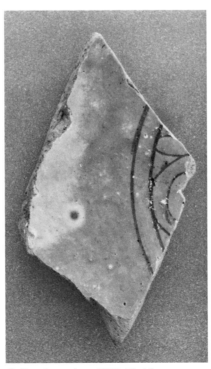

e. Bowl IPB 68-7   f. Bowl or plate IPB 68-15   g. Bowl or plate IPB 68-8

PLATE 42

b. Drain through the East Fortress Wall, from south

a. Fortress Tower 2, Graves 1 and 2 from east

PLATE 43

c. Fortress Tower 6, stairway, from east

a. Fortress Tower 6 from southwest

b. Fortress Tower 6, stairway, from north

PLATE 44

a. Fortress Tower 10 from southeast

b. Fortress Tower 10 from east

c. Fortress Tower 10, detail, from southeast

d. Fortress Tower 10, interior

PLATE 45

a. Bowl IPB 72-1

b. Jug or amphora IPB 72-2

c. Cooking pot IPR 69-246

d. Glaze-painted bowl IPB 69-5

e. Imitation lustre-ware bowl IPB 69-24

PLATE 46

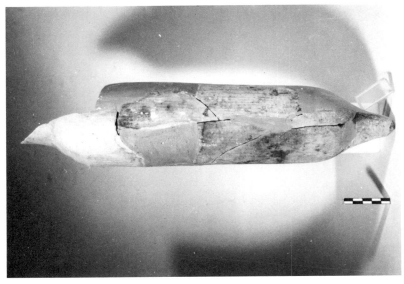

c. Amphora IPB 72-8

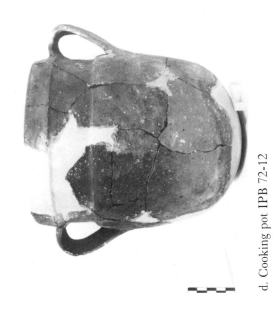

d. Cooking pot IPB 72-12

a. Fortress Tower 17, north tower wall, from south

b. Fortress Tower 17, doorway from south